ILEX FOUNDATION SERIES 21

CYRUS THE GREAT

Also in the Ilex Foundation Series

CYRUS THE GREAT

LIFE AND LORE

Edited by
M. Rahim Shayegan

Ilex Foundation
Boston, Massachusetts

Center for Hellenic Studies
Trustees for Harvard University
Washington, D. C.

Distributed by Harvard University Press
Cambridge, Massachusetts, and London, England

Cyrus the Great: Life and Lore
Edited by M. Rahim Shayegan

Published by Ilex Foundation, Boston, Massachusetts and The Center for Hellenic Studies, Trustees for Harvard University, Washington, D.C.

Distributed by Harvard University Press, Cambridge, Massachusetts and London, England

Production editor: Christopher Dadian
Cover design: Joni Godlove
Printed in the United States of America

Cover image: Collated line drawing of an heirloom seal from the Persepolis Fortification Archive attributed to "Kuraš the Anzanite, son of Šešpeš [Teispes]," presumably Cyrus I, king of Anšan, Cyrus the Great's grandfather and namesake. (After Garrison 2011, fig. 1).

Library of Congress Cataloging-in-Publication Data

Names: Shayegan, M. Rahim, editor.
Title: Cyrus the great : life and lore / edited by M. Rahim Shayegan.
Other titles: Ilex Foundation series ; no. 21.
Description: Boston, Massachusetts : Ilex Foundation ; Cambridge,
  Massachusetts : Center for Hellenic Studies, 2018. | Series: Ilex
  Foundation series ; no. 21 | Includes bibliographical references.
Identifiers: LCCN 2018058557 | ISBN 9780674987388 (alk. paper)
Subjects: LCSH: Cyrus, the Great, King of Persia, -530 B.C. or 529 B.C. |
  Achaemenid dynasty, 559-330 B.C.
Classification: LCC DS282 .C98 2018 | DDC 935/.05092 [B] --dc23
LC record available at https://lccn.loc.gov/2018058557

CONTENTS

Acknowledgments

It is an agreeable duty to acknowledge the many whose help has been crucial in the completion of the present volume, which represents the revised proceedings of an international conference on Cyrus the Great, his Life and reception, held in October 2013 at UCLA.

First, I wish to express my sincere gratitude to the colleagues who generously contributed to the volume and forbearingly tolerated the inevitable vagaries of the editing and production process. I owe a debt of thanks to the many colleagues who partook in the conference as speakers, moderators, and respondents: Aaron Burke, Elizabeth Carter, Kathlyn (Kara) Cooney, Michael Cooperson, Jacco Dieleman, Domenico Ingenito, Sarah Morris, Ali Mousavi, and Gregory Nagy.

I am grateful to the Farhang Foundation and IHF America for their liberal support of the conference, which coincided with the tour of the Cyrus Cylinder in the Americas. My appreciation of the Semnani Family Foundation for its gracious assistance.

My gratitude to Olga M. Davidson and the editorial board of the Ilex Foundation for accepting this volume for publication in their series, in partnership with the Harvard Center Hellenic for Studies. My thanks to Niloo Fotouhi, the Executive Director of Ilex Foundation, for her superb stewardship throughout; and to Chris Dadian for his expert knowledge and obliging patience during the editorial and production process. My thanks also to Jake Nabel for his invaluable help in proofreading, and preparing the index.

I would like to express my appreciation for friends and colleagues, whose fellowship and wit have been a source of solace and joy: Arash Afshar, Maria Brosius, Kara Cooney, Touraj Daryaee, Olga M. Davidson, Magali Delmas, Lothar von Falkenhausen, Shiva Falsafi, Babak Farzami, Sharon Gerstel, Mahnaz Moazami, Anahita Naficy Lovelace, Reem Hanna-Harwell, Domenico Ingenito, Gregory Nagy, Azita Panahpour, Jim Lovelace, Robert Rollinger, Hamid Sabi, David Schaberg, Amir Soltani, Rolf Schneider, William Schniedewind, Romain Wacziarg, and Josef Wiesehöfer.

My deep affection for Daryush, Farideh, Roxaneh, Taraneh, Mehrdad, Cyrus and Darius (der Jüngere), and my love to my Troika: Shiva, Turandot, and Anusha.

This volume is dedicated to my father, Daryush Shayegan,
le meilleur chevalier du monde.

Introduction

M. Rahim Shayegan
University of California, Los Angeles

THE EDITED VOLUME *Cyrus the Great: Life and Lore* re-contextualizes in light of recent scholarship Cyrus' founding act and epoch, while examining his later reception in antiquity and beyond. The one whom Jacob Burckhardt in his *Weltgeschichtliche Betrachtungen* so preciously has called "das große Phantasieobjekt Cyrus"[1] remains an enigmatic figure, whose thrusting into world history, impact, and demise remain shrouded in mist. The wide-ranging contributions assembled in the present volume, as well as a new critical edition and English translation of the Cyrus Cylinder, may hence permit a more adequate evaluation of Cyrus' impact on his own age, and more clearly gauge his imprint on posterity. Among the many themes addressed in the present volume are: the complex dossier of Elamo-Persian acculturation; the Mesopotamian antecedents of Cyrus' edict and religious policy; Cyrus' *Baupolitik* at Pasargadae and the idiosyncratic genesis of Persian imperial art; the Babylonian exile, the Bible, and the First Return; Cyrus' exalted but conflicted image in the later Greco-Roman world; his reception and programmatic function in genealogical constructs of the Hellenistic and Arsacid periods; and finally Cyrus' conspicuous and enigmatic evanescence in the Sasanian and Muslim traditions.

Increasingly, with a better understanding of the Elamite civilization, and its bearing on the Persian ethnos before the empire, the idea of Cyrus' line, the Teispids,[2] being a partially acculturated royal house, has gained traction.[3] To no lesser extent, the accelerated exploration of the Persepolis Elamite archive, a better understanding of Elamite cultual practices and the use of Elamite as an administrative language under the Achaemenids, as well as the persistence of Neo-Elamite iconography in early Achaemenid

---

1. "Die Könige von Medien, obwohl ihrer nur vier sind, machen uns ungeduldig, weil wir so wenig von ihnen wissen, während das große Phantasieobjekt Cyrus bereits vor der Tür zu warten scheint"; Burckhardt 2000, 528 (= 256–257).

2. More recently on the Teispids, see Rollinger 2017 and Rollinger 2014.

3. See Potts 2016, 304–313; more recently and with discussion of older literature, see Henkelman 2011, 584; Henkelman 2008, 41–57; Henkelman 2003; Tavernier 2011; and Shayegan 2012, 9–93.

glyptic imagery,[4] have strengthened this view. Whereas there is merit in perceiving Cyrus and the Teispids as being exposed to the Elamite element, which may partially explain the use of the title of "king of Anšan" by Cyrus and his forebears, or account for the continued support for the religious services of Elamite divinities by the Persepolitan administration, a corrective paying heed to other influences, or the singularity of the Persian cultural element may be required. Several essays in the present volume, which are fully summarized below, provide a more balanced view of Cyrus' world, by emphasizing the importance of Mesopotamian *Vorlagen* for Cyrus' edict and politico-religious projections (and actions); as well as Median, Lydian, and Ionian precedents in the formation of the Persian art and architecture.

In particular, we are reminded that the process of Elamite and Persian acculturation (if indeed as pronounced as has been assumed in recent scholarship) was probably not as seamless, in view of the hostilities that the Teispid house's foray into Anšan perforce caused to the Neo-Elamite polity (Waters in this volume). Nor is the use of the title of "king of Anšan" by Cyrus the Great (and his ancestors?) inevitably a sign of Elamite induced acculturation, for other political motivations may have necessitated it. The use of this title in the Cyrus Cylinder (and other Babylonian documents) may well have been in response to the mental exigencies of a Babylonian audience, which possibly perceived royal power as inherently associated with the prerogatives of an urban setting, prompting Cyrus' scribes to befit that mold by associating him prominently with the venerable city of Anšan (Stronach and Waters in this volume). Another reason Cyrus' scribes could have chosen to emphasize the Persian king's Anšanite pedigree might have been the desire to equate him and his Elamite/Anšanite army (traditionally known in Babylonia as the *destroyers* of Ur III) with the wild hordes of the Ummān-Manda who were presaged to inflict harm on the wicked king Nabonidus (Schaudig in this volume).

The traces of Elamite acculturation are also faint when it comes to Cyrus' building activities in Pasargadae, introducing a new artistic expression. The models for Cyrus' architectural design and artistry are to be found overwhelmingly in the art and architecture of Assyria, Lydia, and Ionia. Although Assyrianizing influences are visible in Persian sculpted imagery at Pasargadae and the hydraulic installations of its gardens may have been inspired by Western Anatolian and possibly Elamite precedents, Pasargadae's artistic conception as a whole appears to have augured a new imperial style that reflected Persian identities (Stronach, Boucharlat, and Brosius in this volume).

4. Still Garrison and Root 2001; and more recently Garrison 2018.

The tendency to accommodate the social and religious practices of conquered peoples when projecting the king's narrative, in order, to the extent possible, to befit their intellectual disposition, is among the main tenets of Cyrus' political philosophy. It perforce permeates the realm of the religious. When the Cylinder reports on Cyrus' establishing a privileged relation with Marduk (as his chosen one), on whose behest he restituted the gods of the land of Sumer and Akkad, or when it affirms his bringing relief to the exhaustion and toil suffered by the Babylonian citizenry, Cyrus is shown acting within the mold expected from Babylonian kings (see Pongratz-Leisten in this volume). It is not surprising that Cyrus was also represented as YHWH's chosen one in texts associated with Deutero-Isaiah, written under the impression of Jerusalem's and Judah's devastation in the late sixth century. In this context Cyrus' scribes might have sought to facilitate his identification with the Messiah, namely, as YHWH's instrument, who could enable the return of the exiled and secure the re-establishment of the temple (see Sweeny in this volume). In this vein, one might wonder, whether Cyrus endeavored to preserve (and enhance?) the position of the priesthood (as he did with the Babylonian elites), in return for their making him the Messiah, which allowed the priesthood to supersede the Davidian line as the leaders of the Jews during the Second Temple period, but also Cyrus to appear as the benefactor of its restoration (see Schniedewind in this volume).

Intriguing are also the radically opposite receptions of Cyrus in (late) antiquity and the early Muslim period. Cyrus' presence is felt more vividly in the Hellenistic and Greco-Roman world, but more discretely in the proper Iranian traditions. Many factors have contributed to Cyrus' evanescence in Iranian antiquity, among others the discontinuation (following the demise of Cambyses and Bardiya) of the Teispid house already in the early Achaemenid period consequent upon the usurpation of Dareios, who although folding Cyrus' line into his own, seems to have been ultimately responsible for Cyrus' diminishing renown. The exaltation of Cyrus as an archetypal prince is well attested in the works of classical authors, who have dramatized Cyrus' figure, bestowed it with features belonging to fictional heroes, and thereby contributed to its continuous presence in the world of classical antiquity. It seems likely that the narratives of Herodotus, Xenophon, and Ctesias were themselves recipients of a variety of Cyrus-legends that were expressly put into circulation by Cyrus' entourage as a means to reach new target audiences and enhance Cyrus' relevance (see Brosius and Beckman in this volume).

It is hence not surprising that Cyrus' persona received a favorable reception among Roman literati and grandees, who may have identified with this cosmopolitan figure worthy of *imitatio* (see Schlude in this volume). Cyrus' reception in the Hellenistic and Arsacid worlds is fraught with complexities. On the one hand, we find him in the genealogical constructs of sundry (minor) Greco-Persian dynasts, as a token of legitimizing their royal ambitions, on the other hand, Cyrus' repute having already suffered a reverse in the Achaemenid period, we witness another displacement occurring, when the Arsacid royal house, on the strength of its own political success, eventually turned as the source of its legitimacy to its eponymous founder Aršak, whose ascent might have sealed Cyrus' slide into obscurity in Iranian lands (see Olbrycht in this volume). Thus, even without the imposition of a Mazdean inspired worldview on Sasanian historiography, which had the effect of inducing a historical amnesia among the Sasanian elites, Cyrus' consignment to the *oubliettes d'histoire* might still have been inevitable (see Daryaee in this volume). What ultimately survived from Cyrus and the Achaemenids in the early new Persian literary traditions are themes and reflexes their *res gestae* share with the Iranian (oral) epic traditions, which have also informed the epic traditions collected in the *Šāhnāme* (see Davidson in this volume).

The study of Matt Waters examines a number of toponyms and technical terms pertaining to early Persian and Elamite history, in order to show the great variability of our historical reconstruction of Cyrus' age, when perforce relying on scarce and opaque evidence. Among the specific terms discussed are the use of the toponyms *Anšan* and *Parsu(m)aš* and how they designated changing realities of the political expanse the Elamite and Persian *ethnē* contolled. Waters begins his essay with the discussion of *Anšan* and *Parsu(m)aš* (the latter as a designation of the polity associated with the Persians probably before their expansion into Anšan) and persuasively argues that, on the basis of two letters (ABL 961 and ABL 1311+) dating to Assurbanipal's reign and reporting hostilities between the Persians and Elamites – assuming these conflicts were reflective of Persian expansion into Anšan under the Tesipids – the notion of Persian and Elamite acculturation in the seventh century seems to have been less seamless: "Why these groups were fighting [is] unknown. It is tempting to connect this activity to early Persian expansion, under Cyrus the Great's predecessors, but there is no way at present to substantiate this. In any event, it would be misguided to assume that processes of Elamite-Persian ethnogenesis proceeded seamlessly." Another intriguing word is *liblibbu* as attested in the Cyrus Cylinder, and how its versatility prevents a more precise determination of the generational gap separating Cyrus the Great from his ancestor Teispes, for it signifies "(great-) grandfather," or "(great-) great-grandfather." Another term discussed by Waters is the word *ṣiḫru* "young/insignificant" in Naboni-dus' Sippar Cylinder, when reporting on Cyrus overthrowing the Medes. There is a general consensus that in Nabonidus' Cylinder, Cyrus, the "king of Anšan" is presented as an instrument of Marduk/the gods, who would remove the Median threat, for Nabonidus to proceed with his building ac-tivities. However, the word *ṣaḫri* following *arassu* "his servant" intrigues: does it mean when referring to Cyrus, that the king of Anšan was Marduk's/ the gods' *young* servant, or more likely Marduk's/the gods' *insignificant* ser-vant. A final investigation concerns the duality of meanings embedded in the verb *nadû* "to erect; to fall into ruin" that describes the sanctuaries to which Cyrus, in his Cylinder, ordered the statues of gods to be returned; that is, whether these sanctuaries were "established" long ago, or "had fallen into ruin" long ago. According to Waters the choice of *nadû* by Cyrus' scribes was intentional: "The ambiguity embedded within the word *nadû* allowed emphasis of two things in this context: the temples were not only ancient but also neglected by the inept and unworthy Nabonidus. Cyrus may thus be allowed to have demonstrated his respect for Babylonian norms through both the correction of previous offense as well as his acknowledgement and maintenance of a long-standing, proper tradition."

The chapter by David Stronach on Cyrus, Anšan and Assyria, aims at providing a much welcome corrective to the concept of Elamite-Persian acculturation, which has gained much traction in recent scholarship. This means that, while acknowledging the impact of the Elamite element in the genesis of the Persian *ethnos*, the importance of Assyrian – as well as Median, Lydian, and Ionian (among others) – precedents in the formation of Persian art and architecture (as well as political ideology) under the early Achae-menids should also be taken into consideration. Stronach meticulously examines a number of well-known indices to exhibit a more nuanced picture of Teispid/Achaemenid borrowing under Cyrus. The analysis of the seal im-pression PFS 93*, which shows a horseman with spear defeating (Elamite?) enemies, with the inscription "Kuraš the Anšanite, son of Šešpeš," possibly the namesake ancestor of Cyrus the Great, is revealing in this context. The seal's iconography Stronach connects – in this following Garrison's work[5] – with elements of Assyrian, rather than Elamite Susian, art, which presumes a link between objects and artifacts circulating in Assyria and Anšan,[6] rather than between Anšan and Susa in mid-seventh century BCE. The inscription of PFS 93*, which at first glance seems to confirm the (Anšanite) Elamite pedigree of the early Teispid line, was more indicative of the Persian desire

5. See Garrison 2011.
6. See Garrison 2011, 397, 400.

under Cyrus I to lay definitive claim over Anšan as "the inalienable, well-favored home of the Teispid royal house," against possible Susian Elamite pretensions. The later use of the title of "king of Anšan" by Cyrus II the Great – among others in the Cyrus Cylinder – while addressing a Babylonian audience, responded to Mesopotamian mental sensibilities that viewed the royal power as inherently associated with the prerogatives of urban settings. Cyrus' recourse to the "city of Anšan" as the locus of his royal power would have thus allowed to cast Cyrus' rule into the mold of Mesopotamian structures of power, thereby rendering it more imminently acceptable to Babylonian recipients. More importantly, Stronach discusses Assyrianizing influences in Pasargadae, especially the adoption, at the heart of Cyrus' newly established capital, of Assyrian inspired apotropaic sculptures and anthropomorphic figures in Gate R and Palace S. He argues that the important presence of Assyrian sculpted imagery, albeit revisited to accommodate Persian identities (and interwoven with elements from other vanquished cultures),[7] was still an important testimony to Cyrus' view of himself as heir to the prestigious Assyrian power, which is further underlined by Cyrus' express reference to Assurbanipal's precedence in the Cyrus Cylinder.

Pasargade – and the origins of its architectonic and artistic styles – is also the subject of Rémy Boucharlat's thought-provoking study. Boucharlat not only makes us aware of the political will, and organizational dexterity, behind the building of Pasargadae, which appears even more remarkable in light of Cyrus' absence from the site, but also evinces a glimpse at the technical difficulties in erecting the palace and its extended gardens. Among the fascinating particularities of Pasargadae, some already known, and others more pertinently revealed during recent surveys, are the absence of fortifications, which in contrast to the walled cities of Mesopotamia, might have indicated that "Cyrus felt the heart of his empire was totally secure, or perhaps wanted to demonstrate the peaceful character of his Persian homeland." Another intriguing discussion by Boucharlat relates to Pasargadae's landscaped park, its geometrical design and expanse (at variance with the less regimented Assyrian gardens set on hills), and its prominence in the overall conception of the site. Although the query about the origins of the Achaemenid garden remains inconclusive, Pasargadae seems to represent one of the earliest examples of the Persian "paradise." In order to create the expansive gardens of Pasargadae in the midst of the arid setting of Dašt-e

7. See also Stronach 1997, 43: "The combination of the figure's Syro-Phoenician-style Egyptianizing *hmhm* crown, Elamite robe with an Ionian rosette border, and Neo-Babylonian stylistic elements, all expressed within the Assyrian tradition of winged genii, appears to represent a deliberate attempt to co-opt the visual traditions of recently conquered regions in order to create a single, powerful, protective image."

Moyān, extensive and sophisticated hydraulic structures, combining a series of dams, reservoirs, and irrigation canals were implemented, whose *disiecta membra*, construction technology, and material (use of Western Anatolian stone cutting rather than backed bricks), may have pertained to elements known from other sites (among others Choga Zanbil), but which as a system appears to be a Persian novelty. A similar philosophy seems to have been at work, according to Boucharlat, in the artistic and architectonic conception of Pasargadae's edifices and imagery that represented a novel imperial style, which was the result of a deliberate collection of techniques and styles assembled from the four corners of the empire, synthesized through the prism of a unique Persian conception by Cyrus and possibly his new multi-ethnic imperial elite.

Hanspeter Schaudig's contributions to the present volume are twofold: a new critical edition and English translation of the Cyrus Cylinder that presents a number of intriguing departures from past editions, and a very careful interpretation of its content and the main sources for its composition. One of Schaudig's more intriguing departures is his exploration of the Cyrus Cylinder's indebtedness to Babylonian literary models, such as the *Babylonian Epic of Creation* (*Enūma elîš*) and the *Esaĝil Chronicle*. Among the main motifs the Cyrus Cylinder shares with the *Enūma elîš* is the theme of the king's good heart, that is, Marduk's placing – by virtue of his capacity to probe the thoughts and hearts of gods and men – a righteous king in an exalted position, to do his bidding ("Marduk, the great lord, who takes care of his people, saw with pleasure his good deeds and *his righteous heart* [emphasis mine]"[8]). The theme of Cyrus' righteous and wide heart in the Cylinder is, as Schaudig elucidates, an allusion to Marduk's name (and function) as *Šazu* in the *Enūma elîš*, that is, as the "one who knows the Heart," and "the one who checks the minds" (of gods/and kings), and was thus likely a theme elaborated by Babylonian scholars who had recourse to the olden "*Šazu*-theology," in order to emphasize Cyrus' being chosen by Marduk. Other equally dominant topoi of the Cyrus Cylinder, such as the removal of a disobedient king, and the restoration of gods to their temples, also occur in the *Enūma elîš*, and complement the theme of the righteous restorer Cyrus, whose heart Marduk has probed. Both of these topics are, as Schaudig persuasively demonstrates, more fully developed in the so-called *Esaĝil Chronicle*, whose main aim is to instruct Babylonian kings of the proper conduct towards Marduk and Babylon: neither is Marduk to be neglected (through improper cults and rites) and opposed (by creating a "counterfeit" shrine rivaling the Esagil temple in Babylon); nor are the people of Babylon to be oppressed by wick-

---

8. Cyrus Cylinder, ll. 13–14. Schaudig in this volume.

ed kings, which could prompt Marduk to unleash the wrath of barbarian enemies against them. By emphasizing Cyrus' Anšanite credentials, rather than his Persian ancestry, the Babylonian scholars redacting the Cyrus Cylinder were eager to equate the "Anšanite" (Elamite) king and his men (who were known in Babylonian annals as the destroyers of the Third Dynasty of Ur) with Marduk's forebodings about barbarian hordes of Gutians and the Ummān-Manda being unleashed against a wicked king (= Nabonidus) as divine punishment. Indeed, as Schaudig puts it, the Babylonian scholars "required the terms 'Anšan' and 'Ummān-Manda,' in order to create the tension between on the one hand the slaughter and devastation that was expected to occur, and on the other hand the miraculously peaceful course of events, which eventually unfolded in Babylon proper."

Beate Pongraz-Leisten's essay also treats the Cyrus Cylinder, but her query is geared towards its social and religious tenor. In a nutshell, she examines whether Cyrus' reported benevolence towards the people and gods of Babylon(ia) is a feature unique to the Persian king, or whether it has precedents in the polytheistic world of the ancient Near East, which she relates to the inherently city-centric political culture of the Sumero-Babylonian world. She begins her study with the general observation that southern Mesopotamia forming primarily a congeries of city-states, albeit bestowed with an overarching cultural tradition, the cities' elites were evidently self-confident and self-reliant, hence prompting rulers seeking supra-regional power to meet their economic wants and preserve their social status. However, conquerors such as Narām-Sîn of Akkad (first half of third millennium BCE) would ascribe their victories and control of numerous cities directly to the city gods (rather than to their entente with the metropolitan elites), thereby rendering the divinities the privileged interlocutors between the cities and the king. In Narām-Sîn's direct evocation of the divinities, Pongraz-Leisten sees the beginning of the same tradition that eventually led to the socio-religious discourse adopted by the Cyrus Cylinder. Therein, Cyrus already in the introductory sections, establishes a privileged relationship with Marduk (who has chosen him), as well as with the gods of the land of Sumer and Akkad. These being restituted to their sanctuaries at Marduk's behest, are implored by Cyrus (as was the case with Narām-Sîn before) to bless him, and solicit Marduk and his son Nabû to grant him a long life: "May all these gods, which I restored to their sacred cities, ask daily Bēl and Nabû to grant me a long life, they may speak blessings for me, and they may say to Marduk, my lord: 'Of Cyrus, the king who reveres you and Cambyses, his son, [*guard their lives!*] May they be the provisioners of our shrines until ⌜distant⌝

days!'"[9] Moreover, as Pongraz-Leisten further argues, the Cyrus Cylinder is mindful to emphasize that the king put an end to the duress endured by the citizens of Babylon under Nabonidus: "I brought relief to their exhaustion" and "did away with their toil" (*anhūssun upaššiha ušapṭir sarmašunu*), hence implying that the privileged status of Babylon's citizenry and priesthood was to be preserved and in doing so Cyrus was complying with the expectations of the city elites.

Marvin Sweeney examines the dichotomy of receptions to which the personality of Cyrus the Great and the Achaemenid dynasty have given rise in biblical traditions. On the one hand, the books of Isaiah, Ezra-Nehemiah, and the Chronicles, which mention Cyrus by name, view the Persian monarch favorably (in Isaiah even exaltedly); on the other hand, minor prophecies of the book of Twelve Prophets, such as Haggai and Zechariah, regard the Achaemenid house with hostility, as an obstacle to overcome, in order to reinstate the house of David in Israel. The reasons for this duality of views constitute the core of Sweeny's investigation. He intriguingly posits that distinct political and social conditions during the prophecy of Deutero-Isaiah, or the post-exilic experience of the prophets Haggai and Zechariah, could have been responsible for the different perceptions of Persian dominion in the Biblical traditions. Thus, the texts associated with Deutero-Isaiah in the sixth century were composed at a time when the awareness of Israel's and Judah's defeat by the Assyrian empire in the late eighth century, as well as the experience of exile in the wake of the Babylonian conquest and devastation of Jerusalem and Judah in the late sixth century, were still vivid. In such a constellation, the texts of "Deutero-Isaiah call for the identification of YHWH with the Persian empire" by showing that Cyrus is in essence YHWH's instrument, partaking in God's grander design to facilitate the return of the exiled, the rebuilding of Jerusalem, and the restoration of its temple. In this light, with Cyrus acting at the behest of YHWH, the notion of Judean political independence became less relevant. Sweeney further argues that the hostility towards the Achaemenid dynasty, as implicitly manifest in the prophecies of Zechariah and Haggai – which mention the second year of Dareios, but do not refer to Cyrus by name – might have been occasioned by political vicissitudes experienced in the first year of Dareios' seizure of power, when he fought numerous battles against the "liar-kings" challenging Persian rule throughout the empire. In this context, thus Sweeny, the prophecies of Zechariah and Haggai having internalized the political turmoil within the empire, might have interpreted it as a sign of YHWH's

---

9. Cyrus Cylinder, ll. 33–36, see Schaudig in this volume.

renouncing the Achaemenid house, and instead embracing the restoration of the Davidic monarchy, that is, seeking Judean independence from Persian rule, and in this possibly following in the footsteps of secessionary insurrections early during the reign of Dareios. Sweeny concludes that with the overthrow of the Persian monarchy obviously not occurring, the prophecy of "Zechariah went on to be read as apocalyptic literature anticipating the triumph of YHWH in a distant future."

In his study, William Schniedewind argues that the Persian province of Yehud, which Cyrus inherited following the conquest of the Babylonian empire, represented a "post-collapse society" with limited economic, political, or military value to the Persian empire. Schniedewind, on the basis of recent archeological research, provides a persuasive survey of elements substantiating the reality of a post-collapse society in sixth-century Judea: among them, a precipitous demographic decline; the absence of monumental architecture (with the resumption of monumentality occurring in the post-exilic Persian period in the fifth and fourth centuries); the disappearance of markers for (foreign) trade, particularly imported Greek pottery; and the thrift, already under Babylonian rule, of administrative documents (that only proliferate in the archaeological records of the fourth and third centuries), which indicates the lack of a coherent administration in sixth century Yehuda. All this, argues Schniedewind, shows that "the political structures from the late Iron Age were obviously dismantled by the Babylonian destruction," and Cyrus had indeed inherited a post-collapse society. Schniedewind's essay further considers the motivations that may have led the Judean exiles to return to a post-collapse society. Several elements seem to have been of marked relevance in this First Return: (1) a strong attachment to the Judean identity among the exilic communities of Babylonia; (2) possible economic hardship suffered in Babylonia, due to reduced land allotments occasioned by inheritance divisions and accelerated taxes, as well as encouragement by the Persian authority to migrate; (3) and possibly an unawareness among the Jews of the First Return of the harsh realities awaiting them in their historical homeland. With the scions of the Davidic house, among them Zerubbabel – who was granted royal allowances (that possibly perdured under Persian rule) in Babylon – likely to have returned back to Babylon in view of the grim conditions of life in Yehud, it is conceivable, thus argues Schniedewind, that the agents for the reconstruction of the Second Temple community were not the representatives of the Davidic line, but the priesthood. These in return projected upon Cyrus the leadership role preserved theretofore for the house of David (by making Cyrus the Messiah), de facto displacing the Davidides as the leaders of the Jews during the Second Temple period. Schniedewind summarizes this in the following terms: "I suspect that the royal princes like Zerubbabel would have returned to their Babylonian situation as soon as they could. In this respect, the appropriation of the figure of Cyrus as true anointed of Israel should probably not be merely seen as a nefarious plot by the priests to usurp the leadership role from the Davidides. The priests were the architects of a new Temple community, and Cyrus was the patron who enabled the restoration."

Daniel Beckman investigates variations on the legend of Cyrus' birth in the narratives of Herodotus, Ctesias, and Xenophon, which, as he posits, were projections tailored for the consumption of distinct target audiences and served specific political agendas. Beckman begins his argumentation with the observation that as an upstart Cyrus repurposed Babylonian ideological and literary norms to assuage his act of conquest and present himself in the continuity of Mesopotamian royal traditions. In the same way as Cyrus in his lifetime adopted the intellectual and ideological garb of vanquished cultures, the legend of his birth, following his demise, was to experience a comparable journey, and undergo transformations for purposes of political propaganda. The narratives of Herodotus, Xenophon, and Ctesias have captured variations pertaining to the Cyrus legend both during his lifetime and following his demise; as such they are case studies in the continued relevance of Cyrus' image and the imperative of controlling the "popular understanding of his life" as a crucial element in controlling the Persian throne.

Maria Brosius, in a sweeping survey, discusses the evidence for Cyrus' life, identity, and deeds. She argues that the multiple layers of information constituting Cyrus' identity renders the historical personage ever more elusive and mysterious. This notwithstanding, Brosius is able to reconstruct, on the strength of ancient Near Eastern evidence, a probable picture of Cyrus' identity. His immediate ancestors, thus posits Brosius, established an Anšanite (Anzanite) royal house, which, in spite of Elamite ascendency, appears to have forged a distinct Persian/Teispid character, also visible in a new Anzanite art form. This secure Persian/Teispid identity (which Brosius calls Cyrus' *Sitz im Leben*) did not hinder him from assimilating and borrowing from other civilizations, so that he may "be perceived as a king who continued the greatness of the kings of Assyria, as well as that of Lydia, and even Media and Elam." The most intriguing aspect of Brosius' study pertains to her analysis of the narratives of classical sources on Cyrus, which represent yet another ontological layer in Cyrus' identity. The dramatization of Cyrus' life in classical authors exhibits a number of key traits with modern fictional heroes. Indeed, Greek narratives in their "descriptions of the heroic, fictional figure of Cyrus ... used techniques comparable to those still used today by creators of fictional modern heroes: a mysterious personal background, a nobility of character, a complex personality, an able fighter who, at the same time, exercises self-control and uses cunning and diplomacy to maximum effect." What further completes Brosius' remarks is the observation that the very existence of the rhetorical elaborations by our classical sources may not dissipate the reality that important elements of Cyrus' legend was probably inspired by Cyrus' own propaganda, which intended "to imbed his rule in the history of royal predecessors."

Marek Jan Olbrycht's study provides an overview of the links established in the greater Iranicate world by the (post-)Hellenistic dynasties – including the Seleucids, Arsacids, as well as the Pontic and Commagenian kingdoms – with the Achaemenids and the figure of Cyrus. In particular, Olbrycht sheds light on the motivation of Seleucid and Parthian rulers to associate their royal houses with the Achaemenid dynasty and the figure of Cyrus (whom he considers to belong to the Achaemenid house, rather than to a distinct Teispid line). Intriguingly, Olbrycht posits that the Arsacids' connection with the Achaemenids and Cyrus may have been less pronounced or grandiloquent (in contrast to the claims made by the rulers of Commagene and Pontos), for already by the early second century BCE, the Arsacid considered their eponymous founder Arsaces I as the real source of their political power and legitimacy. Since the Parthians were forging the first Iranian empire following the demise of the Achaemenids, and, what is more, deemed their imperial aspirations to be on a par with past Achaemenid achievements, they might have felt no urgency to engage in genealogical constructs involving the Achaemenids. Thus, the Parthians, according to Olbrycht, although not forgetful of the Achaemenids and Cyrus, were still in no dire need of them. Instead they had rooted their imperial ideology in the figure of Arsaces: "The Arsacids were able to develop a universal imperial ideology of their own. Their chief point of reference was Arsaces, not his links, real or fictive, with the Achaemenids. It is striking that the Arsacids harked back to the Achaemenids in many respect, but their claim to Achaemenid descendance was sporadic, and their connection to Achaemenid satraps as forebears non-existent."

Jason Schlude's contribution explores the reception of Cyrus (and ancient Persia) in authors of the late Republic and early Empire. He observes that while references to Cyrus the Great are sparse among Roman literati, there is still a valuable substratum that informs the contrasting and complex Roman views on ancient Iran. Schlude argues that in contrast to the Roman perception of the Parthian East as an undesirable *alter orbis*, or an imperial *other*, against which Rome defined herself, the more favorable reception of Cyrus in Roman thinking prompts us to uncover different layers in Roman thought vis-à-vis the Arsacid Orient and Iran altogether. In short, the figure of Cyrus was revered by Romans, although they understood him to be linked with the Parthian foe and neighbor (the new "Persians"). The association of Cyrus with Parthians seems to have in time created and encouraged a level of familiarity with, and respect for, the Arsacids – a conclusion in step with the trend of some of the more recent observations made on the basis of the material culture: "In the end, while Roman views of Cyrus the Great shed no new historical light on the career of the Persian king, they nevertheless demonstrate that in his afterlife Cyrus remained a significant part of the ancient Mediterranean consciousness and imperial history."

In his essay, Touraj Daryaee explores a wide range of evidence pertaining to the Sasanian reception of Cyrus and the Achaemenids. He shows the extent to which Jewish and Armenian traditions had kept memories of the historical Cyrus, which ought to have in return afforded a viable path of transmitting this knowledge to the dominant Persian ethno-class. Moreover, since Middle Iranian and Iranian Muslim literary traditions, or the extant inscriptions of the *fratarakā* and the Dārāyānids, also exhibited some knowledge of the Achaemenid past (although not of Cyrus *expressis verbis*), then, thus inquires Daryaee, why did not the Sasanians possess a historical knowledge of the Achaemenids? The answer to this question he finds in the nature of Sasanian historiography in late antiquity: "As Armenia's ancient history received a 'Christian orientation,' and later as Islamic history received a 'Quranic orientation,' one can argue that Iranian history took on a 'Zoroastrian/Avestan worldview.'" For Daryaee an epic and historical narrative refashioned by the Zoroastrian worldview, with the purpose of justifying Sasanian rule had relegated the Achaemenids to obscurity, including Cyrus the Great. Of the Achaemenid Great Kings merely a faint reflex personified in the personage(s) of Dārā(y) ī Dārāyān remained; Achaemenid monuments instead were associated with mytho-epic heroes and paladins. Although Cyrus continued to be remembered by Iranian Jewish and Christian communities, the empire's dominant Persian ethno-class had allowed him to fall into desuetude.

Within the present volume, Olga M. Davidson analyzes an episode of the *Šāhnāme* of Ferdowsi pertaining to the would-be king Key Xosrō and reveals its thematic affinity with both Achaemenid inscriptions and the Cyrus Cylinder. In the said episode of the *Šāhnāme*, Key Xosrō is shown demolishing a fortress infested by demons, so he may establish a magnificent fire temple and give rise to a new city. Among the themes this *Šāhnāme* episode shares with the Achaemenid inscription of King Xerxes (XPf) is that of the hero/prince being granted sovereign power over other rivals by divine support: in XPf, the crown prince Xerxes is given preference over his potential challengers on account of Ahuramazdā's explicit wish (*A^huramazdām avaθā kāma āha* "Ahuramazdā thus wished it"); similarly, Key Xosrō, who is competing for the status of crown prince against his contender Farīborz, obtains the divine grace (*farr*). Another shared theme between Key Xosrō and Xerxes relates to the evil they both oppose. In his famous *Daiva*-Inscription (XPh), Xerxes is reported converting a "den of demons (*daivas*)" (*daivādāna-*) into an abode of worship for Ahuramazdā – who shall be worshiped in "the right time and following the proper ritual," or "according to order up in the height" (*artācā barzmaniy(a)*); similarly, Key Xosrō converts the fortress of demons (*dīvs*) into a holy abode, centered on the holy Fire of Gošnasp. In a final analogy, Davidson detects in the presence of a letter dictated by prince Key Xosrō to a scribe reflexes of a universalizing declaration, the wording of which echoes elements of Cyrus' foundational inscription. Such an influence, she argues, "affected the Iranian oral traditions, and from there the Achaemenid inscriptions, and, eventually the *Šāhnāme* itself."

Bibliography

Burckhardt, Jacob. 2000. *Werke: Kritische Gesamtausgabe.* Vol. 10. C. H. Beck/ Schwabe & Co.

Garrison, Mark B. 2018. *The Ritual Landscape at Persepolis: Glyptic Imagery from the Persepolis Fortification and Treasury Archives.* Studies in Ancient Oriental Civilization 72. The Oriental Institute of the University of Chicago.

Garrison, Mark B. 2011. "The Seal of 'Kuraš the Anshanite, Son of Šešpeš (Teispes), PFS 93*: Susa – Anšan – Persepolis." In *Elam and Persia*, edited by Javier Álvarez-Mon and Mark B. Garrison, 375–405. Eisenbrauns.

Garrison, Mark B., and Margaret Cool Root. 2001. *Seals on the Persepolis Fortification Tablets.* Vol. I (1/2): *Images of Heroic Encounter.* Oriental Institute Publications 117. The Oriental Institute of the University of Chicago.

Henkelman, Wouter F. M. 2011. "Cyrus the Persian and Darius The Elamite: A Case of Mistaken Identity." In *Herodot und das persische Reich / Herodotus and the Persian Empire: Akten des 3. Internationalen Kolloquiums zum Thema 'Vorderasien im Spannungsfeld klassischer und altorientalischer Überlieferungen, Innsbruck 24.-28. November 2008*, edited by Robert Rollinger, Brigitte Truschnegg, and Reinhold Bichler. Classica et Orientalia 3, ser. eds. Reinhold Bichler, Bruno Jacobs, Giovanni B. Lanfranchi, Robert Rollinger, et al., 577–634. Harrassowitz.

———. 2008. *The Other Gods Who Are: Studies in Elamite-Iranian Acculturation Based on the Persepolis Fortification.* Achaemenid History 14. Leiden: Nederlands Instituut voor het Nabije Oosten.

———. 2003. "Persians, Medes, and Elamites: Acculturation in the Neo-Elamite Period." In *Continuity of Empire (?): Assyria, Media, Persia*, edited by Giovanni B. Lanfranchi, Michael Roaf, and Robert Rollinger, 181–231, table 2, pls. 9–15. History of the Ancient Near East – Monographs V. S.A.R.G.O.N. Editrice e Libreria.

Potts, Daniel T. 2016. *The Archaeology of Elam: Formation and Transformation of an Ancient Iranian State*. Second edition. New York: Cambridge University Press.

Rollinger, Robert. 2017. "Monarchische Herrschaft am Beispiel des teispidischachaimenidischen Großreichs." In *Monarchische Herrschaft im Altertum*, edited by Stefan Rebenich, 189–215. Schriften des Historischen Kollegs, Band 94. Walter de Gruyter.

———. 2014. "Das teispidisch-achaimenidische Großreich: Ein 'Imperium' avant la lettre?" In *Imperien und Reiche in der Weltgeschichte: Epochenübergreifende und globalhistorische Vergleiche*. Vol. I: *Imperien des Altertums, Mittelalterliche und frühneuzeitliche Imperien*, edited by Michael Gehler and Robert Rollinger, 149–192. Harrassowitz Verlag.

Shayegan, M. Rahim. 2012. *Aspects of History and Epic in Ancient Iran: From Gaumāta to Wahnām*. Hellenic Studies Series 52. Center for Hellenic Studies.

Stronach, David. 1997. "Anshan and Parsa: Early Achaemenid History, Art, and Architecture on the Iranian Plateau." In *Mesopotamia and Iran in the Persian Period: Conquest and Imperialism, 539–331 BC: Proceedings of a Seminar in Memory of Vladimir G. Lukonin*, edited by John Curtis, 35–53. British Museum Press.

Tavernier, Jan. 2011. "Iranians in Neo-Elamite Texts." In *Elam and Persia*, edited by Javier Álvarez-Mon and Mark B. Garrison. Eisenbrauns, 191–261.

The Text of the Cyrus Cylinder

Hanspeter Schaudig
University of Heidelberg

T HE BARREL-SHAPED BAKED CLAY CYLINDER inscribed with a proclamation in the name of Cyrus king of Anšan – and henceforth king of
Babylon – was found at the site of ancient Babylon in spring 1879.
Once taken to the British Museum in London, together with numerous other
texts, it was identified and presented to the public in November 1879 (Taylor
2013). The cylinder was probably undamaged when it was found. However,
it appears to have been broken already at the site of Babylon before ship-
ping. A rather large fragment of the original cylinder was acquired some
twenty-five years later on the art market and was incorporated into the Nies
Babylonian Collection of Yale University at New Haven. It was identified as
a fragment of the Cyrus Cylinder in the early 1970s,[1] and eventually joined
to the cylinder in the British Museum. Between December 2009 and January
2010, Wilfred G. Lambert and Irving Finkel discovered a copy of the text of
the cylinder on fragments of a clay tablet in the Babylonian collection of the
British Museum.[2]

Sources

A: Cyrus Cylinder: London, BM 90920; handcopies: H. C. Rawlinson and
T. G. Pinches, *The Cuneiform Inscriptions of Western Asia.* Vol. 5 (London
1880), pl. 35; Schaudig 2001, figs. 58–59.

+ Fragment, now joined to BM 90920 (filling a gap, lines 36–44): formerly
New Haven, Yale University, NBC 2504; handcopy: J. B. Nies and C. E.
Keiser, *Historical, Religious and Economic Texts and Antiquities.* Babylonian Inscriptions in the Collection of James B. Nies, Vol. II (New Haven
1920), pl. 21, no. 32.

B: Fragments of a clay tablet with a copy of the cylinder (photographs in
Finkel 2013a, 19):
B₁: London, BM 47134 = lines A 1–2, 42–45.
B₂: London, BM 47176 = lines A 34–37.

1. Berger 1975, 192–234.
2. Finkel 2013a, 15–26, and Finkel 2013b, 129.

Recent editions of the cylinder can be found in Schaudig 2001, 550–556, Finkel 2013a, 4–7 (translation), and Finkel 2013b, 129–135 (transliteration). Judging from the distribution of the text in lines A 33–36 and 43–44, the copy (B_{1-2}) appears to have arranged the text like the cylinder in long, individual lines. Only the last line (A 45) has been extended with large signs and free space, and split into two (B_1 rev. 4′-5′). The beginning of the text (A 1–3) is badly broken, but we can deduce from the preserved bits, and the overall character of this type of Babylonian royal inscriptions, that its content pertained to Babylonia having suffered in the past from the wrath of its tutelar deity, Marduk, because of some unnamed sin. The historical background is probably to be sought in the troubled years following the death of Nebuchadnezzar II in 562 BCE, when Babylonia experienced a period of unstable reigns and coups d'état. Fueling Marduk's anger and surely without divine approval (A 3 + B_1 obv. 3), a lowly and incompetent person (i.e. Nabonidus, r. 556–539 BCE) was elevated by unnamed powers to rule the land. His crimes and sacrileges provoke another wave of Marduk's wrath that washes Nabonidus away, with the aid of Marduk's pious servant, Cyrus.

Transliteration

A (1) [*ì-nu* (. . .) ^{d}*amar-utu* ....
.. *ú-ša*]*k-ni-šu*

B_1 (obv. 1) [*ì-nu* (. . .) ^{d}*amar-ut*]*u lugal kiš-šat an-e u ki-tì* ⌜x⌝[. . . . . .]

A (2) [. . . . .
ki-i]*b-ra-a-tì*

B_1 (obv. 2) [. . . . . . *šá ki-ma sa-b*]*a-si-šú ú-nam-m*[*u-ú* . . . . . .]³

A (3) [. . . . . *i-na la*] ⌜*šà-bi-šu*⌝¹⁴ *gal ma-ṭu-ú iš-šak-na*
a-na e-nu-tu ma-ti-šú

3. For this use of *kīma* and the same topos, compare: *kīma uzzi ilima īteppuš māta* "in accordance with the wrath of the god (Marduk) he (Senacherib) maltreated the country" (Nabonidus, Babylon Stela, I:18′-19′; see Schaudig 2001, 516).

4. Finkel 2013, 4, 130, suggests to restore the term "[first]born" ([*ṣīt*] *libbīšu*) here in A 3, meaning Nabonidus' son Belshazzar who had been put in charge as a governor by his father. I think it is highly unlikely to introduce this secondary figure so early in the text, if at all. Furthermore, since the restored term **ṣīt libbi* would be in fact feminine, the following attribute *gal = rabû* "great / old(est)," which is preserved, does not speak in favor of this restoration. The attribute should be **rabītu* (= *gal-tú*, etc.). But since a feminine attribute to go with the term "firstborn (son)" sounds awkward, the term *ṣīt libbi* as a rule does not take attributes. Besides, the passive voice in the verb (*iššakna* "he was installed") indicates that the author tries to avoid discussing the question as to who was to blame for this miscast. In fact, it would have been the god Marduk himself. But this was no option, of course. In contrast, Nabonidus commits all his misdeeds actively in this text.

B₁ ⁽ᵒᵇᵛ· ³⁾ [. . . . . . *a-n*]*a uz-zi-*⌜*šú*⌝ ⌜x⌝-[. . . . . .]

A ⁽⁴⁾ ⌜*ù*⁇⌝ [. . . . .]-*ši-li ú-ša-áš-ki-na ṣe-ru-šu-un*

A ⁽⁵⁾ *ta-am-ši-li é-saĝ-íl i-te-*[*pu-uš-ma* . . . . -*t*]*i*⁇ *a-na úri*ᵏⁱ *ù si-it-ta-a-tì ma-ḫa-za*

A ⁽⁶⁾ *pa-ra-aṣ la si-ma-a-ti-šu-nu ta-*[*ak-li-im la me-si* . . . *la*] *pa-liḫ* u₄-*mi-ša-am-ma id-de-né-eb-bu-ub ù* ⌜*a-na ma-ag*⌝-*ri-tì*

A ⁽⁷⁾ *sat-tuk-ku ú-šab-ṭi-li ú-l*[*a-ap-pi-it pél-lu-de-e* . . . *iš*]-*tak-ka-an qé-reb ma-ḫa-zi pa-la-ḫa* ᵈ*amar-utu lugal diĝir*ᵐᵉˢ *i*[*g-m*]*ur kar-šu-uš-šu*

A ⁽⁸⁾ *le-mu-ut-ti uru-šu* [*i-t*]*e-né-ep-pu-*⌜*uš*⌝ u₄-*mi-ša-am-*⌜*ma x x*⌝ [. . . *ùĝ*]ᵐᵉˢ-*šú i-na ab-ša-a-ni la ta-ap-šu-úḫ-tì ú-ḫal-li-iq kul-lat-si-in*

A ⁽⁹⁾ *a-na ta-zi-im-ti-ši-na* ᵈ⁺*en-líl diĝir*ᵐᵉˢ *ez-zi-iš i-gu-ug-m*[*a* . . .] *ki-su-úr-šu-un diĝir*ᵐᶜˢ *a-ši-ib šà-bi-šu-nu i-zi-bu al-*⌜*ma*⌝-*an-šu-un*

A ⁽¹⁰⁾ *i-na ug-ga-ti-ša ú-še-ri-bi a-na qé-reb šu-an-na*ᵏⁱ ᵈ*amar-utu t*[*i-iz-qa-ru* ᵈ⁺*en-líl diĝir*ᵐ]ᵉˢ *us-sa-aḫ-ra a-na nap-ḫar da-ád-mi ša in-na-du-ú šu-bat-su-un*

A ⁽¹¹⁾ *ù ùĝ*ᵐᵉˢ *kur šu-me-ri ù uri*ᵏⁱ *ša i-mu-ú ša-lam-ta-áš ú-sa-*⌜*aḫ*⌝-*ḫi-ir ka-*⌜*bat*⌝-[*ta-áš*] *ir-ta-ši ta-a-a-ra kul-lat ma-ta-a-ta ka-li-ši-na i-ḫi-iṭ ib-re-e-ma*

A ⁽¹²⁾ *iš-te-ʾe-e-ma ma-al-ki i-šá-ru bi-bil šà-bi-ša it-ta-ma-aḫ qa-tu-uš-šu* ⁱ*ku-ra-áš lugal uru an-ša-an it-ta-bi ni-bi-it-su a-na ma-li-ku-tì kul-la-ta nap-ḫar iz-zak-ra šu-*⌜*um-šú*⌝

A ⁽¹³⁾ *kur qu-ti-i gi-mir um-man-man-da ú-ka-an-ni-ša a-na še-pi-šu ùĝ*ᵐᵉˢ *ṣal-mat saĝ-du ša ú-ša-ak-ši-du qa-ta-a-šú*

A ⁽¹⁴⁾ *i-na ki-it-tì ù mi-šá-ru iš-te-né-ʾe-e-ši-na-a-tì* ᵈ*amar-utu en gal ta-ru-ú ùĝ*ᵐᵉˢ-*šú ep-še-e-ti-ša dam-qa-a-ta ù šà-ba-šu i-ša-ra ḫa-di-iš ip-pa-li-i*[*s*]

A ⁽¹⁵⁾ *a-na uru-šu ká-diĝir*ᵐᵉˢ ᵏⁱ *a-la-ak-šu iq-bi ú-ša-aṣ-bi-it-su-ma ḫar-ra-nu tin-tir*ᵏⁱ *ki-ma ib-ri ù tap-pe-e it-tal-la-ka i-da-a-šu*

A ⁽¹⁶⁾ *um-ma-ni-šu rap-ša-a-tì ša ki-ma me-e íd la ú-ta-ad-du-ú ni-ba-šu-un* ᵍⁱˢ*tukul*ᵐᵉˢ-*šu-nu ṣa-an-du-ma i-ša-ad-di-ḫa i-da-a-šu*

A ⁽¹⁷⁾ *ba-lu qab-li ù ta-ḫa-zi ú-še-ri-ba-áš qé-reb šu-an-na*ᵏⁱ *uru-šu ká-diĝir*ᵐᵉˢ ᵏⁱ *i-ṭi-ir i-na šap-ša-qí* ⁱᵈ⁺*nà-ní-tuku lugal la pa-li-ḫi-šu ú-ma-al-la-a qa-tu-uš-šú*

A ⁽¹⁸⁾ *ùĝ*ᵐᵉˢ *tin-tir*ᵏⁱ *ka-li-šu-nu nap-ḫar kur šu-me-ri u uri*ᵏⁱ *ru-bé-e ù šak-kan-nak-ka ša-pal-šu ik-mi-sa ú-na-áš-ši-qu še-pu-uš-šu iḫ-du-ú a-na lugal-ú-ti-šú im-mi-ru pa-nu-uš-šú-un*

A ⁽¹⁹⁾ *be-lu ša i-na tu-kul-ti-ša ú-bal-li-ṭu mi-tu-ta-an i-na pu-uš-qu ù*

ú-de-e ig-mi-lu kul-la-ta-an ṭa-bi-iš ik-ta-ar-ra-bu-šu iš-tam-ma-ru
zi-ki-ir-šu

A   (20)   a-na-ku ¹ku-ra-áš lugal kiš-šat lugal gal lugal dan-nu lugal tin-tir^ki
lugal kur šu-me-ri ù ak-ka-di-i lugal kib-ra-a-ti er-bé-et-tì

A   (21)   dumu ¹ka-am-bu-zi-ia lugal gal lugal uru an-ša-an dumu dumu
¹ku-ra-áš lugal gal luga[l u]ru an-ša-an šà-bal-bal ¹ši-iš-pi-iš lugal
gal lugal uru an-šá-an

A   (22)   numun da-ru-ú ša lugal-ú-tu ša ^d⁺en u ^d⁺nà ir-a-mu pa-la-a-šu a-na
ṭu-ub šà-bi-šú-nu iḫ-ši-ḫa l[uga]l-ut-su e-nu-ma a-n[a q]é-reb tin-
tir^ki e-ru-bu sa-li-mi-iš

A   (23)   i-na ul-ṣi ù ri-ša-a-tì i-na é-gal ma-al-ki ar-ma-a šu-bat be-lu-tì
^damar-utu en gal šà-bi ri-it-pa-šu ša ra-⌈im⌉ tin-tir^ki ši-m[a]⌈-a-tiš⌉
⌈iš-ku?-na⌉-an-ni-ma u₄-mi-šam a-še-ʾa-a pa-la-⌈aḫ⌉-šú

A   (24)   um-ma-ni-ia rap-ša-a-tì i-na qé-reb tin-tir^ki i-ša-ad-di-ḫa šu-ul-ma-
niš nap-ḫar ku[r šu-me-ri] ⌈ù⌉ uri^ki mu-gal-[l]i-tì ul ú-šar-ši

A   (25)   ⌈uru^ki⌉ ká-diĝir-ra^ki ù kul-lat ma-ḫa-zi-šu i-na ša-li-im-tì áš-te-ʾe-e
dumu^meš tin-tir[^ki . . . š]a ki-ma la šà-[bi ding]ir-ma ab-šá-a-ni la
si-ma-ti-šú-nu šu-ziz-⌈zu¹⌉

A   (26)   an-ḫu-ut-su-un ú-pa-áš-ši-ḫa ú-ša-ap-ṭi-ir sa-ar-ma-šu-nu a-na ep-
še-e-ti-[ia dam-qa-a-ti] ^damar-utu en ga[l]-ú iḫ-de-e-ma

A   (27)   a-na ia-a-ti ¹ku-ra-áš lugal pa-li-iḫ-šu ù ¹ka-am-bu-zi-ia dumu ṣi-it
šà-bi-[ia ù a-n]a nap-ḫ[ar] um-ma-ni-ia

A   (28)   da-am-qí-iš ik-ru-ub-ma i-na šá-lim-tì ma-ḫar-ša ṭa-bi-iš ni-it-t[a-al-
la-ak i-na qí-bi-ti-šú] ṣir-ti nap-ḫar lugal a-ši-ib bára^meš

A   (29)   ša ka-li-iš kib-ra-a-ta iš-tu tam-tì e-li-tì a-di tam-tì šap-li-tì a-ši-ib
n[a-gi-i né-su-tì] lugal^meš kur a-mur-ri-i a-ši-ib kuš-ta-ri ka-li-šú-un

A   (30)   bi-lat-su-nu ka-bi-it-tì ú-bi-lu-nim-ma qé-er-ba šu-an-na^ki ú-na-áš-
ši-qu še-pu-ú-a iš-tu [uru nina? ^k]i 5 a-di uru aš-šur^ki ù mùš-eren^ki

A   (31)   a-kà-dè^ki kur èš-nu-nak uru za-am-ba-an uru me-túr-nu bàd-diĝir^ki

5. Following Reade 1998, 65, I myself (Schaudig 2001, 553) and Finkel 2013b, 132, restored
"Babylon" here in the break, as the place from which the statues were sent. However, this is
probably wrong. The preposition ištu "from" in line 30 is in fact too far removed from the verb
utīr "I restored" in line 32, in order to indicate the place from where the statues returned.
Furthermore, one should expect ana "to" as the preposition that goes with the verb turru "to
restore" (see ana ašrišunu in l. 32), not adi "until/as far as." I think that the grammatical arch
ištu ... adi ... adi pāṭ "from ... until ... and even as far as" describes the vast geographical area of
the cities to which the deported gods and the people were returned. So, we should look for a
city north or east of Aššur to be restored here in the break. This is probably not Ḫarrān, since
Nabonidus had already prided himself on having restored the city, its temple, and deities.
Neither should we expect Jerusalem, because of the city's insignificance in those days. Thus,
Nineveh is indeed an option again, after having been correctly removed by Finkel 1997, and
Reade 1998, 65 from the immediately following, misread portion of the text.

a-di pa-aṭ kur qu-ti-i ma-ḫa-z[a e-be]r-ti ⁱᵈidigna ša iš-tu paⁱ-na-ma
na-du-ú šu-bat-su-un

A   (32)   diĝirᵐᵉˢ a-ši-ib šà-bi-šú-nu a-na áš-ri-šu-nu ú-tir-ma ú-šar-ma-a šu-
bat da-rí-a-ta kul-lat ùĝᵐᵉˢ-šú-nu ú-pa-aḫ-ḫi-ra-am-ma ú-te-er da-
ád-mi-šú-un

B₂   (1′)   [. . . . .] ⌜x x⌝ [. . . . .]

A   (33)   ù diĝirᵐᵉˢ kur šu-me-ri ù uriᵏⁱ ša ᴵᵈ⁺nà-ní-tuku a-na ug-ga-tì en
diĝirᵐᵉˢ ú-še-ri-bi
a-na qé-reb šu-an-naᵏⁱ i-na qí-bi-ti ᵈamar-utu en gal i-na ša-li-im-tì

B₂   (2′)   [. . . . . a-n]a u[g-ga]-tì en diĝirᵐᵉˢ ú-še-ri-⌜bi⌝ [. . . . .]

A   (34)   i-na maš-ta-ki-šu-nu ú-še-ši-ib šu-ba-at ṭu-ub šà-bi «ut» kul-la-ta
diĝirᵐᵉˢ ša ú-še-ri-bi
a-na qé-er-bi ma-ḫa-zi-šu-un

B₂   (3′)   [. . . . . šu-ba-at ṭu-u]b šà-bi kul-lat diĝirᵐᵉˢ šá ú-še-r[i-bi . . . . . .]

A   (35)   u₄-mi-ša-am ma-ḫar ᵈ⁺en ù ᵈ⁺nà ša a-ra-ku u₄ᵐᵉˢ-ia li-ta-mu-ú lit-taz-
ka-ru a-ma-a-ta du-un-qí-ia ù a-na ᵈamar-utu en-ia li-iq-bu-ú ša
ⁱku-ra-áš «áš» lugal pa-li-ḫi-ka u ⁱka-am-bu-zi-ia dumu-šú

B₂   (4′)   [. . . . .] ⌜u₄⌝ᵐᵉˢ-ia li-ta-mu-ú lit-taz-ka-ru a-[ma-a-ta du-un-qí-ia . . .
. . .]

A   (36)   ⌜x-⌝[x x x]⌜-x⌝ šu-nu lu-ú ⌜za-ni-ni⌝ ⌜bára⌝-[(i)]-⌜ni⌝ ⌜a-na u₄-um⌝
⌜sù⌝ᵐᵉˢ
[gi-m]ir ùĝᵐᵉˢ tin-tirᵏⁱ ⌜ik-tar-ra-bu⌝ lugal-ú-tu kur-kur ka-li-ši-na
šu-ub-ti né-eḫ-tì ú-še-ši-ib

B₂   (5′)   [. . . . .]⌜x⌝ ⌜šu-nu⌝ lu-ú za-ni-ni bára-i-ni a-na ⌜u₄ᵐᵉˢ⌝ r[e-e-qu-tì . .
. . . .]

A   (37)   [. . . . . kur-]giᵐᵘˢᵉⁿ 2 UZ-TURᵐᵘˢᵉⁿ·<ᵐᵉˢ> ù 10 tu-gur₄ᵐᵘˢᵉⁿ·ᵐᵉˢ
e-li kur-giᵐᵘˢᵉⁿ UZ-TURᵐᵘˢᵉⁿ·ᵐᵉˢ ù tu-gur₄ᵐᵘˢᵉⁿ·ᵐᵉˢ

B₂   (6′)   [. . . . .] ⌜x x x x⌝ [. . . . .]

A   (38)   [. . . . . u₄-m]i-šam ú-ṭa-aḫ-ḫi-id bàd im-gur-ᵈ⁺en-líl bàd
gal-a ša tin-tirᵏ[ⁱ ma-aṣ-ṣ]ar-⌜ta⌝-šú du-un-nu-nù áš-te-ʾe-e-ma

A   (39)   [. . . . .] ka-a-ri a-gur-ru šá gú ḫa-ri-ṣi ša lugal maḫ-ri i-p[u-
šu-ma la ú-ša]k-⌜li-lu⌝ ši-pi-ir-šu

A   (40)   [. . . . . la ú-ša-as-ḫi-ru uru] ⌜a⌝-na ki-da-a-ni ša lugal

       ma-aḫ-ra la i-pu-šu um-man-ni-šu di-ku-u[t ma-ti-šu i-na / a-na q]
       *é-⌈reb⌉ šu-an-na*ᵏⁱ

A   ⁽⁴¹⁾ *[......... i-na esir-ḫád-rá-]⌈a⌉ ù sig₄-al-ùr-ra eš-ši-iš e-pu-uš-ma*
       [ú-šak-lil ši-pir-ši]-in

A   ⁽⁴²⁾ *[............ ᵍⁱˢig*ᵐᵉˢ ᵍⁱˢ*eren maḫ]*ᵐᵉˢ *ta-aḫ-lu-up-tì zabar as-ku-*
       *up-pu ù nu-ku-š[e-e pi-ti-iq e-ri-i e-ma ká*ᵐᵉˢ*-š]i-na*
B₁   ⁽ʳᵉᵛ. ¹′⁾ *[.....] ⌈x x⌉ [......]*

A   ⁽⁴³⁾ *[ú-ra-at-ti .... š]i-ṭi-ir šu-mu šá ᴵan-šár-dù-ibila*
       *lugal a-lik maḫ-ri-[ia šá qer-ba-šu ap-pa-a]l-sa*ᴵ
B₁   ⁽ʳᵉᵛ. ²′⁾ *[.....] ⌈ᴵ⌉an-šár-dù-i[bila ......]*

A   ⁽⁴⁴⁾ *[.................]⌈x x x⌉[......... ba-la-aṭ u₄*ᵐᵉˢ *ru-q]ú-tì*
B₁   ⁽ʳᵉᵛ. ³′⁾ *[...... ú-tir a-na áš-r]i-⌈šú⌉ ᵈamar-utu en gal ba-l[a-aṭ u₄*ᵐᵉˢ *ru-qú-*
       tì]

A   ⁽⁴⁵⁾ *[.............................]⌈x x x⌉[.. a-na d]a-rí-a-tì*
B₁   ⁽ʳᵉᵛ. ⁴′⁾ *[...... la-bar bala]-⌈e⌉ a-na ši-ri-ik-t[ì šu-úr-kam]*
B₁   ⁽ʳᵉᵛ. ⁵′⁾ *[...... a-na-ku lu-ú lugal mu-ṭi-ib]* *šà-bi-ka a-na [da-rí-a-tì]*

Colophon (B₁ only)

B₁   ⁽ʳᵉᵛ. ⁶′⁾ *[ki ka mu-sa-re-e šá ᴵku-ra-áš lugal ká-diĝir-ra*ᵏⁱ *šá-ṭir-ma b]a-ar*
       im ᴵníĝ-ba-ᵈamar-utu ⌈a⌉ [...]

B₁   ⁽ʳᵉᵛ. ⁶′⁾ [Written and ch]ecked [according to an inscription of Cyrus
       king of Babylon].
       The tablet (belongs) to Qīšti-Marduk son of [PN₂ ...]

Translation (A and B combined):

    ⁽¹⁾ [When (...) Mardu]k, the king of the whole of heaven and
       earth, ... subju]gated
    ⁽²⁾ [...... who] laid waste [*the land* in accordance with] his (=
       Marduk's) [wr]ath [................... the regions] of the
       world
    ⁽³⁾ [...... t]o his (= Marduk's) anger [... and without (the consent)
       of] his great heart, a low and unworthy man (= Nabonidus) was
       installed as lord of his (= Marduk's) country.

(4) [. . . . .] . . . . (Nabonidus) imposed on them.

(5) He ma[de] a counterfeit of (Marduk's temple) Esaĝil [. . . . .] . . . for (the city of) Ur and the rest of the sacred cities,

(6) rites, which were inappropriate to them (i.e. the sacred cities and the gods), [improper] sac[rifices . . .]. He spoke [*insolence*] every day and was not afraid (of Marduk's wrath). As an insult,

(7) (Nabonidus) brought the daily offerings to a halt and inter[fered with the rites. He s]et up [. . .] in the midst of the sacred cities. In his heart he br[oug]ht to an end the worship of Marduk, king of the gods.

(8) He [d]id yet more evil to (Marduk's holy) city every day. [. . . . He *tormented*] its [people], he brought ruin on all of them by a yoke without relief.

(9) At their complaints, the Enlil-of-the-gods (= Marduk) became furiously enraged a[nd . . . . *Nabonidus violated*] their (= the gods') sacred territories, (and so) the gods who dwelt therein deserted their shrines.

(10a) Arousing (Marduk's) wrath, (Nabonidus then) had (the statues of) the gods brought into Babylon (from their proper cities).

(10b-11) But Marduk, the l[ofty Enlil-of-the-god]s, relented and felt pity for the cities whose dwelling-places were lying in ruins. He made up [his] mind and had mercy on the people of Babylonia who had become like (living) dead. (Marduk) scanned and checked all the countries,

(12) looking for a righteous king, dear to his heart, and finally he took with his very hand Cyrus, king of the city of Anšan, and calling his name, he appointed him to be king of the entire world.

(13-14) (Marduk) made bow down at (Cyrus') feet the land of the Gutians and all of the Ummān-Manda. And all the people that (Marduk) had given into his hands, (Cyrus) tended most carefully like a shepherd in truth and righteousness. Marduk, the great lord, who takes care of his people, saw with pleasure his good deeds and his righteous heart.

(15) He commanded (Cyrus) to set out for Babylon, he made him take the way to Tintir (= Babylon), and, like a friend and companion, he walked at his side.

(16) (Cyrus') vast troops whose number, like the water in a river, could not be counted, marched at his side, girt with their weapons.

(17) Without any fight or battle (Marduk) had him enter Babylon and saved his city Babylon from hardship. (Marduk) delivered into (Cyrus') hands Nabonidus, the king who would not revere him.

(18) All the people of Babylon, the entire land of Sumer and Akkad (= Babylonia), nobles and governors, bowed down before (Cyrus) and kissed his feet, with shining faces they rejoiced at his kingship.

(19) Sweetly they hailed him as the lord through whose help they had come to life again from the perils of death, praising his name as the one who has saved them all from distress and disaster.

(20) I am Cyrus, the king of the world, the great king, the mighty king, the king of Babylon, king of the land of Sumer and Akkad, the king of the four quarters of the world,

(21) son of Cambyses, the great king, king of the city of Anšan, grandson of Cyrus (I), the great king, kin[g of the c]ity of Anšan, descendant of Teispes, the great king, king of the city of Anšan,

(22a) eternal scion of kingship, whose rule Bēl (= Marduk) and Nabû dearly love, whose k[in]gship they desired for their own delight.

(22b) When I entered Babylon in peace, (23) I took up my lordly abode in the royal palace amidst jubilation and rejoicing. Marduk, the great lord, bestowed on me as my destiny that wide heart of mine, (as a token) of someone who loves Babylon, and so I do revere him every day.

(24) My vast troops walked around in Babylon in peace, and I did not permit anybody to frighten (the people of) the land of S[umer] and Akkad.

(25) Of Babylon and all its sacred places I took care in peace and sincerity. The people of Babylon [. . .], onto whom (Nabonidus) had imposed an inappropriate yoke against the wil[l of the g]ods,

(26) I brought relief to their exhaustion and did away with their toil. Marduk, the great lord, rejoiced at [my good] deeds, and

(27–28a) sent friendly blessings to me, Cyrus, the king who reveres him, to Cambyses, my son, the fruit of [my] loins, as well as to all my troops, and so we w[alked] in peace and happiness before him.

(28b–30a) [At (Marduk's)] august [command] all the kings of the entire world, those who are seated on thrones, living in [distant] coun[tries] from the Upper to the Lower Sea (= from the

Mediterranean to the Persian gulf) as well as the kings of Amurru (= Arabia), dwelling in tents, (all these kings) brought their heavy tribute and kissed my feet in Babylon.

(30b) From [the city of Nineveh?] to the city of Aššur and Susa,

(31–32) (to) Akkad, the land of Ešnunna, the towns Zabbān, Meturnu, Dēr, and as far as the region to the land of the Gutians, the sacred cities on the [ot]her side (= east) of the Tigris, which had been laying in ruins since days of old, I returned (the statues of) the gods who used to dwell therein and had them live there for evermore. I (also) gathered their (former) people and brought them back to their habitations.

(33–34) And (the statues of) the gods of the land of Sumer und Akkad, which Nabonidus – to the anger of the lord of the gods – had brought into Babylon, I had them dwell in peace in their beloved sanctuaries at the command of Marduk, the great lord. May all these gods, which I restored to their sacred cities,

(35) ask daily Bēl and Nabû to grant me a long life, they may speak blessings for me, and they may say to Marduk, my lord: "Of Cyrus, the king who reveres you and Cambyses, his son,

(36) [*guard their lives!*] May they be the provisioners of our shrines until ⌈distant⌉ days!" [A]ll of the people of Babylon blessed my kingship, and I took care that all the countries live in peace.

(37) [. . . . . one go]ose, two ducks and ten wild doves in addition to the goose, ducks, and wild doves (already assigned for the meal of Marduk)

(38a) [. . . . .] I ordered to be delivered (to the temple) eve[ry d]ay.

(38b) As to the wall Imgur-Enlil, the great wall of Babylon, I sought to increase its [secu]rity.

(39) [. . . . .] The quay made of baked brick on the bank of the city moat, which an earlier king had bui[lt but not com]pleted,

(40) [. . . . ., which did not yet surround the city] outwards, a work an earlier king had not completed, his troops, the contingent [of his country . . . . into] Babylon.

(41) [. . . . . with asphal]t and baked brick I built (the walls) anew and [completed the]m.

(42) [. . . . . hu]ge [door-leaves made of cedar-wood], covered with bronze, thresholds and door fitt[ings, made of ore, (43) I set up (42) in all] their [gates].

(43) [. . . . . An in]scription of Assurbanipal, a former king, [which I fou]nd [therein,]
(44) [I *treated it respectfully* and put it back into] its [plac]e [*together with my own inscription.*] Marduk, great lord! (45) [May you grant me] as a gift (44) a [lon]g [life],
(45) [. . . . . and an enduring reig]n! [May I be the king who pleases] your heart for evermore!

Bibliography

Berger, P.-R. 1975. "Der Kyros-Zylinder mit dem Zusatzfragment BIN II Nr. 32 und die akkadischen Personennamen im Danielbuch." *Zeitschrift für Assyriologie und Vorderasiatische Archäologie* 64:192–234.

Finkel, I. 1997. "No Nineveh in the Cyrus Cylinder." *Nouvelles Assyriologiques Brèves et Utilitaires,* no. 24.

———. 2013a. "The Cyrus Cylinder: the Babylonian Perspective." In *The Cyrus Cylinder: The King of Persia's Proclamation from Ancient Babylon,* edited by I. Finkel, 4–34. London.

———. 2013b. "Appendix: Transliteration of the Cyrus Cylinder Text." In *The Cyrus Cylinder: The King of Persia's Proclamation from Ancient Babylon,* edited by I. Finkel, 129–135. London.

Reade, J. 1998. "Greco-Parthian Nineveh," *Iraq* 60:65–83.

Schaudig, H. 2001. *Die Inschriften Nabonids von Babylon und Kyros' des Grossen samt den in ihrem Umfeld entstandenen Tendenzschriften: Textausgabe und Grammatik.* Alter Orient und Altes Testament, Band 256. Münster.

Taylor, J. 2013. "The Cyrus Cylinder: Discovery." In *The Cyrus Cylinder: The King of Persia's Proclamation from Ancient Babylon,* edited by I. Finkel, 35–68. London.

Cyrus Rising:
Reflections on Word Choice, Ancient and Modern[1]

Matt Waters
University of Wisconsin-Eau Claire

ASKED FOR THIS CONFERENCE to discuss the history of the early Persian period, herein are (re)considered some of the relevant historiographic issues associated with Cyrus the Great's rise. Construction of a cohesive historical narrative for the Neo-Elamite period, c. 1000–550 BCE, remains a challenge. A variety of data testifies to the cultural components of the so-called Persian-Elamite ethnogenesis, but the extant archaeological and especially documentary evidence is disjointed.[2] This is especially the case for that last formative century, roughly delineated by the Assyrian invasions of Susiana during the early 640s and Cyrus the Great's early campaigns in the 550s. It remains to be determined how Cyrus the Great's forebears, labeled by Cyrus in his Cylinder as kings of Anshan, fit into the geopolitical milieu of multiple kingdoms – coterminous with various tribal-based groups in southwestern Iran in the late seventh and early sixth centuries.[3] Thus, to resort to some clichéd but apt phraseology, we are in a dark age, for which the barest indicators of political history remain mostly static – a variety of "known unknowns" awaiting additional evidence. In the meanwhile, advances in publishing Assyrian, Babylonian, and Elamite material promote further insights on these antecedents' impact on Achaemenid imperial institutions and ideology.

1. This is a modified version of a paper given 28 October, 2013, at the *Cyrus the Great: Life and Lore* conference, submitted in March 2015. Thanks to UCLA Iranian Studies, the Farhang Foundation, IHF America, the Semnani Family Foundation and M. Rahim Shayegan for their hospitality.
2. See Miroschedji 1985, 1990, and 2003; Vallat 1996; Potts 2016, Chapter 8; Waters 2000 and 2013; Tavernier 2004; Carter 2007; Henkelman 2003 and 2008, Chapter 1; the contributions in Álvarez-Mon and Garrison 2011; Boucharlat 2013. Extant Neo-Elamite royal inscriptions, primarily dedications found in temple contexts, are thin on details of chronology, problems of translation and interpretation aside. The lack of chronological markers in Neo-Elamite royal inscriptions anticipates the same lack in Achaemenid royal inscriptions – Darius I's Bisitun Inscription being an exception, but even that inscription has several timeless elements.
3. See among others Henkelman 2012, 933–935.

The present paper will consider the import of word choice – both in ancient texts and in modern translation – in particular, and how it impacts the historiography of this period. A short example of the phenomenon is the translation of the Akkadian verb *dâku*, represented by the logogram GAZ, in the Nabonidus Chronicle. At issue is whether Cyrus killed, or just defeated (column ii, line 17), a particular king in 547. Similarly, whether Cyrus killed (even "slaughtered" in some translations), or, again, just defeated, the Babylonian army (or people) after his victory at Opis in 539 (column iii, line 14).[4] Interpretation of Cyrus' actions after his victory may take different turns based on how the verb *dâku* is translated in these contexts.

Thus, translation (word choice) of one word or phrase –those basic philological issues with which we still grapple – has significant repercussions for historical interpretation. That is hardly a new or profound observation, quite the opposite. But it is an observation particularly appropriate for historians attempting to untangle such a convoluted period from often sketchy evidence pertaining to a variety of documentation, of different genres and different languages: royal inscriptions, chronicles, administrative documents, and sealing inscriptions, from a chronological range encompassing more than 200 years.

Specific examples discussed in this paper include: geographic labels that appear to shift over time with regard to areas they designate; whether Cyrus was the great-grandson, or a descendant – however the latter is to be understood (the word *liblibbu* in the Cyrus Cylinder) – of Teispes; whether the temples that Cyrus restored after his conquest of Babylonia were age-old, or had been abandoned for a long time (the word *nadû* in the Cyrus Cylinder); and whether Cyrus was insignificant or merely young (the word *ṣiḫru* in Nabonidus' Sippar Cylinder) when he overthrew the Medes. And, finally, what significance may be attributed to Cyrus' adaptation of Babylonian idiom in his short royal inscription from Ur.

Consideration of most of the issues highlighted here is hardly new – another understatement – they have occupied modern scholarship for generations. To torture this data, yet again, for additional insights may strike some as a fool's errand, and I confess myself suspicious that that is the reason Rahim Shayegan invited me to speak at this conference. Regardless, we persist in these pursuits, since Cyrus the Great's formation of the first Persian empire is so fundamentally important in world history, and so many important questions remain unresolved.

---

4. Akkadian *nišū* ("people") has its own ambiguities, see CAD vol. 11/II (N), 284–286 11/2. CAD 3 (D), 35–43 for *dâku*; compare translations of Grayson 1975, 107–109; Glassner 2004, 236–237; Kuhrt 2007, 50–51; and Lambert 2007. Line numbering follows Grayson's edition.

Anshan and Parsa

Cyrus tells us in his Babylonian inscriptions – both the Cyrus Cylinder and the Ur brick inscription – that he was king of Anshan. Why "Anshan"? The most straightforward answer to that question is because this was precisely what he was: the king of Anshan; Anshan as a geographic label applied both to an ancient Elamite city and the surrounding region.[5] Cyrus' use of the title "king of Anshan" in Babylonian inscriptions seems an odd choice; it is a title that was not used, as far as we can tell, for centuries and even then with only few examples.[6] Anshan occurs rarely in Neo-Elamite and even less in Neo-Assyrian texts and in the latter only through the early seventh century.

From the late eighth century, a new entry appears among attested Assyrian toponyms, Parsumash – or Parsumashians, the ethnonym – referring to Persia(ns) in Fars. Parsumash in Fars was a place distinct from the province of Parsua in the central western Zagros, the latter northwest of the Mahidasht.[7] The earliest reference to Parsumash is an intriguing one, a report dating to the reign of Sargon concerning the Elamite-Assyrian struggle

5. It has been proposed that the use of URU (Akkadian determinative for a city) with Anshan in the Cyrus Cylinder implies something more than scribal variation or inconsistency, since Anshan is elsewhere preceded by the KUR determinative (Cyrus' Ur brick, Nabonidus' Sippar Cylinder) or no determinative at all (Nabonidus Chronicle); see Henkelman 2003, 193–194 and 2011, 610–612; Potts 2011; Zournatzi forthcoming. It is unrealistic to expect consistency across various texts (from different locales and periods), especially when the toponym may refer to a city or to a region. Sometimes consistency is lacking within the same text; for example, the Nabonidus Chronicle (ii 3) applies the determinative KUR before *Agamtanu* (Ecbatana), whereat it is described as a "royal city" (*āl šarrūtu*). Not only does the determinative differ, the orthography of Anshan varies as well: [URU]*an-ša-an* in the Cyrus Cylinder; [KUR]*aš-ša-an* in the Ur brick (with archaizing signs); and *an-šá-an* in the Nabonidus Chronicle (no determinative). The [KUR]*an-za-an* in the Sippar Cylinder is the only spelling that matches the typical Elamite orthography [h]*an-za-an* (e.g. as used in PFS 93*). Cyrus' use of the title "king of Anshan" has significance beyond a geographic description, but it is difficult to see how the variation in orthography, or the use of either URU or KUR determinative before the toponym, is germane in those considerations.

6. See references and discussion at Potts 2005, 14–15; and note also Briant 2002, 16–18 and 23. For different perspectives on Cyrus' choice of title, compare Vallat 2011; Zournatzi forthcoming; Stronach 2013. The standard Middle Elamite title "king of Anshan and Susa" is found in inscriptions of only two Neo-Elamite kings, Shutruk-Nahhunte II and Atta-hamiti-Inshushinak; most Neo-Elamite inscriptions contain only the unadorned title "king." For variations on the use of "Anshan and Susa" in royal title, e.g. that of Hallutash-Inshushinak, see Waters 2000, 27; for the confusion between the forms of Shutruk- and Shutur-Nahhunte, see Waters 2000, Appendix B and Tavernier 2004 with references, note also Shayegan 2011, 277.

7. Levine 1974, 112; Rollinger 1999; Waters 1999 and 2011; Fuchs 2004. For CT 53 110+, see Fuchs and Parpola 2001, xxxiii and liii, n. 102 with discussion and references xxiv–xxxi.

for Ellipi.[8] The writer reports that the Elamite king (i.e. Shutruk-Nahhunte II), en route to Bit-Bunakki, located somewhere north of Susa and east of Der, dispatched a messenger to Parsumash to determine if a specific individual – whose name is broken away save its ending: *-yâ* – will mobilize (*dekû*) troops.

Is this indicative of some sort of Elamite-Persian cooperation against Assyria? Whether or not that was the case, note that the word "cooperation" in the preceding question is speculation – a word choice based on an interpretation of a broken and isolated context. Further, even if the word choice is appropriate, there is currently no way to discern whether any such "cooperation" was mandatory or voluntary. If one extrapolates from Shutruk-Nahhunte II's use of the title "king of Anshan and Susa" that he controlled parts of Fars, it is likely that this included Persian (i.e. Parsumashian) subjects. That prospect is further supported by the much-discussed reference of the Elamite forces arrayed against Sennacherib at the Battle of Halule in 691. Sennacherib's annals list a number of places and peoples under the aegis of the Elamite king Humban-menanu. Both Parsuash, a variant of Parsumash, and Anshan are listed as separate entities, first in a long list.[9] Since Assyria controlled the areas north of Ellipi at this time, including the province of Parsua, it is understood that both Sargon's and Sennacherib's Parsu(m)ash must be in Fars. If the Elamite king Humban-menanu was able to draw support from both Anshan and Parasu(m)ash, it stands to reason that his influence there, if not sovereignty, was a given.

Correspondence from Ashurbanipal's reign – sporadic, tantalizing, but more than forty years after Halule – alludes to tension between Elamites and Persians in the Zagros foothills toward Fars. There are references to Persians raiding the area around Hidalu, transport of prisoners, and skirmishes between Elamite and Persian forces; the Assyrians differentiate the two ethnonyms. In a letter addressed to Ashurbanipal (ABL 961), its author (whose name is broken away) urges the king to confirm the Persian raids with Marduk-šar-uṣur, a prominent official, and to send the Elamites Tammaritu and Kudurru to secure the area.[10] The context is sometime after 653 when Elam became, briefly, an Assyrian province. The threat from these Persians was significant, there is a note of crisis in the same letter's plea for assistance (reverse, lines 2–6). The action described in another letter (ABL

---

8. See CT 53 110+ published as SAA 15, no. 129.
9. Grayson and Novotny 2012, 182, no. 22, v. 44 (and other inscriptions, see indices under "Anzan").
10. ABL 961+, obverse, lines 8–15, published in Waterman 1930, 167.

1311+) appears to be related to that of ABL 961.[11] In 1311+, the general Bēl-ibni reports to Ashurbanipal that Persians have been plundering (*ḫabātu*) the areas of the Šallukeans and Hidalu, in opposition to Tammaritu.[12]

Much remains opaque in the two letters, but it is difficult to read these sections any other way than describing friction between groups of Persians and Elamites. How are we to situate such conflict(s) into an overarching process of Elamite-Persian acculturation? The who (beyond the generic ethnonyms), the how, and, most importantly, the why these groups were fighting are unknown. It is tempting to connect this activity to early Persian expansion under Cyrus the Great's predecessors, but there is no way at present to substantiate this. In any event, it would be misguided to assume that processes of Elamite-Persian ethnogenesis proceeded seamlessly. Though we cannot delineate the process during the several decades of the late seventh century and into the sixth, subsequent documentary evidence and material culture demonstrate the result.[13]

One manifestation of that dynamic is a seal impression (PFS 93*) from the Persepolis Fortification Archive: it belongs to Cyrus the Anshanite, the son of Teispes.[14] This sealing and accompanying inscription, generally attributed to Cyrus the Great's grandfather, is a vivid reminder of the Elamite roots of Cyrus' dynasty. The Cyrus of PFS 93* labels himself an "Anshanite" (or, as also translated, "of Anshan").[15] This label offers historians an indirect link to Cyrus the Great's preference in royal title, "king of Anshan" – though the significance of any proposed link vis-à-vis the traditional Elamite title "king of Anshan and Susa" is not straightforward.

In his Cyrus Cylinder,[16] Cyrus tells his audience that Marduk chose him, the king of Anshan, as his instrument. After Cyrus has adopted traditional Assyrian and Babylonian royal epithets, he rehearses his lineage through three generations, each labeled "king of Anshan."[17] What that meant in geopolitical terms is unclear. One must consider the possibility that Cyrus may have exaggerated his predecessor's titular prestige – this is, by adding the appellative "great king, king of Anshan" to his progenitors' names through

---

11. See ABL 1311+, lines 17–27. For ABL 1311+, dated to the late 650s or early 640s, see DeVaan 1995, 311–314; and Waters 2000, 74–75.

12. For *Marduk-šar-uṣur*, see Frame 1992, 158–159,178–179; and Baker 2001, 728–729 with references; also Waters 2000, 59.

13. See especially Root 2011.

14. Also a much discussed artifact, see Garrison 2011.

15. The identification of this Cyrus with Cyrus of Parsumash, also much debated, is left aside here. See Waters 2011 and Henkelman 2011, 601–604 for discussion and references; for attestations of the name Cyrus, see Tavernier 2007, 528–529.

16. Finkel 2013, line 12.

17. Finkel 2013, lines 12 and 21, respectively.

Teispes. It was essential, after all, for Cyrus to have been of an eternal line, a perpetual seed, of kingship (*zēru dārû ša šarruti*),[18] just as it was for his Babylonian predecessors to be so – the phrasing is traditional. It was, likewise, just as important for Darius to claim the same later, with the same phrasing in the Babylonian version of his Bisitun Inscription (DB §4). Continuity of royal ancestry, along with continuity of tradition, was of paramount importance.

The term in the Cyrus Cylinder, line 21, that describes Cyrus' relationship to Teispes is written logographically ŠÀ.BAL.BAL, Akkadian *liblibbu*. Word choice matters in translation, because the term's application was fluid. The *Chicago Assyrian Dictionary* (CAD) cites examples of this word in reference to grandfather (by Ashurbanipal for Sennacherib), great-grandfather (by Adad-nirari I for Ashur-uballit), great-great-grandfather (by Sin-shar-ishkin for Sargon), and descendant (for some ninth-century kings, or earlier). Which translation of *liblibbu* is appropriate in the Cyrus Cylinder? "Descendant" is the safe choice in this context for such a versatile word, especially in this case since we have no external confirmation for Cyrus' line beyond his own testimony.[19] Thus, the precise degree of generational separation between Cyrus the Great and Teispes has become a matter of debate.

We lack Achaemenid-period parallels, since the typical formulation in inscriptions of Darius I and his successors is "son of" x, "son of" y... or "father of" x, "father of" y, etc. In an inscription from Susa (A²Sa), Artaxerxes II refers specifically to his great-great-grandfather, i.e. Darius I, with the Akkadian AD.AD.AD-ya.[20] This iteration must be translated somewhat loosely – on

18. Finkel 2013, line 22. The expression *zēru dārû ša šarruti* (NUMUN [*zēru*] *dārû ša* LUGAL-*utu*) is comparable to NUMUN *dārû*, which occurs in the Babylonian version of Darius' inscription at Bisitun (DB Bab. §4); for the Babylonian version, see Voigtlander 1978, 12. See also the Elamite passage of Bisitun (DB El. §3) – ᵛNUMUNᵐᵉˢ ᵛ*nukami* [ᵛSUNKIⁱᵖ] – and the Old Persian *hacā paruviyata hayā amāxam taumā xšāyaθiyā āha* (From of old our line has been kings). For the Elamite version, see Grillot-Susini, Herrenschmidt, and Malbran-Labat 1993, 20; for the Old Persian version, see Schmitt 2009, §3, 37–38. Further, as several commentators have noted, the Cyrus of PFS 93* does not call himself a king. When considered with Cyrus' genealogy in the Cyrus Cylinder and the royal titles given to his predecessors, the anomaly begs reconciliation; see Waters 2011, 292; and Stronach 2003, 255.

19. CAD 9 (L), 180, see Nielsen 2011, 75–76 for wider uses of the term and note Henkelman 2011, 602, n. 71 citing Rollinger 1998. Translating "descendant": Schaudig 2001, 555; Michalowski 2006, 479; Kuhrt 2007, 71; Finkel 2013, 6. Translating "great-grandson": Berger 1975, 197; Lecoq 1997, 183; Brosius 2000, 11; Waters 1996, 13.

20. Hand copy in Weissbach, 1891, 159–160, and following plate. Weissbach notes on page 160 that his copy is after ("nach"), Loftus, *Inscriptions from Susa*, Plates 1–5, 1852. See Old Persian *apanayāka-maiy* translated by Kent 1953, 154 as "(my) great-great-grandfather (see also entry at 168); Lecoq 1997, 273 translates "mon ancêtre"; more recently see Schmitt 2014, 80 who translates "Ururgroßvater," with further literature; for a diachronic discussion of *apanayāka-* (<*apa-niyāka-*) in Iranian inscriptions, see Shayegan 2011, 18–19. For the text of A2Sa, see

the parallel with *liblibbu* – as "father of my fathers" or allowed that an extra "AD" is missing, as the literal formulation falls one generation short.

Cyrus and the Overthrow of the Medes

Nabonidus' Sippar Cylinder, in two fully preserved copies and multiple fragments of others, provides an important perspective on Cyrus' conflict with the Median king Astyages.[21] Nabonidus, in describing his concern for the restoration of the Eḫulḫul temple (of Sin) in Sippar, found in the Medes both a cause of and an impediment to this work. The Medes in this inscription became the stereotypical enemy in Mesopotamian tradition, the Ummān-Manda, bogeymen created by the gods as an instrument to punish wrongdoers manifest in inscriptions dating from the Akkadian period onward.[22] Nabonidus' choice to cast the Medes as the barbaric Ummān-Manda (LÚÉRIN-*manda*) as responsible for the appalling state of the temples allows him to take credit for their restoration. Cyrus, the king of Anshan, is also an instrument of the gods, whereby the threat of the Medes will be removed, so that Nabonidus may commence with the important work of rebuilding.

Cyrus' overthrow of Astyages and the Medes is well known from the classical tradition, mainly via Herodotus. His account portrays Cyrus as a grandson of Astyages, through Astyages' daughter Mandane's marriage to a Persian named Cambyses (Hdt.1.107). This story has long been recognized as one in which the main point, historicity aside, was to link Cyrus to the Median dynastic tradition, thereby legitimizing his reign. Nabonidus' account offers another perspective, one replete with historical significance for understanding the relationship between Cyrus and Astyages.

Column i, lines 26–28 reads:[23]

> ... *ina šalulti MU.AN.NA ina kašadu ušatbūniššumma* ᵐ*Kuraš LUGAL* ᴷᵁᴿ*Anzan* ÌR-*su ṣaḫri ina ummanišu iṣutu* LÚÉRIN-*manda rapšati usappiḫ*

> ... in the third year, they (the gods) caused to rise Cyrus, the king of Anshan,

---

Schmitt 2009, A2Sa §2, 192.The Elamite *appanuyaka* is simply a gloss of the OP; see Hallock 1969, 669 and Hinz and Koch 1987, 20.

21. The cylinder's content deals mainly with temple restoration: Eḫulḫul of Sin (Harran); Ebabbar of Shamash and the ziggurat Ekunankugga (both in Sippar); and Eulmash of Anunitum (Sippar); Beaulieu 1989, 34, Inscription 15, and 107–109 and Schaudig 2001, 409–440, Inscription 2.12.

22. See especially for this inscription Rollinger 2003, 301–305; note also Adali 2011.

23. Schaudig 2001, 417.

his young servant, with his small army he scattered the vast
Ummān-Manda ...

Historical interpretation of these lines depends on our understanding of the
characterization of Cyrus therein, word choice in translation. For much of
the twentieth century, the "his" of the phrase "his servant" (ÎR-*su* for *arassu*
(< *ardu-šu*) was understood to mean that Cyrus was Astyages' servant; recent translations have for the most part abandoned that sense, though the
ambiguity lingers.[24] In Assyrian and Babylonian documents, such phrasing
is typically applied to an agent who was the god's servant, in this instance,
the god Marduk's. The preceding verb *ušatbūniššum* refers to a plural subject, i.e. the gods plural, rousing Cyrus. Thus, to apply the singular "his" of
"his servant" to Marduk is not straightforward. However, the entire context
refers to a communication, i.e. a dream, from Marduk, so it is defensible
(preferable, to my mind) to understand the "his" of "his servant" as, indeed,
referring to Marduk's. Whether we understand Cyrus as subject to Astyages,
or not, of course has enormous impact on historical reconstruction.

Further, the description of the servant (i.e. Cyrus) as *ṣaḫri* also con-
founds; the word has a variety of meanings.[25] Does it mean in this context,
as often translated, "young" (so here), and thus a commentary on Cyrus'
relative age? Or is another meaning to be applied, that of "small" or "insignificant"? Nabonidus' characterization of Cyrus as "insignificant" – if that
is indeed what he meant – may signify little outside the literary context
of this passage. But for historians attempting to piece together this period,
translating "insignificant" has much greater ramifications than considering
Cyrus merely "young."

Temples "abandoned" or "established" (or both?)

Line 31 of the Cyrus Cylinder[26] describes another staple of expected royal
activity, Cyrus' return of the gods to their sanctuaries, *ša ištu pānama nadû*:
sanctuaries "that were established long ago" or "that have been ruined for a
long time." The ambiguity in translation involves mainly the verb, *nadû*, on
which the adverbial phrase *ištu pānama* relies: the question being whether
the sanctuaries were established a long time ago – i.e. a standard commentary on their antiquity – or whether they had been abandoned, in ruins, for

24. Compare Dandamaev 1989, 18, n. 7; Beaulieu 1989, 108–10; Rollinger 1999, 128–32; Briant 2002, 31–32; Rollinger 2003, 298–302; Kuhrt 2007, 56–57, n. 10; Waters 2014, 38–39.

25. See CAD 16 (Ṣ), 179–85 *ṣiḫru* for various examples of each of the meanings. For "young,"
see Briant 2002, 31; and Kuhrt 2007, 56. For "insignificant" (or similar), see Rollinger 1999, 129;
Beaulieu 2000, 311, and n. 7; and Schaudig 2001, 437.

26. Finkel 2013, 6–7 and 132. See also Schaudig in this volume.

a long time – i.e. standard commentary on (meaning: vilification of) Cyrus' predecessor Nabonidus and his neglect of the proper forms.[27] The verb *nadû* carries both connotations, and translations vary.[28]

The same verb, though in different form (N stem, *innadû*), occurs in the Cylinder in line 10 in a context where neglect is more clearly implied.[29] There are several words in Akkadian texts that may be used to describe neglect, abandonment, or dilapidation, and *nadû* is by no means the most common; others frequently used include *labāru*, *anāḫu*, and *enēšu*. Some ambiguity in the Cyrus Cylinder may have been intentional, the word chosen specifically by whoever was responsible for such things – a not insignificant question in its own right but one far beyond the scope of this paper. The ambiguity embedded within the word *nadû* allowed emphasis of two things in this context: the temples were not only ancient but also neglected by the inept and unworthy Nabonidus. Cyrus may thus be allowed to have demonstrated his respect for Babylonian norms through both the correction of previous offense as well as his acknowledgement and maintenance of a long-standing, proper tradition.

Cyrus was of course genuinely concerned with representing himself as a king in the Assyrian and Babylonian mold, as one might expect for a new conqueror of an ancient civilization. It was Cyrus' job to make the invasiveness of a new order (i.e. a foreign king) minimally so. Observance of traditional forms, rites, and expectations was a critical part of smoothing the transition. This observance manifests similarly in Cyrus' display inscriptions from Uruk and Ur. Both these brick stamp inscriptions situate Cyrus in a long line of rulers, who built and restored parts of the Eanna temple complex at Uruk and the temple of Nanna-Suen at Ur – and in both cases the continuity is

27. In this sense, see also Schaudig in this volume who translates this line: "the sacred cities on the [ot]her side (= east) of the Tigris, *which had been laying in ruins* (nadû) since days of old [emphasis mine] ..."

28. In a previous treatment of this passage, I settled on the first option, with some ambivalence; see Waters 2008, especially page 116, with references. This ambiguity is occasionally reflected in translations, e.g. van der Spek 2014, 263, though not discussed. Note in this context other examples for Nabonidus' *damnatio memoriae*, such as Cyrus' defacement of Nabonidus' monuments, judging from the testimony of Verse Account (vi.18–24, translation in Kuhrt 2007, 78) and a specific example manifest by the erasure of Nabonidus' inscription on BM 90837 (see Razmjou 2013, 119, fig. 56).

29. See also Schaudig in this volume, who translates this line: "But Marduk, the l[ofty Enlil-of-the-god]s, relented and felt pity for the cities whose dwelling-places *were lying in ruins* (innadû) [emphasis mine]." CAD 11/1 (N), 99a, with citation of a Nabonidus inscription (published in Schaudig 2001, Nbn. 3.3 Babylon-Stele, 521 and 528), "Ḫarran and Eḫulḫul which were in ruins for 54 years" with cross-reference to the passage in question here. Note also CAD 11/1 (N), 99b for references to temples being founded and bricks being laid using the N stem.

traceable to Naram-Sin more than a millennium and a half before.[30] Beyond the exceptional use of the title "king of Anshan" (Ur brick, line 1), Cyrus is almost indistinguishable from his Mesopotamian predecessors in his use of royal titles and epithets. That of course was not an accident.

Cyrus adopted traditional titles such as "king of the world" (Cyrus Cylinder, line 20; Ur brick, line 1[31]; Verse Account of Nabonidus, v. 4[32]), "king of the four quarters" (Cyrus Cylinder, line 20); and "king of lands" (ubiquitous in economic and administrative documents). These expressions of universality follow long-standing paradigms. Babylonian and especially Assyrian precedents are legion, almost bewildering in their colorful variety.[33] The traditional title "king of lands" (usually written with a doubled KUR in Assyrian and Babylonian texts) retained its cachet through the Achaemenid period, though its restoration in Cyrus' brick inscription from Uruk, line 1, is problematic, as we shall see below.

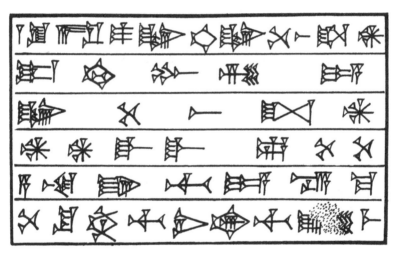

Fig. 1: Hand copy of Ur brick, Gadd 1928, Plate XLVIII, Nr. 194, page xix.

30. George 1993, 114, no. 653 has a list of kings who left inscriptions at the Temple of Nanna-Suen, with references, likewise for the Eanna temple complex at Uruk, pages 67–68.

31. Schaudig 2001, 549 and 552.

32. Schaudig 2001, 569.

33. For example, Esarhaddon "ruled all the lands" (Frame 1995,178; Esar. B.6.31.12 and Ashurbanipal) "… exercised (my) lordship over (all of) the lands and (their) far-flung inhabitants …" (Ashurbanipal 11 x 67, courtesy of Jamie Novotny and the Royal Inscriptions of the Neo-Assyrian Period (RINAP) project). See Seux 1967, 292–320 for combinations in title with *šarru* (king).

The Ur brick stamp inscription is for the most part well preserved, one copy housed in the British Museum (BM 118362) and another in the University of Pennsylvania Museum of Archaeology and Anthropology (University Museum Nr. 15348).[34] Its elegant orthography and archaizing signs situate Cyrus in the long line of rulers who built and restored the Temple of Nanna-Suen (É.KIŠ.NU.GÁL), where the inscription was found.

Transliteration:

> ᵐ*ku-ra-áš* LUGAL ŠÁR LUGAL ᴷᵁᴿ*aš-ša-an*
> DUMU ᵐ*kam-bu-zi-ya*
> LUGAL ᴷᵁᴿ*aš-ša-an*
> DINGIR.DINGIR GAL.GAL *kal* KUR.KUR
> *a-na qá-ti-ya* SI.A-*ma*
> KUR *šu-ub-ti né-eh-ti ú-še-šib*

Translation:

> Cyrus, king of the world, king of Anshan, (2) the son of Cambyses, (3) king of Anshan. (4–5) The great gods have delivered into my hands all the lands and (6) I caused the land to live in peace.

With the noted exception of the title "king of Anshan," Cyrus relied on traditional Assyrian and Babylonian phrasing, especially with regard to the gods' support of his rule. The gods granted all the lands (plural, KUR.KUR) to Cyrus, lines 4–5, this is standard issue.[35] The clause *šubti nehti ušešib* in line 6 refers to the establishment of peace and security, also traditional phrasing; it is found as early as in the Old Babylonian period, and it recurs throughout Neo-Assyrian and Neo-Babylonian inscriptions.[36] It is applied in a variety of ways, frequently to describe the settlement of people in their homes and of gods in their sanctuaries; used just so in the Cyrus Cylinder, line 36 (KUR.

---

34. Schaudig 2001, 549 with references. A photo of the inscription is available via the University of Pennsylvania Museum's online database (http://www.penn.museum/collections/object/106677), accessed 2 February, 2015.

35. CAD 10/2 (M), 187a for idiomatic uses of D-stem of *malû* with *ana qatiya*, with many Neo-Assyrian (Asb.) and Neo-Babylonian parallels. See CAD 10/2 (M), 187b for another use of D-stem of *malû* in Cyrus Cylinder, line 17 ("he delivered Nabonidus into his hands," cited in CAD 10/1 (M) 187b as "exceptional"). In Cyrus Cylinder, line 12, when the god Marduk is described as having scoured all the lands (written *matata*, not logographically) to choose Cyrus, Marduk "called him by his name, proclaiming him aloud for the kingship over all of everything" (*it-ta-bi ni-bi-it-su a-na ma-li-ku-tì kul-la-ta nap-ḫa*); see Finkel 2013, 5 for the translation, and 131 for the transliteration.

36. Several examples from Hammurabi and Samsu-iluna, among others, are cited at CAD 1/2 (A), 408a.

KUR *kališina šubti neḫti ušešib*) in the standard reference to establishing peace for all the lands, emphasis on the plural.

Cyrus' adoption of this formula thus is traditional, though in the Ur brick he presents what appears to be a slight variation.[37] Once all the lands (plural) are delivered to Cyrus by the gods, he establishes in peace and security in one land.[38] I readily grant that it is hazardous to make too much of one reference in one inscription, but read literally from lands, plural, to one land, Cyrus offers here a slight variation on the typical expressions of universality that claim dominion over lands. With the preceding caveats in mind, it seems appropriate that any discussion of Achaemenid universality, especially those that focus on an idea of "one world," ought to include some acknowledgement of Cyrus for a nascent manifestation of this perspective, adapted from the older models.[39] The Ur brick phrasing may have been both a variation of an age-old formula as well as the literal truth. As the founder, Cyrus made many lands into one and left an exceptionally tough act to follow.

Appendix: Cyrus' Inscription from Uruk

Cyrus' Uruk brick stamp inscription is known from four exemplars in Neo-Babylonian script found in the Eanna temple complex: one excavated by Loftus in 1850 is housed in the British Museum (BM 90731), and three were excavated by the German team in the 1920s (W 1141, W 1142, and W 1814). Cyrus' epithet in line 1 of the Uruk brick stamp inscription remains in question.

Transliteration (after H. Schaudig)[40]

1) ᵐ*ku-raš* LUGALⁱ(= LÚ) KUR.KUR *ra-'i-im*
2) É.SAG.ÍL u É.ZI.DA
3) A ᵐ*kam-bu-zi-ya*
4) 20 *dan-nu a-na-ku*

---

37. I hesitate to call this formulation "new," though I have yet to find exact parallels in published inscriptions or in an extensive RINAP/ORACC search in October, 2013, facilitated by and thanks to J. Novotny.

38. Published translations of the text differentiate the switch from multiple lands to one land, but, to my knowledge, no one has commented on it; see e.g. Walker 1981, 94; Schaudig 2001, 549; and Kuhrt 2007 74–75.

39. In other words, perhaps this expression may be considered as anticipatory to Darius' use of Old Persian *bumi-* as an expression of dominion over one world. Note Herrenschmidt 1976 (English translation, 2014); Lincoln 2012, 124–25 and 146 has fuller discussion and references. Compare Frye 1977; Briant 2002, 909, and Waters 2016.

40. Schaudig 2001, 548 with references and bibliography. Also Hagen 1894, 214–215; and Delitszch 1894, with hand copy on page 257.

Figure 2. Uruk brick inscription, BM 90731, hand copy from Smith 1873, 148.

Translation

> Cyrus, [king of lands][41], who loves Esangil and Ezida, son of Cambyses, strong king am I.

The London exemplar is defaced, badly worn, just after Cyrus' name, as per George Smith's copy (Fig. 2), so any signs that may have been there are indeterminate. The title "king" was understood to follow the name, but that is simply supplied in the translation without comment.[42] F. Delitzch's copy of the same inscription (Fig. 3) allows neither space nor indication of LUGAL

41. The title "king of lands" is put in brackets here in light of the uncertainty.

42. Smith's drawing is on the plate after J. W. Bosanquet, "On the Date of the Fall of Nineveh and the Beginning of the Reign of Nebuchadnezar at Babylon, B.C. 581," *Transactions of the Society of Biblical Archaeology*, vol. II, 1873, 147–148; translation by H. Rawlinson (p. 148 n. 1).

KUR.KUR in line 1; Hagen's transliteration and translation (pages 214–215) does not include the title "king of lands"; the title is also not included in either F. H. Weissbach's or C. Walker's transliterations of the same.[43]

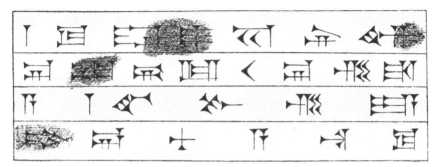

Fig. 3. Uruk brick inscription, BM 90731, hand copy from Delitzsch 1894, 257.

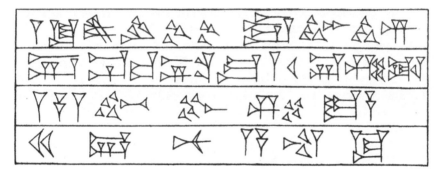

Fig. 4. Uruk brick inscription, hand copy from Schott 1930, plate 31.

The three Berlin exemplars are lost,[44] accessible only via A. Schott's hand copy (Fig. 4), on which Schaudig based his transliteration. Schott's copy plainly represents Cyrus' royal epithet "king of lands" but with the copied LÚ sign read as LUGAL[!] by Schaudig, i.e. the hand copy missing the initial two horizontal wedges for a proper Neo-Babylonian sign for LUGAL. Since Schott's copy cannot be collated, however, one hesitates to make too much of the restored epithet.

43. Weissbach 1911, 8–9 and Walker 1981, 94, No. 115. Walker validates the find spot as Warka (Uruk) despite Bosanquet's assertion that it was from Larsa (page 148, n. 1: "Senkereh"), discovered by Loftus in 1850, and Walker includes the notation: "A copy of BM 90731 is also given in W. K. Loftus and H. A. Churchill, Drawings in Babylonia (manuscript volume in the Department of Western Asiatic Antiquities) pl. XX no. 7." Schaudig 2001, 548, describes the London exemplar as "stark abgerissen." Kuhrt 2007, 74 follows Schaudig's transliteration.

44. Note Schaudig, 2001, 548: "Nach freundlicher Auskunft von Herrn Dr. J. Marzahn nicht in Berlin VA." Dr. Marzahn kindly confirmed the same to me on 4 June, 2014.

Bibliography

Adali, S. 2011. *The Scourge of God: The umman-manda and Its Significance in the First Millennium BC*. Helsinki.

Álvarez-Mon, J. 2013. "Elam in the Iron Age." In *The Oxford Handbook of Ancient Iran*, edited by Daniel T. Potts, 457–477. Oxford.

Álvarez-Mon, Javier, and Mark B. Garrison, ed. 2011. *Elam and Persia*. Winona Lake, Ind.

Baker, H. 2001. "Marduk-šarru-uṣur." In *The Prosopography of the Neo-Assyrian Empire*. Vol. 2/II, L-N, edited by H. Baker, 727–731. Helsinki.

Beaulieu, Paul.-Alain. 1989. *The Reign of Nabonidus, King of Babylon 556-539 B.C.* New Haven.

———. 2000. "The Sippar Cylinder of Nabonidus." In *The Context of Scripture*. Vol. II, edited by W. Hallo and K. L. Younger, 310–313. Leiden.

Berger, P. 1975. "Der Kyros-Zylinder mit dem Zusatzfragment BIN II Nr. 32 und die akkadischen Personnamen im Danielbuch." *Zeitschrift für Assyriologie und vorderasiatische Archäologie* 64:192–234.

Bosanquet, J. W. 1873. "On the Date of the Fall of Nineveh and the Beginning of the Reign of Nebuchadnezar at Babylon, B.C. 581." *Transactions of the Society of Biblical Archaeology* 2:147–148.

Boucharlat, Rémy. 2013. "Southwestern Iran in the Achaemenid Period." In *The Oxford Handbook of Ancient Iran*, edited by Daniel T. Potts, 503–527. Oxford.

Briant, Pierre. 2002. *From Cyrus to Alexander: A History of the Persian Empire*. Translated by Peter T. Daniels. Winona Lake, Ind.

Brosius, Maria. 2000. *The Persian Empire from Cyrus II to Artaxerxes I*. London.

Carter, Elizabeth. 2007. "Resisting Empire: Elam in the First Millennium BC." In *Settlement and Society: Essays Dedicated to Robert McCormick Adams*, edited by E. Stone, 139–156. Los Angeles.

Dandamaev, M. A. 1989. *A Political History of the Achaemenid Empire*. Translated by W. J. Vogelsang. Leiden.

De Vaan, J. M. C. T. 1995. *"Ich bin eine Schwertklinge des Königs": Die Sprache des Bēl-ibni*. Alter Orient und Altes Testament 242. Neukirchen.

Finkel, I. ed. 2013. *The Cyrus Cylinder: The King of Persia's Ancient Proclamation from Babylon*. London.

Frame, G. 1992. *Babylonia 689 - 627 B.C.: A Political History*. Leiden.

———. 1995. *Rulers of Babylonia: From the Second Dynasty of Isin to the End of Assyrian Domination*. Royal Inscriptions of Mesopotamia and Babylonian Periods (RIMB) 2. Toronto.

Frye, R. N. 1977. "Remarks on Kingship in Ancient Iran." *Acta Iranica* 25:75–82.

Fuchs, A. 2004. "Parsua(š)." *Reallexikon der Assyriologie und Vorderasiatischen Archäologie* 10, nos. 5/6, 340–342.

Fuchs, A., and S. Parpola. 2001. *The Correspondence of Sargon II, Part III: Letters from Babylonia and the Eastern Provinces.* State Archives of Assyria 15. Helsinki.

Garrison, Mark B. 2011. "The Seal of 'Kuraš the Anshanite, Son of Šešpeš (Teispes), PFS 93*: Susa – Anšan – Persepolis." In *Elam and Persia*, edited by Javier Álvarez-Mon and Mark B. Garrison, 375–405. Winona Lake, Ind.

George. A. 1993. *House Most High: The Temples of Ancient Mesopotamia.* Winona Lake, Ind.

Glassner, Jean-Jacques. 2004. *Mesopotamian Chronicles*, edited by Benjamin R. Foster. Society of Biblical Literature Writings from the Ancient World, Number 19. Atlanta.

Grayson, A. Kirk. 1975. *Assyrian and Babylonian Chronicles.* Texts from Cuneiform Sources. Locust Valley, NY.

Grayson, A. Kirk, and Jamie Novotny. 2012. *The Royal Inscriptions of Sennacherib, King of Assyria (704-681 BC), Part 1.* Royal Inscriptions of the Neo-Assyrian Period 3/1. Winona Lake, Ind.

Grillot-Susini, Françoise, Clarisse Herrenschmidt, and Florence Malbran-Labat. 1993. "La version élamite de la trilingue de Behistun: une nouvelle lecture." *Journal Asiatique* 281, nos. 1–2:19–59.

Hagen, O. E. 1894. "Keilschrifturkunden zur Geschichte des Königs Cyrus (mit 2 Tafeln: Die Nabûnaʾid Annalen)." *Beiträge zur Assyriologie* 2:205–248.

Hallock, R. 1969. *Persepolis Fortification Tablets.* Oriental Institute Publications 92. Chicago.

Henkelman, Wouter F. M. 2012. "The Achaemenid Heartland: An Archaeological-Historical Perspective." In *A Companion to the Archaeology of the Ancient Near East.* Vol. 2, edited by D. T. Potts, 931–962. Chichester.

———. 2011. "Cyrus the Persian and Darius The Elamite: A Case of Mistaken Identity." In *Herodot und das persische Reich / Herodotus and the Persian Empire: Akten des 3. Internationalen Kolloquiums zum Thema 'Vorderasien im Spannungsfeld klassischer und altorientalischer Überlieferungen, Innsbruck 24.-28. November 2008*, edited by Robert Rollinger, Brigitte Truschnegg, and Reinhold Bichler. Classica et Orientalia 3, ser. eds. Reinhold Bichler, Bruno Jacobs, Giovanni B. Lanfranchi, Robert Rollinger, *et al*, 577–634. Wiesbaden.

———. 2008. *The Other Gods Who Are: Studies in Elamite-Iranian Acculturation Based on the Persepolis Fortification.* Achaemenid History 14. Leiden.

———. 2003. "Persians, Medes, and Elamites: Acculturation in the Neo-Elamite Period." In *Continuity of Empire (?): Assyria, Media, Persia*, edited by Giovanni B. Lanfranchi, Michael Roaf, and Robert Rollinger. History of the Ancient Near East — Monographs V, 181–231, table 2, pls. 9–15. Padova.

Herrenschmidt, Cl. 1976. "Désignations de l'empire et concepts politiques de Darius Ier d'après ses inscriptions en vieux-perse," *Studia Irania* 5:33–65.

———. "Designation of the Empire and Its Political Concepts of Darius I According to Old Persian Records." In *Excavating an Empire: Achaemenid Persia in Longue Durée*, edited by T. Daryaee, A. Mousavi, and K. Rezakhani, 12–36. Costa Mesa, Calif..

Hinz, W., and H. Koch. 1987. *Elamisches Wörterbuch*. Berlin.

Kent, Roland G. 1953. *Old Persian: Grammar, Texts, Lexicon*. American Oriental Series, volume 33. 2nd Revised Edition. New Haven.

Kuhrt, Amélie. 2007. *The Persian Empire: A Corpus of Sources from the Achaemenid Period*. New York.

Lambert, W. G. 2007. "Cyrus' Defeat of Nabonidus." *Nouvelles Assyriologiques Brèves et Utilitaires*, note 14.

Lecoq, Pierre. 1997. *Les incriptions de la Perse achéménide: Traduit du vieux perse, de l'élamite, du babylonien et de l'araméen*. L'aube des peuples. Paris.

Levine, L. 1974. "Geographical Studies in the Neo-Assyrian Zagros-II." *Iran* 12:99–124.

Lincoln, B. 2012 *"Happiness for Mankind": Achaemenian Religion and the Imperial Project*. Leuven.

Michalowski, P. 2006. "The Cyrus Cylinder." In *The Ancient Near East: Historical Sources in Translation*," edited by M. Chavalas. Malden, Mass.

de Miroschedji, Pierre. 2003. "Susa and the Highlands: Major Trends in the History of Elamite Civilization." In *Yeki bud, yeki nabud: Essays on the Archaeology of Iran in Honor of William M. Sumner*, edited by Naomi F. Miller and Kamyar Abdi. Monograph 48, 17–38. Los Angeles: The Costen Institute of Archaeology, UCLA.

———. 1990. "La fin de l'Élam: Essai d'analyse et d'interprétation." *Iranica Antiqua* 25:48–95.

———. 1985. "La fin du royaume d'Anšan et de Suse et la naissance de l'empire perse." *Zeitschrift für Assyriologie und verwandte Gebiete* 75:265–306.

Nielsen, J. P. 2011. *Sons and Descendants: A Social History of Kin Groups and Family Names in the Early Neo-Babylonain Period, 747–626 BC*. Leiden.

Potts, Daniel T. 2016. *The Archaeology of Elam: Formation and Transformation of an Ancient Iranian State*. Second edition. New York.

———., ed. 2013. *The Oxford Handbook of Ancient Iran*. Oxford.

———. 2011. "A Note on the Limits of Anšan." In *Elam and Persia*, edited by Javier Álvarez-Mon and Mark B. Garrison, 35–43. Winona Lake, Ind..

———. 2005. "Cyrus the Great and the Kingdom of Anshan." In *Birth of the Persian Empire*, edited by Vesta Sarkhosh Curtis and Sarah Stewart. The Idea of Iran, vol. I, 7–28. London.

Razmjou, S. 2013. "The Cyrus Cylinder: A Persian perspective." In *The Cyrus Cylinder: The King of Persia's Ancient Proclamation from Babylon*, edited by I. Finkel, 104–126. London.

Rollinger, Robert. 2003. "The Western Expansion of the Median 'Empire': A Re-examination." In *Continuity of Empire (?): Assyria, Media, Persia*, edited by Giovanni B. Lanfranchi, Michael Roaf, and Robert Rollinger. History of the Ancient Near East — Monographs V, 289–320. Padova.

———. 1999. "Zur Lokalisation von Parsu(m)a(š) in der Fārs und zu einigen Fragen der frühen persischen Geschichte." *Zeitschrift für Assyriologie und vorderasiatische Archäologie* 89 no. 1: 115–139.

———. 1998. "Der Satmmbaum des Achaimenidischen Königshauses oder die Frage der Legitimität der Herrschaft des Dareios." *Archäologische Mitteilungen aus Iran und Turan* 30: 155–209.

Root, M. C. 2011. "Elam in the Imperial Imagination: From Nineveh to Persepolis." In *Elam and Persia*, edited by Álvarez-Mon, Javier, and Mark B. Garrison, 419–474. Winona Lake, Ind..

Schaudig, Hanspeter. 2001. *Die Inschriften Nabonids von Babylon und Kyros' des Großen: Samt den in ihrem Umfeld entstandenen Tendenzschriften*, edited by Manfried Dietrich and Oswald Loretz. Alter OrientAlter Orient und Altes Testament: Veröffentlichungen zur Kultur und Geschichte des Alten Orients und des Alten Testaments. Münster.

Schmitt, Rüdiger. 2014. *Wörterbuch der altpersischen Königsinschriften*. Wiesbaden.

———. 2009. *Die altpersischen Inschriften der Achaimeniden: Editio minor mit deutscher Übersetzung*. Wiesbaden.

Shayegan, M. Rahim. 2011. *Arsacids and Sasanians: Political Ideology in Post-Hellenistic and Late Antique Persia*. Cambridge.

van der Spek, Robartus J. 2014. "Cyrus the Great, Exiles, and Foreign Gods: A Comparison of Assyrian and Persian Policies on Subject Nations." In *Extraction & Control: Studies in Honor of Matthew W. Stolper*, edited by Michael Kozuh, Wouter F. M. Henkelman, Charles E. Jones, and Christopher Woods. Studies in Ancient Oriental Civilization, Number 68, 233–264. Chicago.

Stronach, David. 2013. "Cyrus and the Kingship of Anshan: Further Perspectives," *Iran* 51:55–69.

————. 2003. "Early Achaemenid Iran: New Considerations." In *Symbiosis, Symbolism, and the Power of the Past*, edited by W. Dever and S. Gitin, 133–144. Winona Lake, Ind.

Tavernier, Jan. 2004. "Some Thoughts on Neo-Elamite Chronology," *Arta* 2004.003.

————. 2007. *Iranica in the Achaemenid Period (ca. 550–330 B.C.): Lexikon of Old Iranian Proper Names and Loanwords, Attested in Non-Iranian Texts*. Orientalia Lovanensis Analecta 158. Leuven.

Vallat, François. 2011. "Darius, l'héritier légitime, et les premiers achéménides." In *Elam and Persia*, edited by Javier Álvarez-Mon and Mark B. Garrison, 263–284. Winona Lake, Ind.

Vallat, François. 1996. "Nouvelle analyse des inscriptions néo-élamites." In *Collectanea Orientalia: Histoire, arts de l'espace et industrie de la terre: Études offertes en hommage à Agnès Spycket*, edited by Hermann Gasche and Barthel Hrouda. Civilisations du Proche-Orient: Série I: Archéologie et Environnement 3, 385–395. Neuchâtel/Paris.

Walker, C. B. F. 1981. *Cuneiform Brick Inscriptions in the British Museum*, London.

Waterman, L. 1930. *Royal Correspondence of the Assyrian Empire*. Vol. II. Ann Arbor.

Waters, Matthew W. 2016. "Xerxes and the Oathbreakers." In *Revolt and Resistance in the Ancient Classical World and the Near East: In the Crucible of Empire*, edited by J. Collins and J. G. Manning, 93–102. Leiden.

————. 2014. *Ancient Persia: A Concise History of the Achaemenid Empire, 550–330 BCE*. Cambridge.

————. 2013. "Elam, Assyria, and Babylonia in the Early First Millennium BC." In *The Oxford Handbook of Ancient Iran*, edited by Daniel T. Potts, 478–492. Oxford.

————. 2011. "Parsumaš, Anšan, and Cyrus." In *Elam and Persia*, edited by Javier Álvarez-Mon and Mark B. Garrison, 285–296. Winona Lake, Ind.

————. 2008. "Cyrus and Susa." *Revue d'Assyriologie et d'Archéologie Orientale* 102:115–118.

————. 2000. *A Survey of Neo-Elamite History*. State Archives of Assyria Studies 16 – Neo Assyrian Text Corpus Project. Helsinki.

————. 1996 "Darius and the Achaemenid Line." *Ancient History Bulletin* 10:11–18.

Weissbach, F. H. 1891. "Die dreisprachige Inschrift von Artaxerxes Mnemon." *Zeitschrift für Assyriologie und verwandte Gebiete* 6:159–160.

————. 1911. *Die Keilinschriften der Achämeniden*. Leipzig.

Zournatzi, A. Forthcoming. "Early Cross-cultural Political Encounters along the Paths of the Silk Road: Cyrus the Great as a 'King of the City of Anshan.'" In *Proceedings of the First International Conference "Iran and the Silk Road" (Tehran, 12–15 February 2011)*, edited by D. Akbarzadeh (ed.). Tehran. [Electronic pre-publication accessed via www.achemenet.com "Publications en ligne, sous presse."]

Abbreviations:

CT 53 = Parpola, Simo, ed. 1979. *Cuneiform Texts from Babylonian Tablets in the British Museum, Part 53: Neo-Assyrian Letters from the Kuyunjik Collection.* Cuneiform Texts from Babylonian Tablets. London.

CAD = *The Assyrian Dictionary of the Oriental Institute of the University of Chicago.*

SAA 15 = Parpola, Simo, and Andreas Fuchs. 2001. *The Correspondence of Sargon II, Part III: Letters from Babylonia and the Eastern Provinces.* State archives of Assyria 15. Helsinki.

Cyrus, Anshan, and Assyria

David Stronach
University of California, Berkeley

O NE OF THE MORE IMPORTANT ADVANCES in Achaemenid studies in recent years has been the progress that has been made in detecting a number of the effects of Elamite-Persian interaction. The gains that have been made in this context have revealed the important role that this process played, especially in terms of its contribution to the literate character of the early Achaemenid world – a world that had its hub in the highlands of southwestern Iran.[1]

This said, care should be taken not to attribute more than is necessary to Elamite antecedents alone. If we look, for example, at the archaeological remains at Pasargadae, the monumental residence and last resting place of Cyrus II (the Great), there is very little sign of any distinct reflection of Elam (with the exception of the fringed robe that is worn by the four-winged figure in Gate R). Instead we see traces of probable Median influence in certain aspects of the varied plans of the columned halls; signs of Lydian and Ionian influence with reference, not least, to state-of-the-art big stone construction; and clear signs of Assyrian influence in a number of the main doorway sculptures.

Cyrus and Anshan

At the same time a new awareness of the presence of an Elamite contribution has persuaded a number of scholars to look afresh at the historical background of Cyrus and his forebears. In this context, particular attention has come to be paid to the Anshan-related titles that Cyrus (559–530 BCE) bestowed on his ancestors in the text of the Cyrus Cylinder; and one close colleague has gone so far as to propose that the titles in question should be taken at face value – and that, based on this and other evidence, Cyrus might be said to have founded "an Anshanite, not a Persian empire."[2]

---

1. For recent studies of Elamite-Persian interaction in the mainly archaeological sphere, see, for example, Potts 2016; Stronach 2005; Álvarez-Mon 2010; and Álvarez-Mon *et al.* 2011. Also, with reference to recent studies in the philological domain, see especially Tavernier 2008: 59–86 and Shayegan 2012, 90–93.

2. Potts 2005, 21.

The titles are presented here in the form that they are given in Finkel's new translation of the text of the Cyrus Cylinder (see also the edition of Schaudig in this volume). In this format, Cyrus defines himself, at the moment he is introduced in the text of the Cylinder, as "king of the city of Anshan" and, with reference to his lineage, he relates that he is the "son of Cambyses, the great king, king of the city of Anshan, grandson of Cyrus, the great king, king of the city of Anshan, descendant of Teispes, the great king, king of the city of Anshan."[3]

Pl. 1. An aerial view of Tal-e Malyan taken in the second half of the 1970s. (After Stronach and Mousavi 2012, pl. 23.)

If we wish to look more closely at the doubts that are currently being raised about the Persian identity of Cyrus (largely on the basis of the nature of the above-mentioned titles), it may be useful to look, in the first place, at the testimony of Tal-e Malyan – a substantial site that is now firmly identified as the long-sought, ancient city of Anshan. In 2005, Daniel Potts put forward the view that this long-occupied site could have formed the physical core of the region in which Cyrus' predecessors lived – and where, in the seventh and early sixth centuries BCE, they could have ruled over a quasi-independent kingdom that was "culturally Elamite, not Persian."[4] In the aerial photograph in Plate 1 it is still possible to make out most of the circuit of the perimeter wall that was used to define the boundaries of the site, at least

3. Finkel 2013, 4–7.
4. Potts 2005, 17.

during the greater part of the third and the second millennia BCE, when Anshan was at the height of its prosperity.

To the objection that Malyan appears to have been more or less abandoned by a date close to 900 BCE,[5] Potts has responded by pointing out that "Tal-e Malyan is a very large mound only a small portion of which has been explored to date. Thus there is every chance that a Neo-Elamite settlement is present somewhere on the site."[6] In contrast to this observation, however, Elizabeth Carter, a longtime member of the Malyan Expedition of the University of Pennsylvania, and an authority on the ceramic sequence from Malyan, assures me that the whole surface of Tal-e Malyan was carefully examined during the time the site was the scene of ongoing excavations during the 1970s, and no trace of an occupation of late seventh to early sixth century date was discovered.[7]

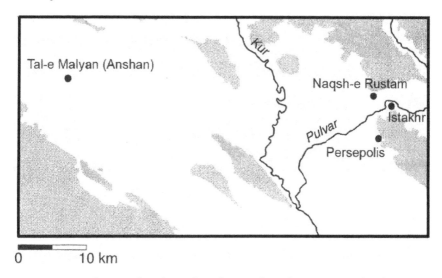

0   10 km

Fig. 1. Map showing the relationship of Persepolis and certain immediately adjacent sites to the extensive mound of Tal-e Malyan.

Also of relevance to the current enquiry is the fact that Tal-e Malyan stands only 50 km WNW of Persepolis (Fig. 1). Accordingly, it is very difficult to see how such a locality, situated on an open, level plain within the "core region" of Fars, could have remained a separate ethno-cultural Elamite enclave in the middle of an increasingly Persian environment.

5. Carter 1994, 66; Carter 1996, 47.
6. Potts 2005, 21.
7. Personal communication.

With reference to other evidence from pre-Achaemenid Fars (that is, from Fars before 550 BCE), special note has to be taken of a remarkable heirloom seal (Fig. 2) that is known from impressions that occur on clay tablets associated with the Persepolis Fortification Archive (dated to between 509 and 493 BCE). In as much as the inscription refers to "Kurash the Anshanite, son of Teispes," the text very possibly names Cyrus the Great's grandfather and namesake (that is, Cyrus I), as well as his great-grandfather. At first glance, therefore, this document might seem to affirm the Anshanite (and hence also the Elamite) affiliations of Cyrus' ancestors. But whether this latter interpretation is the best available one is quite another matter.

Fig. 2. Collated line drawing of an heirloom seal that came to be used in the Persepolis Fortification Archive during the reign of Darius I. (After Garrison 2011, fig. 1.)

To begin with, the mounted horseman in the design could very well have been intended to be a likeness of Cyrus I; and, since the individual who stands before him can be seen to hold up his broken bow (in a gesture of submission that is known to have been used, in part, by the Elamites),[8] the mounted warrior's opponents could quite conceivably have been Elamites. More than this, Garrison has suggested that the original seal was not only an indigenous product of the eastern highlands of southwestern Iran, but that it constituted "the remnants of a nascent 'court style' associated with the Teispid royal house."[9] He goes on to say that the scene in the seal illustrates an exceptional "use of space" that is otherwise attested "in similar spatial arrangements" on the bas-reliefs of Assurbanipal (668–627 BCE).[10] In short, Garrison's remarks would seem to indicate that the model for expressing the growing aspirations of the Teispids did not lie in the direction of charac-

8. Compare Root 2011, 435–436 and fig. 12; also Waters 2011, 291.
9. Garrison 2011, 401.
10. Garrison 2011, 390.

teristic elements that are found in Elamite art, but rather in the direction of certain innovative aspects of late Assyrian art.

In the face of persistent lowland Elamite claims to the throne of "Anshan and Susa," even down to c. 600 BCE,[11] it would in fact seem possible to suppose that the local Persian rulers of mid-seventh-century Fars were willing to lay claim to their own distinctive form of "Anshanite" identity. In this scenario, they presumably sought to demonstrate that the fertile highland region that had long been known as "Anshan" was no longer anything other than the inalienable, well-favored home of the Teispid royal line.[12]

Whether or not such "ancestral" declarations would have been enough to give Cyrus II a strong sense of a latter-day "Anshanite" identity at a date near 539 BCE is, to my mind, far from certain. Instead, it is perhaps more logical to suggest that the Anshan-related titles in the Cyrus Cylinder do not tell us so much about the exact history of Cyrus' ancestral line as they acquaint us with certain ideological and political expectations that Cyrus expected to encounter at the moment that he sought to consolidate his hold on Babylon.[13]

Further support for this latter suggestion comes from an analysis provided by Antigoni Zournatzi.[14] To start with, the latter draws attention to certain of the unusual steps Darius I took to legitimate the restoration of Achaemenid rule in Egypt, even by going so far – on occasion – as to adapt aspects of the official image of Persian royalty to the norms of Egyptian kingship. In this context, she especially refers to the Egyptian formulations of royal authority that occur in hieroglyphic texts that occur on the stone statue of Darius: a statue that was made in Egypt and originally designed for display in Egypt. In particular, the hieroglyphic inscription on the upper surface of the prominent stone base of the statue is not only strictly Egyptian in character, but it makes no reference (as is also the case with reference to the text of the Cyrus Cylinder) to either Persia (at least by this name) or to Ahuramazda. In part, the text in question reads:

> The perfect god, master of the two lands, King of Upper and Lower
> Egypt, Darius – life, prosperity, health! Image made as an exact

11. Henkelman 2003, 193–194.

12. The possibility that Teispes played a significant role in advancing the early fortunes of the Persians is also conceivably reinforced by the fact that Darius I (522–486 BCE), a quintessential Persian ruler, chose to include Teispes in his all-important genealogy in the Bisitun inscription. For DB §2, see Kent 1953, 119; for a recent edition and (German) translation of the text, see Schmitt 2009, 37.

13. Compare Stronach 2013, 55–59.

14. Zournatzi pre-published.

resemblance of the perfect god, master of the two lands, which
his majesty has made so that a monument of himself might be
permanently established and that his person will be remembered with
his father Atum ... for the length of eternity.[15]

Zournatzi goes on to propose that a parallel awareness of local sensibilities could explain references to Cyrus as a "king of the city of Anshan" in
a specifically Mesopotamian setting, especially in a text that was meant to
portray Cyrus – to a quite notable extent – as a stereotypical Mesopotamian
monarch. In support of this proposal, she appeals, not least, to the role that
the venerable Sumerian King List continued to play, even in the late Neo-
Babylonian period, in fortifying a Mesopotamian world view that there was
only "a single divinely sanctioned (and hence legitimate) line of kingship"
and that "the right to rule" was, above all, the prerogative of cities.

With reference to the difficulty of finding a suitable *urban* location in
Fars that could be presumed to meet Mesopotamian expectations in this
regard (at least prior to the completion of the main building program at
Pasargadae, where not a few monuments still remained unfinished at the
time of Cyrus' death), Zournatzi suggests that it may have been thought ad-
visable to invoke the name of Anshan (a city of long renown in the annals of
Mesopotamian history) as the ancestral seat of Cyrus' dynastic line. As she
observes, this solution may have appeared to represent the best available
means of fulfilling the aforementioned "right to rule" and, most particularly,
as the best means of legitimating Cyrus' place "in the native Mesopotamian
continuum of kingship."

Finally, since the Anshan-related titles Cyrus ascribes to himself and his
ancestors in the Cyrus Cylinder cannot be compared to any indisputably
royal title that he, or any other member of his line, is known to have used in
Iran, the only other titles, of which Cyrus has reportedly made use, are two
that came to light during the course of excavations conducted in southern
Mesopotamia. The first title, which occurs on stamped bricks from Ur, follows a good part of the already familiar formula in the Cyrus Cylinder except
that the word "Anshan" is preceded by the determinative for "land" rather
than "city." The brief text reads:

> Cyrus, king of the world, king of Anshan, son of Cambyses, king of
> Anshan. The great gods delivered all the lands into my hands, and I
> made this land to dwell in peace.[16]

15. Kuhrt 2007, 478.
16. Curtis 2013, 47. See also Waters in this volume.

In a still greater departure from the Anshan-related titles, in the Cyrus Cylinder, the second title – one that is known from inscribed bricks from Uruk – omits any mention of Anshan. Instead the text reads:

Cyrus, king of lands, beloved of Esagil and Ezida, son of Cambyses, the mighty king am I.[17]

While it would be hazardous to draw far-reaching conclusions from the presence or the absence of the name of Anshan in one title alone, evidence of another kind from Babylon would appear to stand in accord with a relatively abrupt cessation in the use of the name of Anshan. As local Babylonian documents indicate, the appointment of Cyrus' son and heir, Cambyses, as a "sub-king" of Babylonia did not last for longer than one year.[18] Kuhrt has observed that the reasons for the discontinuation of this latter arrangement are "unknown."[19] Yet one possible explanation for such a change in policy is perhaps not too hard to imagine. It is not at all unlikely that the Persians' local hold on power grew steadily stronger during the first year of Cyrus' reign in Babylon and that various concessions to Babylonian expectations each seemed to lose a large part of their initial, perceived importance.[20]

In sum, there would appear to be a distinct possibility that the Anshan-related titles that are recorded in the Cyrus Cylinder only remained in currency for a distinctly short period of time; that the titles that were given to Cyrus' three named forebears were each examples of titular exaggeration; and that the various references to Cyrus the Great's Anshanite identity (such as would seem to date from either just before or just after the fall of Babylon) were expressly designed to enhance the legitimacy of Cyrus' earliest period of rule in Babylon.[21]

17. Curtis 2013, 47. See also Waters in this volume.
18. Kuhrt 2007, 53.
19. Kuhrt 2007, 53.
20. But the fact that raw tensions would have been in evidence at the moment that Babylon fell to the Persians can hardly be denied. As Beaulieu (2014, 19) has stressed, "the apparent calm" that accompanied this epochal event (at least in the documentation that is available to us) could have masked an "unstable political situation."
21. In case this list of adjustments to the vagaries of Babylonian opinion should impress as something that was hardly necessary in all the circumstances, two particular points need to be made. First, Babylon was very much the "lynchpin" of the Persian realm as Cyrus began to expand his authority in the direction of Egypt. And secondly, there is every reason to take fresh note of P.-A. Beaulieu's (2014, 25) perceptive observation that "within the Persian empire as in all large polities" all politics was "indeed local."

Cyrus and Assyria

If the Anshan-related titles in the Cyrus Cylinder can be seen to have sparked a lively degree of debate, it is interesting to note that an almost equally striking reference to Assurbanipal in line 43 of the same document has so far failed (except in a few salient instances) to attract a like measure of interest. The relevant part of the text of the cylinder – at a point where the text has suffered from considerable damage – appears to be connected to Cyrus' restoration of the well-known Imgur-Enlil wall, that is, the restoration of the great wall of Babylon.[22] Here the text reads: "I saw within it an inscription of Assurbanipal, a king who preceded me."[23]

Following Sennacherib's sack of Babylon in 689 BCE, and following a subsequent about-face in the policies of Assyria, Assurbanipal became engaged in a comprehensive program of restoration at Babylon. Accordingly, as Kuhrt has put matters, "Cyrus' reverent acknowledgement" of Assurbanipal "as his predecessor in pious construction" does much to illuminate Cyrus' wish to cast himself "in the same mould" in the eyes of his new Babylonian subjects.[24]

In a further pertinent observation, Van der Spek suggests that the Assyrian inscription in question could well have been a display inscription, Cylinder L6, in which Assurbanipal dedicated his reconstruction of the walls of Babylon to Marduk, and in which he also described his unique association with Marduk.[25] At the same time, it is necessary to ask if Cyrus' explicit and reverent reference to Assurbanipal was not geared to something more than the expectations of his Babylonian subjects alone. It is noticeable, for example, that the major Mesopotamian titles that Cyrus enumerates in the text of his cylinder "are Assyrian not Babylonian."[26] In addition, there is an important range of archaeological evidence from Pasargadae that deserves to be examined in the broad context of what would appear to have been Cyrus' carefully modulated citation of the "inherited power" of Assyria. But before this latter evidence is reviewed, it may be useful to recall one not insignificant consequence of the Assyrian sack of Susa in 646 BCE. In the wake of this Assyrian triumph, Assurbanipal boasts that:

> Cyrus of Parsumash heard about my victory. He became aware of the might that I wielded with the aid of Assur, Bel, and Nabu, the great

22. Van der Spek 2014, 254.
23. Finkel 2013, 7.
24. Kuhrt 2007, 74.
25. Van der Spek 2014, 247.
26. Van der Spek 2014, 254.

gods my lords, with which I leveled the whole of Elam like a flood. He sent Arukku, his eldest son, with his tribute to Nineveh, the city of my lordship, to pay homage to me. He implored my lordship.[27]

The fact that Arukku, the eldest son of Cyrus (*Kurash* in Akkadian), who is here portrayed as the ruler of Persia (*Parsumash* in Akkadian), was sent as a hostage to the Assyrian court at this juncture is something in keeping, as Waters has pointed out, with "a common practice, a means of assuring good relations between the Assyrians and their subjects or distant neighbors."[28] Further, as various commentators have emphasized, this type of arrangement – one in which exiled princes and their entourages lived at Nineveh for extended periods of time – could have played a significant role in the transmission of cultural knowledge.[29]

The possibility that Arukku, who finds no mention in any other contemporary source, survived to return home is by no means certain. But the indisputable presence of Persian royal "guests" at the Assyrian court, coupled with Garrison's recognition of a late Assyrian "use of space" in the design of the seal of "Kurash the Anshanite, son of Teispes,"[30] could point to an initial Persian interest in Assyrian art that took root in Fars at least as early as the second half of the seventh century BCE.

Whether or not such a conceivable early Persian interest in the nuances of Assyrian art could have had any direct influence on the many choices that were available to Cyrus the Great and his designers three or more generations later may never be known, even if it is far from impossible that this was the case. Not in dispute in any way, however, is the fact that Cyrus chose to borrow and adapt key elements of the apotropaic imagery of – at the very least – late eighth- and seventh-century Assyria.

If we look, for example, at the unmistakably Assyrian-related sculptures from Gate R and Palace S, it would seem more than likely that accomplished designers and craftsmen were sent from Iran to Assyria soon after 547 BCE (presumably with whatever degree of military protection may have been required at the time) in order to acquaint themselves with the precise details of the apotropaic sculptures that were still present – and visible – at such significant, late Assyrian sites as Khorsabad and Nineveh.[31] If anything,

27. Kuhrt 2007, 53–54.
28. Waters 2014, 36. Also, for further notes on the largely prevailing (but by no means unanimous) view that Cyrus the Great's grandfather, whom Cyrus names as "king of Anshan" in the Cyrus Cylinder, is the same as the Cyrus, king of Persia, who is mentioned in the above-cited passage, see especially Waters 2014, 35–37.
29. See, for example, Kawami 1972, 148; Waters 2014, 36.
30. See note 10 above.
31. Compare Stronach 1997, 44; and, more recently, Garrison 2013, 573.

moreover, the subsequent introduction of such protective figures at Pasargadae – a royal site without traditional, static defenses – may only have added to the intimations of authority that came to be attached to such borrowed, fantastical creatures in early Achaemenid times.

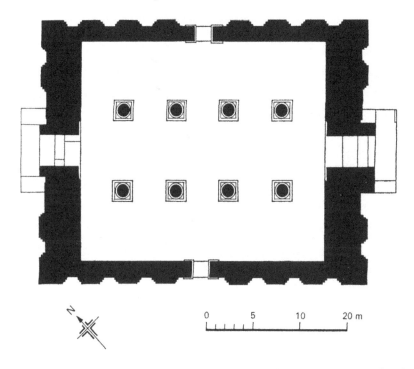

Fig. 3. A reconstructed plan of Gate R at Pasargadae. (After Stronach 2014, fig. 7.)

The sculptures from Gate R are very unevenly preserved. Since the two pairs of massive bull colossi that once guarded the opposed main doorways on the long axis of the structure are now only represented by the not exactly identical plinths on which the inner and outer colossi once stood (Fig. 3), and by a very few surviving fragments of finely carved stone,[32] these no longer extant guardians are perhaps best conceived of as the probable prototypes of the well-known colossi that still flank the Gate of All Lands at Persepolis.[33]

32. See Stronach 1978, 44, n. 7, 55 and pls. 47b and 47c.
33. For further comment on Herzfeld's suggestion that, while a pair of winged bulls flanked the main outer entrance of Gate R, a pair of human-headed bulls faced the palaces, see Stronach 1978, 44.

Fig. 4. Drawing of the four-winged figure at Gate R, Pasargadae. (After Stronach 1978, fig. 25.)

As far as the one nearly intact four-winged figure from Gate R is concerned (Fig. 4), it is important to remember that it was originally one of four larger-than-life-sized, winged anthropomorphic figures that were associated with the building's two opposed side doorways. While one pair of such anthropomorphic guardians has totally disappeared, the one remaining example from the second pair of figures is still visible on a single truncated doorjamb in the northeast doorway (Pl. 2).[34]

Pl. 2. Gate R, Pasargadae. The doorjamb with the relief of the four-winged figure stands at the mid-point of the long northeast wall. Photo: D. Stronach.

This now isolated, upstanding image is undoubtedly derived from a long-familiar type of four-winged Assyrian protective "genius."[35] In fact, Cyrus' version of this guardian figure is visibly updated in that it is shown in a full-profile view and in so far as the traditional Assyrian "bucket and cone" motif is no longer attested. With reference to the four-winged figure's other characteristics, it is of special interest that, whereas the wings retain a largely Assyrian appearance, the short-bearded face was given a Persian

34. For one not improbable explanation for this uneven pattern of preservation, see Stronach 2010 [2014], 9.
35. Compare Stronach 1978, 47–55; Root 1979, 46–49.

physiognomy and the standard Assyrian horned crown and ankle-length dress were each relinquished in favor of non-Assyrian elements. Indeed, it would seem quite possible that the final design for the figure was only approved in the immediate aftermath of Cyrus' capture of Babylon. In this latter context, the introduction of the Egyptian *hemhem* crown (Fig. 4) was almost certainly intended to signal – at an absolute minimum – the sudden expansion of Cyrus' dominions to the border of Egypt; and the presence of a version of a well-known, mid-seventh-century Elamite royal robe (Fig. 4) would appear to illustrate Cyrus' further wish to introduce – at just this moment – a striking visual claim to the briefly significant "Anshanite identity" of his royal line.

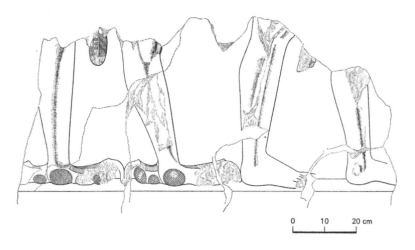

0   10   20 cm

Fig. 5. The extant remains of a doorway relief from Palace S, Pasargadae. The relief shows a likeness of the Assyrian "smiting god" followed by a likeness of the Assyrian "lion-demon." (After Stronach 1978, fig. 34.)

Further sculptures of relevance are located in the opposed northwest and southeast doorways on the long axis of Palace S. Although the figures in question are only preserved in one instance above the level of the knee, the fragmentary figures on the matching doorjambs of the northwest doorway can be seen to have consisted of a likeness of the Assyrian "smiting god," followed by a likeness of the Assyrian "lion-demon" (Fig. 5).[36] This pairing is not only well attested in late Assyrian art, but it is expressly known from doorway reliefs that were associated with Sennacherib's Southwest Palace at Nineveh (Fig. 6).[37]

36. Black and Green 1992, 165–166.
37. Stronach 1997, 44–45.

Fig. 6. A pair of similar images from Sennacherib's Palace at Nineveh. (After
Stronach 1997, fig. 19.)

The pairing of the fish-garbed man and the bull-man that occurs in the
southeast doorway of Palace S (Fig. 7) is not so far attested at any site in
Assyria, even if images of fish-garbed figures are known to have sometimes
stood in the near-vicinity of gateway colossi.[38] On a related issue, the leading
leg of the fish-garbed man (Fig. 7) also illustrates the way, in which Cyrus'
sculptors chose to soften the exaggerated musculature of the original Assyrian models in order to meet the demands of early Achaemenid taste.[39]

Modern reactions to the Assyrianizing character of the Gate R and Palace S reliefs have varied quite considerably. Early in the twentieth century,
Herzfeld already suggested that the long fringed robe of the four-winged
figure in Gate R could be related to Cyrus' known allusions to Anshan and he
also identified the four-winged figure as a guardian genius in the Assyrian
tradition as opposed to a representation of Cyrus himself.[40] But since the

38. Compare Kawami 1972, 147.

39. Note also that Cyrus' borrowings from the late Assyrian corpus of apotropaic imagery
could have done more than a little to inspire Darius I's still more comprehensive sculptural
innovations. With special reference to the extent of "the debt to Assyria" that is detectable at
Persepolis, see, recently, Stronach 2002 and Roaf 2004, 407.

40. For Herzfeld's detailed comments, see, in particular, Sarre and Herzfeld 1910, 155–
160.

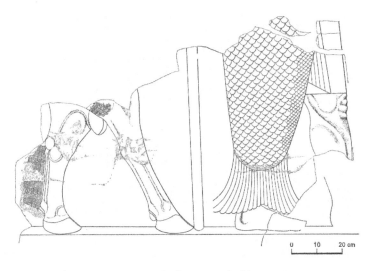

Fig. 7. The extant remains of a doorway relief from Palace S, Pasargadae. The relief shows a fish-garbed man followed by a bull-man. The lower part of the staff of the latter's tall standard is also visible. (After Stronach 1978, fig. 35.)

reliefs in Palace S were only revealed during Ali Sami's excavations in 1950,[41] Herzfeld (d. 1948) was never aware of the presence of any doorway reliefs in this latter construction.

Sami himself was clearly puzzled by the nature of the reliefs that he brought to light in Palace S; and, so far as I can detect, he was unaware of any Assyrian prototypes as such.[42] For Kawami, on the other hand, the presence of the Assyrianizing sculptures at Pasargadae found a possibly logical explanation in the known sequence of Cyrus' conquests. That is to say that, since the basic designs for Gate R and Palace S were almost certainly drawn up some years before the fall of Babylon in 539 BCE, Cyrus was obliged to "resort to Assyrian rather than Babylonian imagery" in order to emphasize "his legitimacy as a ruler."[43] But while this line of thought is not by any means unreasonable, it should be stressed that Cyrus' choices could have been influenced by still other factors. In particular, Kawami's analysis – in this specific case – fails to acknowledge the depth and duration of western Iran's fascination with Assyrian-related imagery from at least the early centuries of the first millennium BCE onwards.[44]

41. Sami 1971, 54.

42. Compare Sami 1971, 58.

43. Kawami 1972, 148, n. 37.

44. Even Elam, a sworn enemy of Assyria both before and during the reign of Assurbanipal, was not totally impervious to this attraction. See especially Álvarez-Mon 2011, 328–334.

At the present time it may in fact be helpful to take note of the vivid adaptations of Assyrian imagery that have begun to come to light in the small but strategically important eighth/seventh-century kingdom of Mannea in the northern Zagros. In this highland polity, which stood directly to the east of Assyria (Fig. 8), excavated glazed bricks (or, better, tiles) from the sites of Rabat Tepe and Qalaichi can be seen to portray winged, crowned, beardless human-headed composite creatures with, on occasion, the bodies of lions or bulls.[45] Indeed, as Reade and Finkel have observed, decorated tiles of this type served to give the indigenous sites of Mannea a distinct "Assyrian veneer."[46]

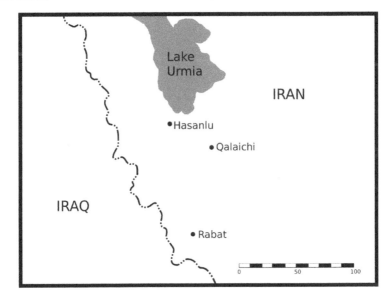

Fig. 8. Map showing the location of Rabat Tepe and Qalaichi in northwestern Iran.

The colorful tiles of this small late Iron Age kingdom also seem to reveal elements of Urartian as well as Assyrian style – a detail that is not without interest in the present enquiry. Above all else, the powerful, northerly kingdom of Urartu chose to borrow many different Assyrian motifs, which were then supplied with separate Urartian affiliations. A similar set of local identities is likely to have obtained with reference to the various Mannean motifs; and, at least in my estimation, a further separate identity for each

45. For a tile from Rabat Tepe, see Pl. 3a (after Heidari 2010, pl. 50, 1; otherwise also illustrated in Kargar and Binandeh 2009, pl. 7) and for a tile from Qalaichi, see Pl. 3b (after Heidari 2010, pl. 50, 2).
46. Reade and Finkel 2014, 594.

Pl. 3a. A decorated tile from Rabat Tepe. Courtesy of R. Heidari. (After Heidari 2010, pl. 50, 1.)

borrowed Assyrian motif could also have existed in Fars, where some knowledge of Assyrian imagery may date back, as we have seen, to at least the second half of the seventh century BCE. In other words, two of Cyrus' more important buildings at Pasargadae were intended to showcase a number of the latest and most impressive adaptations of ancient Assyria's sculpted imagery, even if the images in question were most probably furnished with Persian identities.

In conclusion, Cyrus unquestionably viewed himself as an heir to the legacy of prestigious cultures.[47] Furthermore, as Briant has stressed, Cyrus saw himself, still more specifically, as the heir to "ancient Assyrian power."[48] Both of these interpretations may be said to find more than a little support in the text of the Cyrus Cylinder. In the absence of contemporary written documents from Iran, however, only Cyrus' extraordinary building program at Pasargadae provides related evidence of strictly parallel date from the

47. Compare Henkelman 2003, 192.
48. Briant 2002, 44.

Pl. 3b. A decorated tile from Qalaichi. Courtesy of R. Heidari. (After Heidari 2010, pl. 50, 2.)

Persian homeland. And here, remarkably enough, the visual evidence from Pasargadae suggests that Cyrus viewed himself as a direct heir to the heritage, at the least, of Media, Lydia, Ionia, Assyria, Anshan, and even Egypt.

Bibliography

Álvarez-Mon, J. 2010. *The Arjan Tomb at the Crossroad of the Elamite and Persian Empires.* Leuven.

———. 2011. "The Golden Griffin from Arjan." In *Elam and Persia*, edited by J. Álvarez-Mon and M. B. Garrison, 277–373. Winona Lake, Ind.

Álvarez-Mon, J., M. B. Garrison and D. Stronach 2011. "Introduction." In *Elam and Persia*, edited by J. Álvarez-Mon and M. B. Garrison, 1–32. Winona Lake, Ind.

Beaulieu, P.-A. 2014. "An Episode in the Reign of the Babylonian Pretender Nebuchadnezzar IV." In *Extraction & Control: Studies in Honor of Matthew W. Stolper*, edited by M. Kozuh, W. F. M. Henkelman, C. E. Jones, and C. Woods. Studies in Ancient Oriental Civilization, Number 68, 17–26. Chicago.

Black, J., and A. Green. 1992. *Gods, Demons and Symbols of Ancient Mesopotamia*. London.

Briant, P. 2002. *From Cyrus to Alexander: A History of the Persian Empire*. Translated by P. T. Daniels. Winona Lake, Ind.

Carter, E. 1994. "Bridging the Gap between the Elamites and the Persians in Southeastern Khuzistan." In *Achaemenid History VIII: Continuity and Change: Proceedings of the Last Achaemenid History Workshop April 6–8, 1990 — Ann Arbor, Michigan*, edited by H. W. A. M. Sancisi-Weerdenburg, A. Kuhrt, and M. Cool Root, 65–95. Leiden.

Carter, E. 1996. *Excavations at Anshan (Tal-e Malyan): The Middle Elamite Period*, University Museum Monograph 82. Philadelphia.

Curtis, J. 2013. *The Cyrus Cylinder and Ancient Persia: A New Beginning for the Middle East*. London.

Finkel, I. L., ed. 2013. *The Cyrus Cylinder: The King of Persia's Proclamation from Ancient Babylon*. London.

Garrison, M.B. 2011. "The seal of Kuraš the Anzanite, Son of Šešpes (Teispes), PFS 93*: Susa – Anšan – Persepolis." In *Elam and Persia*, edited by J. Álvarez-Mon and M. B. Garrison, 375–405. Winona Lake, Ind.

———. 2013. "Royal Achaemenid Iconography." In *The Oxford Handbook of Ancient Iran*, edited by D. T. Potts, 566–595. Oxford.

Heidari, R. 2010. "Hidden Aspects of Mannean Rule in Northwestern Iran." *Armenian Journal of Near Eastern Studies* 5, no. 2:147–151.

Henkelman, Wouter F. M. 2003. "Persians, Medes, and Elamites: Acculturation in the Neo-Elamite Period." In *Continuity of Empire (?): Assyria, Media, Persia*, edited by G. B. Lanfranchi, M. Roaf, and R. Rollinger. History of the Ancient Near East — Monographs V, 181–231, table 2, pls. 9–15. Padova.

Kargar, B., and A. Binandeh 2009. "A Preliminary Report of Excavations at Ribat Tepe, Northwestern Iran." *Iranica Antiqua* 44:113–129.

Kawami, T.1972. "A Possible Source for the Sculptures of the Audience Hall, Pasargadae," *Iran* 10:146–148.

Kent, R. G. 1953. *Old Persian: Grammar, Texts, Lexicon*. American Oriental Series, volume 33. 2nd Revised Edition. New Haven.

Kuhrt, A. 2007. *The Persian Empire. A Corpus of Sources from the Achaemenid Period*. London.

Potts, D.T. 2005. "Cyrus the great and the Kingdom of Anshan." In *Birth of the Persian Empire*, edited by V. S. Curtis and S. Stewart. The Idea of Iran, vol. I, 7–28. London.

———. 2016. *The Archaeology of Elam: Formation and Transformation of an Ancient Iranian State*. Second edition. New York.

Reade, J., and I. Finkel 2014. "Between Carchemish and Pasargadae: Recent Iranian Discoveries at Rabat." In *From Source to History: Studies on Ancient Near Eastern Worlds and Beyond, Dedicated to Giovanni Battista Lanfranchi on the Occasion of his 65th Birthday on June 23, 2014*, edited by S. Gaspa, A. Greco, D. Morandi Bonacossi, S. Ponchia, and R. Rollinger, 581–596. Münster.

Roaf, M. 2004. "Persepolis," *Reallexikon der Assyriologie und vorderasiatischen Archäologie* 10: 393–412.

Root, M.C. 1979. *The King and Kingship in Achaemenid Art: Essays on the Creation of an Iconography of Empire*. Acta Iranica 19 — Textes et Mémoires 9. Leiden.

———. 2011. "Elam in the Imperial Imagination: From Nineveh to Persepolis." *Elam and Persia*, edited by Javier Álvarez-Mon and Mark B. Garrison, 419–474. Winona Lake, Ind..

Sami, A.1971. *Pasargadae. The Oldest Imperial Capital of Iran.* Shiraz.

Sarre, F., and E. Herzfeld. 1910. *Iranische Felsreliefs: Aufnahmen und Untersuchungen von Denkmälern aus alt- und mittelpersischer Zeit*. Berlin.

Schmitt, R. 2009. *Die altpersischen Inschriften der Achaimeniden: Editio minor mit deutscher Übersetzung*. Wiesbaden.

Shayegan, M. R. 2012. *Aspects of History and Epic in Ancient Iran: From Gaumāta to Wahnām*. Edited by Gregory Nagy. Hellenic Studies Series 52. Washington, D.C./Cambridge.

Stronach, D. 1978. *Pasargadae: A Report on the Excavations Conducted by the British Institute of Persian Studies from 1961 to 1963*. Oxford.

———. 1997. "Anshan and Parsa: Early Achaemenid History, Art and Architecture on the Iranian Plateau." In *Mesopotamia and Iran in the Persian Period: Conquest and Imperialism 539–331 BC*, edited by J. Curtis, 35–53. London.

———. 2002. "Icons of Dominion: Review Scenes at Til Barsip and Persepolis." *Iranica Antiqua* 37:373–402.

———. 2005. "The Arjan Tomb: Innovation and Acculturation in the Last Days of Elam." *Iranica Antiqua* 40:179–196.

———. 2010 [2014]. "Solomon at Pasargadae: Some New Perspectives," *Bulletin of the Asia Institute* 24:1–14.

———. 2013. "Cyrus and the Kingship of Anshan: Further Perspectives." *Iran* 51:55–69.

Stronach, D., and A. Mousavi, eds. 2012. *Ancient Iran from the Air.* Mainz.

Tavernier, J. 2008. "Multilingualism in the Fortification and Treasury Archives." In *L'archive des Fortifications de Persépolis: États des questions et perspectives de recherches,* edited by P. Briant, W. F. M. Henkelman, and M. W. Stolper. Persika 12, 59–86. Paris.

van der Spek, R. J. 2014. "Cyrus the Great, Exiles, and Foreign Gods: A Comparison of Assyrian and Persian Policies on Subject Nations." In *Extraction & Control: Studies in Honor of Matthew W. Stolper,* edited by M. Kozuh, W. F. M. Henkelman, C. E. Jones, and C. Woods. Studies in Ancient Oriental Civilization, Number 68, 233–264. Chicago.

Waters, M.W. 2011. "Parsumash, Ansan and Cyrus." In *Elam and Persia,* edited by J. Álvarez-Mon and M. B. Garrison, 285–296. Winona Lake, Ind.

———. 2014. *Ancient Persia. A Concise History of the Achaemenid Empire, 550-330 BCE.* Cambridge.

Zournatzi, A. Pre-published. "Early Cross-cultural Political Encounters along the Paths of the Silk Road: Cyrus the Great as a 'King of the City of Anshan.'" In *Proceedings of the First International Conference "Iran and the Silk Road" (Tehran, 12-15 February 2011),* edited by D. Akbarzadeh. Tehran. Electronic pre-publication available at: http://www. achemenet.com/document/ZOURNATZI_Cyrus_of_Anshan.pdf

The Magnanimous Heart of Cyrus:
The Cyrus Cylinder and its Literary Models

Hanspeter Schaudig
University of Heidelberg, Germany

> If indeed with any prince history seems to turn into poetry,
> it is with the founder of the Persian empire, Cyrus. Just see
> this divine sprout, conquerer and legislator of the nations,
> as portrayed in the writings of the Hebrews or Persians, by
> Herodotus or Xenophon. It is beyond doubt that the latter
> writer of historical belles-lettres, being already inspired by
> his teacher to write a Cyropaedia, did collect genuine reports
> on him on his expeditions throughout Asia. But since Cyrus
> had long passed away, these reports in Asian manner would
> not speak of him but in the hymnical tone of praise that is
> so particular and customary to any of the reports of these
> nations about their kings and heroes."
>
> Johann Gottfried Herder, *Ideen*
> *zur Philosophie der Geschichte der*
> *Menschheit* (Weimar 1784), 12th book,
> IInd chapter: Medes and Persians.

WHEN HERDER WROTE THESE LINES on Cyrus "the Great," he still had to rely completely on the reports of the classical authors. It was only about a century later that in the loamy ruins of Babylonian cities vast amounts of cuneiform documents were found that could give first-hand reports on Cyrus and the events connected to his name and fame. As we shall see, not only was Xenophon's *Cyropaedia* more poetry than reality, but already the Babylonians had cast the figure of Cyrus and events surrounding his rule into the molds of their own religious literature. The words of Herder about history transformed into poetry still hold true. The Babylonian sources, and above all the Cyrus Cylinder itself, are by no means dull and dry documents listing mere facts, but elaborate and refined literature. Using the experience of styling history for more than two millennia, this literature had woven the "facts" into a glittering and silky image of "historical truth" that was intended to last. The stories of the Jews and the

Greeks were in turn but reflections of the literary-historical masterpiece the Babylonians created.

The few pieces of information about Cyrus that we are inclined to consider as sober and plain facts are told quickly. Our main source is a Babylonian chronicle that lists the data and events pertaining to the reign of the last Babylonian king Nabonidus and those of his Persian adversary Cyrus.[1] Cyrus was the son of Cambyses I and inherited from his father the rulership over Persia, as well as the status of a vassal to the Median king Astyages. But in 550 BCE, Cyrus rebelled against Astyages. He took his overlord captive and looted his royal city Ecbatana. During the following decade, Cyrus seized Lydia ruled by king Croesus.[2] In the summer of 539 BCE, Cyrus moved against Babylonia. He defeated the Babylonians at Opis and took Sippar without a battle. Again without fighting, his troops entered Babylon, led by Cyrus' general Gaubarva on October 12, 539 BCE. The reign of Nabonidus was thereby brought to an end, and Nabonidus made captive. Cyrus entered Babylon in triumph only two weeks later, on October 29. According to the report given by the Babylonian-Greek writer Berossos,[3] Cyrus treated Nabonidus, the vanquished opponent – an old man of about 80 years – magnanimously: instead of slaying him, he exiled him from Babylonia to Carmania in the east where Nabonidus spent the rest of his life. This magnanimity seems indeed to have been a trait of Cyrus, since it has parallels in his treatment of the Median king Astyages and, at least according to well-known Greek *historiettes*, Cyrus' treatment of Croesus of Lydia. Cyrus pardoned his former enemies after they had been defeated. However, we should bear in mind that this kind of noble behavior was not an exception at all in the ancient Near East. At the same time there were many defeated foreign kings living in the palace at Babylon in exile, among them the last king of Judah, Jehoiachin. Recently, Bert van der Spek has demonstrated in detail that the politics of the Persian rulers towards their subjects and vassals were in fact a faithful continuation of the politics of their Assyrian and Babylonian predecessors.[4]

Now we shall have a closer look at the famous text that first praised the magnanimous heart of the great Cyrus: The Cyrus Cylinder.[5] It is a barrel-

1. The following events summarized after the Nabonidus Chronicle (Grayson 1975, 104–111, chronicle 7) and an inscription of Nabonidus (Schaudig 2001, 417, no. 2.12 1 I 26–29).

2. This event had formerly been dated to 547 BCE because of a misread line in the Nabonidus Chronicle (Grayson 1975, 107, chronicle 7, II 16). However, as Oelsner (1999–2000, 378–379) has demonstrated, this line of the chronicle deals with U[rartu], the land of Ararat, not with Lydia.

3. Verbrugghe and Wickersham 1996, 61, F10a.

4. Van der Spek 2014.

5. Editions and translations of the Cyrus Cylinder can be found in Schaudig 2001, 550–

shaped, solid cylinder of baked clay, 23 cm long and 8 cm in diameter at each end. It is not completely preserved, but fragmented. The cylinder is inscribed with a text of forty-five lines in the Babylonian language and script. Cylinders of this kind had been in use in Babylonia for more than two millennia. Being building inscriptions, their main and original purpose was to document for posterity that a certain building work had been done by a certain king, serving the gods. To that end numerous inscribed tablets, cylinders, or prisms were physically embedded into the foundations and the brickwork of the ancient buildings. So the "original" part of the present inscription is the rather short and dull part at the very end (part 10: lines 38b–45, see below), reporting that king Cyrus had done some repair on the famous and sacred wall of Babylon. As demonstrated by Jonathan Taylor, the Cyrus Cylinder itself had also been probably placed as a building inscription into the wall of Babylon, the wall Imgur-Enlil.[6] Apart from the present cylinder, there are certainly still dozens of cylinders of the same kind enclosed in the brickwork of the wall that Cyrus restored. Up to now, however, the present cylinder is the only extant one reproducing the inscription by Cyrus.

However, it is well known that these inscriptions were not just buried within the foundations of temples, palaces, and city walls, but that copies were kept in archives and libraries, so the texts could be read and studied.[7] Thus, it came as a pleasant, but not a complete surprise when some years ago Wilfred G. Lambert and Irving Finkel discovered a copy of the text of the cylinder on fragments of a clay tablet in the Babylonian collection of the British Museum.[8] This shows the text had very probably been circulating in Babylonian society, and those parts of the text that did not merely deal with the building process might have been put down on other objects such as royal stelae, enabling the distribution of the proclamation to a wider audience.

So, although these cylinders originally were in fact building inscriptions, the Babylonian kings increasingly used them to provide historical reports on major events of their rule. These historical reports ultimately became the larger and also more interesting parts of the inscriptions. In the present case, Cyrus, king of Persia, reported how he had become king of Babylonia by seizing the city of Babylon in October 539 BCE and deposing the Babylonian king Nabonidus (556–539 BCE). Up to that moment, Nabonidus had been the legitimate king of Babylonia, so the attack of Cyrus had to

---

556, Finkel 2013a, 4–7 (translation), Finkel 2013b, 129–135 (transliteration), and Schaudig in this volume.

6. Taylor 2013, 58–59.

7. See, among others, Schaudig 2001, 46–47 for the inscriptions of Nabonidus.

8. Finkel 2013a, 15–26, and Finkel 2013b, 129.

be justified. This was done by demonstrating that Nabonidus had offended the gods and that Cyrus had been choosen and sent by the angry god Marduk himself. Nabonidus had in fact been tied in a bitter deadlock for years with the most influential priesthood of Marduk, the traditional head of the Babylonian pantheon, because Nabonidus venerated the moon-god Sîn as the "King of the Gods" at the expense of Marduk. The Babylonian priesthood finally resolved the situation by opening the gates of Babylon to Cyrus, hailing him as the "savior" from the "tyranny" of Nabonidus.[9]

The inscription of the cylinder is a brilliant literary reading of the events, written by sophisticated Babylonian scribes in the name of Cyrus in a beautiful and flowery Babylonian. The text can be divided into the following parts:

Part	Lines	Content
1	lines 1–11a	Nabonidus king of Babylon is a blasphemous tyrant, despising Marduk king of the gods, neglecting the shrines, and oppressing the people.
2	lines 11b–16	The merciful god Marduk chooses Cyrus as the savior from the tyranny of Nabonidus.
3	lines 17–19	Babylon, the holy city, falls without any fighting into the hands of Cyrus, assisted miraculously by Marduk himself; Nabonidus is taken captive.
4	lines 20–22a	Cyrus introduces himself to the reader, providing his royal pedigree.
5	lines 22b–28a	Cyrus settles in Babylon as king.
6	lines 28b–30a	Cyrus receives the tribute of the world in Babylon.
7	lines 30b–32	Cyrus restores the gods of various eastern, Trans-Tigridian regions, which had been carried off by Babylonian kings in previous wars, to their temples.
8	lines 33–36	Cyrus restores the gods of Babylonia, which had been brought into Babylon by Nabonidus (for safety), to their temples in Babylonia.
9	lines 27–38a	Cyrus increases the offerings for the temple of Marduk.
10	lines 38b–45	Cyrus restores the wall of Babylon.

9. This is clear from the strong support that "god Marduk" offered to Cyrus according to the narrative of the Cyrus Cylinder authors. Of course, it was not the god himself, but his human staff – his "priesthood" in the widest sense – in Babylon.

In the Cyrus Cylinder, the original and actual building inscription forms only a rather short segment at the very end of the text (part 10: ll. 38b-45). Before it goes a part that explains why the good king Cyrus of Anšan came to replace the wicked Nabonidus as king of Babylonia (parts 2–3: ll. 11b-19). And at the beginning of the inscription there is a lengthy part that lists the many crimes and sacrileges of the former king Nabonidus (part 1: ll. 1–11a). The Cyrus Cylinder, thus, is a good example of how the original format of a genre – a building inscription – can be changed, even distorted, in order to convey a new and completely different piece of information.

Since in line 43 of the Cyrus Cylinder a reference is made to an inscription of the Assyrian king Aššurbanipal, which had come to light during the restoration of the wall of Babylon by Cyrus, modern scholars have been looking for similarities between the texts that might indicate that the cylinder of Aššurbanipal had been used as a model.[10] The inscription of Aššurbanipal, to which the cylinder refers, was probably one of the numerous cylinders of this king dealing with his own restoration of the walls of Babylon.[11] However, the Babylonian scribes were of course completely capable of producing one of their traditional building inscriptions without any physical model. After all, these texts consisted mainly of standard expressions and stock phrases.

There are of course some features that the cylinders of Aššurbanipal and Cyrus have in common, but their similarity is rather superficial. Both are massive clay cylinders with lines running all over their whole widths, with no division into columns.[12] Admittedly, we know this feature best from cylinders of the Late Neo-Assyrian kings like Sargon II, Sennacherib, or Aššurbanipal. The cylinder inscriptions of the Late Babylonian kings were rather organized in two or three columns. But here the similarity ends, since the signs of the Aššurbanipal cylinder are archaizing, and the signs of the Cyrus Cylinder are Neo-Babylonian. Among the many classical stock phrases used by either text, there seems to be only one phrase that might have been inspired by the Aššurbanipal text. That is a phrase using an infinitive construction with *maṣṣarta dunnunu* telling us that each king had "strengthened the security or the fortifications" of Babylon. However, this similarity is not very specific, as the following demonstrates:

---

10. Harmatta 1974; Kuhrt 1983, pp. 88–92; Michalowski 2014.

11. Frame 1995, no. B.6.32.1.

12. Photographs of the Cyrus Cylinder, of one of the Aššurbanipal cylinders mentioned above, and of two cylinders of Nebuchadrezzar and Nabopolassar can be found in Taylor 2013, 65, for comparison.

Aššurbanipal on the walls Imgur-Enlil and Nēmetti-Enlil:

aššu maṣṣarti Esaĝil u ešrēt Bābil dunnuni[13]

in order to increase the security of Esaĝil and the (other) sanctuaries of Babylon

Cyrus on the wall Imgur-Enlil:

[maṣṣ]artašu dunnuna ašte''ēma[14]

I sought to increase its [secu]rity

Another element is the selection and order of royal titles. Both texts use the string "great king, strong king, king of the world, king of Assyria / Babylonia, king of the four quarters." Titles of this kind are indeed typical for Assyrian royal inscriptions, but Cyrus' predecessor, Nabonidus had also been using them. The order he uses is in fact closer to the Assyrian model than the one used by Cyrus, who puts *šar kiššati* "king of the world" in front. So this may not serve as an argument for the bearing of Aššurbanipal's cylinder on the wording of the Cyrus Cylinder. The scribes of Cyrus could have easily adopted the titles from Nabonidus directly, as we may observe:

Aššurbanipal: *šarru rabû šarru dannu šar kiššati šar GN šar kibrāti erbetti*[15]
Nabonidus: *šarru rabû šarru dannu šar kiššati šar GN šar kibrāti erbetti*[16]
Cyrus: *šar kiššati šarru rabû šarru dannu šar GN šar kibrāti erbetti*[17]

The most surprising element that seems to justify the assumption that Cyrus styled himself as a successor of the Assyrian kings, rather than of the Babylonian kings, is not the alleged similarity of certain stock phrases, but the plain fact that Cyrus mentions the Assyrian king Aššurbanipal by name at all, just as Nabonidus had done. So it is not a matter of literary adaption or styling but of "name-dropping."[18] As we shall see, the literary models of the Cyrus Cylinder are to be found in another genre. The text of the Cyrus Cylinder actually refers to the Babylonian *Epic of Creation* (*Enūma elîš*) and to the *Esaĝil Chronicle*.

Since the cylinder explains why Cyrus had to replace his – until then legitimate – predecessor, the text belongs to the genre of apologies. There

---

13. Frame 1995, 198, no. B.6.32.1, ll. 19–20.
14. Cyrus Cylinder, l. 38; Schaudig 2001, 554; Finkel 2013b, 133.
15. See e.g. Frame 1995, 197, no. B.6.32.1, l. 3.
16. Schaudig 2001, 415, no. 2.12, ll. 1–2.
17. Cyrus Cylinder, l. 20; Schaudig 2001, 552; Finkel 2013b, 131.
18. In this respect, I find it rather difficult to ascribe to one of these stock phrases like "I found an inscription of RN$_{xy}$" such a meaning as Michalowski 2014 does. It is not the "biography of a sentence" but rather the "afterlife of a name."

are similar apologies in the ancient Near East, and their main argument is that the former king either never had divine support or had lost it in the meantime. For example, Nabonidus himself once explained in this way why Lā-abâš-Marduk, the legitimate son and successor of king Neriglissar, had to be removed from the throne. According to Nabonidus, Lā-abâš-Marduk sat on the throne "against the will of the gods," and furthermore, he displayed a bad character and "would not show proper behavior":

> *Lā-abâš-Mar[duk] mār^ušu ṣaḫr[u] lā āḫiz riddi kīma lā libbi ilīma ina kussî šarrūti ūšimma*[19]
>
> Lā-abâš-Mar[duk], (Neriglissar's) little son who would not show proper behavior, ascended the royal throne without divine consent.

Very close to the formulation of the Cyrus Cylinder is a text of the Assyrian king Sargon II, which explains why his brother and predecessor lost the throne. Shalmaneser V, dubbed in the text as "he who did not fear the King of the Universe (that is, Aššur)," had imposed corvée labor on the citizens of the holy city of Aššur. In consequence, "the Enlil of the gods (that is, Aššur) overthrew his reign in the rage of his heart," and appointed Sargon instead:[20]

> (32) *lā pāliḫ ša[r] gimri ana āli šu'āti qā[ss]u ana lemutti ūbilma*
>
> He who did not fear the Kin[g] of the Universe brought [h]is han[d] to that city for evil.
>
> (32–33) *[eli] nišīšu ilku tupšikku marṣ[i]š i[šku]n i[mt]ani ṣābī ḫupšiš*
>
> He griev[ous]ly im[pos]ed corvée and forced labor [upon] its people, (and) so c[ount]ed them as people of serf status.
>
> (34) *Enlil ilānī ina uggat libbīšu palâšu ⌈iskip⌉*
>
> The Enlil of the gods (that is, Aššur) overthrew his reign in the rage of his heart.

In the ancient Near East, many holy cities like Aššur, Nippur, or Babylon enjoyed privileges such as freedom from taxation and from service for the king, since they were entirely to serve their tutelar deities.[21] Hence, in the end the grievous sin of Shalmaneser solely consisted in imposing taxes.

---

19. Nabonidus, Babylon Stela, IV:37′–42′; Schaudig 2001, 517.
20. The following after Saggs 1975, 14–15, the "Aššur Charter," ll. 32–34.
21. On this concept of *kidinnu* "divine protection" and *kidinnūtu* "privileged status," see Reviv 1988 and Pongratz-Leisten 1997.

The sins of Nabonidus also fit into this scheme. According to the Cylinder his main fault consisted in his no longer being fearful of Marduk, the king of the gods. This is the reason why "he laid his hands on Babylon with evil intent." He made "a copy, a counterfeit of Esaĝil," the temple of Marduk and the center of the universe. This accusation aims at the fact that Nabonidus indeed fostered the cult of the Syrian moon god of Ḥarrān as king of the gods and had restored the temple of this god at Ḥarrān. Furthermore, Nabonidus is said to have introduced "inappropriate cultic pratices" and to have "cut the offerings." And last, but not least, he oppressed the people of Babylon and "ruined them by a yoke without relief."[22] Like Shalmaneser, Nabonidus had imposed taxes on the rich temples and cities of Babylonia. This was deemed a sacrilege and so god Marduk went into action. Just as Marduk once had saved the gods, his fathers, from hardship in olden days, he now saved his city Babylon from the hardship imposed by Nabonidus. The rare phrase used in the Cyrus Cylinder – īṭir ina šapšāqi (he saved from hardship) – is a clear allusion to a verse from the Babylonian Epic of Creation (Enūma elîš) which is dedicated to Marduk as the king of the universe:

| Enūma elîš: | (Marduk ša) ilānī abbīšu | īṭiru | ina | šapšāqi |

(Marduk who) saved the gods, his fathers, from hardship

(Enūma elîš VI:126; Kämmerer and Metzler 2012, 271)

| Cyrus Cylinder: | (Marduk) ālšu Bābil | īṭir | ina | šapšāqi |

(Marduk) saved his city Babylon from hardship

(Cyrus Cylinder, l. 17; Schaudig 2001, 552; and Schaudig in this volume)

There is also another quote from Enūma elîš in a formula, wherein Cyrus and Cambyses are called upon to perfom the duties held by the office of the "provider of the temples" of Babylonian gods:

Enūma elîš: atta lū zāninu parakkīni

May you be the provisioner of our shrines!

(Enūma elîš V:115; Kämmerer and Metzler 2012, 241; Lambert 2013, 102)

---

22. See the list of Nabonidus' sacrileges from lines 5–9 of the Cyrus Cylinder in my text and translation in this volume. After he had taken the throne of Babylon, Cyrus undid the regulations imposed by Nabonidus: "The people of Babylon, [...] onto whom (Nabonidus) had imposed an inappropriate yoke without divine consent – I (Cyrus) brought relief to their exhaustion and did away with their toil" (Cyrus Cylinder, ll. 25–26).

Cyrus Cylinder: *šunu lū zāninū parakkīni*
May they be the provisioners of our shrines!
(Cyrus Cylinder, l. 36; Finkel 2013b, 132)

The office of the "provider of the temples" (*zāninu*) is the most important office and title of the Neo-Babylonian kings, an office which Nabonidus is said to have fullfilled only reluctantly or perhaps not at all. And there are more allusions to *Enūma eliš*. The Cyrus Cylinder states that Marduk saw with joy the good deeds and the "righteous heart" of Cyrus. According to the Cylinder it was Marduk himself who had created and bestowed that "wide heart" upon the king, as his destiny:[23]

(14) *Marduk (...) epšētīšu damqāti u libbašu išāra ḫadîš ippali[š]*

Marduk (...) saw with pleasure his good deeds and his righteous heart.

(23) *Marduk (...) libbī ritpāša ša rāʾim Bābil ⌜šīmātiš iškunannîma⌝*

Marduk (...) bestowed on me as my destiny that wide heart of mine, (as a token) of someone who loves Babylon.

This motif harkens back to earlier examples. Indeed, Nabopolassar, who like Cyrus had seized the Babylonian throne very much as a usurper without any hereditary claim to it, instead stressed the qualities of his good character:[24]

(8) ᵈ*Šà-zu bēl mūdû libbi ilānī ša šamê u erṣeti* (9) *ša tākalāt nišī ibarrû kayyāna* (10) *(...) ša libbīya ibrēma* (11) *ina māt abbanû iškunanni ana rēšēti*

(8) Šazu (= Marduk), the lord who knows the heart of (or: among) the gods, (9) who constantly checks the inner mind of the people, (10) (...) scanned the (thoughts) of my heart and (11) placed me in the land where I was born in the most exalted position.

All this emphasis on the good heart of Babylonian kings is rooted in a

---

23. The following from the Cyrus Cylinder, ll. 14, 23; Schaudig 2001, 552–3; Finkel 2013b, 131.

24. The following quote is from the Eḫursaĝtila cylinder of Nabopolassar (Langdon 1912, 66, Npl. no. 4, ll. 8–11; Da Riva 2013, 58, NaplC12/1: 8–11 + variants; same phrase in Nabopolassar's Imgur-Enlil cylinder: Da Riva 2013, 94, NaplC32: I 15–20). The term *tākaltu* "stomach / innards" (Starr 1983, 53–54) means the "inside," the "mind" of the people, very much like *libbu* "heart" and *kabattu* "liver." The imagery is taken from extispicy, performed by the god Marduk on living humans here, not on slaughtered sheep, as the human diviner would do.

particular capacity of Marduk which becomes manifest in one of his holy Sumerian names. In *Enūma elîš*, Marduk's eighteenth name is: "Šazu, that is, 'He-Who-Knoweth-the-Heart,' he who checks the mind." It is Marduk who has the power to observe and check (*barû*) the thoughts of the heart (*ša libbi*) of gods and men. The righteous and wide heart of Cyrus is a motif created by Babylonian scholars on the basis of the *Šazu*-theology. The other main topics of the Cyrus Cylinder can equally be derived from the explanations of Marduk's holy names in *Enūma elîš*. Further variants of the name *Šazu*, that is, *Šazu-Zisi*, *Šazu-Suḫrim*, *Šazu-Zaḫrim* qualify Marduk as "the one who punishes the evil-doer, the one who subjugates the disobedient, the one who uproots his enemies and who thwarts their plans." And finally Marduk is also the one "who restores the gods, who have left their shrines, to their proper places":[25]

(35)	*Šazu* (ᵈšà-zu) *mūdē libbi ilānī ša ibarrû karša*	(Marduk's name is also:) *Šazu*, He-Who-Knoweth-the-Heart of (or: among) the gods, he who checks the mind,
(36)	*ēpiš lemnēti lā ušeṣṣû ittīšu*	who does not let a (single) evil-doer escape his (punishment)
(38)	*mukanniš lā māgiri*	who subjugates the disobedient
(43)	*nāsiḫ ayyābī*	who uproots the enemies
(44)	*musappiḫ kipdīšunu*	who thwarts their plans
(53)	*ša napḫar ilānī munnabtī ušēribu ešressun*	who restored all the gods, who had taken flight, to their shrines

These two topics, the removal of the disobedient and the restoration of the gods to their temples, are the main themes of the Cyrus Cylinder. Before the eyes of a Babylonian, who faithfully believed in Marduk, the power and meaning of his holy name *Šazu* had become reality through the fall of Nabonidus and Cyrus' rise as a benevolent restorer.

The punishment of Nabonidus itself follows closely a scheme set up by another text from the circles of the priests of Marduk. That text is the so-called *Esaĝil Chronicle*, from the early first millennium BCE.[26] This chronicle

25. The following after *Enūma elîš* VII:35–53; Kämmerer and Metzler 2012, 288–291; Lambert 2013, 126.

26. Formerly also known as *Weidner Chronicle*; editions by Grayson (1975, 145–151, no. 19), al-Rawi (1990), and Glassner (2005, 263–269, no. 38). I quote the text after my own reconstruction which will appear in my book, *Explaining Disaster*.

aims at teaching Babylonian kings the proper behavior towards Marduk and Babylon. The text apparently builds on material from the late third and early second millennia, but in the way it has come down to us, it is clearly a work of the early Neo-Babylonian period. The main topic of the chronicle is the status of the god Marduk. The reader is informed that, supplanting Enlil, Marduk has risen to the head of the pantheon. Marduk is not to be ignored or even opposed. This is the rather simple and straightforward moral which the author wants us to learn.

To strengthen his point, the author gives a short summary of the history of earlier kings of Babylonia and how they fared. The kings and their deeds are briefly introduced and assessed. The sole line of argument runs along the question as to whether they had either heeded Marduk, or not. Good kings secure a good life and rule the world, bad kings are deposed or killed. Obviously, there are more bad kings than good kings, and so the narrative culminates in the final "disaster of Ibbi-Sîn" (*šaḫluqti Ibbi-Sîn*), when Marduk wrathfully rejected Babylonia, and had it sacked by barbarian hordes from the east.

The text demonstrates that any offence committed would be punished by Marduk harshly, but justly. No evildoer would escape his wrath. Sometimes, bad kings are simply deposed from office, sometimes they have to face illnesses, or invading barbarian hordes. At the end of the story, we see Marduk losing his temper: since kings would not learn their lessons, death penalties increase, and finally disaster strikes during the reign of king Ibbi-Sîn of Ur. This is when the gods leave their shrines, go into exile and deliver the land to destruction.

Among the kings' sins, we may distinguish two distinct groups: one represents offenses committed against the holy city of Babylon, or its people; and the other are ritual transgressions in various food offerings destined to Marduk:

Line	King of	City	Conduct	Offence	Punishment
(41)	Akka	(Kiš)	bad	graves?	kingship taken
(42)	Enmerkar	Uruk	bad	people	barbarians invading
(45)	Gilgameš	(Uruk)	good		
(48)	Puzur-ilī	Akšak	bad	fish offerings	kingship taken
(53)	Ku-Baʾu	(Kiš)	good		
(56)	Ur-Zababa	(Kiš)	bad	wine offerings	kingship taken

Line	King of	City	Conduct	Offence	Punishment
(57)	Šarru-kīn	Akkade	good ›› bad	city of Babylon	sleeplessness
(62)	Narām-Sîn	(Akkade)	bad	people	barbarians invading
(64)	Gutians		bad	fish offerings	kingship taken
(65)	Utu-ḫeĝal	(Uruk)	good ›› bad	city of Babylon	death
(70)	Šulgi	(Ur)	bad	purification rites	leprosy
(72)	Amar-Sîn	(Ur)	bad	bull offerings	death
(74)	Šu-Sîn	(Ur)	good		
(75)	Ibbi-Sîn	(Ur)	poor wretch	(sin of Šulgi)	disaster

The individual examples are dominated by mirror elements, that is, by rewards and punishments that are commensurate with the original misdeed, or virtuous act. Sometimes, these mirror elements display a highly philological character. That means the correspondence is in particular an expression or verb that describes the action or events. There is a nice example of applied Sumerology in the legend about the barmaid, Ku-Baʾu, who provided the fishermen of Marduk with "bread and water," that is, *akala u mê* in Akkadian, and *ú a* "fodder (and) water" in Sumerian. In the form *ú-a* the Sumerian term – and its Akkadian counterpart *zāninu* "the provider of a temple" – is also a royal title, in fact, the most important title of the Late Babylonian kings who were *zānin Esaĝil* "the providers of Esaĝil." Thus, when still a barmaid, Ku-Baʾu proved herself competent, and worthy of serving Marduk and his temple. As a consequence, she was also deemed fit to hold kingship for Marduk, and to rule all the world. Her reward mirrors her pious deed. Another philological example revolves about the idea of "taking something away." When the Gutians took away (*ekēmu* in Akkadian) a fish that was to be offered to Marduk, the god in turn took away their rule (*ekēmu* again). Sometimes the correspondence is more illustrative: when Šulgi defiled and sullied the holy purification rites, his body was sullied with leprosy in turn.

Philological Examples:

Puzur-ilī	takes (*ekēmu/nakāru*) the fish	kingship is taken (**ekēmu/nakāru*)
Ku-Baʾu	provides bread and water (**ú-a*)	obtains the office of the provider (**ú-a*)

Ur-Zababa	alters (*šupêlu*) the wine offerings	is exchanged (**šupêlu*) for Sargon
Sargon	changes his attitude (**nakāru*)	Bēl changes his attitude (*nakāru*) and people become hostile (*nakāru*)
Gutians	take away (*ekēmu*) the fish	kingship is taken (*ekēmu*)
Utu-ḫeĝal	touches Esaĝil (*qāta wabālu*)	is carried off (*wabālu*) by a river

Illustrative Examples:

Enmerkar	harms the PEOPLE (of Babylon)	has to face enemy HORDES
Sargon	gets TIRED of Marduk	is stricken with SLEEPLESSNESS
Narām-Sîn	harms PEOPLE of Babylon	has to face enemy HORDES
Amar-Sîn	alters the OXEN for the offering	dies from a sandal (made of COW-HIDE)
Šulgi	SULLIES the rites	is SULLIED (by leprosy)

Kings who dare oppress the "people of Babylon" are punished by hostile "people" or "masses," that is, barbarian enemy hordes sent against them by Marduk. Such is the punishment of Enmerkar and Narām-Sîn:

(42) *Enmerkar šar Uruk nammaššê ušalpitma*
Ummān-Manda ša apil kalbati š[ū idkâššumma]

Enmerkar, the king of Uruk, wrecked the people,
and so [he (= Marduk) summoned up against him] the Ummān-Manda, who was the son of a bitch.[27]

These phrases are repeated nearly verbatim in the description of the sin and the punishment of Narām-Sîn of Akkade:

27. In this imagery, the Ummān-Manda – or the leader or ancestor – are singularized.

(62)   *Narām-Sîn nammaššê Bābil ušalpitma adi šinīšu ummān Qutî
        idkâššumma*

Narām-Sîn wrecked the people of Babylon,
(and so) he (= Marduk) summoned up against him
the horde of the Gutians, for a second time (after he had done so
with Enmerkar).

As we can see, offending the good people of Babylon will conjure up the
foreign peoples against the wicked king as a divine "mirror punishment."
We also see that the Ummān-Manda "the hordes of the Manda" and the
ummān Qutî "the hordes of the Gutians" are virtually interchangable elements, meaning merely "barbarian hordes." In the story of Narām-Sîn, we
can see another feature of Marduk's perfect verdicts. The punishment may
happen again, for a second time, in correlation with (reaction to) the crime
perpetrated. When Narām-Sîn offended the people of Babylon, Marduk sent
barbarian hordes against him for a second time, after Marduk had done so
already with Enmerkar, who in a similar manner had offended the people.

      As an expression of perfect divine justice, the punishments have a
strong tit-for-tat character. The "mirror principle" we see working in this
chronicle is a kind of divine retaliation. As an expression of that divine law
code, these punishments would recur regularly. The same offence would call
for the same punishment. For the Babylonian audience of that chronicle,
learning from history meant applying the rule learnt from the examples of
kings of old to contemporaneous events.

      Now it is time to turn to Nabonidus and his fate again. According to the
ideologues, scholars, and priests of Marduk, he had committed sin upon sin.
He was the culmination of his wicked predecessors:

Sins of Nabonidus (Cyrus Cylinder)		Sins of King$_{xy}$ (Esaĝil Chronicle)
(5)	*tamšīl Esaĝil īte[pušma ...]* "he ma[de] a counterfeit of Esaĝil"	= Sargon of Akkade (*Esaĝil Chronicle*, l. 60)
(6)	*paraṣ lā simātīšunu* "rites inappropriate to them (: the gods)"	= Šulgi (*Esaĝil Chronicle*, ll. 70–71)
(7)	*sattukkī ušabṭil* "he brought the daily offerings to a halt"	= Ur-Zababa & Amar-Suʾena (*Esaĝil Chronicle*, ll. 56, 72)

Sins of Nabonidus (Cyrus Cylinder)		Sins of King$_{xy}$ (Esaĝil Chronicle)
(8)	*lemutti ālīšu [īt]eneppuš ūmišamma* "he [d]id yet more evil to his city every day"	= Utu-ḫeĝal (*Esaĝil Chronicle*, l.69)
(8)	*[... niši]šu ina abšāni lā tapšuḫti uḫalliq kullassin* "he brought ruin to all of his [people] by a yoke without relief"	= Enmerkar & Narām-Sîn (*Esaĝil Chronicle*, ll.42, 62)
(9)	*ana tazzimtīšina Enlil ilānī ezziš īgugm[a ...]* "at their complaints, the Enlil-of-the-Gods became furiously enraged a[nd ...]"	

Among these sins, Nabonidus had committed the sin of Sargon of Akkade (twenty-fourth cent. BCE) when he restored the temple of the moon-god at Ḥarrān and decorated it excessively and unduly, creating a copy, a counterfeit of the true center of the world, the temple Esaĝil at Babylon. The *Verse Account* (ca. 539 BCE) sharply rebukes Nabonidus for having built and decorated the temple Eḫulḫul at Ḥarrān as a copy rivaling Esaĝil. The text puts the following quote into Nabonidus' mouth:[28]

(II:6′) *ana Ekurri ešša tamšīl simāti lumeššil*
(II:7′) *Eḫulḫul lumbi zikiršu ana ṣâti*

I will make a shrine, rivaling Ekur (= the main temple Esaĝil) as a counterpart of its (holy) insignia, I will call its name "Eḫulḫul," (to last) for evermore!"

The *Esaĝil Chronicle* and similar texts have it that Sargon tore out the soil from the pit of Babylon and that he built a rivaling "counterpart" (*gabarû*, from Sumerian *gaba-ri* "rival") of Babylon, next to Akkade:[29]

28. Verse Account, Col. II:6′–7′; after Schaudig 2001, 567. The same text also rebukes Nabonidus for decorating Eḫulḫul exactly like Esaĝil: *rēma ekda kīma Esaĝil ušaṣbit pānuššu* "he installed a fierce bull in front of it, just like (the bull installed in) Esaĝil" (Verse Account, Col. II:15′; after Schaudig 2001, 567).

29. The following quote from the Esaĝil Chronicle, line 60. The same story is told in a liver omen from the library of Aššurbanipal, see Koch 2005, 226–227, § 3.

(l. 60) šū amāt Bēl iqbûšu ima[ššīma] eper šatpīšu issuḫma
         miḫrat Akkade āla īpušma Bābil ana šumīšu ib[b]i

But he (= Sargon) for[got] about the word that Bēl had told him,
he took earth from its (= Babylon's) pit and built a city opposite
to Akkade, and (also) cal[led] it "Babylon".

The *Chronicle of Early Kings* (first mill. BCE) calls Sargon's deed expressly a
"sacrilege" (*ikkibu*):[30]

(18) *eper e(s)sê ša Bābil issuḫma*
(19) *itê Akkade gabarâ Bābil īpuš*
(20) *ana ikkib īpušu bēlu rabû Marduk īgugma*

He tore out the soil from the pit of Babylon and
next to Akkade he built a counterpart of Babylon.
At the sacrilege he committed the great lord Marduk became
enraged.

Nabonidus committed also the sin of Šulgi of Ur (twenty-first cent. BCE),
that is, he did not keep the divine rites in order, but changed them and introduced improper cults:[31]

(l. 70) *ana Šulgi mār Ur-Namma šarrūt kiššat mātāti iddin(šum)ma*
(l. 71) *parṣīšu ul ušaklil šuluḫḫīšu ulàʾīma annašu ina zumrīš[u i]štakkan*

(Marduk) gave the kingship over all the lands to Šulgi, the son
of Ur-Namma.
(Šulgi, however,) did not perform his rites perfectly, but defiled
his purification rites,
(and so Marduk) made his sin manifest in his body (in form of a
skin disease).

The *Religious Chronicle from Uruk* (ca. fourth cent. BCE) blames Šulgi for the
same sacrilege, but transfers the setting from Marduk of Babylon to its own
Urukean sky-god Anu. Interestingly, it also blames Šulgi for having reverred
the moon-god Sîn in an excessive and improper way, just like Nabonidus had
done:[32]

(13) *[pa]raṣ Anūti uṣurāti ša Uruk*

---

30. The following quote after Grayson 1975, 153–154, chronicle 20, A:18–23; Glassner 2005, 270–271, ll. 18–23.
31. The following quote from the Esaĝil Chronicle, lines 70–71.
32. The following quote after Glassner 2005, 288–289, obv. 13–17.

(14)   [n]iṣirti ummânī ša lā simāt unakk[irma]
(15)   [pa]llāḫ Sîn bēl Uri ištur[ma]
(16)   [ina p]alêšu narâ surrāti ṭuppi šillāti
(17)   [ša šul]uḫḫī ilūti išṭurma īzib

(Šulgi) altered the [ordi]nances of the office of Anu,
the regulations of Uruk, the [s]ecret of the scholars in an
unbefitting way, [and]
he wrote (instead the order) to [re]vere Sîn the lord of Ur.
[In] his [r]eign he wrote and left (to posterity)
a stela (full) of lies, and a tablet of blasphemy
[dealing with] the divine rites of [puri]fication.

Nabonidus also committed the sins of Ur-Zababa (ca. twenty-fourth cent.
BCE) and Amar-Su'ena (twenty-first cent. BCE) when he cut the offerings.
The following quotes are all taken from the Esaĝil Chronicle:

(l. 56)   Ur-Zababa karānī maqqâti ša Esaĝil ana Šarru-kīn šāqîšu šupella
iqb[i]

Ur-Zababa tol[d] Šarru-kīn his cupbearer to alter (that is, to cut)
the wine libations of Esaĝil.

(l. 72)   Amar-Su'ena mārušu alpī rabûti ša nīq zagmukki ša Esaĝil ušpēlma

Amar-Su'ena, his son, altered (that is, reduced the number, or
quality, of) the great bulls for the offering of the New Year's
festival of Esaĝil.

Nabonidus committed the sin of Utu-ḫeĝal (twenty-second cent. BCE) when
he laid his hands on Babylon with evil intent:[33]

(l. 69)   Utu-ḫeĝal šukudakku qāssu ana ālīšu ana lemutti ūbilma
nāru šalamtašu itb[al]

Utu-ḫeĝal the fisherman touched his (= Marduk's) city with evil
intent, and in reaction, the river car[ried] off his corpse.

And finally, Nabonidus commited the sins of Enmerkar of Uruk (legendary, perhaps thirtieth cent. BCE) and Narām-Sîn of Akkade (twenty-third

33. Admittedly, this is a weak argument here, since the sin of Nabonidus is not precisely
modelled on the characteristic phrase using qāta wabālu (to lay one's hand upon something).
Instead, the authors of the Cyrus Cylinder used the phrase lemutta epēšu "to do evil": lemutti
ālīšu [īt]eneppuš ūmišamma "(Nabonidus) [d]id yet more evil to his city every day" (Cyrus Cylinder. l. 8; Schaudig 2001, 552; Finkel 2013b, 130).

cent BCE), that is, he oppressed and wrecked the people of Babylon. And it is literally "at their complaints,"[34] that is, following the complaints of the people, that Marduk went into action. That is why he summoned the mythical hordes of the Gutians and the Ummān-Manda as a "mirror punishment," just as he had done before twice in the cases of Enmerkar and Narām-Sîn:

(42)   *Enmerkar šar Uruk nammaššê ušalpitma*
        Ummān-Manda ša apil kalbati š[ū idkâššumma]

        Enmerkar the king of Uruk wrecked the people,
        and so [he (= Marduk) summoned up against him]
        the Ummān-Manda, who was the son of a bitch.

(62)   *Narām-Sîn nammaššê Bābil ušalpitma adi šinīšu ummān Qutî*
        idkâššumma

        Narām-Sîn wrecked the people of Babylon,
        (and so) he (= Marduk) summoned up against him
        the horde of the Gutians, for a second time (after he had done
        so with Enmerkar).

Bearing the punishment of Enmerkar and Narām-Sîn in mind, it is important to observe that the authors of the Cyrus Cylinder speak of Cyrus' army and vassals as the "Gutians and Ummān-Manda."[35] According to the Cyrus Cylinder, the god Marduk sent these "barbarian hordes" against Nabonidus, led by Cyrus "king of Anšan."[36] Later civilizations knew Cyrus, king of Persia, who conquered Babylonia with his Median allies. So why did the Babylonian "priests" – or rather public relations officers – who drew up the text of the Cylinder, used the terms "Anšan, Gutians, Ummān-Manda," instead of the

34. Cyrus Cylinder, l. 9: *ana tazzimtīšina*, Schaudig 2001, 552; Finkel 2013b, 131.
35. Cyrus Cylinder l. 13: *māt Qutî gimir Ummān-Manda* "the land of the Gutians and all of the Ummān-Manda" (Schaudig 2001, 552; Finkel 2013b, 131).
36. In the cylinder, Cyrus is called *Kūraš šar āl Anšan* (Cyrus king of the city of Anšan; l. 12, Schaudig 2001, 552; Finkel 2013b, 131). The title *šar āl Anšan* (king of the city of Anšan) appears three times with his ancestors in his genealogy (ibidem, l. 21). The variant title *šar māt Aššan* (king of the land of Anšan [/Aššan]) is used twice in a brick inscription of Cyrus from Ur (Schaudig 2001, 549, ll. 1, 3). So, in Babylonian sources, Cyrus' title "king of Anšan" is spelled with the determinatives – or rather determining nouns – eri = *ālu* 'city' and kur = *mātu* 'land' indiscriminately. Apart from Anšan, the determinatives eri = *ālu* 'city' and kur = *mātu* 'land', respectively *šadû* mountain', interchange freely in a wide range of foreign names in Neo-Babylonian texts, such as the Medes, the city or the land of Gaza, the land Ḫumē, Lydia, and even Mount Amanus (Schaudig 2001, 231–232). According to archaeological investigations, the Marv Dasht plain, including the city of Anšan, became deserted roughly from the tenth century BCE onwards (Miroschedji 1990, 53; Carter 1994, 65; Waters 2000, 16). However, from the Babylonian perspective, the alternation between "city of Anšan" and "land of Anšan" has no bearing on the question whether the city proper was deserted by then or not.

more neutral terms "Persia" or "Media"? When the question is addressed, it is often stated that these terms are archaizing and historical. This is always a good choice to make in Assyriology. And it is true in the sense that these terms have a history. But it does not mean that they are simply older versions of "Persia" or "Media," as we shall see.

First, let us take a short glance at the map. Anšan is modern Tall-e Malyān in Fars, known best as a political power in the late third and early second millennium.[37]

The land of the Gutians was located roughly north of Elam in the Zagros mountains, east of the Tigris. They, too, were known best in the third millennium, when they were even credited with installing a Gutian dynasty in Mesopotamia which is held to have finished off the dynasty of Akkade.[38]

To the Ummān-Manda we should not assign a place on the geographic map, since they do not belong there, but rather to the Babylonian mental map and literature. There might have been actual people or regions that were called Mandu or Manda in the third and early second millennia and these may have given rise to the term "Manda troops," but this is of no concern to us in the present discussion.[39] The Ummān-Manda proper appear on the scene in the Old Babylonian period as the classic foes of Narām-Sîn of Akkade in the literary tradition, in the composition known as the *Cuthean Legend*.[40] According to this story, the Ummān-Manda are alien, beast-like, semi-demonic, yet vulnerable warriors, created by the gods. Enlil sends them against Narām-Sîn, who faces them in three battles and finally turns them back. However, he does not kill them, which provides an etiological explanation for agressors like the Ummān-Manda, attacking Mesopotamia from time to time, be they Cimmerians, Scythians, or be they Medes. In the time of Nabonidus, the Ummān-Manda meant the Medes. And so the term Ummān-Manda is regularly and straightforwardly translated with "hordes of the Medes" and "Median troops" in modern literature.[41] Although this translation is not all wrong, it is not all right, either. It misses an important point. At first sight, the equation with the Medes seems to be perfectly justified. After all, the terms Medes and Ummān-Manda alternate in the *Fall of Nineveh Chronicle*, as does the name Cyaxares and the title "king of the Ummān-Manda."[42] Similarly, in the inscriptions of Nabonidus, the term

37. Summer 1987–1990.
38. Hallo 1957–1971; Cooper 1983, 30–33.
39. See the overview by Goodnick Westenholz 1997, 226 and Adalı 2011, 32.
40. See Goodnick Westenholz 1997, 265–266 and Adalı 2011, 43–71 on the Ummān-Manda as the classical enemies of Narām-Sîn in the *Cuthean Legend*.
41. So did I, too, in my translations of the inscription of Nabonidus and Cyrus the Great: Schaudig 2001, p. 714, s.v. Ummān-Manda (here:) "Meder-Haufen".
42. Zawadzki 1988.

Ummān-Manda clearly designates the Medes, and their king Astyages is called "king of the Ummān-Manda" on several occasions.[43] Yet, although the term Ummān-Manda could designate the Medes, it meant more than the Medes. By calling the Medes – or in Neo-Assyrian sources the Cimmerians[44] – "Ummān-Manda", the texts assigned to them a certain role in the Assyro-Babylonian mental universe, operated by gods. The term "Ummān-Manda" was not an ethnographical term, denoting semi-nomadic people roaming along with wagons and archers riding on horseback, but it was a religious-historical term, designating barbarians created by Enlil who were to come down upon Mesopotamia from time to time – instead of another flood – in order to punish wicked kings at Enlil's command. Thus, translating Ummān-Manda simply with "the Medes" is historizing mythology, whereas the Babylonians were in fact mythologizing history.

Cyrus' official title "king of Anšan" was his;[45] there was no other. The title "king of Persia," which was given to him – later – in the *Nabonidus Chronicle*,[46] one that Cyrus himself never used, is on the one hand a description of his actual status after the deposition of Astyages, and on the other hand a reflection of the modern title "king in / of Persia," used later by Dareios I.[47] Cyrus had inherited the title "king of Anšan" from his ancestors, for example from his grandfather, Cyrus I, who calls himself on his seal "Cyrus, the Anšanite, Son of Teispes."[48] The title "king of Anšan and Susa" (or the other way round), was among the foremost titles borne by various Elamite kings from the Old-Elamite to the Neo-Elamite period.[49] So the official title of Cyrus was indeed "king of Anšan." However, the important question is, what sentiments did that title arouse in the minds of the Babylonian audience, when used in conjunction with the terms "Gutians and Ummān-Manda"? It might have been an honorific title in Elam, but after all, the Cyrus Cylinder is not a Persian or Anšanite text. It is a Babylonian text, written by Babylonians for Babylonians, in Babylonia in Babylonian. And for Babylonians, the term Anšan was

43. See the examples in Schaudig 2001, 714 s.v. *Ummān-Manda*.
44. See Adalı 2011, 107–132.
45. See note 36 above.
46. Grayson 1975, 107, no. 7, II:15, as opposed to "king of Anšan," Grayson 1975, 107, II:1.
47. Schaudig 2001, 26–27; Henkelman 2003, 193. For Dareios using the title "king in Persia" see e.g. DB § 1 (Schmitt 2009, 37). The two inscriptions of Ariaramnes (brother? of Cyrus) (AmHa) and Arsames, his son, (AsHa), which also display the title "king in Persia," (Schmitt 2009, 33–34; 34–35) are quite probably later Achaemenid compositions ascribed to early Persian kings (see Schmitt 1999, 105–111).
48. Henkelman 2003, 193; Kuhrt 2010, 54–55, no. 3 with fig. 3.2.
49. On the history of the title *sunkik Anšan Šušunka* (king of Anšan and Susa), see the discussion by Shayegan 2011, 283–284, with a list of rulers on pages 265 (Ebarat II, ca. eighteenth cent. BCE), and 269–277 (Middle and Neo-Elamite periods).

closely connected to at least two major devastations of Babylonia. The more recent one had occurred in the twelfth century, when Šutruk-Naḫḫunte I and his son Kutir-Naḫḫunte II, "kings of Anšan and Susa," had conquered Babylonia.[50] The destruction wrought by these kings must have been considerable. Their rule in Babylonia gave rise to a group of texts known today as *Chedorlaomer-Texts*, lamentations bewailing the disaster done to the cult centers of Babylonia. Among the most famous misdeeds was the abduction of a statue of Marduk to Susa. In one of these texts, Kutir-Naḫḫunte, the evildoer, is closely connected to the Ummān-Manda, as is later Cyrus. The god Enlil himself calls Kutir-Naḫḫunte and the barbarian hordes of the Ummān-Manda to smash Babylonia:[51]

(rev. 21') *ayyū Kudur-nuḫuĝa [ē]piš lemnēti*
(rev. 22') *idkâmma Ummān-Manda [ispu]n māt Enlil*

Which one is Kudur-nuḫuĝa (that is, Kutir-Naḫḫunte), the evil-[d]oer?"
(Enlil then) summoned the Ummān-Manda,
[and he devasta]ted the land of Enlil.

The more ancient disaster – in relation to which the later Babylonian conquest by Šutruk-Naḫḫunte and Kutir-Naḫḫunte appeared very much like a recurrence – was the famous "Ibbi-Sîn Disaster," the *šaḫluqti Ibbi-Sîn* as it is called in Babylonian sources.[52] At the end of the third millennium BCE, the once famous Third Dynasty of Ur was wiped out by barbarian hordes from the Iranian mountains, from Elam and Anšan. The city of Ur was taken, looted, and destroyed. The august temples were spoiled, and even the statues of the gods residing in them were carried off as prisoners. And with them the hapless king Ibbi-Sîn was taken in fetters to Anšan, from where he was not to return, and where he was eventually to die. The devastation of Sumer holds the place of one of the worst destructions ever in Babylonia's memory.

So, a "king of Anšan" leading the "Ummān-Manda" against Babylonia could not presage anything good. It could mean nothing but uttermost disaster. The Babylonian scholars who drafted the text of the Cyrus Cylinder were

50. On the Elamite raid into Babylonia and the end of the Kassite dynasty see Brinkman 1968, 88–89.

51. The following quote after Lambert 1994, 70, rev. 21'-22'; see also Adalı 2011, 163–165. It is of course clear that the Ummān-Manda cannot mean the Medes here, but any kind of barbarian, eastern, Elamite invaders.

52. The memories of this event were kept alive mainly by cultic lamentations and historical omens; see among others Michalowski 2011, 210–215. My forthcoming study *Explaining Disaster* will deal in detail with the literary texts which this catastrophe has brought forth.

not interested in a Persian king leading his Median and Trans-Tigridian allies against Babylonia. What they needed was a king of Anšan bringing down the hordes of the Gutians and the Ummān-Manda against a wicked king as a divine punishment. Of course, Cyrus came with this title, but the scholars of Marduk seized their chance and fitted "Cyrus, king of Anšan" and the terms "Gutians" and "Ummān-Manda" into their worldview, which was permeated by religious and mythical thought. They needed the Ummān-Manda to turn Nabonidus into a new Narām-Sîn or Enmerkar in the tradition of the *Esaĝil Chronicle*, and they needed them, as a means to paint the picture as black as possible. They required the terms "Anšan" and "Ummān-Manda," in order to create the tension between on the one hand the slaughter and devastation that was expected to occur, and on the other hand the miraculously peaceful course of events that eventually unfolded in Babylon proper.

When Cyrus king of Anšan crossed the Tigris with the troops of the Gutians and the Ummān-Manda, this meant absolute terror for the Babylonians. At the end of the third millennium, Anšan and Elam had wiped out the empire of the famous Third Dynasty of Ur. At the end of the second millennium, Šutruk-Naḫḫunte and his son Kutir-Naḫḫunte, "kings of Anšan and Susa," had eliminated the Kassite dynasty. Assisted by the Ummān-Manda, they had devastated Babylonian cities and temples. With Cyrus, yet another king of Anšan had arisen who was marching with the barbarian hordes of the Gutians and the Ummān-Manda towards Babylonia. This could only signify complete and utter destruction.

In order to appreciate fully the surprise of the Babylonians when the king of Anšan, the Gutians, and the Ummān-Manda entered Babylon peacefully and paid his hommage to Marduk and Esaĝil, we should translate these elements into a tale about the king of the Huns leading Gog and Magog against Rome, and turning all of a sudden into a woolly lamb at the gates of Saint Peter's Basilica.

The capture of Babylon by Cyrus was quite a remarkable event in its own right. But it turned into a miracle induced by Marduk himself when the Babylonians presented their reading of history on the basis of the *Enūma elîš* and the *Esaĝil Chronicle* to account for the "righteous heart of Cyrus," and the punishment of the wicked Nabonidus. Before the eyes of the Babylonians, their sacred scriptures had been fulfilled.

Bibliography

Adalı, S. F. 2011. *The Scourge of God: The Umman-manda and its Significance in the First Millennium BC*. State Archives of Assyria, Studies 20. Helsinki.

Al-Rawi, F. N. H. 1990. "Tablets from the Sippar Library, I. The 'Weidner Chronicle': A Supposititious Royal Letter concerning a Vision." *Iraq* 52:1–13, plate 1.

Brinkman, J. A. 1968. *A Political History of Post-Kassite Babylonia, 1158–722 B.C.* Analecta Orientalia 43. Rome.

Carter, E. 1994. "Bridging the Gap between the Elamites and the Persians in Southeastern Khuzistan." In *Continuity and Change: Proceedings of the Last Achaemenid History Workshop, April 6–8, 1990 – Ann Arbor, Michigan*, edited by H. Sancisi-Weerdenburg, A. Kuhrt and M. Cool Root, 65–95. Achaemenid History VIII. Leiden.

Cooper, J. S. 1983. *The Curse of Agade*. Baltimore.

Da Riva, R. 2013. *The Inscriptions of Nabopolassar, Amēl-Marduk and Neriglissar*. Studies in Ancient Near Eastern Records 3. Berlin.

Finkel, I. 2013a. "The Cyrus Cylinder: the Babylonian perspective." In *The Cyrus Cylinder: The King of Persia's Proclamation from Ancient Babylon*, edited by I. Finkel, 4–34. London.

———. 2013b. "Appendix: Transliteration of the Cyrus Cylinder Text." In *The Cyrus Cylinder: The King of Persia's Proclamation from Ancient Babylon*, edited by I. Finkel, 129–135. London.

Frame, G. 1995. *Rulers of Babylonia: From the Second Dynasty of Isin to the End of Assyrian Domination (1157–612 BC)*. The Royal Inscriptions of Mesopotamia – Babylonian Periods 2. Toronto.

Glassner, J.-J. 2004. *Mesopotamian Chronicles*. Edited by Benjamin R. Foster. Society of Biblical Literature Writings from the Ancient World, Number 19. Atlanta: Society of Biblical Literature.

Goodnick Westenholz, J. 1997. *Legends of the Kings of Akkade: The Texts*. Mesopotamian Civilizations 7. Winona Lake.

Grayson, A. K. 1975. *Assyrian and Babylonian Chronicles*. Texts from Cuneiform Sources 5. Locust Valley.

Hallo, W. W. 1957–1971. "Gutium (Qutium)." *Reallexikon der Assyriologie und vorderasiatischen Archäologie* 3: 708–720.

Harmatta, J. 1974. "Les modèles littéraires de l'édit babylonien de Cyrus." In *Hommage Universel*. 3 vols. Vol. I. Acta Iranica 1 – Commémoration Cyrus: Actes du Congrès de Shiraz 1971, 29–48. Téhéran/Liège: Bibliothèque Pahlavi; distributed by E. J. Brill.

Henkelman, W. F. M. 2003. "Persians, Medes, and Elamites: Acculturation in the Neo-Elamite Period." In *Continuity of Empire (?): Assyria, Media, Persia*, edited by Giovanni B. Lanfranchi, Michael Roaf, and Robert Rollinger. History of the Ancient Near East – Monographs V, 181–231, table 2, pls. 9–15. Padova: S.A.R.G.O.N. Editrice e Libreria.

Kämmerer, Th. R. and K. A. Metzler. 2012. *Das babylonische Weltschöpfungsepos Enūma elîš.* Alter Orient und Altes Testament, Band 375. Münster.

Koch, U. S. 2005. *Secrets of Extispicy. The Chapter Multābiltu of the Babylonian Extispicy Series and Niṣirti bārûti Texts mainly from Aššurbanipal's Library.* Alter Orient und Altes Testament, Band 326. Münster.

Kuhrt, A. 1983. "The Cyrus Cylinder and Achaemenid Imperial Policy." *Journal for the Study of the Old Testament* 25:83–97.

———. 2010. *The Persian Empire. A Corpus of Sources from the Achaemenid Period.* London.

Lambert, W. G. 1994. "The Fall of the Cassite Dynasty to the Elamites: An Historical Epic." In *Cinquante-deux réflexions sur le Proche-Orient Ancien : Offertes en hommage à Léon De Meyer,* edited by H. Gasche. Mesopotamian History and Enviroment – Occasional Publications 2, 67–72. Leuven.

———. 2013. *Babylonian Creation Myths.* Mesopotamian Civilizations 16. Winona Lake.

Langdon, S. 1912. *Die neubabylonischen Königsinschriften.* Vorderasiatische Bibliothek 4. Leipzig.

Michalowski, P. 2011. *The Correspondence of the Kings of Ur: An Epistolary History of an Ancient Mesopotamian Kingdom.* Mesopotamian Civilizations 15. Winona Lake.

———. 2014. "Biography of a Sentence: Assurbanipal, Nabonidus, and Cyrus." In *Extraction & Control: Studies in Honor of Matthew W. Stolper,* edited by M. Kozuh, Wouter F. M. Henkelman, Ch. E. Jones, and Ch. Woods. Studies in Ancient Oriental Civilization, Number 68, 203–210. Chicago.

de Miroschedji, P. 1990. "La fin de l'Élam: Essai d'analyse et d'interprétation." *Iranica Antiqua* 25: 47–95.

Oelsner, J. 1999–2000. "Review of R. Rollinger. *Herodots babylonischer Logos.* Innsbruck: 1993." *Archiv für Orientforschung* 46–47:373–380.

Pongratz-Leisten, B. 1997. "Das 'negative Sündenbekenntnis' des Königs anläßlich des babylonischen Neujahrsfestes und die *kidinnūtu* von Babylon." In *Schuld, Gewissen und Person. Studien zur Geschichte des inneren Menschen,* edited by J. Assmann and Th. Sundermeier. Studien zum Verstehen fremder Religionen, Band 9, 83–101. Gütersloh.

Reviv, H. 1988. "*kidinnu*: Observations on Privileges of Mesopotamian Cities," *Journal of the Economic and Social History of the Orient* 31:286–298.

Saggs, H. W. F. 1975. "Historical Texts and Fragments of Sargon II of Assyria: (I) The 'Assur Charter.'" *Iraq* 37:11–20.

Schaudig, H. 2001. *Die Inschriften Nabonids von Babylon und Kyros' des Grossen samt den in ihrem Umfeld entstandenen Tendenzschriften: Textausgabe und Grammatik*. Alter Orient und Altes Testament, Band 256. Münster.

———. Forthcoming. *Explaining Disaster: Tradition and Transformation of the "Catastrophe of Ibbi-Sîn" in Babylonian Literature*. Alter Orient und Altes Testament, Band 370. Münster.

Schmitt, R. 1999. *Beiträge zu altpersischen Inschriften*. Wiesbaden.

———. 2009. *Die altpersischen Inschriften der Achaimeniden: Editio minor mit deutscher Übersetzung*. Wiesbaden.

Shayegan, M. R. 2011. *Arsacids and Sasanians: Political Ideology in Post-Hellenistic and Late Antique Persia*. Cambridge.

van der Spek, R. J. 2014. "Cyrus the Great, Exiles, and Foreign Gods: A Comparison of Assyrian and Persian Policies on Subject Nations." In *Extraction & Control: Studies in Honor of Matthew W. Stolper*, edited by M. Kozuh, W. F. M. Henkelman, Ch. E. Jones, and Ch. Woods. Studies in Ancient Oriental Civilization, Number 68, 233–264. Chicago.

Starr, I. 1983. *The Rituals of the Diviner*. Bibliotheca Mesopotamica 12. Malibu.

Summer, W. M. 1987–1990. "Maljān, Tall-e (Anšan)." *Reallexikon der Assyriologie und Vorderasiatischen Archäologie* 7:306–320.

Taylor, J. 2013. "The Cyrus Cylinder: Discovery." In *The Cyrus Cylinder. The King of Persia's Proclamation from Ancient Babylon*, edited by I. Finkel, 35–68. London.

Verbrugghe, G. P., and J. M. Wickersham. 1996. *Berossos and Manetho: Introduced and Translated*. Native Traditions in Ancient Mesopotamia and Egypt. Ann Arbor.

Waters, M. W. 2000. *A Survey of Neo-Elamite History*. State Archives of Assyria, Studies 12. Helsinki.

Westenholz, A. 1999. "The Old Akkadian Period: History and Culture." In *Mesopotamien. Akkade-Zeit und Ur III-Zeit*, edited by P. Attinger und M. Wäfler. Annäherungen 3. Orbis Biblicus et Orientalis 160/3, 15–117. Fribourg.

Zawadzki, S. 1988. "Umman-manda: Bedeutung des Terminus und Gründe seiner Anwendung in der Chronik von Nabopolassar." In *Šulmu: Papers on the Ancient Near East Presented at the International Conference of Socialist Countries (Prague, Sept. 30 - Oct. 3, 1986)*, edited by P. Vavroušek and V. Souček, 379–387. Prague.

"Ich bin ein Babylonier":
The Political-Religious Message of the Cyrus Cylinder

Beate Pongratz-Leisten
New York University

IN JUNE 24, 1963, AT THE HEIGHT OF THE COLD WAR, John F. Kennedy stood on a platform facing the Berlin Wall, the most visible symbol of Soviet oppression and the world's division into East and West, and delivered a speech that captivated the world. During his speech Kennedy uttered the immortal lines "two thousand years ago, the proudest boast was *civis romanus sum*, 'I am a Roman citizen.' Today in the world of freedom, the proudest boast is *Ich bin ein Berliner* ['I am a citizen of Berlin']." With these words Kennedy embraced the fate of the citizens of Berlin and boosted the morale of a people living in a city surrounded by barbed wire – an exclave situated deep within the Eastern bloc. He not only cemented the view that the city was irrevocably part of the free Western world, but also embraced the identity of a city that once served as the cultural and political capital of a nation. In evoking both their past and their current political situation, Kennedy won the hearts of the people of Berlin and of the world; women and men who witnessed this speech still remember it as the most incisive statement of the period after World War II.

Kennedy's strategic boosting of the morale of Berlin's citizenry can be traced back to a long tradition of superpowers and conquerors deliberately seeking the support of people who once had been their enemies, but had been defeated. This example from modern politics will serve as a model for my investigation of Cyrus' carefully drafted rhetoric in the so-called Cyrus Cylinder, which was created to commemorate the restoration of the city walls of Babylon after his conquest of Babylonia. Cyrus the Great, founder of the Persian empire, had managed to bring former Median territory under his control, including Fars in southern Iran, parts of Central Asia to the east and westwards to the Halys River in Anatolia. He extended these dominions by adding" the adjoining areas of the Lydian Kingdom further west in the 540s and "the Neo-Babylonian Empire, which embraced the entire Fertile Crescent (from the Persian Gulf to the Egyptian frontier) in 539.[1] The empire

---

1. Kuhrt 2007, 169.

created by Cyrus was the largest the world had yet seen and had no rivals for most of its duration. Adding Babylonia to his dominion, Cyrus not only considerably enlarged his territory and augmented his economic resources, but also inherited a cultural tradition going back thousands of years.

The Cyrus Cylinder reveals that Cyrus, following in this in the footsteps of other conquerors before him, had decided to comply with certain traditions of ancient Near Eastern city culture by performing specific royal gestures that responded to the expectations of the local urban elites. The Babylonian Chronicles inform us that he installed his son Cambyses as king of Babylon on the occasion of the New Year festival,[2] a gesture that acknowledged the paramount role Babylonia was playing among the Persian provinces. He relied equally heavily on existing administrative structures of Babylonia, acknowledging the organization of power in place, and undertook major building activities in the city, which included the restoration of the city walls. It is within this cultural-political context that we must interpret the Cyrus Cylinder.

Various scholars, foremost among them János Harmatta,[3] had already recognized that the contents of the Cylinder could not have been drawn up at the Persian court or chancellery as, at the moment when Cyrus rose to hegemonic power in the ancient Near East, Persian scribes could not yet rely on literary models drawn up in Persia itself. Moreover, the Cyrus Cylinder was not only written in Babylonian cuneiform, but its literary structure also reveals strong similarities with the Babylonian building inscriptions. In other words, the scribe(s) or scholar(s) who composed the Cylinder on behalf of Cyrus was (were) steeped in Babylonian literary traditions and familiar with both the style of royal building inscriptions and the typical rhetorical features of their discourse.[4] The identity of that scholar, as shown by Irving Finkel in his most recent edition of the Cyrus Cylinder,[5] can be even further narrowed down to somebody who had access to the building inscriptions installed one century earlier by the Assyrian king Ashurbanipal in Babylon. The Assyrian cylinders differed in their physical shape from their Babylonian counterparts in that they used only one column, exactly the form used for the Cyrus Cylinder.[6] Moreover, not only does Cyrus mention an inscription of Ashurbanipal at the end of his text, but also the overall image drawn of the Persian conqueror as overlord of the Babylonians relied on an

2. For the *Nabonidus Chronicle*, see Grayson 1975, 104–111. Discussion further below.
3. Harmatta 1974, 31; Kuhrt 1983.
4. See also Schaudig in this volume, who argues that the Cyrus Cylinder was also emulating the *Babylonian Epic of Creation* (*Enūma eliš*) and the *Esaĝil Chronicle*.
5. Finkel 2013.
6. Finkel 2013, 67.

Assyrian antecedent, even while revealing unique traits that can only be attributed to the time of Cyrus. In other words, the Cyrus Cylinder as testament to the king's victory over Babylon was steeped in the well-established scribal tradition of the kings of the late Assyrian period.

The Cylinder, with its long history of reception, has had many lives serving the Iranian as well as the Jewish people as an icon of identity.[7] As with many objects throughout history such an appropriation was and is made possible only by selective readings and interpretations, which do not necessarily take into account the object's original historical context.

In what follows my focus will be on the religious implications of the Cylinder. One aspect determining my investigation will be whether the structure of the divine world, which was polytheistic in nature in ancient Mesopotamia, has contributed to the discourse as reflected in the text. In pursuing this question, I would like to ask whether the notion of tolerance towards the Babylonian gods and people, which has been defined as a particularly characteristic feature of Cyrus, is indeed unique, or whether it should rather be considered a typical trait of polytheistic systems in the ancient Near East. In order to understand how polytheism worked and what exactly Cyrus' rhetoric was intended to convey, it is necessary to take a closer look at the construction of identity in antiquity as it was shaped in its relations to the divine. Contrary to our modern notion of individuality, a person's identity in antiquity was very much determined by his/her social network, which even reached into the divine world through the practice of ancestor worship.

Such ancestor worship is attested far back in human history,[8] with the oldest burials dating between 200,000 and 40,000 BCE.[9] Richly decorated bodies in the cemeteries of the Epipaleolithic Natufian villages in the hills of the Mediterranean coast, dating to approximately 12,500 BCE, reveal the cultic care with which the Natufian people treated their dead.[10] The burial practices of the Late Natufian people in Jericho appear to include the separate reburial of skulls of adults. This and the later plastering of such skulls with inlaid cowrie-shell eyes indicate the performance of an ancestor cult of selected members of the community who were ranked higher in the social hierarchy and considered important for the construction of identity. Such care for the dead continues through the history of the Fertile Crescent into the historical periods, as attested by the archaeological evidence for the *kispum* offering,[11] found in the numerous bowls lined up on benches in the

7. Curtis 2013; Razmjou 2013.
8. Cauvin 2000; Renfrew and Morley 2009.
9. Lichter 2007, 247.
10. Mithen 2006, 32–34.
11. On the *kispum*, see Tsukimoto 1985 and Jacquet 2012.

royal tombs located under the Middle Bronze Age palace in Qatna,[12] or by the richly decorated tombs of Assyrian queens excavated at Nimrud.[13] The fundamentally revolutionary aspect of such finds from the prehistoric periods is that it reflects cultural "adaptive behavior," which contributed to a "socially transmitted knowledge,"[14] such as that represented by the commemoration of the dead, which reinforced metaphorically the community of the living[15] and secured its permanence.

In historical times, the ancestors, together with the family god and, on a larger scale, the patron deity of the city and the local pantheon, represented the spatial and historical dimensions of identity. The importance of the local temple as an economic center, and of the patron deity as its owner, is reflected in the particular manner in which the city's name was written. In the archaic period the writing frequently consisted in the combination of the *sign* for sanctuary and the *name* of the patron deity, as attested in the so-called city seals. Examples of such writing are: èš-utu (sanctuary of [the sun god] Utu/Shamash) for the city of Larsa; èš-ùri (sanctuary of [the moon god] Nanna) for Ur; and èš-mùš (sanctuary of [the goddess] Ishtar) for the city of Zabalam. It is primarily on the basis of the paramount role played by the temple as an economic institution fostering social differentiation and hierarchies that we can explain such types of city names. Such writing further indicates that these communities had a strong sense of communal identity bound up with their patron divinities. Moreover, the existence of a city god (Sum. dingir-uru/Akk. *il āli*) per se, furthermore, that divinity's function in securing military security, political stability, and economic prosperity (see also the secondary ᵈlamma-uru, a protective genius of the city), as well as the celebration of a festival called "day of the city god" (*ūm ili āli*), all together reveal the central importance of patron deities for the city as a community and by extension for the individual.[16] While we have archaeological and textual evidence for the cult of the protective *genius* and family god,[17] it is difficult to determine the role major deities of the local pantheon of the city or even supra-regional deities played in the daily life of the individual. To some degree, the choice of theophoric names permits inferences

12. Al-Maqdissi, Dohmann-Pfälzner, Pfälzner, Souleiman 2003, 211–218.

13. Damerji 1998.

14. Cauvin 2000, 19; Sperber and Hirschfeld 2004; Tomasello 2000.

15. Cauvin 2000, 20.

16. The distinction between the major gods or even chief god of a city and the "god of the city" is not always clear, see Selz 2011.

17. Larsa period evidence indicates that the protective genius acted as an intermediary between the individual and the divine sphere, as statuettes of Lamma figures were found together with a female deity in a street sanctuary at Ur (Wiseman 1960; van der Toorn 1996).

on the role of these divinities;[18] the public processions during the major festivals offered an opportunity for the individual to see and perhaps interact with the gods of the pantheon.

In its most complex structure, then, the social network of the individual consisted of the family, divine ancestors, the protective genius, the personal god or family god, the local pantheon, major deities of the supra-regional pantheon, and, finally, the chief god. All of these contributed to determining personal and religious identity. Religion thus operated as a resource for constructing the self as an embedded entity in the multilayered relationships of one's social network, which extended into the divine world.

The other important aspect of polytheism in Mesopotamia is that Sumero-Babylonian culture was primarily a city culture. An important aspect of Mesopotamian history is that there never was any enduring political unification in Mesopotamia until the Persian conquest in the mid-first millennium BCE. When territorial or imperial systems collapsed, the cities represented the basis, from which political organizations re-emerged. Thus, from its beginnings the south politically consisted of a congeries of city states, and culturally of an overarching cultural tradition. The social structure of the early Mesopotamian cities was determined by a mixture of tribal and urban elements, the latter playing out in the diversification of labor, social stratification, and the concentration of wealth in the hands of a few. Indeed, the interesting historical phenomenon Marc van de Mieroop has observed for Mesopotamia is that, "with the progressive territorial expansion of the political units" into empires "the cities and their representatives gained increased political independence."[19] This political independence was grounded in an economic independence, which was based on private entrepreneurship.

Such political constellations contributed to the strong self-confidence of the cities and their elites, which explains why every ruler who aimed at exercising supra-regional control sought to accommodate their interests, in order to earn their collaboration. In their inscriptions, however, conquerors would ascribe their achievement of supra-regional control to the gods, rather than to their interaction with the metropolitan elites.

Such religious-ideological rhetoric appears in an inscription of King Narām-Sîn of Akkad, who extended the borders of the Akkadian empire to hitherto unseen dimensions. After having successfully crushed a revolt of various Sumerian city states in the south, King Narām-Sîn projected the

18. Harris 1972; Beaulieu 1992, esp. 54–55; Edzard 1998.

19. This "is the reverse of the currently predominant view that Mesopotamian history evolved from a 'primitive democracy' to a totalitarian state headed by an all-powerful king"; see Van de Mieroop 1997, 133.

vision of a unified territory under divine control, as recorded in an inscription on the so-called Bassetki Statue, which was named for the village close to Mosul where the statue was found. The following includes a few salient passages:

> Naram-Sin, the Mighty,
> King of Akkade:
>
> *Summary of the great revolt* (ll. 5–19)
> When the Four Quarters (of the world)
> all together revolted against him,
> he won nine battles in only one year.
> through the love Ishtar showed to him,
> he captured the kings
> who had risen against him.
>
> *Request for deification* (ll. 20–56)
> Because he preserved
> the base of his city
> in these times of crisis,
> (the citizens of) his city
> asked
> from Ishtar in Eanna (in Uruk),
> from Enlil in Nippur,
> from Dagan in Tuttul,
> from Ninhursag in Kesh,
> from Ea in Eridu,
> from Sin in Ur,
> from Shamash in Sippar,
> (and) from Nergal in Kutha
> that he be the god of their city
> and they built a temple for him
> in the midst of Akkade.[20]

Having violently suppressed the rebellion of the cities, Narām-Sîn asked nothing less than the acknowledgment by those established political and cultic centers of his elevation to divine status and his acceptation as the "god of Akkad."[21] Instead of engaging in conversation with the elites of the

---

20. Translation: Kienast 2003, 244.

21. The title "god of Akkad" is attested in several inscriptions of seal impressions, a seal a plaque and a hemispherical bowl dedicated either by his servants, or family members. See Frayne 1993, E2.1.4.2003, E2.1.4.2013, E2.1.4.2014, E2.1.4.2020, E2.1.4.2023 (seal impressions); E.2.1.4.53 (seal cylinder); E2.1.4.2018 (plaque); E2.1.4.2007 (bowl).

conquered cities, however, Narām-Sîn claimed that the elites of his own city had addressed the respective patron deities of the conquered cities, thereby insinuating that: (1) a consensus between him and his own community had been reached; and (2) a further understanding was achieved with the patron deities of the conquered cities, who were evoked as representatives of the political and religious elites.

In this ideological discourse, then, the patron deities were turned into active players in promoting the creation of a unified territory under hegemonic control. Military and political success were presented as a result of the relationship established between the gods and the king, thus tying Narām-Sîn's action as an individual ruler into the general cosmic order as it originated with the gods.[22] Narām-Sîn's inscription thus stands at the beginning of a longstanding tradition that shaped such religious-ideological discourse, one that was reiterated through millennia well into the sixth century BCE as revealed by the discovery of the Cyrus Cylinder.

Let us turn now to the cylinder itself and consider the claims made by the Persian king.[23] The first larger section including, ll. 1–14, denounces the former Neo-Babylonian ruler Nabonidus for his wicked deeds with regard to Marduk's temple Esagila, his interruption of the regular offerings, and his imposition of heavy labor duties and taxes on the citizens of Babylon. According to the text, Marduk first raged at the laments of the people and the abandoned cult centers and then took mercy on his people's suffering and turned to look for a suitable ruler. His choice fell upon Cyrus, king of Anshan, and he named him king of the totality and caused him to triumph over the Gutians and the Medes (*Ummān-Manda*). Pleased by the good deeds of the Persian king, Marduk ordered him to take the road to Babylon, which the king entered in triumph and without battle amid public rejoicing.

Note that after this introduction, which follows entirely Sumero-Babylonian reasoning with regard to the choice of the ruler, a genealogy and titulary of Cyrus follow, and then the inscription stresses first the king's reverence paid daily to Babylon's patron deity Marduk – and boasts in tandem Cyrus' fair and benevolent treatment of Babylon's citizens (I quote after the most recent translation offered by Hanspeter Schaudig):

> (25)   Of Babylon and all its sacred places I took care in peace and
>   sincerity. The people of Babylon [...], onto whom (Nabonidus) had
>   imposed an inappropriate yoke against the wil[l of the g]ods,

22. Pongratz-Leisten 2015.
23. See also Schaudig in this volume.

(26)   I brought relief to their exhaustion and did away with their toil.
Marduk, the great lord, rejoiced at [my good] deeds ...

In this passage, Cyrus takes pains to emphasize that the citizens of Babylon went unharmed when his troops entered the city. Even more important,
however, is his statement that he "brought relief to their exhaustion" and
"did away with their toil" (*anhūssun upaššiha ušapṭir sarmašunu*). What exactly
does Cyrus refer to with that statement? In my view, Cyrus here elicits a royal gesture known to have been performed by the Assyrian kings when they
managed to gain control over Babylonia, a gesture which implied a guarantee
of the privileged status of the city of Babylon. In earlier royal inscriptions the
kings referred to this status with various terms that all implied freedom from
forced labor for royal projects and tax exemption (*andurāru, kidinnūtu, šubāru,*
and *zakûtu*).[24] Cyrus' boast of his positive treatment of the citizens of Babylon
must thus be seen in the context of the special status that this city – together
with the ancient cultic centers of Sippar, Nippur, and Ur – enjoyed in the
history of Babylonia. That this status was still known at the time of Cyrus is
evident from the reference in one of the Babylonian chronicles to Cyrus' son
going, on the fourth day of Nisannu, into the *Nabû ša hare* temple in Babylon
and celebrating the New Year festival probably together with his father.[25] On
the fourth day, this festival included the so-called negative confession of the

---

24. Lemche 1979; Charpin 1987; Lion 1993; Leemans 1946; Reviv 1988. In addition to
andurārum and *kidinnu*, the terms *šubarrû* and *zakûtu* are used to circumscribe the privileges of
the citizens of particular cities, as in the *Advice to a Prince*, also known as *Babylonischer Fürstenspiegel*; see Lambert 1960, pls. 31, 32 and pages 110–115; Cole 1996, 268–274; Hurowitz 1998;
Diakonoff 1965; Civil 1982. For the most recent translation, see Foster 2005, 867–869.

25. Andrew George, after having collated the respective tablet BM 35382 reconstructed
the relevant passage as follows: ud 4^{kam} ^{m}kam-bu-zi-ia māru(dumu) šá ^{m}k[u-raš] ^{25} a-na é.níg.
gidar.kalam.ma.sum.mu *ki illiku*(gin) ^{lú}é.gidru ^{d}nabû(nà) haṭṭi(níg.gidar) m[āti(kur) iddinaššu?
^{m}ku-raš?] ^{26} *ki illiku*(gin) *ina* ^{túg}lu-bu-uš-tu_{4}!(BI) elamti(elam.ma)^{ki} qātī(šu)^{min} ^{d}nabû(nà) iṣ-[bat x]
x[...] ^{27} [^{giš}az-m]a-re-e u ^{kuš}iš-pat^{meš} iš[ši(íl)-ma? i]tti(ki) mār(dumu)-šarri(lugal) ana kisalli(kisal)
[ūrida(e_{11})^{da}?] ^{28} [ultu(ta)? līb-bi? bī]t(é) ^{d}nabû(nà) ana é.sag.gíl ishur(nigin)^{ur} kurunna(KAŠ.TIN)
ina mahar(igi) ^{d}bēl(en) u mār(dumu) x [. . . iggi/û . . .], "When on the 4th day (of Nisannu) Cambyses, the son of Cyrus, went to Eniggidar-kalamma-sumu, the official of the Sceptre House of
Nabû (or the *šangû*-priest of Nabû?) [gave him] the Scepter of the [Land]. When [Cyrus] came,
in Elamite attire he [took] the hands of Nabû [. . .] lances and quivers he picked [up, and] with
the crown-prince [he came down] into the courtyard. He (or possibly they) went back [from the
temple] of Nabû to E-sagil. [He/they libated] ale before Bēl and the Son of [. . .]"; see George
1996, 380. The important position of Cambyses as governor in Babylon is further accentuated
by the fact that Cyrus chose to mention him twice in the cylinder, once after the description
of the peaceful entering of the Persian army into Babylon in line 27, stating that not only he
himself, but also his son received Marduk's blessing; and the other time, when Cyrus stated
their taking care of the regular provisioning for the temples of Babylon in line 35.

king reaffirming the gods and the elites of Babylon that he did not touch upon Marduk's temple and the privileges of the citizens of Babylon. The Babylonian New Year festival is generally thought of as the celebration of Marduk's elevation to the rank of the supreme god of the Babylonian pantheon; there is, however, another crucial aspect to it, namely, its guaranteeing every year anew the tax exemption and freedom accorded to the citizens of Babylon. Indeed, the ritual text contains two prayers addressed by the priest to the gods Marduk and his consort Zarpanitu that explicitly refer to the privileged citizens (ṣabē kidinni) of Babylon. The fact that this plea for the maintenance of elite privileges appears in the last two lines of the prayer addressed to Marduk already on the morning of the second day of the festival – so even before the king appeared as an active participant – shows that the kidinnu-status of the privileged citizens was a central aspect to be negotiated during the festival.[26] The respective passage of the prayer reads as follows:

31   To Esagila, your temple turn your face!
32   Establish freedom from service (šubarru) for the citizens of
      Babylon, (your) privileged subjects (ṣābē kidinnu)![27]

The demand of Babylon's elites reappeared in the prayer addressed by the high priest to Zarpanitu on the fourth day of the festival, in which Marduk's consort was requested to assume a mediating role on behalf of the citizens in the divine assembly:[28]

263   Decree the fate of the king who reveres you,
264   Prolong the life of the citizens of Babylon, (your) privileged
       subjects,
265   Intercede for them in front of the king of the gods, Marduk.[29]

Only following the temple's purification did the king perform his famous humiliation before Marduk. This rite, known as the "negative confession" of the king, was probably meant to counterbalance royal intervention in the economic affairs of the temples, managed by families holding offices in the institution, and guarantee their privileged status. Both Piotr Michalowski[30] and I[31] have argued that all kings, native or foreign, had to perform this ritual.

---

26. Kuhrt 1987, 38.
27. Linssen 2004, 224.
28. For the role performed by the goddesses on behalf of the king, in the theogamies referred to in royal inscriptions, see Pongratz-Leisten 2008.
29. Linssen 2004, 224.
30. Michalowski 1990, 393.
31. Pongratz-Leisten 1997; and Pongratz-Leisten 2014.

This interpretation is based on the content of the "negative confession," as the king swears in the presence of Marduk and his priest that he has neither infringed upon the cult of Marduk nor upon the privileges of the elites:

419 He will place them (the royal insignia) [on] a seat. He (the priest) will go out and strike the cheek of the king.

420 He will place [the king (?)] behind him. He will make him enter before Bēl.

421 [After (this)?] he will pull his ears, make him kneel on the ground.

422 [Together w]ith(?) the king he will say this once:

423 [I did not] sin, o lord of the lands, I was not neglectful of your divinity,

424 [I did not] destroy Babylon, I did not command its dispersal,

425 [I did not] make Esagila tremble, I did not forget its rites,

426 [I did not] struck the cheek of any privileged citizen,

427 [...] I did [not] bring about their humiliation

428 [I have been taking ca]re of Babylon, I have not destroyed its outer walls.[32]

After his re-enthronement the king is slapped a second time, probably as an oracular action.[33]

It seems the significance of the second slapping lies in the precariousness of the office of rulership, which was considered a "loan from the gods, not a permanent gift, and would become forfeit should its holder sin against the established order."[34] Again central to the "negative confession," therefore, is the maintenance of the social order as originally ordained by the gods. With attending the *akītu*-festival of Babylon, the Persian king and his son thus made a powerful statement of complying with the expectations of the city elites.

Another central statement from the Cyrus Cylinder recounts the Persian king's allowing the return of the gods of various cities located in Assyria and the eastern Tigridian region, as well as those of Sumer and Akkad to their original home. Unusually, at least in the context of earlier royal inscriptions, Cyrus emphasizes that he also let return the people of these regions:

(30b) From [Babylon] to the city of Aššur and Susa,

(31-32) (to) Akkad, the land of Ešnunna, the towns Zabbān, Meturnu, Dēr and as far as the region to the land of the Gutians, the sacred cities on the [ot]her side (= east) of the Tigris, which had been laying in ruins since days of old, I returned (the statues of) the gods who

32. Text follows Linssen 2004, 215–233; see also Thureau-Dangin 1921, 144, ll. 415–428.
33. Smith 1982, especially 93.
34. Kuhrt 1987, 38.

used to dwell therein and had them live there for evermore. I (also) gathered their (former) people and brought them back to their habitations.

(33-34) And (the statues of) the gods of the land of Sumer und Akkad, which Nabonidus – to the anger of the lord of the gods – had brought into Babylon, I had them dwell in peace in their beloved sanctuaries at the command of Marduk, the great lord.[35]

It is exactly this passage that has been embraced by Jews as a historical reference to the return of the ancient Israelites from their exile and the restoration of their cult in Jerusalem. The situation is not so clear, however, as Jerusalem is not mentioned among the cities, and as the reference to the "people" probably also implied the respective temple personnel serving the cult of divinities, and possibly even war prisoners, since the temples in addition to their function as cultic institutions were also large economic entities. Moreover, the return of deities under Cyrus is also mentioned in the Babylonian Chronicles without any mention of the "people." The presence of these various divinities at Babylon notably should not be read as necessarily implying that a kidnapping of gods was performed by Nabonidus; he may well have brought these deities to Babylon in the face of the Persian threat.

The introductory section of the Cyrus Cylinder, elaborating on the misdeeds of Nabonidus vis-à-vis Babylon and the cult of Marduk, as well as the subsequent paragraphs recounting the positive deeds of the conqueror Cyrus in this regard, place the relationship between the Persian king and the city of Babylon and its cult of Marduk at center stage. Only towards the end does the Cyrus Cylinder refer to the restoration work performed on the city walls, demonstrating that the king's interaction with the citizens and the temple was deemed central to his dealings with Babylon and considered crucial to gain the support of the powerful Babylonian elites.[36]

Given all this background and context, how are we to judge the content of the Cyrus Cylinder? Is it all empty rhetoric? The Babylonian chronicles as additional sources of historical information suggest not. The Cyrus Cylinder – with a rhetoric that strives to meet not only the expectations prescribed by tradition, but also those fostered by the contemporaneous Babylonian elites – provides us with the portrayal of a statesman, who strategically responded to the manifold socio-historical conditions of the Babylonian capital. The Cyrus Cylinder thus stands in line with Ashurbanipal's earlier cylinder, and Antiochos' later one, all testifying to the longevity of the image of the ideal conqueror who endeavors to interact properly with local traditions, as well as meet the demands of the citizenry, which the inscription addressed.

35. See Schaudig in this volume.
36. Kuhrt 1983, 90.

This message was carefully constructed with the help of local scholars, and it could well be that it was primarily produced to satisfy a divine audience and that Cyrus never saw or knew of it, the goal being rather to provide written testimony of his perpetuation of the harmonious balance between earthly kingship and cosmic order according to the Sumero-Babylonian world view. The correspondence between King Ashurbanipal and his scholars, revealing a statesman who was actively involved in his image-making, however, suggests Cyrus may have taken an active role in the crafting of this cylinder's message. Whether the Cyrus Cylinder reflects some historical truth, unfortunately, remains uncertain and so should not be of primary relevance to modern interpretation. What is evident and what in my view is of greater interest is to see how conqueror and conquered alike strove to represent the new king of Babylon under the guise of a time-honored tradition.

Bibliography

Al-Maqdissi, M., H. Dohmann-Pfälzner, P. Pfälzner, and A. Souleiman. 2003. "Das königliche hypogeum von Qatna." *Mitteilungen der Deutschen Orientgessellschaft* 135:189–218.

Beaulieu, Paul-Alain. 1992. "Antiquarian Theology in Seleucid Uruk." *Acta Sumerologica* 14:47–75.

Cauvin, J. 2000. *The Birth of the Gods and the Origin of Agriculture.* Cambridge/New York.

Charpin, D. 1987. "Les décrets royaux à l'époque paléo-babylonien : À propos d'un ouvrage récent." *Archiv für Orientforschung* 34:36–44.

Civil, M. 1982. "Appendix to E. Reiner, 'The Babylonian *Fürstenspiegel* in Practice.'" In *Societies and Languages of the Ancient Near East Studies in Honour of I. M. Diakonoff,* edited by I. Michailovich Diakonov, 320–326. Warminster.

Cole, S. 1996. *The Early Neo-Babylonian Governor's Archive from Nippur.* Chicago.

Curtis, J. 2013. "The Cyrus Cylinder: The Creation of an Icon and its Loan to Tehran." In *The Cyrus Cylinder,* edited by I. Finkel, 85–103. London and New York.

Damerji, M. S. B. 1998. *Gräber assyrischer Königinnen aus Nimrud.* Jahrbuch des Römisch-Germanischen Zentralmuseums 45, Mainz.

Diakonoff, I. M. 1965. "A Babylonian Political Pamphlet from about 700 B.C." *Assyiological Studies* 16:343–349.

Edzard, D. O. 1998. "Name, Namengebung. B. Akkadisch." *Reallexikon der Assyriologie* 9, Berlin and New York, 103–116.

Finkel, I. 2013. *The Cyrus Cylinder.* London and New York.

Foster, B. R. 2005. *Before the Muses.* Bethesda.

Frayne, D. 1993. *Sargonic and Gutian Periods 2334-2113 BC.* Toronto.

George, A. 1996. "Studies in Cultic Topography and Ideology." *Bibliotheca Orientalis* 53:363-395.

Grayson, A. K. 1975. *Assyrian and Babylonian Chronicles.* Texts from Cuneiform Sources. Locust Valley, NY.

Harmatta, Janos. 1974. "Les modèles littéraires de l'édit babylonien de Cyrus." In *Hommage Universel.* 3 vols. Vol. I. Acta Iranica 1 – Commémoration Cyrus: Actes du Congrès de Shiraz 1971, 29-48. Téhéran/Liège: Bibliothèque Pahlavi.

Harris, R. 1972. "Notes in the Nomenclature of Old Babylonian Sippar." *Journal of Cuneiform Studies* 24:102-104.

Hurowitz, V. 1998. "Advice to a Prince: A Message from Ea." *State Archives of Assyria Bulletin* 12:48-53.

Jacquet, A. 2012. "Funerary Rites and the Cult of the Ancestors during the Amorite Period: the Evidence of the Royal Archives of Mari." In *(Re-) Constructing Funerary Rituals in the Ancient Near East: Proceedings of the First International Symposium of the Tübingen Post-Graduate School "Symbols of the Dead" in May 2009*, edited by Peter Pfälzner, Herbert Niehr, Ernst Pernick, and Anne Wissing, 123-136. Wiesbaden: Harrassowitz.

Kienast Burkhart. 2003. "Inscription of Sargon: Foundation of the Akkadian Empire (2.89)." In *Context of Scripture.* Vol. 2, edited by W. Hallo and K. L. Younger, 243. Leiden/Boston.

Kuhrt, A. 1983. "The Cyrus Cylinder and Achaemenid Imperial Policy." *Journal for the Study of the Old Testament* 25: 83-97.

———. 1987. "Usurpation, Conquest and Ceremonial: from Babylon to Persia." In *Rituals of Royalty: Power and Ceremonial in Traditional Societies*, edited by D. Cannadine and S. Price, 20-55. Cambridge.

———. 2007. "Cyrus the Great of Persia: Images and Realities." In *Representations of Power*, edited by M. Heinz and M. H. Feldman, 169-191. Winona Lake.

Lambert, W. G. 1960. *Babylonian Wisdom Literature.* Oxford.

Leemans, W. F. 1946. "*Kidinnu* : Un symbol de droit divin babylonien." In *Symbolae ad jus et historiam antiquitatis pertinentes Julio Christiano Van Oven dedicatae*, edited by M. David. Leiden, 36-61.

Lemche, N. P. 1979. "Andurārum and Mīšarum: Comments on the Problem of Social Edicts and their Application in the Ancient Near East." *Journal of Near Eastern Studies* 38:11-22.

Lichter, C. 2007. "Geschnitten oder am Stück? Totenritual und Leichenbehandlung im jungsteinzeitlichen Anatolien" In *Die ältesten Monumente der Menschheit.* Badisches Landes Museum Karlsruhe, 246-257. Stuttgart.

Linssen, M. J. H. 2004. *The Cults of Uruk and Babylon.* Leiden/Boston.

Lion, B. 1993. "ARM XVII,2: Race d'une andurârum au début du règne de Zimrilim?" *Nouvelles Assyriologiques Brèves et Utilitaires* 1993/111.

Michalowski, P. 1990. "Presence at the Creation." In *Lingering over Words: Studies in Ancient Near Eastern Literature in Honor of William L. Moran*, edited by T. Abusch, J. Huehnergard, and P. Steinkeller, 381–396. Atlanta.

Mithen, S. 2006. *After the Ice.* Cambridge, MA.

Pongratz-Leisten, B. 1997. "Das 'negative Sündenbekenntnis' des Königs anläßlich des babylonischen Neujahrsfestes und die *kidinnūtu* von Babylon." In *Schuld, Gewissen und Person*, edited by J. Assmann and T. Sundermeier, 83–101. Gütersloh.

———. 2008. "Sacred Marriage and the Transfer of Divine Knowledge: Alliances between the Gods and the King in Ancient Mesopotamia." In *Sacred Marriages*, edited by M. Nissinen and R. Uro, 43–73. Winona Lake.

———. 2014. "Bad Kings in the Literary History of Mesopotamia and the Interface between law, Divination, and Religion." In *From Source to History. Studies on Ancient Near Eastern World and Beyond. Dedicated to Giovanni Battista Lanfranchi on the Occasion of his 65th Birthday on June 23, 2014*, edited by S. Gaspa, A. Greco, D. Morandi Bonacossi, S. Ponchia, and R. Rollinger, 527–548. Münster.

———. 2015. *Religion and Ideology in Assyria.* Berlin and Boston.

Razmjou, S. 2013. "The Cyrus Cylinder: A Persian Perspective." In *The Cyrus Cylinder*, edited by I. Finkel, 104–125. London and New York.

Renfrew, C., and I. Morley. 2009. *Becoming Human: Innovation in Prehistoric Material and Spiritual Culture.* Cambridge.

Reviv, H. 1988. "*kidinnu*: Observations on Privileges of Mesopotamian Cities." *Journal of the Economic and Social History of the Orient* 31:286–298.

Selz, G. J. 2011. "Stadtgott." *Reallexikon der Assyriologie* 13, 75–78. Berlin.

Smith, J. S. 1982. "A Pearl of Great Price and a Cargo of Yams: A Study in Situational Incongruity." In *Imagining Religion. From Babylon to Jonestown*, edited by J. Z. Smith, 90–101. Chicago/London.

Sperber, D., and L. A. Hirschfeld. 2004. "The Cognitive Foundations of Cultural Stability and Diversity." *Trends in Cognitive Science* 8, 1:40–46.

Thureau-Dangin, F. 1921. *Rituels accadiens.* Paris.

Tomasello, M. 2000. *The Cultural Origins of Human Cognition.* Cambridge, MA.

Tsukimoto, Akio. 1985. *Untersuchungen zur Totenpflege* (kispum) *im alten Mesopotamien.* Kevelaer and Neukirchen.

Van de Mieroop, M. 1997. *The Ancient Mesopotamian City.* Oxford and New York.

van der Toorn, K. 1996. *Family Religion in Babylonia, Ugarit, and Israel. Continuity and Changes in the Forms of Religious Life.* Leiden and New York.

Wiseman, D. J. 1960. "The Goddess LAMA at Ur." *Iraq* 22:166–171.

Cyrus and Post-Collapse Yehud

William Schniedewind
University of California, Los Angeles

T
HE PERSIAN PROVINCE OF YEHUD that Cyrus the Great inherited from the Babylonians was a "post-collapse society."[1] Cyrus did not inherit much of economic, political, or military value in the Babylonian province of Yehud. In this respect, the well-known "Return to Zion" trumpeted in the Bible both at the end of the Books of Chronicles and the beginning of the Book of Ezra was not all it appeared to be, though not for the reasons raised in recent biblical scholarship discussing the so-called "Myth of the Empty Land."[2] This paper describes some demographic and economic aspects of the Babylonian province of Yehud that Cyrus inherited upon his conquest of Babylon, and also discusses some historical and theological aspects of the First Return of the Jews. This historical and archaeological context should inform the way we date and read the biblical literature of the neo-Babylonian and early Persian period. It is this context of a post-collapse society in Persian Yehud that gives rise to the figure of Cyrus as a new messiah, or "anointed one," as well as the replacement of the Davidic leadership of the post-exilic community by a priestly leadership.

"Post-collapse society" is a term coined by Joseph Tainter in his book *The Collapse of Complex Societies*.[3] Tainter followed up this book with a couple of more recent articles summarizing and refining the concept.[4] According to Tainter, when societies collapse, they exhibit some general characteristics. These characteristics include decline in population, monumental construction, and political fragmentation. These are aspects of ancient societies that can be seen and measured in the archaeological record. The consequences of collapse are also evident in the area of literature, which is of special interest to biblical scholarship. Avraham Faust takes up Tainter's description in his book *Judah in the Neo-Babylonian Period: The Archaeology of Desolation*.[5] Faust argues that all the characteristics of the province of Yehud in the sixth

---

1. See Tainter 1988, 1999; Faust 2012, 174–175.
2. Barstad 1996.
3. Tainter 1988.
4. Tainter 1999; Tainter 2000.
5. Faust 2012.

century bear the marks of a post-collapse society. Faust explains how the destructions and the demographic decline in Judah after the Babylonian invasions brought about social changes and disintegration as well as the end of Iron Age cultural markers.

The archaeological aspects of the Yehud that Cyrus inherited correspond to a post-collapse society. The first aspect of collapse that Tainter emphasized is the decline of population. Tainter writes,

> Whether as cause, consequence, or both, depopulation frequently accompanies collapse. Not only do urban populations decline, so also do the support populations of the countryside. Many settlements are concurrently abandoned.[6]

Estimates for the population decline in Judah after the Babylonian invasions certainly follow this model. Scholars estimate that the overall population decline in Judah was as much as 85-90%.[7] There is some debate about the exact numbers among scholars, but there is no question that the region witnessed a precipitous decline in population. To be sure, it is difficult to measure the population precisely, but these estimates have remained consistent over the past two decades, as more and more excavation and survey data have become available. This type of decline is exactly what Tainter envisions in his anthropological overview of post-collapse societies that often show depopulation between 75 and 90%[8]. The archaeological record for a dramatic decline in population is quite important because it undermines a significant trend in biblical scholarship that was marked by Hans Barstad's book *The Myth of the Empty Land*.[9] Barstad essentially argued that the significance of the Babylonian conquest of Jerusalem and Judah was overstated and that life continued as it had before for most of the people of the land. The last couple decades of archaeological research has now completely invalidated this position, yet there remains a certain persistence of the theory (mostly because of the dating of much of the composition and editing of biblical literature to the Babylonian and Persian periods).

In addition to population decline, Tainter noted that in post-collapse societies "there is an end to monumental construction."[10] This observation also tracks well with the archaeological record from the Babylonian and

6. Tainter 1999, 1021, as cited by Faust (2012, 169).
7. Estimates vary considerably, but the overall patterns are most critical. See recently A. Faust 2012, 119–148; I. Finkelstein 2010, 45–46.
8. Tainter 1999, 1010, cited in Faust (2012,169).
9. Barstad's book was followed and supported by the edited volume from the "European Seminar in Historical Methodology"; see Grabbe 1998.
10. Tainter 1999, 1024; Faust 2012, 170.

Persian periods in Yehud. There is almost no monumental architecture that has been excavated in the region. Certainly, nothing from the sixth century BCE and Persian architecture mostly begins to appear later in the fifth and fourth centuries BCE along the coast.[11]

The disappearance of monumental architecture can certainly be associated with political, social, and territorial fragmentation, which is the third of Tainter's criteria for post-collapse societies.[12] In the province of Yehud, evidence of trade as marked particularly by Greek imported pottery almost completely disappears.[13] The political structures from the late Iron Age were obviously dismantled by the Babylonian destruction. Indeed, it would have been almost impossible for the political structures to continue with the general depopulation. The administrative personnel and skills necessary for complex political and economic structures disappeared. This is evident, for example, in the dearth of written artifacts from the Babylonian period. In their monumental compendium, *The Yehud Stamp Impressions*, Lipschits and Vanderhooft give evidence for some ad hoc administrative writing particularly connected with the site of Ramat Rahel,[14] but the evidence remains meager for the sixth and fifth centuries. More specifically, however, they date the emergence of these "early types" of seal impressions only to the Persian period – that is, to the late sixth century BCE and not to the Babylonian period. Most notably, the script changes from Hebrew to the Aramaic script, and "no paleo-Hebrew letter forms appear,"[15] which would be consistent with Persian administration. Moreover, administrative documents begin to flourish again in the archaeological record in the fourth and third centuries BCE.

In sum, there is little evidence from epigraphic remains of a coherent administration under Babylonian rule. It seems first to develop under the early Persian rule and flourish in the late Persian period.

It has been argued by a few scholars that the situation in Benjamin, that is, the region just north of Jerusalem, was different. This interpretation seems to be based in part on a reading of the biblical texts (for example, 2 Kgs 25:23-26; Jer 40:6- 42:22), which imply a Babylonian administration in the region around Mizpah. The site is identified with Tell en-Nasbeh, which was excavated by Frederic Badè in the 1930s, but only published by Jeffrey Zorn in his doctoral dissertation.[16] Zorn emphasized the Babylonian phase

11. See discussions by Carter, Stern, Jamieson-Drake, Finkelstein, Faust.
12. Tainter 1999, 1023.
13. Faust 2012, 73-92..
14. Lipschits and Vanderhooft 2011, 81-252.
15. Lipschits and Vanderhooft 2011, 251..
16. Zorn 1993.

of the site in his assessment. Settlement continuity at a few urban sites has been suggested by many scholars, and it is thought that Benjamin became a locus for the Babylonian administration of Yehud. The archaeological evidence, however, is more equivocal than it first seems. While it is clear that the region of Benjamin was not destroyed in great conflagrations, it is equally evident that the region eventually experienced the same overall population decline discernible elsewhere in Yehud. Avi Faust writes, "Small and rural Iron Age sites in Benjamin did not continue to exist in the Persian period, and most probably ceased to exist in the sixth century. Out of sixteen rural sites north of Jerusalem … only two exhibit possible continuity into the Persian period."[17] Even Oded Lipschits notes the precipitous fall in population.[18]

The question thus is when exactly did the population decline occur? Was the apex of this depopulation in the sixth century or in the fifth century? Some scholars have suggested that the urban settlements in Benjamin continued while the rural sector was decimated, but this is an unlikely scenario. The rural settlements forms the backbone of support for the urban society in antiquity – the urban cities cannot continue to flourish if the rural section is decimated. Faust notes, "The situation after the Babylonian destruction at Timnah (Mazar and Panitz-Cohen 2001, 282) might illuminate the situation in many urban sites. The last Iron Age town there was quite large, and was destroyed in massive conflagration – the debris were more than one meter deep. At Timnah, however, evidence for reoccupation was found only in one area, in the form of an agricultural installation. Mazar and Panitz-Cohen concluded that "this was a brief phase and may indicate that a few farmers lived in the ruined town for a short while in the early 6th century."[19]

The continuity theory in the settlements of Benjamin is critical to Barstad's *Myth of the Empty Land*, but it – ironically – is itself biblically centered. For example, in Jer 40:6, we read, "Jeremiah went to Gedaliah son of Ahikam at Mizpah, and stayed with him among the people who were left in the land," and the following verse notes that "the king of Babylon appointed Gedaliah son of Ahikam governor in the land, and committed to him men, women, and children, those of the poorest of the land who had not been taken into exile to Babylon." Gedaliah reportedly encourages the people to "stay in the land" (v. 9), and it mentions that "all the Judeans who were in Moab, among the Ammonites, and in Edom … returned from all the places which they had been scattered to the land of Judah and to Gedaliah at Miz-

17. Faust 2012, 211.
18. Lipschits 2003, 349.
19. Faust 2012, 234..

pah" (vv. 11-12). Unfortunately for these refugees, Gedaliah is murdered and the region apparently returned to turmoil.

One of the more unfortunate misinterpretations of the Benjamin region's prominence is rooted in outdated archaeological interpretation of the major destructions of the late Iron Age. The problem can be illustrated in an article by Ernst Axel Knauf,[20] who observed that the site of Bethel is mentioned seventy-one times in the Hebrew Bible and sought to explain why. Relying on earlier misunderstandings of the archaeology of this site from Kelso,[21] he suggested that Bethel was occupied well into the Babylonian period. Consequently, Bethel must have been a locus for the literary production of the Hebrew Bible during the Babylonian period.[22]

As Finkelstein and Singer have shown in a more recent article,[23] this interpretation is based on a fundamental misunderstanding of the archaeology of the Iron IIB and IIC periods that was prevalent in the 1960s. In short, the more recent archaeological pottery typology from the excavations at Lachish distinguished a pottery typology for the neo-Assyrian destructions in 701 – the Iron IIB – from that pertaining to the Babylonian invasions in the early sixth century – the Iron IIC. The early excavations of Bethel relied on the old Albrightian pottery typology that attributed the 701 BCE destruction to a century later in 597 BCE. Unfortunately, the site of Bethel was never reevaluated on the basis of the new pottery chronology until the article by Finkelstein and Singer in 2009. They demonstrate that the site of Bethel went into decline in the seventh century BCE, and that "it was probably uninhabited or almost deserted in the Babylonian and Persian periods;"[24] as a result, they logically associate "the proposed scribal activity at Bethel with its period of prosperity in the Iron IIB."[25] In other words, there is no basis for continuity of settlements in Benjamin.

The region of Benjamin – particularly, the site of Bethel – was already impacted by the neo-Assyrians invasions. Although the region was not devastated by Babylonian invasions in the early sixth century BCE, it was certainly impacted by earlier neo-Assyrian invasions and had not fully recovered in the seventh century BCE. Archaeological surveys make it clear that by the Persian period – that is, by the end of the sixth century – the region experienced the same severe depopulation as the rest of the prov-

20. Knauf 2006.
21. Kelso 1968.
22. Also Blenkinsopp 2003.
23. Finkelstein and Singer 2009.
24. Finkelstein and Singer 2009, 45.
25. Finkelstein and Singer 2009, 44.

ince of Yehud.[26] Even in Benjamin, Cyrus inherited what was a post-collapse society.

The situation of Jewish exiles in Mesopotamia during the Persian Empire is also becoming clearer. For example, we find many Jewish names in a variety of texts from the fifth and fourth centuries BCE. The most well known of these is the Murashu Archive, a group of Babylonian legal and economic texts from Nippur dating to the late fifth century BCE. The corpus is often cited for the presence of non-Babylonian groups and names, presumably peoples that were resettled by the Babylonians as part of imperial policy. These names include many names that seem to be Jewish names like Shabbatai, Haggai, Minyamîn, and other names with the Yahwistic theophoric suffix.[27] More recently, Laurie Pearce and Cornelia Wunsch have published an extensive collection of documents from Judean exiles in Babylonia, and they write that "a strong sense of Judean identity and attachment to their cultural and religious heritage emerges from the name-giving patterns preserved across as many as four generations of exilic life."[28] At the same time, they note that many Judean exiles had the status of settlers, and thus were not chattel slaves. They note, however, that by the time of Cyrus their allotments of royal land might have been reduced through inheritance divisions and accelerated taxes that could have served as an incentive to migrate, especially if encouraged by the Persian administration. The situation for the exiles, however, appears to be much better than that awaiting the returnees.

One quite interesting observation that Tainter makes regarding post-collapse societies concerns the literary idealization of a golden age. Tainter observes that a feature of many post-collapse societies is that they treat their past as "a paradise lost, a golden age of good government, wise rule, harmony and peace."[29] Faust has noted the ways this golden age ideal is evident in the Book of Lamentations. For example, Lamentations opens by referring to Jerusalem before its "destruction as 'she that was great among the nations; she that was a princess among the provinces' (Lam 1:1) and as 'the city that was called the perfection of beauty, the joy of all the earth' (Lam 2:15)."[30] Glimpses of this idea can be caught in various other passages that should be dated to the early Persian period. For example, Ezra 3:10-13 describes laying the foundation for the Second Temple, the temple that Cyrus permitted to be rebuilt. The text begins by noting: "When the builders

---

26. Faust 2012, 209-232.
27. See Bickerman 1978; Coogan 1976; Zadok 1977a and Zadok 1977b.
28. Pearce and Wunsch 2014, 3.
29. Tainter 1999, 1028.
30. Faust 2012, 171.

laid the foundation of the temple of the LORD ... all the people responded with a great shout when they praised the LORD, because the foundation of the house of the LORD was laid." However, the text further notes, "many of the priests and Levites and heads of families, old people who had seen the first house on its foundations, wept with a loud voice when they saw this house." Thus, the text concludes, "the people could not distinguish the sound of the joyful shout from the sound of the people's weeping." How shall we understand this? The text reflects nostalgia for the first Temple – for the temple built during the golden age. Other texts about the temple might also be read in this light. For example, in Isaiah 66 – a text usually dated to the late sixth century BCE – the prophet seems to question and even undermine the Second Temple by recalling the building of the first temple: "Thus says the LORD: Heaven is my throne and the earth is my footstool; what is the house that you would build for me, and what is my resting place?" (v. 1). In this text, the prophet quotes from the story that introduces the building of the first Temple by Solomon.

One of the more curious aspects of biblical literature of the early Persian period is the role of Cyrus himself. In Isaiah 45, God refers to Cyrus as his *messiah*, the royal anointed one: "Thus says the LORD to his anointed, to Cyrus, whose right hand I have grasped to subdue nations before him and strip kings of their robes, to open doors before him – and the gates shall not be closed." The special role of Cyrus is further underscored by parallel text in 2Chr 36 and Ezra 1, namely: "In the first year of King Cyrus of Persia, in order that the word of the LORD by the mouth of Jeremiah might be accomplished, the LORD stirred up the spirit of King Cyrus of Persia so that he sent a herald throughout all his kingdom, and also in a written edict." The edict has been widely understood, of course, as applying the decree known from the Cyrus Cylinder specifically to the Jewish people that ushered in the First Return of the Jews, as well as the rebuilding of the Temple.

What is more interesting is the way Cyrus becomes both the fulfillment of the prophetic word as well as the new royal anointed one. This becomes clear when we recast this text with a political question: who loses and who stands to gain from casting Cyrus as the chosen and anointed one? The answer is quite obvious. The Davidic rulers stand to lose as they are no longer necessary, and the priests stand to gain as they replace the Davidides as the political leaders of the post-exilic community. However, Davidic leaders are prominent figures in the early Persian period according to biblical literature. There are two Davidic figures, Zerubbabel, son of Shealtiel, as well as Sheshbazzar, the prince (Ezr 1:8; 5:4). Zerubbabel apparently replaced Sheshbazzar early in the Persian period, and it is under Zerubbabel that the second temple is built (Ezr 3:10-12). Zerubbabel is quite clearly a Davidic descendent, and the prophet Haggai calls him "a signet ring whom the LORD has chosen" (2:23). Sarah Japhet even suggests on the basis of her analysis of the genealogies in Chronicles that Zerubabbel may be the grandson of Jehoiachin, the last king of Judah.[31] However, Zerubbabel's lineage in the Book of Ezra is more obscure, which seems to serve its pro-priestly ideology.

It is noteworthy that the Book of Ezra seems to draw intentionally on the language of Haggai with regard to Zerubbabel for its introduction to the well-known decree of Cyrus. In Haggai 1:14, we read, "the LORD stirred up the spirit of Zerubbabel son of Shealtiel, governor of Judah" – this is the exact same unique language used for Cyrus in Ezra 1:1, and 2Chr 36:22: "the LORD stirred up the spirit of King Cyrus of Persia so that he sent a herald throughout all his kingdom and also a written edict." Moreover, the message of the prophet Haggai to Zerubbabel begins with a reflection about the golden age of the temple – that is, the golden age nostalgia so typical of literature in post-collapse societies. Haggai begins his address: "Who is left among you who saw this house in its former glory? How does it look to you now? Is it not in your sight as nothing?"

Thus, what does the re-appropriation of this language and its application to Cyrus by beginning of the Book of Ezra and the ending of the Book of Chronicles accomplish? Fundamentally, it helps to replace the Davidic scion Zerubbabel with the foreign king Cyrus. More than this, it likely underscores that the Davidides are no longer required for the leadership of the post-exilic community.

Of course, we do have evidence of a propaganda campaign by Cyrus in the cuneiform sources,[32] but the best evidence may actually be in Isaiah 45, where the prophet speaks of Cyrus as the anointed of Yahweh who will conquer all nations before him. In turn, the prophet says that Cyrus will restore the Jewish exiles to their native land. Cyrus may actually have been viewed as a liberator not only by the Babylonians, but also by the Jews. Indeed, the Cyrus Cylinder does suggest a policy of remarkable deference to, and respect for, other ethnic groups and religions. Yet, the depiction of Cyrus as a Jewish messiah also had its local political underpinnings. That is, it served the ambitions of the Jerusalem priesthood who would displace the Davidides as the leaders of the Jews during the Second Temple period.

Finally, I want to reflect on how it is that the Davidic line disappears "quietly into the night," so to speak. In biblical literature, figures of the Davidic line and their descendants – such as Shealtiel, Zerubbabel, the sons

---

31. Japhet 1982.
32. See Schaudig in this volume.

of Jehoiachin, as well as a Davidide named Shenazzar who is mentioned in the genealogies of Chronicles (1Chr 3:18) – play no role in the leadership of the post-exilic community in the fifth century down through the second century BCE. Instead of the Davidides, it would be priestly leadership that rose to power, and this displacement of the Davidides culminated in the Hasmonean kingdom.

The Davidides disappear. What happened to them? For instance, what happened to Zerubbabel? At this point, we can only speculate. There is probably some merit in the very late Rabbinic tradition in *Seder Olam Zuta* from the sixth century CE that suggests Zerubbabel returned to Babylon after completing the temple. Although some scholars have doubted the historicity of the First Return, we have no basis to disregard the biblical accounts. Indeed, it seems quite likely that the purpose of the Cyrus Cylinder was to stoke some euphoria among various communities and that this would have occasioned a group of Judean exiles to return to Yehud in the hopes of restoring a community in their homeland. Undoubtedly, however, the reality that they met when they returned was not what they expected. They returned to a post-collapse society, to a land devoid of population and economic infrastructure. It was a hard life to which they returned, especially for people like Zerubbabel.

We know something of the fate of the royal family while they were still in Babylon from the excavation in the 1930s. In the Ishtar Gate, Ernst Weidner excavated 290 tablets dating between 595 and 570 BCE, of which four mention several Judeans affiliated with the royal court. Most notably, Tablet 28178, a list of rations, reads as follows: "6 liters (of oil) for Jehoiachin, king of the land of Judah, 2 1/2 liters for the 5 princes of Judah, 4 liters for the 8 men of Judah." This actually accords well with the fate of Jehoiachin, the last Judean king in 2Kgs 25:27-30; we read that the Babylonian king was kind to him and released him from prison and that he came "to dine regularly in the king's presence" and that "a regular ration was given to him." Apparently, the Judean princes lived in one of the southern palaces of Babylon with a royal allowance. If this was indeed the case, then returning to Yehud would been a rude awakening. Indeed, one may wonder how interested the Judean princes would have been in leaving their pleasant situation in Babylon for the harsh reality of the province of Yehud. On the other hand, it seems unlikely that the Jews of the First Return understood much of what awaited them when they returned to their homeland. I suspect that the royal princes like Zerubbabel would have returned to their Babylonian situation as soon as they could. In this respect, the appropriation of the figure of Cyrus as true anointed of Israel should probably not be merely seen as a nefarious plot by the priests to usurp the leadership role from the Davidides. The priests were the architects of a new Temple community, and Cyrus was the patron who enabled the restoration.

Literature Cited

Barstad, Hans M. 1996. *The Myth of the Empty Land: Study of the History and Archaeology of Judah During the Exile Period*. Oslo.

Bickerman, E. J. 1978. "The Generation of Ezra and Ethnic Minorities in Babylonia." *Proceedings of the American Academy of Jewish Research* 45:1-18.

Blenkinsopp, J. 2003. "Bethel in the Neo-Babylonian Period." In *Judah and the Judeans in the Neo-Babylonian Period*, edited by O. Lipschits and J. Blenkinsopp, , 93-107. Winona Lake.

Coogan, Michael David. 1976. *West Semitic Personal Names in the Marašû Documents*. Harvard Semitic Monographs 7. Missoula.

Faust, Avraham. 2012. *Judah in the Neo-Babylonian Period: The Archaeology of Desolation*. Cambridge.

Finkelstein, Israel. 2010. "The Territorial Extent and Demography of Yehud/Judea in the Persian and Early Hellenistic Periods." *Revue Biblique* 117:45–46.

Finkelstein, Israel and L. Singer-Avitz. 2009. "Reevaluating Bethel." *Zeitschrift des Deutschen Palästina-Vereins* 125:33-48.

Grabbe, L. (ed.). 1998. *Leading Captivity Captive. 'The Exile' as History and Ideology. Journal for the Study of the Old Testament, Supplement Series, 278* and European Seminar in Historical Methodology, 2. Sheffield.

Japet, Sara. 1982. "Sheshbazzar and Zerubbabel–against the Background of the Historical and Religious Tendencies of Ezra-Nehemiah." *Zeitschrift für die alttestamentliche Wissenschaft* 91 (1982):55-98.

Knauf, Ernst Axel. 2006. "Bethel: The Israelite Impact on Judean Language and Literature." In *Judah and the Judeans in the Persian Period*, edited by O. Lipschits and M. Oeming, 291-349. Winona Lake.

Kelson, James Leon. 1968. *The Excavation of Bethel (1934-1960)*. American Schools of Oriental Research, Volume 39.

Lipschits, Oded, and David S. Vanderhooft. 2011. *The Yehud Stamp Impressions*. Winona Lake.

Lipschitz, O. 2003. "Demographic Changes in Judah between the 7th and the 5th Centuries BCE." In *Judah and the Judeans in the Neo-Babylonian Period*, edited by O. Lipschits and J. Blenkinsopp, 323-376 Winona Lake.

Mazar, A., and N. Panitz-Cohen. 2001. *Timnah (Tel Batash) II: The Finds from the First Millennium BCE*. Qedem 42. Monograph Series of the Institute of Archaeology, Hebrew University of Jerusalem, Jerusalem.

Pearce, Laurie E., and Cornelia Wunsch. 2014. *Documents of Judean Exiles and West Semites in Babylonia in the Collection of David Sofer*. Ithaca, New York.

Tainter, Joseph. 1988. *The Collapse of Complex Societies*, Cambridge.

———. 1999. "Post-Collapse Societies." In *Companion Encyclopedia of Archaeology*, edited by Graeme Barker, 988-1039. London.

———. 2000. "Problem Solving: Complexity, History, Sustainability." *Population and Environment* 22:3-41.

Zadok, Ran. 1977a. "On Five Biblical Names." *Zeitschrift für die alttestamentliche Wissenschaft* 89:266-268.

———. 1977b. "Iranians and Individuals Bearing Iranian Names in Achaemenian Babylonia." *Israel Oriental Studies* 7:89-138.

Zorn, J. R. 1993. *Tell en Nasbeh: A Re-evaluation of the Architecture and Stratigraphy of the Early Bronze Age, Iron Age and Later Periods*. Unpublished Doctoral Dissertation, University of California Berkeley.

Contrasting Portrayals of the Achaemenid Monarchy in Isaiah and Zecharia

Marvin A. Sweeney
Claremont School of Theology and Academy
for Jewish Religion California

I

INTERPRETERS GENERALLY PRESUME a favorable view of King Cyrus of Persia and the Achaemenid Empire in the Hebrew Bible. The accounts of Cyrus' decree allowing Jews to return to the land of Judah to reconstruct the Jerusalem Temple in Ezra 1:1-4 and 2 Chronicles 36:22-23 are well-known passages in the Hebrew Bible that articulate a magnanimous policy towards Jews and Judaism by the Achaemenid monarch, like that found for other nations in the famed Cyrus Cylinder.[1] Likewise, the references to Cyrus in Isaiah 44:28 and 45:1, in which the anonymous Judean prophet of the exile commonly known as Second Isaiah identifies him as YHWH's Messiah and Temple builder, indicates that Cyrus was viewed very favorably in at least one of the major prophetic books of the Hebrew Bible.

But such a view does not tell the entire story. Isaiah, Ezra-Nehemiah, and Chronicles are the only biblical books that mention Cyrus by name – and they do indeed view him favorably – but other prophetic books found in the Book of the Twelve Prophets, Haggai and Zechariah, point to a very different view of Cyrus and the Achaemenid monarchy as foreign rulers that must be overthrown so that the house of David might once again be restored as the true monarchy in Israel. Haggai 2:20-23, speaking at the outset of the reign of Darius, calls for YHWH to overthrow the kingdoms of the nations and to install Zerubbabel ben Shealtiel, the grandson of the last Davidic king Jehoiachin ben Jehoiakim, as YHWH's signet ring, or monarch. Likewise, Zechariah 11, attributed to Haggai's contemporary Zechariah ben Berechiah ben Iddo, announces YHWH's establishment of a worthless shepherd, apparently a reference to Darius, who will be brought down by the sword as part of YHWH's victory over the nations at Zion.

---

1. For a recent translation of the Cyrus Cylinder, see Finkel 2013; and Schaudig in this volume.

Such a view points to a debate in the Hebrew Bible concerning Cyrus and the Achaemenid monarchy. Whereas the Book of Isaiah views Cyrus as YHWH's chosen monarch, the Book of the Twelve views the Achaemenid monarchs as obstacles to YHWH's plans for the future of the Jewish people. This paper therefore examines both Isaiah and the Book of Zechariah in order to illustrate the contrasting portraits of the Achaemenid monarchy in the prophetic books of the Hebrew Bible.

II

Modern critical biblical scholarship correctly views the prophetic Book of Isaiah as a composite literary work.[2] Indeed, the references to King Cyrus in Isaiah 44:28 and 45:1 play a major role in that view. Isaiah ben Amoz is identified in the book as a prophet who lived and spoke during the late-eighth century BCE reigns of the Judean Kings, Uzziah, Jotham, Ahaz, and Hezekiah, when the Assyrian empire made its first incursions into the land of Israel, ultimately destroying Israel and subjugating the kingdom of Judah. The references to the sixth century monarch, Cyrus of Persia, raised questions concerning the authorship and date of the prophetic Book of Isaiah. As early as the third-sixth centuries CE, the Talmudic rabbis identified Isaiah as an edited work, composed by King Hezekiah and his colleagues (b. Baba Batra 14b-15a), and the twelfth-century commentator, Abraham Ibn Ezra, recognized the possibility of later authorship beginning in Isaiah 40. Eighteenth- and nineteenth-century scholars followed suit by recognizing that the book of the eighth century BCE prophet had been supplemented with material that presupposed the Babylonian exile of the sixth century BCE in Isaiah 13-14; 21; and 40-66.[3] The classic critical model emerged in Bernhard Duhm's 1892 commentary on Isaiah, in which he identified three major prophets in the book: First or Proto-Isaiah in Isaiah 1-39, which represented the work of the eighth-century prophet, Isaiah ben Amoz; Second or Deutero-Isaiah in Isaiah 40-55, which represented the work of an anonymous sixth-century prophet of the Babylonian exile; and Third or Trito-Isaiah in Isaiah 56-66, which identified these problematic chapters as the work of another anonymous prophet of the post-exilic or Persian period.[4] Duhm's model still stands as the foundation for modern critical scholarship on Isaiah, although many of its elements have been considerably modified. My own commentary on Isaiah 1-39, for example, identifies a seventh-century

2. For recent overviews of research on Isaiah, see Sweeney 1993; Sweeney 1996b; Sweeney 2016b; Kim 2008; Melugin 2008; and Stromberg 2011.

3. E.g. Gesenius 1820-21.

4. Duhm 1892.

BCE edition of the book produced during the reign of the Judean monarch, Josiah ben Amon, to support his program of religious reform and national restoration.[5]

Turning to the work of Deutero-Isaiah in Isaiah 40–55, these chapters are formulated as part of the larger vision of Isaiah ben Amoz in Isaiah 1-66.[6] Following the portrayal of the Assyrian invasions, the destruction of Israel, the subjugation of Judah, and the anticipation of future restoration in Isaiah 1–39, Isaiah 40–55 is especially concerned with the question of YHWH's integrity as G-d of Israel and of all creation. Questions concerning YHWH's role as G-d of Israel and all creation would have been prompted by Israel's and Judah's defeat by the Assyrian empire and its god, Assur, in the late-eighth century and by the defeat and exile of Jerusalem and Judah by Babylon and its god, Marduk, in the late-sixth century BCE. Insofar as Deutero-Isaiah identifies YHWH's purposes with the rise of Cyrus and the Achaemenid empire, Deutero-Isaiah attempts to show that YHWH's plans for worldwide sovereignty are now being realized with Cyrus' ascension to the throne of the Babylonian Empire in 539 BCE and his subsequent decree to allow Jews to return to Jerusalem to rebuild the Jerusalem Temple.

Deutero-Isaiah puts forward a number of arguments to support his contentions that YHWH's sovereignty, and fidelity to the covenant, are now being realized.[7] The arguments follow a brief introductory section in Isaiah 40:1–11 that portrays YHWH's approach to Jerusalem through the desert, in order to bring about the restoration of the city and the return of its people. Each of the arguments is formulated as oracular poetry that concludes with a brief hymnic section glorifying YHWH. It may be that the work of Deutero-Isaiah was composed for liturgical performance in the Temple or another suitable public venue. The first argument is that YHWH is the master of creation in Isaiah 40:12–31; the second is that YHWH is master of human events in Isaiah 41:1–42:13; the third is that YHWH is the redeemer of Israel in Isaiah 42:14–44:23; the fourth is that YHWH will use Cyrus of Persia for the restoration of Zion in Isaiah 44:24–48:22; and the fifth is that YHWH is restoring Zion in Isaiah 49:1–54:17. Isaiah 55 was composed as a concluding section for Deutero-Isaiah that reflects upon YHWH's covenant with Israel. We will return to this below.

First, we may focus on Isaiah 44:24–48:22, which explicitly mentions Cyrus as YHWH's messiah and Temple builder.[8] The passage represents con-

5. Sweeney 1996a.
6. For discussion of texts in Isaiah 40–66, see Sweeney 2016a.
7. For discussion, see Sweeney 1988.
8. Sweeney 1988, 76–81.

stitutes the announcement that YHWH shall use Cyrus for the restoration of Jerusalem and Judah.

Isaiah 44:24–45:8 may be further divided in three constituent units. The first is the oracle to Israel in Isaiah 44:24–28, which argues that YHWH will use Cyrus for the restoration. The second is the oracle to Cyrus in Isaiah 45:1–7, which constitutes a royal commission for Cyrus to undertake the task. The third is the concluding hymn in Isaiah 45:8, which closes the subunit.

The relevant language in the oracle to Israel in Isaiah 44:24–28 reads as follows:

> Thus says YHWH, your Redeemer, who formed you in the womb;
> I am YHWH, who does everything, who alone stretches out the heavens;
> Who myself spreads out the earth (v. 24).
> Who cancels the signs of diviners, and makes fools of augurers;
> Who turns back the wise, and frustrates their knowledge (v. 25).
> Who establishes the word of His servant, and fulfills the counsel of His messengers (v. 26a).
> Who says to Jerusalem, You shall be inhabited; and to the cities of Judah, You shall be rebuilt, and its ruins, I will restore (v. 26b).
> Who says to the Deep, Be dry, and I will dry up your streams (v. 27).
> Who says to Cyrus, (He is) my shepherd, and he will accomplish my purposes.
> And he will say to Jerusalem, You will be rebuilt, and to the Temple, You will be refounded (v. 28).

Here, YHWH establishes credentials as the creator of heaven and earth, who has greater knowledge, wisdom, and power than the wisest of humans, who is able to restore Jerusalem and Judah just as YHWH can dry up the sea, and who therefore has the power to commission Cyrus to carry out the divine task of rebuilding Jerusalem and the Temple. Such an act is particularly important and controversial because unlike the monarchs of the House of David, Cyrus is a foreign king who acts at YHWH's behest. Normally, the monarchs of the House of David would carry out such tasks, but because YHWH is the creator, YHWH may use a foreign king in place of the monarchs of the House of David to rebuild Jerusalem and reestablish the Temple.

Cyrus acts as YHWH's chosen monarch just as David did five centuries earlier. Cyrus' role as YHWH's chosen monarch is evident in the following oracle to Cyrus in Isaiah 45:1–7, which commissions him as YHWH's royal servant:

Thus says YHWH to Cyrus, His Anointed One,
Whose right hand I have grasped to tread down nations before him,
To open doors before him so that gates would not remain closed (v. 1).
I walk before you, and I level splendor,
And doors of bronze I shatter, and bars of iron I cut down (v. 2).
And I will give to you the treasures of darkness and hidden hoards,
So that you will know that I am YHWH, the G-d of Israel, who calls
    your name (v. 3).
For the sake of my servant, Jacob, and Israel, my chosen one,
I call your name, I confirm you though you do not know Me (v. 4).
I am YHWH, and there is no other, beside Me, there is no god;
I gird you, though you do not know Me (v. 5).
So that they will know, from east to west, that there is none but Me
I am YHWH, there is no other (v. 6).
The former of light and creator of darkness,
Who makes peace and creates evil,
I, YHWH, do all these things (v. 7).

This oracle confirms that Cyrus will serve as YHWH's anointed monarch, just as David did some five centuries earlier. Again, YHWH's role as creator of the universe enables YHWH to take such action on behalf of the chosen people of Israel. Such an act becomes a revelatory event, that is, YHWH chooses Cyrus to act as YHWH's anointed so that Cyrus – and indeed, Israel and all creation – will know YHWH.

The closing hymn in Isaiah 45:8 calls upon creation to celebrate YHWH's role as creator, thereby confirming the basis for YHWH's unusual and controversial act[9]:

Pour down, O Heavens, from above! And let the skies rain down
    righteousness!
And let the earth open, so victory will multiply and righteousness
    will sprout together!
I, YHWH, have created it!

The balance of the passage in Isaiah 45:9–48:22 constitutes a trial scene, which provides further argumentation in Isaiah 45:9–48:19 supporting YHWH's choice of Cyrus as monarch and Temple builder, followed by another closing hymn in Isaiah 48:20–22.

The decision to announce YHWH's choice of the Persian King Cyrus as YHWH's monarch and Temple builder comes against the background of the

9. See also Matheus 1990, 73–77.

demise of the House of David by the late-sixth century BCE. Although descendants of the last legitimate Davidic monarch of Judah, King Jehoiachin ben Jehoiakim, were undoubtedly alive in 539 BCE when Cyrus ascended the Babylonian throne and decreed that Jews could return to Jerusalem to rebuild the Temple, the Book of Isaiah does not envision a Davidic monarch. This decision is all the more remarkable given First Isaiah's basis in Davidic/Zion covenant ideology and his anticipation of an ideal Davidic king. Deutero-Isaiah's decision to recognize Cyrus as YHWH's king has consequences for Davidic ideology.[10] Indeed, these consequences are apparent in Isaiah 55:1–13, an exhortation to the exiled people of Israel/Judah to join YHWH's covenant that was originally written as the conclusion for Deutero-Isaiah's work. The prophet's exhortation is especially noteworthy in that it redefines the Davidic covenant tradition so that YHWH's eternal covenant is no longer made with the royal House of David to ensure that Davidic sons would sit on the throne in Jerusalem forever. Instead, the covenant is made with the people of Israel who are offered the eternal covenant of David if they will return to YHWH. Isaiah 55:3–5 makes these points clear:

> Incline your ear, and come to Me! Hear that you may live!
> And I will make with you an eternal covenant,
> Based on the enduring fidelity promised to David (v. 3).
> Behold, I made him a witness of peoples,
> A leader and commander of nations (v. 4).
> Behold, you will call a nation that you do not know,
> And a nation that does not know you.
> Unto you it will run, for the sake of YHWH, your G-d,
> And for the Holy One of Israel, who has glorified you (v. 5).

Altogether, the texts that we have examined in Deutero-Isaiah call for the identification of YHWH with the Persian empire. They assert that YHWH, as creator of heaven and earth, has commissioned Cyrus as YHWH's monarch and Temple builder to act on YHWH's behalf to return the exiled peoples of Israel and Judah back to Jerusalem, where they will rebuild the ruined city and restore the Holy Temple. Such statements presume the acceptance of Cyrus' – and Persian – sovereignty as an expression of the plan and will of YHWH. Essentially, Deutero-Isaiah gives up the notion of Judean political independence by asserting that Cyrus reigns over Jerusalem and Judah at YHWH's behest.

Such a position is carried over into later editions of the Book of Isaiah as well. The final sixty-six chapter form of the Book of Isaiah continues to

10. See Sweeney 1997.

eschew the House of David as YHWH's ruling monarch and views Cyrus as YHWH's legitimate king. By the conclusion of the book in Isaiah 66, Trito-Isaiah identifies YHWH as the true monarch, which of course leaves open the continued role of the Persian Achaemenid monarchy as YHWH's chosen monarch over Israel and Judah. Such a position is in keeping with the per-spectives of the Book of Ezra-Nehemiah and the Book of Chronicles. Both Ezra and Nehemiah are Jews who are appointed for service in Jerusalem by the Achaemenid monarchy, and there is no hint of resistance to Persian rule as the Temple is constructed and dedicated and turned into the center of Jewish life in the Persian period. Chronicles likewise shows no resistance to Persian rule. Insofar as the book views the Temple as the holy center of creation, Cyrus' decree at the end of the book to rebuild the Temple inaugu-rates a new era in the history of creation.[11] But this time, instead of a Davidic monarch, Israel/Judah will have a Persian monarch who will see to the res-toration of the people to the land and to the rebuilding of the Temple.

III

When we turn to Zechariah, we encounter two critical issues that are analo-gous to those encountered in Isaiah. First, Zechariah is part of the larger Book of the Twelve Prophets. The Book of the Twelve Prophets includes twelve smaller prophetic books that are read together as one book in the Jewish form of the Bible. Consequently, Zechariah must be read in relation to its context in the Book of the Twelve.[12] Second, Zechariah is often viewed as a composite text like that of Isaiah, insofar as Zechariah 1–8 is read as the work of Zechariah the prophet, whereas Zechariah 9–14, or perhaps Zecha-riah 9–11 and 12–14, is read as the work of later anonymous prophets known to scholars as Second and possibly Third Zechariah.[13] We must examine each of these issues to understand Zechariah.

Zechariah appears as the eleventh book among the Book of the Twelve Prophets, which includes, in the Masoretic Hebrew version of the text, Hosea; Joel; Amos; Obadiah; Jonah; Micah; Nahum; Habakkuk; Zephaniah; Haggai; Zechariah; and Malachi. Although critical scholarship has generally treated these prophets as twelve discrete prophetic books through most of the twentieth century, more recent literary studies have begun to examine their character as a single and yet composite prophetic book, much like Isa-

---

11. For a study of the Jerusalem Temple as the holy center of creation in ancient Judean thought, see Levenson 1984.

12. For discussion of the Book of the Twelve Prophets, see Sweeney 2005c; Sweeney 2000; Alberta et al. 2012; Redditt and Schart 2003.

13. For discussion of Zechariah, see Sweeney 2000, 2:559–709.

iah. One result of such work is the recognition that the Book of the Twelve presents a prophetic overview of Israel's, Judah's, and especially Jerusalem's experience of invasion, destruction, exile, and reconstruction from the eighth through the fifth centuries BCE, culminating in the period of Achaemenid rule.

The second is the recognition that the Book of the Twelve Prophets covers the same issues and periods as the Book of Isaiah, but it frequently challenges Isaiah's viewpoints and proposes alternative understanding of divine purpose.[14] An example emerges in Isaiah's presentation of the famed "swords into plowshares" passage in Isaiah 2:2–4, which presents an image of the nations and Israel streaming to Jerusalem to learn divine instruction and to make world peace. Isaiah's understanding of this oracle is that both the nations and Israel must submit to YHWH's worldwide sovereignty to achieve such an ideal. The Book of the Twelve offers another view in which the ideal vision of "swords turned into plowshares" emerges only after Israel and YHWH confront and defeat the nations that oppress Israel. To that end, Joel 4:9–21 calls for plowshares to be turned into swords so that the nations that oppress Jerusalem might be defeated.[15] Micah 4–5 envisions the rise of a new Davidic King who will defeat the nations that oppress Jerusalem to achieve the ideal vision of peace.[16] The citation of a rewritten form of the ideal swords into plowshares oracle in Zechariah 8:20–23 precedes Zechariah 9–14, which portrays YHWH's battle against the nations who will finally recognize YHWH as world sovereign at Mt. Zion in Jerusalem.[17]

Although none of these examples mentions Cyrus or the Achaemenid monarchy by name, we may observe that Zechariah follows Haggai, Zechariah's prophetic contemporary at the time of the building of the Second Temple in Jerusalem. The brief Book of Haggai argues that the reconstruction of the Jerusalem Temple will bring a variety of benefits from YHWH. In his last oracle in Haggai 2:20–23, the prophet calls for the overthrow and destruction of the kingdoms of the nations, which in Haggai's historical context refers to the Achaemenid Persian monarchy that ruled Judah at the time.[18] He also calls for the establishment of a figure named Zerubbabel ben Shealtiel as YHWH's "signet ring." Insofar as Zerubbabel ben Shealtiel was the grandson of Jehoiachin ben Jehoiakim, the last legitimate ruling monarch of the Judean dynastic House of David, such an oracle functions as a

14. See esp. Bosshard-Nepustil 1997.
15. Sweeney 2005b.
16. Sweeney 2005a.
17. Sweeney 2005d.
18. Sweeney 2000, 2:549–555.

cryptic call for the restoration of the royal House of David once the Achaemenid dynasty is overthrown. Such a view obviously challenges Isaiah's call for recognition of Cyrus as YHWH's Temple builder and anointed monarch.

When we turn to Zechariah, the introduction to the book in Zechariah 1:1 immediately points to an intertextual relationship with the Book of Isaiah. Zechariah 1:1 identifies the prophet as Zechariah ben Berechiah ben Iddo, and places him in the second year of King Darius of Persia, when construction on the Second Temple commenced. The identification of the prophet as Zechariah ben Berechiah ben Iddo presents a problem, insofar as the references to the prophet in Ezra 5:1 and 6:14 refer to him as Zechariah bar Iddo, the Aramaic equivalent of Zechariah ben Iddo.[19] Many scholars presume that there is some textual corruption at this point that resulted in the loss of the reference to Berechiah. Others presume that reference to Zechariah's grandfather is an acceptable naming convention at the time. But there is another explanation for Zechariah's name. Isaiah 8:1–4 makes reference to a certain Zechariah ben Yeberechiah, who is a signed witness to the birth of Isaiah's symbolically named son, Maher Shalal Hash Baz, "the spoil speeds, the prey hastens," whose name points to impending judgment against Israel and Judah. The name Zechariah ben Yeberechiah is quite similar to Zechariah ben Berechiah ben Iddo. Indeed, Yeberechiah is a theophoric name based on the third masculine singular imperfect (future) verbal statement, "YHWH will bless," whereas Berechiah is a theophoric name based on the third masculine singular perfect (past) verbal statement, "YHWH has blessed." When read intertextually, the two names relate to each other as indications of the impending and realized fulfillment of YHWH's prophecies, that is, in Isaiah 8:1–4, Zechariah ben Yeberechiah signals the impending fulfillment of YHWH's word of judgment against Israel and Judah, whereas in Zechariah 1:1, Zechariah ben Berechiah ben Iddo signals the past fulfillment of YHWH's word of judgment against Israel and Judah. Isaiah employs the name to signal future judgment; Zechariah uses the name to signal judgment that has already taken place. The use of a symbolic name to indicate aspects of the prophet's message is a frequent feature of the work of Isaiah ben Amoz. The citation of earlier prophets to illustrate aspects of Zechariah's message is likewise a frequent feature of the Book of Zechariah. In sum, Zechariah's true name is Zechariah ben/bar Iddo, but the book deliberately identifies him as Zechariah ben Berechiah ben Iddo to indicate Zechariah's role as the figure who represents the fulfillment of Isaiah's earlier prophecies.

Such a role is crucial for understanding the book of Zechariah. Zechariah announces that the time of punishment has been realized and that the time

19. Sweeney 2000, 2:569–570.

for the reconstruction of the Temple and the restoration of Jerusalem and Judah – and the consequences that will ensure – has begun. Zechariah 1–6 presents Zechariah's visions concerning the significance of the construction of the Temple in Jerusalem, namely, the reconstruction of the Jerusalem Temple signals YHWH's plans to restore divine sovereignty over the world, particularly over the city of Babylon, from which the Persians ruled their western empire. Zechariah 7–8, commonly read as the conclusion to Zechariah 1–6 in diachronic readings of the book, functions as the introduction to Zechariah 9–14 in synchronic readings of the book as whole. Zechariah 7–8 details YHWH's return to Jerusalem, culminating in the oracle of Zechariah 8:20–23, which reworks elements of the Isaian swords into plowshares passage in Isaiah 2:2–4 and the Isaian reference to Emmanuel, "G-d is with us," in Isaiah 7:14 to portray the many peoples and strong nations that will come to entreat YHWH Sebaoth at the newly reestablished Temple in Jerusalem.

The portrayal of YHWH's battle against the nations that oppress Jerusalem and Judah then follows in the oracular units of Zechariah 9–11 and 12–14. Most scholars correctly view Zechariah 9–14 as later compositions that have been appended to Zechariah 1–8, but they fail to understand the function of these chapters in relation to what precedes. They are not haphazardly appended; rather, they are intentionally appended to illustrate YHWH's plans to liberate Jerusalem and Judah from foreign oppression and to establish divine sovereignty over the entire world. Furthermore, Zechariah 9–14 cryptically portrays the Achaemenid Persian empire as the foreign oppressor that YHWH must overthrow.

Many past scholars argued that Zechariah 9–14 was the product of a Jewish apocalypticist of the Hellenistic period, based on two principal observations. The first was the view that the approach of the king portrayed in Zechariah 9 must refer to Alexander the Great. The second was the view that the reference to Jews fighting Greeks in Zechariah 9:13 must refer to Jewish resistance to Alexander's approach. Neither argument holds up. Zechariah 9 portrays the approach of the king from the land of Hadrach, Damascus, and Hamath, before proceeding down the Mediterranean coast, that is, from Aram, which is the route that one would take when traveling from Mesopotamia to Judah.[20] But Alexander approached from Asia Minor before heading south toward Judah via the Mediterranean coast. The approach of the king is better understood as the approach of a Mesopotamian monarch, such as Darius on his march down the Mediterranean coast to put down revolt in Egypt in 517 BCE. The portrayal of Jews fighting Greeks likewise does not apply to Alexander. Josephus (*AJ* 11.329ff; cf. b. Yoma 69a) relates that when

20. For discussion, see Sweeney 2000, 2:660–662.

Alexander came to Jerusalem during the course of his campaign of conquest, he was welcomed into the city by the Jews. He then proceeded to present offerings to YHWH at the Jerusalem Temple and to grant the Jews protection and privileges as loyal vassals. The portrayal of Jews fighting Greeks in Zechariah 9:13 better portrays Jews who joined Darius' campaign against Greece following his expedition to Egypt in 517 BCE.

This brings us to the oracle concerning the three shepherds in Zechariah 11. Zechariah 11 presents a series of oracles that portray a process in which three shepherds who were expected to tend the sheep are hidden away so that YHWH might raise a new shepherd who will be destroyed when he does not tend the sheep. Interpreters have correctly understood that the passage employs the common metaphor of shepherds to portray the leadership of Judah and YHWH's plans to make changes. Past interpreters have also generally understood that the leaders are themselves Judean, but we must observe that there is a distinction between the first three shepherds in vv. 4–14 who are hidden away, leaving the prophet to tend the people, and the next worthless shepherd of vv. 15–17 who feasts upon the sheep rather than tend to them and thereby earns punishment by the sword against his arm and right eye.

Given the setting of the book in the early Persian period when the Temple was rebuilt, we may observe the presence of Zerubbabel ben Shealtiel, who is named in Zechariah 4, as the royal figure of the House of David who oversaw the construction of the Second Temple.[21] Zerubbabel was the grandson of Jehoiachin ben Jehoiakim, the last legitimate monarch of the House of David, who was deposed by the Babylonians in 597 BCE and sent into Babylonian exile to spend the rest of his life. Neither he nor his sons ever resumed Davidic rule in Jerusalem, but we have already seen above that Haggai anticipated the restoration of Zerubbabel to the Davidic throne. This never happened. Although Zerubbabel presided over the reconstruction of the Temple at the outset of the building in 520 BCE, he was absent at the dedication of the newly-constructed Temple in 515 BCE.

Many speculate that Zerubbabel was supposed to be the royal figure seated on a throne with a priest beside him in Zechariah's final vision in Zechariah 6, but Joshua ben Jehozadak, the High Priest, assumes that role, although the imagery calls for a royal figure.[22] No one knows what happened to Zerubbabel, although it is certainly possible that Darius would have taken action against him when he passed by Judah in 517 BCE on his way to put down the revolt in Egypt. Zerubbabel was a vassal of Darius who was identi-

21. Byer 1992.
22. Sweeney 2000, 2:623–634.

fied as YHWH's new monarch once the throne and might of the nations was overthrown. Therefore, Darius may well have given Zerubbabel the "honor" of leading the first assaults against the Egyptian rebels, or even taken him on his subsequent campaign against Greece. In such a scenario, it is easy to imagine that Darius found a way to dispose of Zerubbabel and thereby leave Judah without its anticipated Davidic king. Insofar as Zerubbabel was the grandson of Jehoiachin, that would account for the hidden character of the three shepherds or kings, namely, Jehoiachin, Shealtiel, and Zerubbabel, leaving Judah and Israel leaderless and tended by the prophet.[23]

The worthless shepherd of vv. 15-17 who will devour the sheep and suffer punishment by the sword against his arm and right eye then would be Darius. The language used to describe the worthless shepherd recalls the language used to describe Cyrus in Isaiah 44:28, where YHWH calls Cyrus, "my shepherd." Isaiah 41:2 portrays YHWH's victor from the east, that is, Cyrus, as the one who makes the sword of his enemy like dust, and Isaiah 45:1 states that YHWH grasps Cyrus' right hand to tread down nations before him. The identification of Darius as the worthless shepherd of Zechariah 11:15-17 then makes sense insofar as the following material in Zechariah 12-14 describes the process in which YHWH, accompanied by the House of David, defeats the nations that oppress Jerusalem and Judah. Zechariah 13:7-9 portrays the downfall of YHWH's shepherd and YHWH's restored relationship with the people who survive the ensuing conflict, who will once again declare, "YHWH is my G-d!" The final scene in Zechariah 14 portrays YHWH's defeat of the nations at Jerusalem and the nations' recognition of YHWH at Jerusalem during the festival of Sukkot. Darius's downfall paves the way for Judah and the nations to recognize YHWH's sovereignty in Jerusalem. This is not the peaceful scenario of Isaiah 2:2-4; rather it represents the uprising against the oppressor anticipated by the Book of the Twelve.

IV

In sum, our comparison of the portrayal of Cyrus in the Book of Isaiah and Darius in the Book of Zechariah points to very different views of the Achaemenid dynasty in these prophetic books. The Book of Isaiah calls for political submission to the Persian empire. It portrays Cyrus as YHWH's chosen messiah and Temple builder at the conclusion of the Babylonian exile when Cyrus authorized the return of Jews to Jerusalem following his accession to the throne in 539 BCE to restore the Jerusalem Temple and Jewish life in the land of Judah. Cyrus' act is not recorded in the Cyrus Cylinder, but it is in keeping with his policies depicted therein. When the time came actually to

23. Contra Sweeney 2000, 2:675–683.

build the Temple, Cyrus was dead and Darius was the new Achaemenid monarch. Darius suffered major challenges to his rule and fought for years at the outset of his reign to put down revolt against his rule. The Book of Zechariah – and Haggai – therefore differ from Isaiah insofar as they see the turmoil of their time as a sign that YHWH was about to depose the Achaemenid monarchy and thereby open the way for the restoration of the Davidic monarchy and Judean political independence from Persian rule. Such an overthrow was never achieved, and Zechariah went on to be read as apocalyptic literature anticipating the triumph of YHWH in a distant future.[24]

24. I am indebted to my research assistant, Dr. Pamela J. Nourse, for her careful reading of my manuscript. Any errors are my own.

Bibliography

Alberta, Rainer et al. eds.. 2012. *Perspectives on the Formation of the Book of the Twelve: Methodological Foundations – Redactional Processes – Historical Insights*. Berlin.

Bosshard-Nepustil, Erich. 1997. *Rezeptionen von Jesaja 1–39 im Zwölfprophetenbuch: Untersuchungen zur literarischen Verbindung von Prophetenbüchern in babylonischer und persischer Zeit*. Freiburg.

Byer, Bryan E. 1992. "Zerubbabel," *Anchor Biblical Dictionary*, volume VI:1085–1086.

Duhm, Bernhard. 1892. *Das Buch Jesaia*. Handkommentar zum Alten Testament – 3 Abteilung, 1 Band: Die prophetischen Bücher. Göttingen.

Finkel, Irving, ed. 2013. *The Cyrus Cylinder: The King of Persia's Proclamation from Ancient Babylon*. London.

Gesenius, Wilhelm. 1820–21. *Der Prophet Jesaia: Übersetzt und mit einem vollständigen Philologisch-kritischen und historischen Commentar begleitet*. 4 vols. Leipzig.

Kim, Hyun Chul Paul. 2008. "Recent Scholarship on Isaiah 1̥39." In *Recent Research on the Major Prophets*, edited by Alan J. Hauser, 118–141. Sheffield.

Levenson, Jon D. 1984. "The Temple and the World," *Journal of Religion* 64:275–298.

Melugin, Roy F. 2008. "Isaiah 40–66 in Recent Research: The 'Unity' Movement." In *Recent Research on the Major Prophets*, edited by Alan J. Hauser, 142–194. Sheffield.

Matheus, Frank. 1990. *Singt dem Herrn ein neues Lied: Die Hymnen Deuterojesajas*. Stuttgart.

Redditt, Paul and Aaron Schart, eds. 2003. *Thematic Threads in the Book of the Twelve*. Berlin.

Stromberg, Jacob. 2011. *An Introduction to the Study of Isaiah*. London.

Sweeney, Marvin A. 1988. *Isaiah 1-4 and the Post-Exilic Understanding of the Isaianic Tradition*. Berlin.

———. 1993. "The Book of Isaiah in Recent Research," *Currents in Research: Biblical Studies* 1:141–162 Sheffield.

———. 1996a. *Isaiah 1-39: With an Introduction to Prophetic Literature*. Grand Rapids.

———. 1996b. "Re-evaluating Isaiah 1–39 in Recent Critical Research." *Currents in Research: Biblical Studies* 4:79–113. Sheffield.

———. 1997. "The Reconceptualization of the Davidic Covenant in Isaiah." In *Studies in the Book of Isaiah: Festschrift Willem A. M. Beuken*, edited by J. van Ruiten and M. Vervenne, 41–61. Louvain.

———. 2000. *The Twelve Prophets*. 2 vols. Collegeville, MN.

———. 2005a. "Micah's Debate with Isaiah." In *Form and Intertextuality in Prophetic and Apocalyptic Literature*. Forschungen zum Alten Testament 45:210–221. Tübingen.

———. 2005b. "The Place and Function of Joel in the Book of the Twelve." In *Form and Intertextuality in Prophetic and Apocalyptic Literature*. Forschungen zum Alten Testament 45: 189–209. Tübingen.

———. 2005c. "Sequence and Interpretation in the Book of the Twelve." In *Form and Intertextuality in Prophetic and Apocalyptic Literature*. Forschungen zum Alten Testament 45: 175–188. Tübingen.

———. 2005d. "Zechariah's Debate with Isaiah." In *Form and Intertextuality in Prophetic and Apocalyptic Literature*. Forschungen zum Alten Testament 45:222–235. Tübingen.

———. 2016a. *Isaiah 40-66*. Grand Rapids, MI.

———. 2016b. "Isaiah." In *Encyclopedia of the Bible and its Reception*, edited by D. C. Allison, et al. Vol. 13: 297–305. Berlin and Boston.

Cyrus and Pasargadae:
Forging an Empire – Fashioning "Paradise"

Rémy Boucharlat
CNRS – Lyon University

> How can we explain this sudden outburst into history by a
> people and a state hitherto practically unknown? How can
> we explain not only that this people could forge military
> forces sufficient to achieve conquests as impressive as they
> were rapid, but also that, as early as the reign of Cyrus, it had
> available the technological and intellectual equipment that
> made the planning and building of Pasargadae possible?[1]

ECENT FIELDWORK IN THE PASARGADAE AREA has provided new data on Cyrus' first residence in Iran. These have deeply enriched what we already knew of Cyrus' achievements, showing his activity was much more ambitious than expected and, at the same time, more complicated than assumed during the formative period of the Achaemenid empire, when Cyrus was far from Fārs.

The more we work on Pasargadae, the more we are astonished by the history of the site building, as it is better known today.[2] Cyrus' achievements in Pasargadae raise many questions. Two of them are particularly puzzling when we measure what the king accomplished within two decades. His plan extended much beyond the well-known monuments we can admire today. The picture of Pasargadae should now include not only the site itself, but also the whole region. The two following questions, otherwise clearly expressed in Pierre Briant's sentence placed as epigraph, should be kept in mind in this contribution that emphasizes the new features recently brought to light.

- How and when was Cyrus able to envision and build his residence, as well as control the progress of the work, since he was more often than not away from Fārs, very engaged in conquering and securing his empire, as well as organizing its management?

1. Briant 2002, 13.
2. The new picture we can draw today owes much to the results of the surveys (field walking, topographic, aerial photography, and above all geomagnetic surveys) carried out between 1999 and 2008 by an Iranian and French team. See Benech, Boucharlat, and Gondet 2012. For a more general presentation, see Boucharlat 2011.

- To what extent was Cyrus in a position to envision and execute the construction of Pasargadae, for which he selected several different traditions of the Near East and western Asia Minor, and was at the same time able carefully to integrate them within his project that included many Iranian and/or Persian features?[3]

These pages do not pretend fully to answer these questions. The geography and chronology of Cyrus' conquests may be a part of the explanation for the second question, the so-called "influences," which are very likely intentional borrowings from various parts of his empire. Some of these foreign elements are well known, such as the Ionian column basis, or the ashlar masonry of Tall-e Takht, to mention only a few of them. Others are borrowed traits from Mesopotamian art, which some of the Persian elite already knew, and Elamite traditions, which were actually part of the local culture. The latter raises the question of the Persians before Cyrus. As evinced by recent discoveries of pre-Achaemenid elite graves between Fārs and Susiana, there was a well-informed and educated Irano-Elamite (= Persian) elite in the decades preceding Cyrus, or even one century earlier. I do not treat this issue here, but it should be nonetheless borne in mind.[4]

Forging an Empire Far from Pasargadae

After 560, Cyrus started expanding the Persian kingdom, which certainly was not *merely* populated with nomads and shepherd tribes. Around 553 BCE, Cyrus defeated the Median army, maybe in the Pasargadae plain according to some authors (Strabo 15.3.8). Did he start to build Pasargadae soon thereafter? In order to settle the site, he had first to bring water and to plan for minimal settings accommodating his family, the court, guards, not to speak of the hundreds of masons and workers who would be employed at the site when the building activity started.

In the following years, Cyrus went to conquer Asia Minor, especially the western part of it, that is, Croesus' Lydian kingdom with its capital in Sardis. That conquest alone consumed much time. By 545 BCE, Cyrus had vanquished the Lydian kingdom, and he continued his subjugation of the West by subduing the Ionian cities. The takeovers required careful preparation and the participation of allied troops, which in turn demanded a preparation time of up to several months. Therefore, Cyrus had to remain in these areas for some time, in order to organize the administration of these provinces.

Cyrus eventually went back to Persia, but only for a while, for his pres-

---

3. Stronach 2008 has offered a very clear picture of Cyrus' building program.
4. See Álvarez-Mon and Garrison 2011, with ample references.

ence was required in the East to secure that part of the Iranian world, which probably was encompassed in the political sphere of the former Median polity. Later on, Cyrus conquered Babylon. According to the Cyrus Cylinder, Cyrus made a peaceful entry into Babylon in 539 BCE,[5] but we know that it was preceded by battles and negotiations,[6] a period to be counted in terms of months. After 539, the former immense Neo-Babylonian kingdom had to be integrated into the new Achaemenid administration. Cyrus in all likelihood stayed in Mesopotamia often, or for longer periods of time. Xenophon (*Cyr.* 8.6.22) states that Cyrus spent seven months of the year there, because Babylonia and the western regions were of primary importance for the empire. Finally, during his last years, and until his death in 530 BCE, Cyrus was far away from Persis, extending his conquests into Central Asia.

To sum up, during his last twenty years Cyrus could not have resided for any long period at Pasargadae. Therefore, in his absence he must have delegated the building of Pasargadae, the management of the region, and the administration of Fārs to his representatives. The question as to how the empire was structured and organized during the first decades of Achaemenid rule has not hitherto been addressed in a satisfactory manner, and I do not think extant archaeological data could help in this respect.

Pasargadae before Cyrus

There is no archaeological evidence for a previous occupation of Pasargadae in the centuries preceding Cyrus. According to ancient and recent surveys of the site itself and salvage excavations in the Tang-e Bulaghi valley nearby (2005–2007),[7] there is a chronological gap in the occupation between the fourth millennium and the Achaemenid period. There is absolutely no evidence of any pre-Achaemenid occupation corresponding to the emergence of Persian power. The same situation occurs for the whole of central Fārs, and this is certainly one of the major challenges for Iranian history.

The Beginnings

As mentioned above, the first imperative for the development of the Pasargadae site would have been to secure a reliable water supply. The Pulvar

---

5. For the text of the Cyrus Cylinder, see Schaudig in this volume.

6. A case in point is the Nabonidus Chronicle reporting on Cyrus' killing in Opis: "In the month Tešrit, Cyrus having joined battle with the army of Akkad at Upû (Opis) on the bank of the Tigris, the people of Akkad fell back. He [Cyrus] pillaged and massacred the population. The fourteenth, Sippar was seized without struggle. Nabonidus fled"; (Glassner 2004, no. 26, iii.12–15; 236–237).

7. See the five reports on the Achaemenid sites in Tang-e Bulaghi edited by Boucharlat and Fazeli Nashli 2009; Boucharlat 2011, 566–572; and Boucharlat 2014.

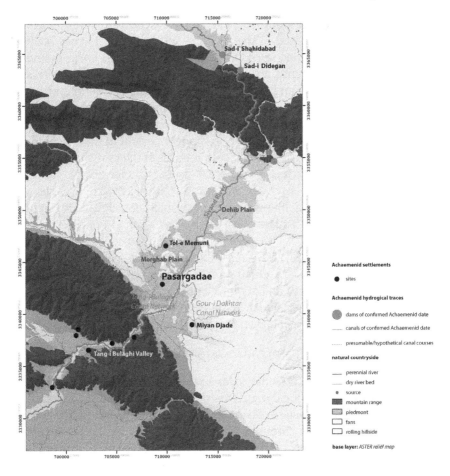

Fig. 1. Map of the Pasargadae area showing the hydraulic installations, dams and canals from the Achaemenid period (S. Gondet, Iran-France Joint expedition Persepolis-Pasargadae, 2016).

river is far from the central part of the site (ca. 1 kilometer) and is deeply incised (ca. 6 meters) below the surface. Certainly, the very first operation would have been to dig a canal, in order to divert the course of the Pulvar river, which must, judging from the point from which the river deviates today, have been roughly the same in the past. Recent investigations have demonstrated that the stream flowing in the central part of the site is not natural, but its bed was dug and protected by built embankments (which can be seen in the center of Fig. 2).

The first stone buildings were started after the conquest of Anatolia and the Ionian coast that supplied masons and workers for the construction work in Pasargadae. We still do not have an adequate understanding of where the king and his retinue resided at Pasargadae, nor how the residential area was structured. Even for the later period our knowledge remains limited. We possess no further information on administrative buildings initiated by Cyrus, or on the dwellings.

Fig. 2. General view of the central part of the site taken from a kite facing north (B.-N. Chagny, Iran-France Joint expedition Persepolis-Pasargadae, 2001).

During his conquest, Cyrus had the opportunity to observe the architecture and imagery used in diverse parts of his empire. He collected techniques, iconographic elements, and decorative motifs, which he wanted to implement in his homeland. These borrowed elements were chosen so they could be integrated and transformed in a project that also included Persian components. This whole project from its original conception through its implementation with external and local elements was very ambitious. The ultimate aim was probably to exhibit in his residence the diversity and the resources of his new empire, as Darius would do some decades later in Persepolis.

This process is well illustrated by many examples that display elements borrowed from other cultural contexts, such as Greek techniques and elements in palatial architecture; and Assyrian-inspired iconography

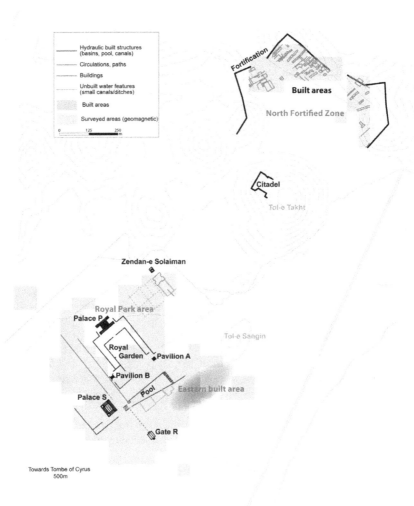

Fig. 3. Map of Pasargadae showing the results of the geophysical prospections 1999-2015 (Gondet, Iran-France Joint expedition Persepolis-Pasargadae, 2016).

in the realization of the winged genius, or reliefs on the doorjambs, of the columned halls. In the following, I shall describe a few more examples to illustrate Cyrus' sophisticated and ambitious plans. Needless to say, I do not always have an explanation for the entire process, nor a clear answer on the origin of the described elements. These are:

• The quite new layout of the residence and the problem of the elusive nature of the city of Pasargadae.

- The implementation of stonemasonry techniques in a region with no prior tradition of stone architecture.

- Sophisticated hydraulic engineering in the Pasargadae area that was also quite novel for the region of Fārs.

The Residence and the City

There was no previous city in Pasargadae, or, as a matter of fact, in the whole of Fārs, as far as we know. Daniel Potts' hypothesis that views the site of Malayan as Cyrus' place of extraction is interesting, but highly speculative, since it is not based on any known archaeological evidence.[8] In the eastern plain of modern day Khuzestan between the lowland and the highlands, graves pre-dating Cyrus' time have been found (near Behbāhān and near Rām-Hormoz) that belong to members of elites in local chiefdoms, about whose way of life (nomadic or sedentary) we know little.[9] Were they the rulers of actual towns? Rare Neo-Elamite and Mesopotamian written sources may point to existing towns in the plains and valleys, but they have been rarely located with precision, with the exception of such sites as Susa and Tepe Bormi; for all of them both layout and size are poorly known.[10]

This situation raises the question: from which models did Cyrus draw his inspiration for planning Pasargadae? The layout is still partly unknown, especially for the housing of the population, but the visible or detected components do not resemble anything we know in the Near East. The first striking original trait is the absence of a rampart, either a city wall or a wall delimiting and protecting the royal quarters. Ernst Herzfeld cautiously posited the existence of a rampart on the south side of the site, but he observed that it would not have been connected to the monumental Gate R nearby. As a matter of fact, the recent geomagnetic survey has confirmed that these were possibly dwellings rather than a defensive wall (Fig. 2 bottom). Compared to the strongly walled cities of Babylonia and Assyria, Pasargadae offers a completely different picture, as does Persepolis although built a few decades later.[11] The absence of a bulwark remains to be explained. Herzfeld's

8. Potts 2005, 21.

9. For the grave near Behbāhān, see Alizadeh 1985; for that near Rām-Hormoz, see Shishegar 2015.

10. Carter and Stolper 1984, 187–189. For the late Neo-Elamite period (NE III 647–539) Potts 2016, 282–305; Miroschedji 2003; Álvarez-Mon and Garrison 2011. Despite the important discoveries of the two famous elite graves, these references published in last three decades show there is no real progress of our knowledge of the Neo-Elamite settlements in southwest Iran. The sites of Tol-e Nurābād and Tol-e Sepid, which have been recently investigated, are rather large mounds, but the surface of the archaeological sites does not correspond to a large city.

11. See Boucharlat forthcoming; contra Mousavi 1992, who emphasizes the importance of

theory of Pasargadae as a kind of campsite can no longer be maintained; instead we have to think more along the lines David Stronach envisages for Pasargadae's establishment: "it may prove possible to think in terms of a subtle and carefully conceived master plan."[12] Moreover, one may assume that Cyrus felt the heart of his empire was totally secure, or perhaps he wanted to demonstrate the peaceful character of his Persian homeland. This assumption is strengthened by the symbolic entrance to the royal quarter, an impressive isolated building with four large doors with the decorated doorjambs (only the winged figure has survived) and the columns topped with animal capitals found by Herzfeld (Fig. 4).

No part of the Gate points to a defensive structure. Since the British and Iranian excavations at Pasargadae in the 1950–1970s, the garden that is set in the central part of the site has garnered much attention. Gardens in the Near East have long been known, and are first linked with temples. Beginning with the late second millennium BCE, gardens were created by Assyrian kings primarily for their own pleasure.[13] However, none of the representations of gardens on the Neo-Assyrian reliefs can be compared with the geometrical design of the Pasargadae garden. The Assyrian gardens are set on a hill, often topped by a small open pavilion, where streams and trees are in irregular positions. Conversely the garden of Pasargadae is located in a flat area and shows a geometric design strongly emphasized by stone channels. The stone buildings are not in the middle, but put outside.[14] Therefore the garden appears to be more important than the relatively modest hypostyle buildings. Once again, when we compare the respective importance of both elements, Pasargadae is definitely different from the Assyrian cities, including the newly founded ones created ex nihilo by the Assyrian kings.

Another important component is also related to the landscaped central part of the site. The geomagnetic survey revealed that the canal was transformed near the bridge into a huge trapezoidal pond some 200 meters long, more than 50 meters wide, and only 1.50 meter deep (Fig. 2). Given the strong contrast of the geomagnetic map, the embankment seems to be made of dressed stones. Such a large pond is totally unknown in earlier royal gardens in Mesopotamia, Anatolia, and Egypt.

---

the "three ramparts" mentioned by Diodorus Siculus (17.71, 3–8) and considers Persepolis to have been initially a "strong military fortress" (Mousavi 1992, 221).

12. Stronach 1978, 44; and Stronach 2008, 154, contra Herzfeld 1935, 28 – followed later by Hansman 1972, 110 – whose hypothesis of a kind of Persian campsite in the nomadic tradition(?) is no longer acceptable.

13. Stronach 1990.

14. The geomagnetic survey conducted on the major part of the inner garden has not revealed any building.

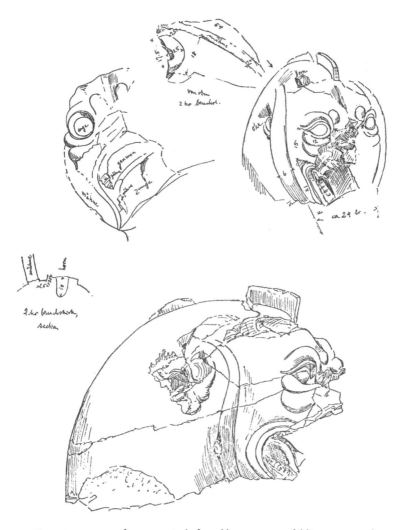

Fig. 4. Fragments of stone capitals found by Ernst Herzfeld in 1929 in Palace P (Calmeyer 1981, fig. 6, E. Herzfeld's drawing, Archives E. Herzfeld, Freer Gallery, Washington, DC, D-1187).

The geometric layout designed by Cyrus goes beyond the central part. Geomagnetic tests carried out on three hectares between the central garden and the tower of Zendān-e Soleymān have detected a grid delineating squares. The meshes are not all of the same size, measuring 30 to 60 meters a side. The grid very likely corresponds to a network of channels and ditches, maybe lined by rows of trees. From this test, we assume a large part of the plain or the whole flat area between the platform and the tomb of Cyrus might have been an immense landscaped park organized with rectilinear lines of ditches and trees. This reconstruction clearly recalls the description of some paradises by the Greeks authors (for example, Xenophon, *Oec.* 4.20–25). Pasargadae may offer the earliest examples of a paradise, the celebrated Persian invention.

Such a geometric layout being in striking contrast with the gardens, as represented on Assyrian bas-reliefs, its origin should be sought elsewhere. The Ionian/Greek garden is not a good candidate given its small size.[15] Can we envisage its origin in the gardens of the royal residences of Anatolian kingdoms? This is an open question until we have more information on their layout.

The main part of the site belongs to the royal area with only a few stone constructions. Consequently, we are not yet able to define the nature of Pasargadae's "urbanism," if there was an urban center at all. We know almost nothing about the town. An area for housing the population and workers should have existed somewhere. One of the hypotheses is to locate it within the "outer" polygonal defensive wall. Here the geomagnetic survey has detected a series of large buildings following the same general orientation (Fig. 4). However, the size of the blocks, 20 to 40 meters long, rather points to barracks, or storage buildings. The location and shape of the town remain a pending question, but we may state with confidence that Pasargadae was definitely not built based on the model of Mesopotamian cities. Neither the distribution of palatial buildings, nor the internal layout, have any resemblance to the compact Assyrian palaces organized around courtyards. The only possible illustration of Pasargadae's influence can be seen on discrete Achaemenid structures at the Karacamirli site in Azarbaijan, where, for the moment, we may compare the loose distribution of the official buildings on the site, the simple surrounding wall, the propylaeum, that is, the isolated monumental gate, and more.[16]

Implementation of Foreign Stone Techniques: Creating a Persian Architecture

Until the Achaemenids, the overwhelming construction material in southwestern Iran was brick, mainly mudbrick. The use of baked brick was restricted to important constructions such as temples, but baked brick also occurred occasionally as the raw material for foundations, and in sewers.

15. On Greek gardens, see Nielsen 1999. In Egypt and Mesopotamia, there are gardens containing rows of trees set at regular intervals along alignments. However, the size of these gardens is much smaller than the garden of Pasargadae.
16. See Knauß, Gagošidse, Babaev 2013.

The introduction of stone architecture hence must have come from outside of Fārs and modern day Khuzestān. The conquest of the Urartian territory preceded that of Asia Minor, but most of the stone techniques and decoration are not borrowed from Urartu, but from western Anatolia, that is, the Lydian kingdom and the Ionian cities. Therefore, stone architecture in Pasargadae postdates these events.

Cyrus certainly visited several Greek cities and their temples, visually the most striking achievements of Greek architecture. From this exposure, Cyrus and his engineers(?) might have selected some components and implemented them for quite different purposes in buildings at Pasargadae, affecting their layout plan, elevation, and architectural details. To mention but a single example: the hypostyle hall (used in Pasargadae) was unknown to the Greeks; the stone column rows, however, were borrowed from the Greek porticoes, but implemented in the Iranian way for the central hall, as we see it in the arrangement of wooden columns in central Zagros sites, such as Nush-e Jān or Godin Tepe. In Pasargadae, the two rows of stone columns flanking the sides of the two palaces (Palace P and Palace S) are not arranged in emulation of the sole Greek portico, but are built in a novel, distinct way, either fronting the central, rectangular columned hall on two sides (Palace P), or on all four sides (Palace S).

After the conquest of Babylon, the Persians came into direct contact with Mesopotamian art, but we know today that they had already encountered Mesopotamian artistry some decades prior to the Persian dominion of the region, as demonstrated by a number of artifacts found recently in elite burials in an area between Fārs and southwest Iran.[17]

In Assyria, monumental mudbrick buildings had probably fallen into decay following the fall of Nineveh, but most likely stone sculptures were still partly preserved and visible. The four-winged genius at the Gate R of Pasargadae illustrates this selection of traditional Mesopotamian iconography (the two pairs of wings), beside the Elamite motif, which is displayed by the genius' dress, and the Egyptian crown. Animal busts (horse, bull, and lion), or protomes, found in fragments in Gate R and Palace S, also betray Mesopotamian influence in the iconography, but the idea of placing them, in the garb of zoomorphic capitals, at the column's top is definitely Persian.

The borrowing of non-Persian components has been precisely and adequately analyzed.[18] However, a number of questions still remain, namely, the genesis of Cyrus' tomb, as well as the origin and function for the Zendān-e Soleymān tower.

17. See footnote 7.
18. Among many studies, see Calmeyer's considerations on the Babylonian and Assyrian elements in Pasargadae and Persepolis (Calmeyer 1994).

Sophisticated Hydraulic Engineering: Questions of Its Origin

Water played a major role in Pasargadae, but its importance was underestimated until recent fieldwork. Water is not only present in the stone watercourses of the garden, but along its southeastern side in the well-built canal, as revealed by the geomagnetic survey. The visitor arriving through the monumental isolated Gate R could see it after some 200 meters. Such an abundance of water in this semi-arid landscape was certainly very impressive. Moreover, the water level was apparently constantly maintained thanks to a series of six water gates at both ends of the large pool (Fig. 5).[19] That device may be related to Neo-Assyrian technology and to the water sluice gates in Choga Zanbil.[20] The latter is much older (second half of the second millennium BCE), and was probably no longer visible in the sixth century BCE, when the site had been abandoned. An Urartian, or Neo-Assyrian origin for this hydraulic technology is highly probable.

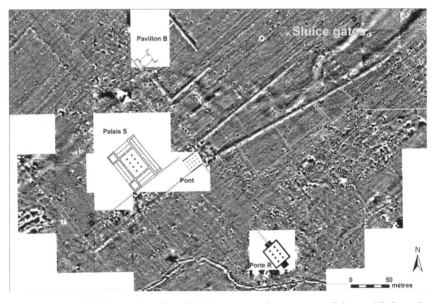

Fig. 5. Detail of the series of small sluice gates at the entrance of the pool (adapted from Benech, Boucharlat, Gondet 2012, fig. 9).

19. The interpretation of this part of the geomagnetic image, as well as the section of the canal downstream after flowing along Palace S, ought to be checked by future surveys and excavations.
20. Ghirshman 1968, 96–100, figs. 38–39, pls. xli–lxii.

However, this feature could only work if the water flow deriving from the Pulvar river was regularly maintained. In view of the variation of the river throughout the year, owing to snowmelt in the spring and the drought in late summer and fall, the engineers must have regulated the river flow upstream. As a matter of fact, there are testimonies of half a dozen dams on the Pulvar river and some of its tributaries up to 20 kilometers north of Pasargadae. Dating the dams to the Achaemenid period is highly likely, and certain for at least two of them. They were planned to function as a large catchment control measure. Very likely this series of dams was intended to control the water flow: retaining water in the spring in huge natural reservoirs of millions of cubic meters, then providing a continuous flow in the dry season. From the map drawn by W. Kleiss, an Iranian and French team visited the remains of the dams, and studied two of them in the Safā Shahr plain at an altitude of 2100 meters above sea level. The clearing and sounding carried out in the years 2008 and 2009 revealed very sophisticated devices of ashlar masonry set into the dam made of earth and stones. These devices are so exceptional that we are at a loss what they were built for![21]

The excavated dam at Shahidābād shows a very high quality of stone masonry: well-drafted limestone blocks up to 2.50 meters long, using anathyrosis joining technique without mortar (Fig. 6). The huge, often polished blocks were bonded by means of iron clamps set into a dovetail-shaped or rectangular notch filled with melted lead. This is a highly distinctive Achaemenid masonry which can be seen in the royal constructions at Pasargadae. It is directly inspired by contemporary Lydian and Ionian stone cutting techniques. One of the dams is dated by radiocarbon to the late sixth to early fifth century BCE, and the second dam, lacking the dovetail clamps characteristic of the sixth century stonecraft, is slightly later, but still within the Achaemenid period.

The 20-meter long stone device is set on the top of the first dam (Fig. 7). It consists of a main conduit 0.84 meter wide and 1.56 meter high; then the flow is divided up into six small channels (0.35 meter in width and 0.50 meter in height). Each of these could be closed by a sluice gate (only the slots remain). These channels open into a rectangular basin built of ashlar masonry on three sides, but the rear side is apparently open. In the middle, in a line, three stone pillars very likely supported a roof. Beyond this distal part, a natural channel is still visible stretching a few meters. The masonry points to the early Achaemenid period (no traces of tooth chisel on the stones) and the radiocarbon dates fall between 540 and 480 BCE.

---

21. For a general presentation and geomorphological study, see De Schacht et al. 2012.

Fig. 6. The ashlar masonry of the stone construction on the Shahidābād dam, north of Pasargadae (T. De Schacht, Iran-France Joint expedition Persepolis-Pasargadae, 2008).

Two kilometers downstream, the second dam, which is higher, but less wide, built as it was across a narrow valley, exhibits the same stone device, though installed here at the bottom of the dam. It is badly preserved. On this second dam, we notice the smaller size of the stones and the lack of dovetail clamps.

The stonecutting techniques we observe in Pasargadae originated undoubtedly from western Anatolia, but the hydraulic system is completely unknown in the Greek world. The structure itself is not so different from the "reservoir" in Choga Zanbil, which is made of baked bricks. However, the two systems are exactly inverted: whereas in Pasargadae, the main conduit carries water to the small channels, and then diffuses it into the basin, in Choga Zanbil, the high water level in the lower basin goes up to the small, almost vertical channels, and from there flows into the upper small basin. However, this reconstruction is now seriously questioned.[22] The purpose and

22. Behzad Mofidi Nasrabadi (2007, 25–28, tables 23–24; and 2013, 308–311, table 5) conducted an in-depth analysis of the water canals and devices around the ziggurat and on the middle enclosure wall. Moreover, he noted that water cannot be conducted from the surround-

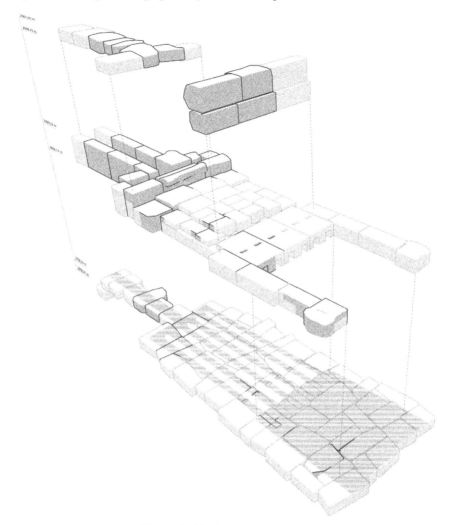

Fig. 7. Axonometry of the Shahidābād stone construction (Y. Ubelmann, Iran-France Joint expedition Persepolis-Pasargadae, 2008).

working of the sophisticated devices near Pasargadae are quite unclear, as is their origin. We may only speculate on the identity of the engineers, or

---

ing plain, which is several meters lower than the level of the city. Mofidi Nasrabadi considers the different water installations on the site aimed to drain run-offs outside the city. Thus, the installation excavated by Ghirshman is just one of three or more components on the gates of the enclosure wall. Nevertheless, this type of sophisticated installation remains unique in southwest Iran before the Achaemenids.

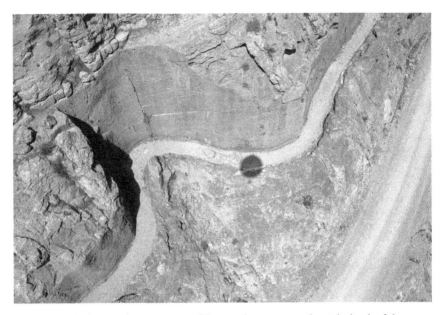

Fig. 8. The long rock-cut section of the canal running on the right bank of the
Pulvar river in the Tang-e Bulaghi taken from a balloon (B.-N. Chagny, Iran-France
Joint expedition Persepolis-Pasargadae, 2008).

from which region of the empire they came. They were certainly not from
Fārs, because of the stone technology they applied. In sum, the survey of the
hydraulic structures in the most developed regions of the empire has not
brought any light to questions about their origin and function.

Looking at the southern part of the region of Pasargadae, evidence for
another Achaemenid hydraulic installation can be seen in the Tang-e Bulaghi valley, two kilometers south of Cyrus' tomb. Here again, stonecutting
was widely used for digging rock-cut canals on both sides of the river in
the narrow parts of the gorge (Fig. 8). In the wider parts of the valleys, the
rock-cut sections are replaced by a kind of earth causeway that supported
the canal itself. The engineers were able to maintain a very gentle general
sloping, a one to two percent gradient, as did Roman engineers much later.
These canals obviously were intended to irrigate dozens of hectares in the
small plain of Bulaghi. Similar important rock-cut canals and tunnels were
in use in Urartu and Assyria in the centuries preceding the Achaemenid
empire. The instruments used to establish almost horizontal channels may
also have come from these regions. As to the chronology of the canals, several clues from the stoneworking techniques point to an Achaemenid date.
Surprisingly, we noted that the canal on the right bank was left unfinished

despite huge investments already made. It is tempting to assume the abandonment of the work coincided with the diminished role of Pasargadae after the demise of Cyrus or maybe of Cambyses, when Darius moved the royal residence in Fārs to Persepolis.

Upon Cyrus' passing, Pasargadae's quiet existence commenced, though it remained a symbolically important dynastic place. Apart from Darius' limited activities on sculptures at Palace P, and the addition of short inscriptions in the name of Cyrus on the two palaces, and Gate R, the main change concerns the Tall-e Takht edifice, which Cyrus left unfinished above the stone platform. Darius built a defensive mud-brick building that seems rather modest in comparison with the huge and careful work of the enormous platform. No doubt, Cyrus was the main actor at Pasargadae, building his residence on an empty space. Between 550 and 530 BCE, he was able to carefully collect architectural, artistic, and technological elements from the various regions of his empire and blend them in the creation of new a personal or Persian style, or concept of art. Summoning engineers, craftsmen, and workers from Anatolia, Mesopotamia, and Syria and dispatching them to Pasargadae, and very likely to Bushehr near Borazjan, was not a difficult task for the king. Conceiving a quite original layout for his residence based upon local and foreign traditions, as well as forging a new architectural vision, and imposing it on a new landscape can hardly have been the work of a single person, who, moreover, was an itinerant king, busily expanding and regulating his nascent empire. The role of a Persian and multiethnic elite, constituted during Cyrus' subjugation of technologically more advanced cultures, was probably very important but remains to be determined.

References

Alizadeh, Abbas. 1985. "A Tomb of the Neo-Elamite Period at Arjān, near Behbahan." *Archäologische Mitteilungen aus Iran* 18:59–73.

Álvarez-Mon, Javier, and Mark B. Garrison, ed. 2011. *Elam and Persia*. Winona Lake, Ind.: Eisenbrauns.

Benech, Christophe; Rémy Boucharlat; and Sébastien Gondet. 2012. "Organisation et aménagement de l'espace à Pasargades: Reconnaissances archéologiques de surface, 2003–2008." *ARTA* 2012.003.

Boucharlat, Rémy. 2011. "Gardens and Parks at Pasargadae: Two "Paradises?" In *Herodot und das persische Weltreich / Herodotus and the Persian Empire*, edited by Robert Rollinger, Brigitte Truschnegg, and Josef Wiesehöfer. Classica et Orientalia 3:557–574. Wiesbaden: Harrassowitz.

———. 2014. "Achaemenid Estate(s) near Pasargadae?" In *Extraction & Control: Studies in Honor of Matthew W. Stolper*, edited by Michael Kozuh,

Wouter F. M. Henkelman, Charles E. Jones, and Christopher Woods. Studies in Ancient Oriental Civilization, Number 68:27–35. Chicago: The Oriental Institute of the University of Chicago.

———. Forthcoming. "Arriving at Persepolis, An Unfortified Royal Residence." In *Festschrift for Margaret C. Root*, edited by Elspeth R. M. Dussinberre and Mark B. Garrison.

Boucharlat, Rémy, and Hasan Fazeli Nashli, ed. 2009. "Tang-i Bulaghi Reports." *ARTA* 2009.002–2009.006

Briant, Pierre. 2002. *From Cyrus to Alexander: A History of the Persian Empire.* Translated by Peter T. Daniels. Winona Lake, Ind.: Eisenbrauns.

Calmeyer, Peter. 1994. "Babylonische und assyrische Elemente in der achaeimenidischen Kunst." In *Continuity and Change : Proceedings of the Last Achaemenid History Workshop, April 6-8,1990 - Ann Arbor, Michigan.* Achaemenid History VIII, edited by Heleen Sancisi-Weerdenburg, Amélie Kuhrt, Root, and Margaret Cool Root, 131–147. Leiden: Nederlands Instituut voor het Nabije Oosten.

Carter, Elisabeth, and Matthew W. Stolper. 1984. *Elam: Survey of Political History and Archaeology.* University of California Publications: Near Eastern Studies, vol. 25. Berkeley/Los Angeles/London: University of California Press.

De Schacht, Tijs; Morgan De Dapper; Ali Asadi; Yves Ubelmann; and Rémy Boucharlat. 2012. "Geoarchaeological Study of the Achaemenid Dam of Sad-i Didegan (Fars, Iran)." *Géomorphologie: Relief, Processus, Environnement,* 1:91–108.

Ghirshman, Roman. 1968. *Tchoga Zanbil (Dur-Untash).* Vol. II: *Temenos, temples, palais tombes.* Mémoires de la Délégation Archéologique en Iran, XL. Mission de Susiane. Paris: Geuthner.

Glassner, Jean-Jacques. 2004. *Mesopotamian Chronicles.* Edited by Benjamin R. Foster. Society of Biblical Literature Writings from the Ancient World, Number 19. Atlanta: Society of Biblical Literature.

Gondet, Sébastien; Kourosh Mohammadkhani; Mahdokht Farjamirad; Nabil Ibnoeirida; Farhad Zare Kordshouli; Hamid Reza Karami; Damien Laisney. 2016. "Field Report on the 2015 Current Archaeological Works of the Joint Iran-French Project on Pasargadae and Its Territory." *International Journal of Iranian Heritage* 1,1:60–87.

Hansman, John. 1972. "Elamites, Achaemenians and Anshan." *Iran: Journal of the British Institute of Persian Studies* 10, no. 1:101–125

Herzfeld, Ernst. 1935. *Archaeological History of Iran,* Oxford: Oxford University Press.

Knauß, Florian S.; Iulon Gagošidse; and Ilyas Babaev. 2013. "Karačamirli: Ein persisches Paradies," *Arta* 2013.004.

de Miroschedji, Pierre. 2003. "Susa and the Highlands: Major Trends in the History of Elamite Civilization." In *Yeki bud, yeki nabud: Essays on the Archaeology of Iran in Honor of William M. Sumner,* edited by Naomi F. Miller and Kamyar Abdi. Monograph 48, 17–38. Los Angeles: The Costen Institute of Archaeology, UCLA.

Mofidi-Nasrabadi, Behzad. 2007. *Archäologische Ausgrabungen und Untersuchungen in Čoǧā Zanbil.* Münster: Agenda Verlag.

———. 2013. *Planungsaspekte und die Struktur der altorientalischen neugegründeten Stadt in Choga Zanbil.* Aachen: Shaker Verlag.

Mousavi, Ali. 1992. "Parsa, A Stronghold for Darius: A Preliminary Study of the Defence System of Persepolis." *East and West* 42, nos. 2–4:203–226.

Nielsen, Inge. 1999. *Hellenistic Palaces: Tradition and Renewal.* Studies in Hellenistic civilization 5. Aarhus: Aahrus University Press.

Potts, Daniel T. 2005. "Cyrus the Great and the Kingdom of Anshan." In *Birth of the Persian Empire,* edited by Vesta Sarkhosh Curtis and Sarah Stewart. The Idea of Iran, vol. I:7–28. London: I. B. Tauris Publishers.

———. 2016. *The Archaeology of Elam: Formation and Transformation of an Ancient Iranian State.* Second edition. New York: Cambridge University Press.

Shishegar, Arman. 2015. *Tomb of the Two Elamite Princesses of the House of King Shutur-Nahunte son of Indada. Neo-Elamite Period, Phase IIIB (ca. 585–539 B.C.).* Tehran: Pažuhešgāh-e Mirās̱-e Farhangī, Sonat-e dastī va Gardešgarī.

Stronach, David. 1978. *Pasargadae: A Report on the Excavations Conducted by the British Institute of Persian Studies from 1961 to 1963.* Oxford: At the Clarendon Press.

———. 1990. "The Garden as Political statement. Some Case Studies from the Near East in the First Millennium B.C." *Bulletin of the Asia Institute* 4:171–180.

———. 2008. "The Building Program of Cyrus the Great at Pasargadae and the Date of the Fall of Sardis." In *Ancient Greece and Iran Iran: Cross-Cultural Encounters,"* edited by Seyyed Mohammad Reza Darbandi and Antigoni Zournatzi. Athens: National Hellenic Research Centre – Hellenic National Commission for UNESCO – Cultural Center of the Embassy of the Islamic Republic of Iran.

Cyrus the Great and Ancient Propaganda

Daniel Beckman
Princeton University

WHO WAS CYRUS THE GREAT? Despite decades of research, we still do not have a definitive answer to this question. Our earliest sources cannot agree on even the basic facts of his life. However, these sources do contain traces of the propaganda created by Cyrus and his officials, intended to shape how his subjects saw him. This paper will attempt to: (a) establish criteria for identifying propaganda captured in Greek histories; and (b) determine how Cyrus' identity would change for different audiences. We shall compare the accounts of Cyrus' birth and early life, as found in the three earliest Greek sources, these being Herodotus' *Histories* (written circa 430–425[1]), Xenophon's *Cyropaedia*, and the known fragments of Ctesias' *Persica* (both early fourth century). The Greek historians were not mouthpieces for Cyrus or his successors, so we should not expect them to repeat the party line uncritically. But within their narratives concerning pivotal moments in Cyrus' life, we may occasionally detect elements of Persian official propaganda.

I begin with a brief consideration of the nature of ancient propaganda, for which I have selected illustrative examples from across the Near East of the first millennium BCE. Next, I will examine the Cyrus Cylinder (c. 539), damaged but otherwise preserved in its original form. This analysis will give us a framework better to understand the narratives of Cyrus' birth and early life in Herodotus, Xenophon, and Ctesias. Our goal is not to determine which version is most accurate, but rather to determine the motivation(s) behind each account.

Propaganda in the Ancient World

In the context of a modern Western democracy, "propaganda" has strongly negative connotations. It suggests a political lie, the misuse of information intended to mislead a group into accepting a given belief or behavior that they might otherwise reject.[2] In an ancient context, however, "propaganda"

---

1. All dates in this section are BCE, unless otherwise noted.
2. Ross 2002; Silverstein 1987; Powell 1982.

must have a broader sense, more akin to "persuasion," as the ruling elites were the source for almost all official information.[3] Following Alan Lloyd, we can define ancient propaganda as "a conscious attempt by a social group to impose or encourage an attitude by exploiting communication media.[4]"

Propaganda must have three components: *sender, message,* and *recipient*.[5] The sender must be an individual or well-defined and unified party. An amorphous and disorganized collection of individuals cannot create a coherent message. In the ancient world, only monarchs, nobles, and religious officials had the capacity to compose and distribute a single, effective message. The sender likely did not compose the message personally, but relied on professional writers, poets, and artists for its composition in their name.[6] The message must conform to the guidelines of a familiar genre, and will rely heavily on symbolic language. When a text conforms to local expectations, the sender can claim to be upholding traditional values or fulfilling traditional roles, and the recipients are more likely to receive it as a product of their own social group, and therefore more acceptable.[7] A well-crafted

3. Ross 2002, 16–17: "The term 'propaganda' was originally associated with propagating or spreading the Christian faith. The word was coined by Pope Gregory XV in 1622 to refer to the *congregio de propaganda* which was an organization of the Roman curia that had jurisdiction over missionary territories ... Propaganda in this sense meant something along the lines of persuasion, preaching, or education."

4. 1982b, 33. There are many competing definitions of propaganda (some of which are listed by Jowett and O'Donnell 2012, 2–7.) I have selected Lloyd's because it does not arbitrarily exclude the possibility of ancient propaganda (as does Ellul 1976) and it is flexible enough to accommodate the various potential sources of propaganda in an ancient society.

5. Ross 2002, 18–20.

6. The realities of archaeology dictate that we are far better informed about written and visual propaganda, but we must remember that propagandistic messages would have been spread orally as well. Liverani 1979, 298–302 suggests that, if we cannot name a specific individual or office responsible for the composition of the message, surely the message originated from the "ruling class" at large (priests, scribes, palace officials). These few highly educated groups would understand the message, with all its literary flourishes and political allusions, better than a peasant would, but nonetheless the core of the message could be spread throughout the realm. Liverani gives the example of Sargon's Letter to Aššur, although preserved as a written document, "would in fact have been read aloud to the god (here more than ever the hypostasis of the whole of Assyria) in a solemn ceremony in the presence of a vast public."

7. Jowett and O'Donnell 2012, 35: "To change old beliefs or to create new ones, a persuader has to build on beliefs that already exist in the minds of the audience. A persuader has to use anchors of belief to create new belief." Porter 2000 examines Esarhaddon's stelae at Til Barsip and Sam'al, erected c. 670 BCE. She demonstrates that, while the stelae in the two cities share much in common, the differences show that the Assyrians were aware of the particularities of the individual communities of their empire, and were able to create nuanced messages crafted to target unique groups of recipients. Specifically, the message sent to Til Barsip, an important trading center and a reliable Assyrian vassal, "was essentially inclusive, encouraging the people of Til Barsip to continue in their loyal support of the Assyrian king and his

propagandistic text targets the audience's emotions, rather than logic, but the text cannot stray too far from truth (or at least commonly believed falsehood) and reason, or it will be rejected wholesale.[8]

A message could take the form of a written or inscribed text, something that could be distributed over great distance and last throughout time without alteration. However, due to the extremely low literacy rates before modern times, a message was more likely to be delivered orally, even if it was composed in written form.[9] Oral traditions are typically not concerned with strict historical accuracy,[10] although modern research has demonstrated

---

heirs (164)." The message sent to Sam'al, less strategically significant and traditionally more independent than Til Barsip, "seems intended as a pointed reminder to potentially disloyal subjects that opponents of Assyria ... would be captured and demeaned (171)."

8. Senders walked the fine line between the effective message and the outright lie. Lloyd 1982b describes the Egyptian *Sesostris Romance*, which was updated several times after foreign conquests of Egypt. Each new version attributed the greatest feats of the foreigners to the Pharaoh Sesostris (Senusret I, reigned c.1971–1926). Thus a "fantasy" was couched in familiar Egyptian terms, and actual historical events were manipulated in the creation of a false history. Likewise, in an analysis of Neo-Assyrian divination texts, Cooley 2014 argues that Esarhaddon manipulated divination practices in such a way that diviners were essentially forced to violate traditional interpretations of celestial phenomena so that any positive omen was claimed as evidence for divine support for Esarhaddon, and any negative omen was either declared irrelevant or was said to apply to a foreign king or land. While we cannot know how the diviners felt about this royal interference with their duties, it is clear that several of them went out of their way to adopt the new methods of divination, even when it required convoluted reinterpretation of celestial movements.

9. When a written text does not specify that it was read aloud, it can be especially difficult to determine how wide an audience may have had access to the message. Porter 1993, 105–117 suggests that Esarhaddon's Nineveh A inscription (for text, translation, and bibliography, see Leichty 2011, 9–26), though interred in the foundations of temples, may have been read to an audience. For an Iranian example, Shayegan 2012, 84–103 argues that Darius' inscription at Bisotun (DB) was originally a written, Elamite composition, which then served as the basis for the Old Persian and Babylonian versions. Further, he argues that Darius specifies that his written message (*dipi-*) is to be read and preserved, and the *oral* content (*ha^nduga-*) of that inscription is to be reported to the people (*kara-*).

10. Vansina 1985 emphasizes that oral traditions are regularly restructured to fit the needs of the current generation of performers and audiences. While there are no laws of restructuring, there are typical patterns: irregularities and unnecessary repetition may be lost; clichés and images could be amplified; events are grouped into epochs; exact numbers are reduced to "few," or "many," or a lucky or unlucky number. See especially Vansina 1985, 162–173, 186–193. Memorization is an obvious factor in the transmission of an oral tradition, but it is not a simple issue of remembering versus forgetting. For example, it is easier to memorize the meaning of a statement or tale, as opposed to the verbatim phrasing of the original. Hence, transmission "is not a reduplicative process, for instance, but a procedure of creative reconstruction (Rosenberg 1987, 81)." Researchers have noted instances where the audience criticizes the accuracy of the tale during the performance: Finnegan 2012, 13–14; Okpewho 2003, 218–224.

that non-literate societies are capable of preserving information accurately for several generations.[11]

Given a particular oral tradition, we cannot know what form it took in previous generations. The variations across different oral cultures admit no universal laws of composition, performance, or transmission, other than that which is dictated by biology. For example, in historical oral traditions, usually the history of the founders is kept, as well as the history of the more recent generations, while mostly everything in between is lost.[12] Whatever the current generation of tellers and hearers deems important is remembered.[13] Herodotus states that he reports "what is said,"[14] from which we can assume that his narrative is based on contemporary accounts in Persia. These were most likely descended from, but not identical with, the original versions from Cyrus' own day.[15] The same assumption holds for Xenophon and Ctesias. The student of the reception of Iranian oral traditions by Greek authors must take the nuanced view that texts, especially in the literate Near Eastern and Greek worlds of the first millennium, are not always strictly either oral or written. In many different traditions, there is a range of interplay that occurs between the orally performed text and a written counterpart.[16] Without knowing more about the specifics of how our Greek

11. Irwin 1981, 67–89 demonstrates that "traditionists" in the Liptako region of West Africa pass on a chronology calculated by dating backwards from the present (as in, "this event took place twenty years ago"). The traditions are not exact, and there are variant traditions, but on the whole, they are internally consistent and agree with other local traditions, as well as information gathered by Western visitors to the region. The Liptako tradition thus accurately preserves reigns and political events, and allows the traditionist to date events of more personal interest, for a period of over 160 years.

12. Vansina 1985, 23–24 calls this phenomenon the "floating gap," as the limit of the span of a tradition moves as the generations go on. I should stress here that we are discussing oral historic traditions, and not epic literature. While the two are not entirely unrelated, we are dealing with the composition and dissemination of a message by a ruling elite for the purpose of maintaining or expanding their power over their subjects. Such a message may be influenced by the literary tropes borrowed from an oral epic tradition, but the two cannot be expected to operate in the same manner.

13. Thomas 1992, especially 108–113.

14. Hdt. 7.152.3.

15. Shayegan 2012, 103–138 speculates that the various classical accounts of Darius' rise to the throne may have been informed by Darius' own oral account (the *haⁿdugā-* mentioned in n. 9 above). The fact that a number of themes found in Herodotus' account, but not DB, also appears in the accession discourse of the Sasanian king Narseh, inscribed at Paikuli (NPi), lends more weight to the idea that Herodotus was informed by an oral, rather than a written, narrative.

16. Finnegan 2005 gives a display of the wide variety of possible interactions between performance and text, from around the world.

historians came into contact with Iranian traditions, we cannot make any more speculations about where their sources fit on the oral-written continuum.[17]

Furthermore, for any message, we have to ask who the intended recipient was. If Greeks were amongst the recipients targeted by Cyrus or later Persians, this would make it more likely that our Greek historians were equipped fully to understand the message. If, however, the messages were aimed solely at non-Greek audiences, then we would expect Greek authors to be more prone to errors and misinterpretations, as they would not be primed to receive the nuances of the message. It is certain that the Great Kings of Persia did, on occasion, make concerted efforts to appeal to Greek sympathies and to seek support from Greek elites.[18] But as we shall see, the messages captured by Herodotus, Ctesias, and Xenophon all would seem to fit better in an Iranian or Mesopotamian milieu, and therefore were unlikely to have had Greeks in mind at the time of composition.

As we examine the Greek accounts of Cyrus the Great, to extract the "original" material will be an ultimately impossible task. However, an understanding of the context of the text can help us determine the sender, recipient, and a general summary of the message. It will also be beneficial to compare our Greek accounts with a Near Eastern account, in this case, the Cyrus Cylinder. The sender and recipient are known, as are its literary and historical contexts, and the message text has been preserved in a fairly complete form. Our analysis will show what to expect from a propagandistic work emanating from Cyrus' court, and this will serve as a model for our analysis of the Greek texts.

The Cyrus Cylinder

In the Cyrus Cylinder, the Persian king claims he was called by the Babylonian god Marduk to restore the proper rituals in the city's temples, and bring peace and prosperity to the citizens. He accuses the previous king, Nabonidus, of failing to uphold the rites due to Marduk. Modern historians

17. Shayegan 2012, 83–108 applies this notion of the oral-literate continuum to Darius' res gestae and its reception by the Greek historians, as well as its impact on later Iranian traditions. As mentioned in note 15, Darius specifically states that he disseminated both a written and oral version of his message. While this illustrates well one possible interaction between written text and performance in the Achaemenid empire, it is not necessarily the case that other royal texts were treated in the same way.

18. For a few examples: Cyrus made an effort to garner support amongst the Ionian Greeks, through the sanctuaries of Apollo at Didyma and Claros (Hdt. 1.157–159; Briant 2002, 37–38); Darius gave political support to tyrants in Ionian *poleis* (Hdt. 4.137); Xerxes appealed to the Argives based on a shared descent from Perseus (Hdt. 7.150).

have taken this as evidence of a religious rift between the Marduk priests and Nabonidus, caused by the latter's excessive patronage of the temple of Sin at Harran. It is unclear if this is historically accurate; Cyrus would have needed a straw man to justify his capture of the city,[19] and the "crimes" of Nabonidus may not have been perceived as such at the time.[20] Besides claiming the support of Marduk, Cyrus pointed to his lineage to establish himself as the legitimate ruler of Babylon. In doing so, he does not once refer to the Median or Persian elements. Instead, he presents himself as the king of Anšan, one of the two capitals of Elam, insinuating a venerable and proud lineage.

Cyrus' message is obvious. He is the savior of the Babylonians, especially the priesthood. It is likely that they were the main recipients, although it may have appealed to the wider elite. His deeds are unequivocally good: his bloodless conquest will restore Marduk's temples, and, perhaps more importantly, make sure that royal patronage flows richly and regularly to the priests. Nabonidus is unequivocally evil: the historical context of his policies is ignored. Cyrus accuses Nabonidus of neglecting the cult of Marduk, and takes credit for restoring the proper sacrifices. But Nabonidus had made the same claims for himself.[21] The crimes with which Nabonidus is charged, and the terms through which Cyrus is praised, are both more or less stock phrases found in accounts of Babylonian regime changes dating back to at least the time of Sargon II. We are dealing not with contemporary unbiased reporting, but *"post eventum* justifications for the defeat of a perfectly legitimate, regular Babylonian ruler."[22]

19. Vanderhooft 2006 and Tolini 2005 give evidence that Cyrus may have had to resort to some violence when taking Babylon. If this was indeed the case, it would have been all the more necessary to emphasize the necessity and benefits of his conquest. In this context, we might keep in mind the report of Cyrus' slaughter of the enemy at Opis, as recorded in the Nabonidus Chronicle: "In the month of Tašrîtu, when Cyrus attacked the army of Akkad in Opis on the Tigris, the inhabitants of Akkad revolted, but he [Cyrus] massacred the inhabitants. The fifteenth day Sippar was seized without battle. Nabonidus fled (ABC iii.12–15 = Grayson 1975, 104–11)."

20. Michalowski 2014, 205–206.

21. In his texts describing his restoration of several temples, he states that Nebuchadnezzar II, grandfather of the king overthrown by Nabonidus, had tried to make a proper restoration. However, the gods had not shown him the original foundations of the temples, so he was forced to make false and therefore structurally unsound surrogates. Nabonidus, loved and aided by the gods, was able to find the foundations (usually laid by a famous predecessor, for example Hammurabi or Naram-Sin) and make a complete and lasting restoration. His intent was to show that he was intelligent, pious, and legitimate, whereas his predecessors, even the great Nebuchadnezzar, were of an unworthy dynasty, deserving to be overthrown. See Schaudig 2010, 155–161.

22. Kuhrt 1990, 143–144. The very fact that Cyrus must spend such energy vilifying Na-

All of this is stated in a form immediately recognizable to the Babylonians. Everything about it was firmly rooted in a long Mesopotamian tradition, and there is nothing about it (besides the name of Cyrus) that can be used to group it with the Achaemenid royal inscriptions.[23] Babylonian, Assyrian, and Sumerian kings had a long history of restoring temples and other structures in Babylon, and preserving their account of this deed by placing an inscribed cylinder in the foundation of that structure. In fact, a fragment of the Cylinder states that Cyrus had found an inscribed cylinder from a previous restoration:

(38b)   As to the wall Imgur-Enlil, the great wall of Babylon, I sought to increase its [secu]rity.

(39)   [. . . . .] The quay made of baked brick on the bank of the city moat, which an earlier king had bui[lt but not com]pleted,

(40)   [. . . . ., which did not yet surround the city] outwards, a work an earlier king had not completed, his troops, the contingent [of his country . . . . into] Babylon.

(41)   [. . . . . with asphal]t and baked brick I built (the walls) anew and [completed the]m.

(42)   [. . . . . hu]ge [door-leaves made of cedar-wood], covered with bronze, thresholds and door fitt[ings, made of ore, (43) I set up (42) in all] their [gates].

(43)   [. An in]scription of Assurbanipal, a former king, [which I fou]nd [therein,]

(44)   [I *treated it respectfully* and put it back into] its [plac]e [*together with my own inscription.*] Marduk, great lord! (45) [May you grant me] as a gift (44) a [lon]g [life],

(45)   [. . . . . and an enduring reig]n! [May I be the king who pleases] your heart for evermore![24]

With these lines, Cyrus draws on Babylonian and Assyrian literary traditions. The reference to Assurbanipal's cylinder, while possibly motived by a genuine discovery, may also have a greater significance. Assurbanipal himself

---

bonidus is a clue that perhaps this view of him was not currently widespread. Nor did it take hold. A case in point being two Babylonian usurpers who at the accession of Darius sought to establish their own legitimacy in Babylon by claiming (truthfully or not) to be the son of Nabonidus (DB 1.77–81; 3.76–83; 4.12–15; 4.28–31; Schaudig 2001, 68.) Kratz 2002, 151 puts the creation of the Verse Account and the Chronicle of Nabonidus after the date of these revolts.

23. Kuhrt 1983, 88; van der Spek 2014, 252–255; and more copiously discussed by Schaudig in this volume.

24. Text and translation follows the new edition by Schaudig in this volume; see also Finkel 2013, lines 38–45.

made a great deal of effort to show respect for Marduk and his cult. Thus, Cyrus' accusations against Nabonidus, and his reference to Assurbanipal, are a clear statement of the divine displeasure at the unworthy Nabonidus, and a promise to the Babylonian elite about what kind of treatment they can expect from Cyrus. Thus, the Cylinder conveys its message through two avenues: for one, Cyrus presented himself to the Babylonians, using Assurbanipal as a model. This was only possibly because the Babylonian priesthood, who composed the text, had access to, and familiarity with, the literary tradition of Assurbanipal, and had been allowed sufficient autonomy by Cyrus to put forward Neo-Assyrian literary customs as a model for Persian proclamations.[25] But regardless of the extent to which Cyrus may have wished to connect himself to Assurbanipal or other Neo-Assyrian rulers, the process of creating an authentic text demanded that the priests make use of models dating back as far the Old Babylonian period in crafting the phraseology of the accusations against Nabonidus and the legitimation of Cyrus.[26]

The form of the Cylinder text was dictated by the requirements of successful propaganda. By claiming to be a pious worshipper of Marduk, Cyrus was identifying himself with the Marduk priests, at least insofar as they had shared interests. He could not claim to be Babylonian himself, but his royal Elamite lineage meant that he was familiar with the customs and expectations of his new subjects. The appropriation of an ancient literary form further established his credentials, and made its arguments more persuasive to his audience.

Herodotus

In Book 1 of his *Histories*, Herodotus tells us that Astyages, King of the Medes, had several dreams that predicted his daughter, Mandanae, would give birth to a son who would overthrow him. In order to prevent this, Astyages married his daughter to Cambyses, a Persian of high rank. Despite this, the dreams continued, and when Cyrus was born, Astyages ordered the child abandoned in the wilderness. The herdsman ordered to carry out the dirty deed faltered at the last moment, and instead raised the boy as his own. The herdsman's wife, Herodotus informs us, was named Spako, which is Median for "dog."[27] When Cyrus grew up, his innate skill and wisdom could not be suppressed by his lowly upbringing, and he soon took his rightful place at his grandfather's court. When he was finally reunited with his parents in Persis, and told his parents how Spako nursed him, they "spread the rumor

---

25. Shayegan 2011, 287–290.
26. See Shaudig, in this volume.
27. Hdt. 1.107–108.

that Cyrus, when he was abandoned, was suckled by a dog, so that their son's salvation would seem more providential to the Persians."[28]

To what extent are these narratives a reflection of Persian propaganda? First, it is obvious that the composer of this tale relied on traditional literary motifs. The motif of the hero exposed as a child is widespread throughout the mythologies of many cultures; Romulus and Remus, Moses, Oedipus, and many others that come effortlessly to mind. This is a clear example of the use of a traditional literary model in a propagandistic text. But whose model(s)? Scholars of classical and Iranian literature have long since connected Cyrus' version to that of Sargon of Akkad, who lived more than 1500 years earlier. According to this fragmentary text, his mother, a priestess, bore him in secret, then set him in a basket in the Euphrates river. Akki, the "drawer of water," found him and raised him as his own.[29] Sargon went on to become king, founder of the dynasty of Agade, and ruling for fifty-five prosperous years. As the Cyrus Cylinder demonstrates, in order to give his rule an aura of legitimacy in the eyes of his Mesopotamian subjects, Cyrus made use of venerable Mesopotamian literary traditions to describe his own life and deeds, so it is possible that he would have adopted Sargon's legend for his own ends. However, there are important variations in the motif, some of which follow cultural divides. Brian Lewis has catalogued seventy-one instances of this motif, and found that in the Semitic tales of Moses and Sargon, the mother of the hero abandons her son, but only because she thinks it is his only chance for safety. In the Indo-European versions, of which Herodotus' Cyrus narrative is an example, the hero is abandoned by someone who wants to destroy the hero.[30] Thus, it is very unlikely that Cyrus' message was crafted for a Mesopotamian audience, with intentional reference to Sargon.

Herodotus himself suggested a second possibility, that Cambyses and Mandanae intentionally manipulated the facts and turned it into a myth to impress the Persians. Herodotus is mistaken here. As we expect from a piece of propaganda, Cyrus defines himself through identity with one party and in opposition to an enemy. Cyrus identified himself with both the Persians and Medes, in opposition to Astyages alone. This narrative may have been composed before Cyrus had overthrown Astyages, and was still trying to build an alliance. Perhaps he calculated that it would be easier to overthrow a single dynast, than to take on the entire Median tribe.

28. Hdt. 1.122.
29. Drews 1974, 389–390; although the text purports to relate the life of Sargon of Akkad, who reigned c.2334–c.2279, scholars are confident that it was composed during the reign of Sargon II, 722–705 (Longman 1991, 55–56).
30. Lewis 1976, 218–318.

The role of the Medes in Near Eastern history, and the realities of the Median "empire," are much debated by scholars. In the archaeological record, there are very few clear traces of the Medes, and indeed scholars have yet to agree on a definite set of criteria for declaring an artifact as "Median."[31] Texts, both Near Eastern and classical, are not much more helpful: while they certainly testify to the existence of the Medes, they give very little reliable information as to what sort of entity they might have represented or to the spatial and temporal boundaries of that entity.[32] With that said, there is no reason to deny that Cyrus could have had biological and cultural links to the Medes. The mystery concerning the Medes in the decades immediately before and after Cyrus impedes our ability to analyze the meaning of the narratives of Cyrus' upbringing at the Median court. In his late-sixth century inscription at Bisotun, the Persian king Darius the Great frequently refers to the Persian and Median troops under his control (*kāra pārsa ut[ā m] āda haya upā mām āha*, "the Persian and Median people in arms that was with me")[33] including Median royal guards,[34] giving clearly the impression that the dominant Achaemenid ethno-classes are the Persians and the Medes. Herodotus also mentions Medes in powerful positions in the Persian empire, such as Datis, one of two commanders of the invasion force sent to destroy Athens and Eretria in 490.[35] This, as well as other indices, suggests that the Medes remained an influential element within the Persian state. It could, however, also indicate that as a distinct and self-conscious ethno-class, they might have viewed Cyrus, who brought an end to Median rule, with some resentment.[36] So, for example, Pierre Briant argued that the stories of Cyrus' Median heritage were Median, anti-Persian propaganda, designed to reveal to Mesopotamian elites the lowly and shallow roots of the Achaemenid

31. For an overview of the problem of Median archaeology, see Genito 2005, especially 324–329. Henkelman 2003 discusses the evidence for Elamite Iranian acculturation, while emphasizing that there is very little evidence at all for a specifically Median presence in the Neo-Elamite period. Kroll 2003, discussing post-Urartian Transcaucasia, has a similar view: the absence of an agreed-upon definition of "Median" art or architecture makes it essentially impossible to argue for the existence of a Median empire, state, or tribe in the region based on archaeological evidence.

32. Sancisi-Weerdenburg 1994; Rollinger 2003; Tuplin 2004.

33. DB 2.18–19.

34. DB 1.13–17.

35. Hdt. 6.94.

36. It is possible that the Median rebel Fravartiš, described in DB 2.13–17, who claimed to be Xšaθrita, son of Cyaxares, may have tried to harness anti-Persian sentiment amongst the Medes. Unfortunately, we know almost nothing about him. It does seem that Darius' eventual punishment of Fravartiš was unusually harsh: "Fravartiš was seized and brought to me; I cut off his nose, ears and tongue, and I put out one of his eyes; at my gate he was held bound, and all the people could look at him. Then I impaled him at Ecbatana (DB 2.70–90)."

monarchy.[37] In the wider Near Eastern world, which could trace its history back to the very foundation of the world, a tribe of Iranian upstarts would have very little legitimacy.

Matthew Waters also places these tales in the "Median milieu" of the early Achaemenid state. However, he argues that the story was most likely crafted by Cyrus or his descendants to stress the essential unity of the Persian and Median groups, and thus convince the Medes that Persian interests were identical with their own.[38] At the present stage of our knowledge, it is difficult to explain the role of the Medes in the Persian state. Still, given what evidence we do have, it is likely that the story of Cyrus' Median heritage was created as an appeal to the Medes.

Throughout Herodotus' *Histories*, the terms "Mede" and "Persian" are used almost interchangeably.[39] Cyrus' empire is perceived as the continuation and extension of the period of Median rule in Asia.[40] We could dismiss this by saying that Herodotus was simply ignorant, and did not differentiate between the two tribes. This would imply that Herodotus received enough information to distinguish between the Medes and Persians, but not enough to understand that distinction. Regardless of whether Herodotus' informants were themselves Medes or Persians, they considered Cyrus to be a mixture of the two. By Herodotus' time, there were many Medes whose fate and wealth were tied up in the success of the Persian empire and it is unlikely that they would actively try to delegitimize it.

Furthermore, if Briant were correct, his interpretation would only make sense if the Medes had created the tale to appeal to the sensibilities of a Mesopotamian audience. But besides the possible connection to the Sargon legend, there is nothing in the Cyrus narratives to suit the expectations of a Mesopotamian audience. The Medes and Persians are the only logical recipients. Cyrus clearly defines his enemy, Asytages, as being exceptionally cruel and abhorred by his subjects: Astyages murdered a child and then fed him to his Median noble father.[41] His crimes only harmed the Medes and Persians, and had no effect on neighboring peoples. Likewise, Cyrus' promises to all his allies concern only the Medes and Persians.[42] Thus, the story

37. Briant 1984, 74–75.
38. Waters 2010, 65.
39. Although Tuplin 1994 argues that the Greeks used "Mede" "when focusing on the empire as an alien, faceless military and political threat." This association was formed because Croesus, master of the Asian Greeks, met his doom when he marched East into Media to punish Cyrus for the conquest of the Median empire.
40. Munson 2009, 458–460.
41. Hdt. 1.119.
42. Hdt. 1.125–126. Unfortunately, this section is clearly a Herodotean creation, as it has

of the rise of Cyrus and his conquest of the Medes had little to offer to a Mesopotamian audience. When Cyrus overthrew Astyages and captured Ecbatana, the Babylonians were interested enough to note it in the so-called Nabonidus Chronicle.[43] But while Cyrus was still courting his fellow Iranians, his messages were targeted at them and them alone. It appears that he was successful: not only did they rally around Cyrus, but also, by the time Pompeius Trogus in the first century BCE reported the story of Cyrus' childhood (as is captured in Justin's *Epitome*), Cyrus had been nursed by an actual dog, not a woman named "Dog."[44]

Xenophon and Ctesias

In the late fifth century BCE, the Persian king Artaxerxes II was forced to fight his own brother, Cyrus (called the Younger) for the throne. Luckily, we have informants from both sides: Xenophon was part of a band of Greek mercenaries hired by Cyrus, while Ctesias served as a physician at the court of Artaxerxes. Both historians were writing for a Greek audience, but their accounts were strongly influenced by what they heard from their respective patrons. Therefore, it is most profitable to compare them side-by-side.

Like Herodotus, Xenophon states that Cyrus was the son of Cambyses the Persian, and grandson of Astyages the Mede. However, in this version, Cambyses is the king of Persia, and Cyrus was raised in his court, never suffering abandonment. Eventually, Astyages invited Cyrus to his court, where he remained until about fifteen years of age. Astyages died a natural death, succeeded by his son Cyaxares. In time, Cyrus came to take the Median throne, but without violence, as in Herodotus. Instead, after winning the support of the army by his valor and wisdom in battle, Cyrus was able peacefully and respectfully to put aside Cyaxares.[45]

Xenophon was writing nearly a century and a half after the death of Cyrus the Great, but Cyrus' biography was never more relevant. This time it was Cyrus the Younger who was the sender, and his message attempted to make use of the reputation of his namesake, himself a usurper. His goal was to bolster his own legitimacy in the eyes of his recipients, the Persian nobles whom he sought as allies. His message can be deduced from a comparison of

Cyrus promise the Persians a life of leisure in exchange for their allegiance; this is part of Herodotus' effort to demonstrate the adverse and decadent effect of luxury on a once hardy people. It is a literary device, and not motivated by historical evidence. See Avery 1978.

43. ABC 7 ii.1.

44. Justin 1.4–6. Fehling 1989, 110–111 argues that the story is not a play on the Iranian "*spaka*/Spako," but on the Greek Κῦρος/κύων, which suggests that the story is a Greek rationalization of a common motif, rather than an authentic Persian tale.

45. Xen. *Cyr.* 5.5.

Xenophon's two works on Persian history, the *Cyropaedia* and the *Anabasis*. There are strong connections between the two works. The first was part history, part meditation on politics, strategy, and religion. In conveying to his Greek readers his own thoughts on ideal kingship, Xenophon used Cyrus as his model. The *Anabasis*, in turn, is an account of Xenophon's own time as a mercenary under Cyrus the Younger. A comparison of the language describing the two men shows that the younger Cyrus was expected to be seen as the embodiment of the virtues of the elder. The *Cyropaedia* is not a history or biography, nor is it a work of total fiction.[46] However one classifies the work, attention should be given to the influence of the propaganda spread by Cyrus the Younger. He, who desired to be king, was at pains to show he would lead a rebirth of the Persian empire. Simultaneously he emphasized the shortcomings of Artaxerxes, especially the loss of Egypt.

Xenophon was not naive, and did not wholly buy into Cyrus' message, nor was the *Anabasis* intended for a Persian audience. A seasoned soldier and politician, Xenophon experienced first-hand the horrors of civil war in Persia. In the *Cyropaedia,* he makes it clear that Cyrus achieved greatness not through good governance and sound political theory, but only by sheer force of will and an innate skill not found in any other king.[47] For all that Xenophon supported Cyrus the Younger and praised his virtue, he was not uncritical in his portrayal. Xenophon makes clear that Cyrus was not responsible for initiating the revolt, but instead was forced to react to Tissaphernes' slanders and insinuations before Artaxerxes. Cyrus' only chance for honorable survival would be to seize the throne himself.[48] Nevertheless Xenophon saw that Cyrus' revolt was a mortal danger not just to Artaxerxes, but to the kingdom itself, and that the only way for a kingdom to remain whole was for the royal family to avoid internal conflicts. The importance of unity within the ruling family is emphasized in the *Cyropaedia*, where Cyrus the Great's final message to his two sons stresses that conflict between brothers will destroy the legitimacy of the dynasty.[49] Xenophon may have been aware of some of Cyrus the Younger's propaganda, but was not willing to repeat it uncritically to his readers.

The figure of Cyrus found in Ctesias' *Persika* is of a very different sort.

46. Hirsch 1985a and Sancisi-Weerdenburg 1985 make the case for authentic Persian elements in the *Cyropaedia*; Tuplin 2012, Lendon 2006, and Stadter 1991, argue that, even if some authentic elements are present, Xenophon has manipulated them for the sole purpose of having a didactic conversation about Greek politics, and was not at all concerned with providing his readers with an accurate depiction of Cyrus and his empire.
47. Xen. *Cyr.* 1.1.4–6, 8.8.1–2; Sage 1994, 165–166.
48. Xen. *An.* 1.1.6–9.
49. Xen. *Cyr.* 8.7.23

Neither his mother nor father are of royal extraction. Instead, his father was Atradates, a thief and a member of the Mardian tribe, a particularly poor and savage band of Iranians.[50] His mother, Argoste, was a goat herder. After Cyrus had begun his rise at the Median court, he was induced to revolt by another tribesman, Oibaras the Cadusian. The latter is so important as being depicted placing the crown on Cyrus' head.[51] Because of a namesake described in Herodotus' account (the Herodotean Oibaras is a groom who devises a ploy to secure the throne for Darius, not Cyrus), we might assume that Ctesias took this character from Herodotus, and then expanded upon it. But it is not enough to consider the chronological order of the two authors. Because Ctesias served at the court of Artaxerxes II, it is assumed that at least some of his information came directly from official sources surrounding the king.

While the Persians still held Cyrus in high regard in the fourth century, it appears that a critical version was present as well. If Cyrus the Younger attempted to establish his legitimacy by comparing himself to the founder of the dynasty, Artaxerxes may have countered this with a message of his own, perhaps suggesting that Cyrus the Elder was not such an illustrious predecessor after all, but the son of a brigand and a goat herder.[52] In contrast, he, Artaxerxes, was the legitimate heir of Darius the Great, whose own impeccable lineage was preserved at Bisotun and recorded by Herodotus.[53] We could speculate that the differing visions of the empire's founder were related to the opposition between the Teispid and Achaemenid branches of the royal family, a rift first brought to light by Darius the Great's over-throw of Bardiya, a legitimate son of Cyrus.[54] However, the fact that Cyrus the Younger was able to use his namesake as a source for his own legitimacy shows that, whatever hostility the Achaemenid line may have felt towards the founder of the empire, Cyrus the Great was still a venerated figure at the end of the fifth century.

Conclusion

In this paper, I set out to investigate the stories concerning the birth and lineage of Cyrus the Great. The different versions collected by Herodotus,

50. F8d 3; Arrian *Anab.* 3.241–43; Q.C. Rufus *Hist. Alex.* 5.6.17ff; Potts 2014, 94–99.
51. F8d 45; Waters 2011.
52. Hirsch 1985b, 73.
53. DB 1.3–6; Hdt. 7.11.
54. Rollinger 1998 and Jacobs 2011 offer full discussions of the possible familial relation-ship between Cyrus and Darius. Regardless of the historical realities, what is of note here is that Darius wished it to be known that he had dynastic legitimacy through Teispes, but not Cyrus.

Ctesias, and Xenophon each show a unique *message* crafted by a particular *sender* for the consumption by one or more specific *recipients*. As the founder of a new dynasty and a new empire, it was vitally important for Cyrus to appeal to the notions of ideal kingship held by his subjects. He could not deny his Persian birth, but he was able to insert himself into whichever traditions dominated in the various communities he conquered: he would be the one restoring the glorious order of the past, and the embodiment of royal virtues, within the targeted culture. We can find other examples of the same strategy at work: Cyrus is declared the Messiah in the Hebrew Bible, following the restoration of the Jews to their Holy Land;[55] Cambyses takes on the titles and functions of a Pharaoh after conquering Egypt;[56] Alexander becomes the half-brother of Darius III.[57] Cyrus' biography continued to be relevant long after his death, and control over the popular understanding of his life was one element of control of the Persian throne. In all these cases, the sender's concern is not so much the truth, as what they want their recipients to believe is true.

55. As argued by Fried 2004, 177–183.

56. Most famously on display in the inscription of Udjahorresnet (Lloyd 1982a); see also Assmann 2002, 367–371, Dillery 2005, 400–403.

57. This appears in medieval Persian literature, such as Nezamī's *Iskandar-Nāmeh*, Tarūsī's *Dārāb-Nāmeh*, and Firdusī's *Shāhnāmeh*. Daryaee 2007; Manteghi 2012.

Bibliography

Álvarez-Mon, Javier. 2013. "Elam in the Iron Age." In *The Oxford Handbook of Ancient Iran*, edited by Daniel T Potts, 457–477. Oxford: Oxford University Press.

Assmann, Jan. 2002. *The Mind of Egypt: History and Meaning in the Time of the Pharaohs*. New York: Metropolitan Books.

Avery, Harry C. 1972. "Herodotus' Picture of Cyrus." *The American Journal of Philology* 93 (4):529–546.

Briant, Pierre. 1984. "La Perse avant l'Empire (un état de la question)." *Iranica Antiqua* 19:71–118.

———. 2002. *From Cyrus to Alexander: A History of the Persian Empire*. Winona Lake, IN: Eisenbrauns.

Carter, Elizabeth, and Matthew W. Stolper. 1984. *Elam: Surveys of Political History and Archaeology*. Berkeley and Los Angeles: University of California Press.

Cooley, Jeffrey L. 2014. "Propaganda, Prognostication, and Planets." In *Divination, Politics, and Ancient Near Eastern Empires*, edited by Alan Lenzi and Jonathan Stökl, 7–32. Atlanta: Society of Biblical Literature.

Daryaee, Touraj. 2007. "*Imitatio Alexandri* and Its Impact on Late Arsacid, Early Sasanian and Middle Persian Literature." *Electrum* 12:89–97.

Dillery, John. 2003. "Manetho and Udjahorresne: Designing Royal Names for Non-Egyptian Pharaohs." *Zeitschrift für Papyrologie und Epigraphik* 144:201–202.

Drews, Robert. 1974. "Sargon, Cyrus and Mesopotamian Folk History." *Journal of Near Eastern Studies* 33 (4):387–93.

Ellul, Jacques. 1973. *Propaganda: The Formation of Men's Attitudes*. New York: Vintage Books.

Fehling, Detlev. 1989. *Herodotus and His "Sources": Citation, Invention and Narrative Art*. Liverpool: Cairns.

Finkel, Irving L. 2013. *The Cyrus Cylinder: The King of Persia's Proclamation from Ancient Babylon*. London: I.B. Tauris & Co Ltd.

Finnegan, Ruth. 2012. *Oral Literature in Africa*. 2nd ed. World Oral Literature Series 1. Cambridge: Open Book Publishers CIC Ltd.

Fried, Lisbeth S. 2004. *The Priest And The Great King: Temple Palace Relations In The Persian Empire*. Winona Lake, IN: Eisenbrauns.

Genito, Bruno. 2005. "The Archaeology of the Median Period: An Outline and a Research Perspective." *Iranica Antiqua* 40:315–340.

Grayson, Albert Kirk. 1975. *Assyrian and Babylonian Chronicles*. Locust Valley, NY: J.J. Augustin.

Harmatta, J. 1971. "The Literary Patterns of the Babylonian Edict of Cyrus." *Acta Antiqua Academiae Scientiarum Hungaricae* 19:217–231.

Henkelman, W. F. M. 2008. *The Other Gods Who Are. Studies in Elamite-Iranian Acculturation Based on the Persepolis Fortification Texts*. Achaemenid History, XIV. Leiden: Nederlands Instituut voor het Nabije Oosten.

———. 2003. "Persians, Medes, and Elamites: Acculturation in the Neo-Elamite Period." In *Continuity of Empire (?): Assyria, Media, Persia*, edited by Giovanni B. Lanfranchi, Michael Roaf, and Robert Rollinger, 73–123. Padova: S.a.r.g.o.n. editrice e libreria.

Hirsch, Steven W. 1985a. "1000 Iranian Nights: History and Fiction in Xenophon's Cyropaedia." In *The Greek Historians: Literature and History: Papers Presented to A.E. Raubitschek,* edited by Michael Jameson, 65–85. Saratoga, CA: ANMA Libri; Dept. of Classics, Stanford University.

———. 1985b. *The Friendship of the Barbarians: Xenophon and the Persian Empire*. Hanover: Published for Tufts University by University Press of New England.

Irwin, Paul. 1981. *Liptako Speaks: History from Oral Tradition in Africa*. Princeton: Princeton University Press.

Jacobs, Bruno. 2011. "'Kyros, der große König, der Achämenide.' Zum verwandtschaftlichen Verhältnis und zur politischen und kulturellen Kontinuität zwischen Kyros dem Großen und Dareios I." In *Herodot und das Persische Weltreich = Herodotus and the Persian Empire: Akten des 3. Internationalen Kolloquiums zum Thema "Vorderasien im Spannungsfeld klassischer und altorientalischer Überlieferungen," Innsbruck, 24.-28. November 2008*, edited by Robert Rollinger, Brigitte Truschnegg, and Reinhold Bichler, 635–663. Wiesbaden: Harrassowitz Verlag.

Jowett, Garth, and Victoria O'Donnell. 2012. *Propaganda and Persuasion*. 5th ed. Thousand Oaks: Sage.

Kratz, Reinhard. 2002. "From Nabonidus to Cyrus." In *Ideologies as Intercultural Phenomena: Proceedings of the Third Annual Symposium of the Assyrian and Babylonian Intellectual Heritage Project, Held in Chicago, USA, October 27-31 2000*, edited by Antonio Panaino and Giovanni Pettinato, 143–156. Melammu 3. Milan: Associazione Culturale Mimesis.

Kroll, Stephan. 2003. "Medes and Persians in Transcaucasia: Archaeological Horizons in Northwestern-Iran and Transcaucasia." In *Continuity of Empire (?): Assyria, Media, Persia*, edited by Giovanni B Lanfranchi, Michael Roaf, and Robert Rollinger, 282–288. Padova: S.a.r.g.o.n. editrice e libreria.

Kuhrt, Amélie. 1983. "The Cyrus Cylinder and Achaemenid Imperial Policy." *Journal for the Study of the Old Testament Journal for the Study of the Old Testament* 8:83–97.

———. 1990. "Nabonidus and the Babylonian Priesthood." In *Pagan Priests. Religion and Power in the Ancient World*, edited by John North and Mary Beard, 119–155. London: Duckworth.

Leichty, Erle. 2011. *The Royal Inscriptions of Esarhaddon, King of Assyria (680-669 BC)*. The Royal Inscriptions of the Neo-Assyrian Period 4. Winona Lake, IN: Eisenbrauns.

Lendon, J. E. 2006. "Xenophon and the Alternative to Realist Foreign Policy: 'Cyropaedia' 3.1.14–31." *The Journal of Hellenic Studies* 126:82–98.

Lewis, Brian. 1976. "The Legend of Sargon: A Study of the Akkadian Text and the Tale of the Hero Who Was Exposed at Birth." PhD dissertation, New York University.

Liverani, Mario. 1979. "The Ideology of the Assyrian Empire." In *Power and Propaganda: A Symposium on Ancient Empires*, edited by Mogens Trolle Larsen, 297–317. Copenhagen: Akademisk Forlag.

Lloyd, Alan B. 1982a. "The Inscription of Udjaḥorresnet: A Collaborator's Testament." *The Journal of Egyptian Archaeology* 68:166–180.

———. 1982b. "Nationalist Propaganda in Ptolemaic Egypt." *Historia: Zeitschrift für Alte Geschichte* 31 (1):33–55.

Longman, Tremper. 1991. *Fictional Akkadian Autobiography: A Generic and Comparative Study*. Winona Lake, IN: Eisenbrauns.

Luckenbill, Daniel David. 1924. *The Annals of Sennacherib*. OIP 2. Chicago, Ill: Univ. of Chicago Press.

Manteghi, Haila. 2012. "Alexander the Great in the Shāhnāmeh of Ferdowsī." In *Alexander Romance in Persia and the East*, edited by Richard Stoneman, Kyle Erickson, and Ian Netton, 161–174. Groningen: Barkhuis.

Michalowski, Piotr. 2014. "Biography of a Sentence: Assurbanipal, Nabonidus, and Cyrus." In *Extraction & Control: Studies in Honor of Matthew W. Stolper*, edited by Michael Kozuh, Wouter Henkelman, Charles E. Jones, and Christopher Woods, Studies in Ancient Oriental Civilizations 68, 203–210. Chicago: The Oriental Institute of the University of Chicago.

Munson, Rosaria Vignolo. 2009. "Who Are Herodotus' Persians?" *Classical World* 102:457–470.

Okpewho, Isidore. 2003. "Oral Tradition: Do Storytellers Lie?" *Journal of Folklore Research* 40 (3):215–232.

Porter, Barbara. 2000. "Assyrian Propaganda for the West: Esarhaddon's Stelae for Til Barsip and Sam'al." In *Essays on Syria in the Iron Age*, edited by Guy Bunnens,, Ancient Near Eastern Studies, Supplement 7, 143–176. Louvain; Sterling, VA: Peeters Press.

———. 1993. *Images, Power, and Politics: Figurative Aspects of Esarhaddon's Babylonian Policy*. Philadelphia: American Philosophical Society.

Potts, Daniel T. 2016. *The Archaeology of Elam: Formation and Transformation of an Ancient Iranian State*. 2nd ed. New York: Cambridge University Press.

———. 2014. *Nomadism in Iran: From Antiquity to the Modern Era*. Oxford University Press.

Powell, Jon T. 1982. "Towards a Negotiable Definition of Propaganda for International Agreements Related to Direct Broadcast Satellites." *Law and Contemporary Problems* 45 (1):3–35.

Rollinger, Robert. 1998. "Der Stammbaum des achaimenidischen Königshauses oder die Frage der Legitimität der Herrschaft des Dareios." *Archäologische Mitteilungen aus Iran und Turan* 30:155–209.

———. 2003. "The Western Expansion of the Median 'empire': A Re-Examination." In *Continuity of Empire (?): Assyria, Media, Persia*, edited by Giovanni B. Lanfranchi, Michael Roaf, and Robert Rollinger, 289–319. Padova: S.a.r.g.o.n. editrice e libreria.

Rosenberg, Bruce A. 1987. "The Complexity of Oral Tradition." *Oral Tradition* 2 (1):73–90.

Ross, Sheryl Tuttle. 2002. "Understanding Propaganda: The Epistemic Merit Model and Its Application to Art." *Journal of Aesthetic Education* 36 (1):16–30.

Sage, Paula Winsor. 1994. "Dying in Style: Xenophon's Ideal Leader and the End of the 'Cyropaedia.'" *The Classical Journal* 90 (2):161–74.

Sancisi-Weerdenburg, Heleen. 1985. "The Death of Cyrus: Xenophon's Cyropaedia as a Source for Iranian History." In *Papers in Honour of Professor Mary Boyce*, edited by H.W. Bailey, A.D.H. Bivar, Jacques Duchesne-Guillemin, and J.R. Hinnells, 459–471. Leiden: E. J. Brill.

———. 1994. "The Orality of Herodotus' *Medikos Logos* or: The Median Empire Revisited." In *Continuity and Change: Proceedings of the Last Achaemenid History Workshop, April 6-8, 1990, Ann Arbor, Michigan*, edited by Heleen Sancisi-Weerdenburg, Amelie Kuhrt, and Margaret Cool Root. Achaemenid History 8, 39–55. Leiden: Nederlands Instituut voor het Nabije Oosten.

Schaudig, Hanspeter. 2001. *Die Inschriften Nabonids von Babylon und Kyros' des Grossen samt den in ihrem Umfeld entstandenen Tendenzschriften: Textausgabe und Grammatik*. Münster: Ugarit-Verlag.

———. 2010. "The Restoration of Temples in the Neo- and Late-Babylonian Periods: A Royal Prerogative as the Setting for Political Argument." In *From the Foundations to the Crenellations: Essays on Temple Building in the Ancient Near East and Hebrew Bible*, edited by Mark J. Boda and Jamie R. Novotny, AOAT 366, 141–164. Münster: Ugarit-Verlag.

Shayegan, M. Rahim. 2011. *Arsacids and Sasanians: Political Ideology in Post-Hellenistic and Late Antique Persia*. Cambridge: Cambridge University Press.

———. 2012. *Aspects of History and Epic in Ancient Iran: From Gaumāta to Wahnām*. Cambridge: Harvard University Press/Center for Hellenic Studies.

Silverstein, Brett. 1987. "Toward a Science of Propaganda." *Political Psychology* 8 (1):49–59.

Stadter, Philip A. 1991. "Fictional Narrative in the Cyropaideia." *The American Journal of Philology* 112 (4):461–491.

Stronach, David. 2001. "From Cyrus to Darius: Notes on Art and Architecture in Early Achaemenid Palaces." In *The Royal Palace Institution in the First Millennium BC: Regional Development and Cultural Interchange between East and West*, edited by Inge Nielsen, 95–111. Athens; Århus; Headington, Oxford; Oakville, CT: Danish Institute at Athens; Distributed by Aarhus University Press.

Thomas, Rosalind. 1992. *Literacy and Orality in Ancient Greece*. Cambridge: Cambridge University Press.

Tuplin, Christopher. 1994. "Persians as Medes." In *Continuity and Change: Proceedings of the Last Achaemenid History Workshop, April 6-8, 1990, Ann*

Arbor, Michigan, edited by Heleen Sancisi-Weerdenburg, Amelie Kuhrt, and Margaret Cool Root, Achaemenid History 8, 235–256. Leiden: Nederlands Instituut voor het Nabije Oosten.

———. 2004. "Medes in Media, Mesopotamia, and Anatolia: Empire, Hegemony, Domination or Illusion?" In *Ancient West & East*, 3, no. 2:223–251. Leiden; Boston: Brill.

———. 2012. "Xenophon's *Cyropaedia*: Fictive History, Political Analysis and Thinking with Iranian Kings." In *Every Inch a King: Comparative Studies on Kings and Kingship in the Ancient and Medieval Worlds*, edited by Lynette Mitchell and Charles Melville, 67–90. Leiden: Brill.

Van der Spek, R. J. 2014. "Cyrus the Great, Exiles and Foreign Gods: A Comparison of Assyrian and Persian Policies on Subject Nations." In *Extraction and Control: Studies in Honor of Matthew W. Stolper*, edited by Wouter Henkelman, Charles Jones, and Christopher Woods, 233–264. Chicago: The Oriental Institute of the University of Chicago.

Vanderhooft, David Stephen. 2006. "Cyrus II, Liberator or Conqueror? Ancient Historiography Concerning Cyrus in Babylon." In *Judah and the Judeans in the Persian Period*, edited by Oded Lipschitz and Manfred Oeming, 351–372. Winona Lake, Ind.: Eisenbrauns.

Vansina, Jan. 1985. *Oral Tradition as History*. Madison, WI: University of Wisconsin Press.

Waters, Matthew. 2010. "Cyrus and the Medes." In *The World of Achaemenid Persia: History, Art and Society in Iran and the Ancient Near East*, edited by John Curtis and St John Simpson, 63–71. London: I. B. Tauris.

———. 2013. "Elam, Assyria, and Babylonia in the Early First Millennium BC." In *The Oxford Handbook of Ancient Iran*, edited by Daniel T Potts, 478–492. Oxford: Oxford University Press.

Cyrus the Great:
A Hero's Tale

Maria Brosius
University of Toronto

I N THE MODERN PERIOD, the classics have continually provided inspiration for writers of fiction, as well as filmmakers. Amidst the wealth of material they are able to draw on exceptional personalities, both historical and fictional, such as Achilles, Alexander the Great, Caesar, and Cleopatra. What is surprising, then, is Cyrus the Great's lack of prominence, despite the fact that he captured the imagination of classical authors, both on account of the story of his upbringing and of his military conquests. He was the founder of the largest empire the world had ever seen in antiquity, long before Alexander the Great was credited with the same achievement – albeit one which enjoyed a much shorter life-span compared to the 230-year duration of Cyrus' realm. The evident fascination with the Persian empire seems to stem from the fact that the preferred perspective – cinematic and otherwise – emanates from the view of the Greek victor, as can be seen in films such as *The 300*,[1] or its spoof version, *Meet the Spartans*,[2] both of which center on the Spartan battle at Thermopylae against the Persian king Xerxes, depicted in a highly exaggerated and unrealistic manner in the two movies, devoid of any resemblance to the historical ruler. Epic films about Alexander the Great, such as the 1956 original and the 2004 version,[3] continue to uphold the praises of the Macedonian, and by extension, Greek hero who conquers the Orient. There is a nagging suspicion that the absence of a film script, which would have carried as its subject the phenomenal conquests and political achievements of the founder of the Persian empire, results from the unease the idea of bringing an eastern hero to the screen still causes.[4]

With this in mind I imagined the figure of Cyrus II as a cinematic hero, and much to my own surprise, discovered unexpected parallels between

---

1. USA 2007, directed by Z. Snyder.

2. USA 2008, directed by J. Friedberg and A. Seltzer.

3. *Alexander the Great*, USA 1956, directed by R. Rossen and *Alexander*, USA 2004, directed by O. Stone.

4. A remarkable exception is the film *Mongol*, which traces the life of the founder of the Mongol empire, Genghis Khan (Russia 2007, directed by S. Bodrow).

Cyrus II and modern-day cinematic heroes. Looking at the key events of Cyrus II's life, as they have been conveyed to us especially through classical sources, our sixth-century conqueror shares a number of key traits with modern fictional heroes. For the present discussion, I have chosen one fictional hero who seems to be particularly apt as a figure of comparison, namely, Jason Bourne, created by Robert Ludlum and the main protagonist of several cinematic blockbusters. The comparison of these figures induces the following two observations. One is the prevailing value and timeless appeal of classical texts in depicting historical heroes – and by the same token of Cyrus' quality as a cinematic hero. The other observation is the need to distinguish between the heroic – but largely fictional – portrait of Cyrus, created already in antiquity, and the historical Cyrus, whom we can grasp most strongly – and most genuinely – in his own creation, the royal complex at Pasargadae.

What does a comparison between the figures of Cyrus and Jason Bourne reveal? Two heroes. Two men in search of an identity. These are two men whose identities become more and more complex, not to say fictional, the more layers of information are being added to their biography. In both cases, different suggestions are being offered as regards their name and background. They are two men who are seemingly of an inherently noble, gentlemanly character, but who, at the same time, possess an unmistakably violent and ruthless streak. They are two heroes about whose upbringing various stories circulate: the childhood of the historical hero, and the training/education of the fictional one. Both seem to have gotten where they are having been manipulated by higher forces: Cyrus II by the Median courtier Harpagus, Jason Bourne by an intelligence officer of sorts, the fictional hero by a covert branch of the CIA. The lifes of both men amount to incredible careers: both traverse their own known worlds (albeit for different reasons) in record time, each in his respective "historical" period. Various stories circulate about the death, real or assumed, of both. Finally, these are two heroes, about whom there is divided opinion as to whether they were virtuous or not.

On the issue of Cyrus' identity, recent scholarship debates the question of his Elamite or Persian ethnicity, considering that the Teispid Cyrus might be of Elamite, rather than Persian background.[5] The more we look into the evidence about Cyrus from Greek, Persian, Elamite, and other Near Eastern sources, the less we seem to be able to get a grasp who Cyrus in fact was. The growing mystery surrounding him began with the dismissal of the

5. Garrison 2011, 375–405; Jacobs 2011, 635–664; Henkelman 2011, 577–634. For the view that Cyrus was a Mede, see Frye 2010, 17–19.

original idea that the figure from the entrance gate at Pasargadae wearing Elamite dress and an Egyptian crown represented Cyrus II. On this point, at least, scholars reached a consensus. An accompanying inscription, which seemingly determined that identification, has been dismissed as a later addition placed there by Darius I.[6] More recently, a deeper engagement into the genesis of the winged figure asserted its Assyrian roots.[7] This fact alone provokes yet another query in our quest to determine Cyrus' identity: by ethnicity Cyrus II may have been Persian, with a strong link to the indigenous Elamite population, but considering the affinity of early Persian art at Pasargadae with Assyria, Cyrus' evocation of Aššurbanipal in the Cylinder,[8] as well as his reliance on Babylonian literature,[9] the concept of Cyrus' symbolic identity becomes relevant. It might indeed be worthwhile considering to what extent Cyrus' ethnicity was of bearing on his "real," rather than the "symbolic," identity he sought to forge by linking himself to Near Eastern predecessors, in whose footsteps he so keenly wanted to follow.

The doorways of Gate R at Pasargadae, which include the figure of the winged genius, were flanked by reliefs of winged bulls known from Neo-Assyrian art.[10] For Stronach, both features were "clearly inspired by Assyrian sculpture, yet here we are not dealing with a replica but rather with an evocation of an established tradition towards a different end."[11] Elsewhere he remarks that the artists of Pasargadae "drew their inspiration from original Assyrian monuments wherever these were still available for inspection."[12] In the Audience Palace, Palace S, we find the remains of stone reliefs representing the type of supernatural beings that are known from Neo-Assyrian palaces, clearly serving as models for the Pasargadae reliefs.[13] But Cyrus went even further in his creation of a royal identity: not only did he link himself with Assyrian predecessors through a careful application of Assyrian artistic elements in Pasargadae, the architecture also established a connection with Lydia and the Ionian Greeks in the use of Ionian columns and, perhaps even

6. Kuhrt 2010, 91; Sekunda 2010, 269.

7. Four-winged genii are known from Assyrian art, especially on the palace reliefs of Ashurnarsipal II (883–859 BCE) at Kalhu/Nimrud and of Sargon II (722–705 BCE) at Dur-Sharrukin. The Assyrian link of the figure from Gate R at Pasargadae was established by Stronach 1978, 51; compare Stronach 2001, 99; Sekunda 2010, 268–271.

8. As well, we may add, Cyrus' modeling his biography on the Sargon legend, if he instigated its dissemination.

9. See Schaudig 2001 for references, especially to the Epic of Creation, *Enūma eliš*, and the Esagil Chronicle. See also Schaudig in this volume.

10. See Stronach and Gopnik 2009.

11. Stronach and Gopnik 2009. See also Stronach's contribution in this volume.

12. Stronach 2001, 99.

13. Stronach and Gopnik 2009; compare Stronach 1997, 44–45; Kuhrt 2010, 90.

more significantly, in modeling his tomb after a Lydian prototype.[14] The founder of the Persian empire claimed the heritage of his conquered lands, Media, Lydia, Babylonia, and accordingly converged their respective royal and palatial designs into an innovative form of Persian royal art.

Until recently, scholars were certain that they had determined his ancestry due to the evocative seal impression found in some Persepolis Fortification tablets, which mentions a certain "Kuraš the Anzanite, son of Šešpeš (Teispes),"[15] who has been identified as Cyrus the Great's grandfather and namesake, Cyrus I. Darius' ascension having raised doubts as to his legitimacy to the throne, Cyrus' ancestry was considered as separate from that of Darius and a justified distinction was made between the early Persians and the Achaemenids.

Most recently, the artistic style of the seal led Mark Garrison to consider it distinct from an early Persian, and the neo-Elamite, style, instead prompting him to identify it as a new art form dubbed "Anzanite," which he considered a style linked to the court of Teispes.[16] If this were to be the case, we would need not only to rethink the attitudes of the early Persians, or those of the Anzanites, towards the Elamites, but also gauge the formers' status compared to the latter. It seems the reattribution of Cyrus I's Cylinder seal and basing it on the models of four "antique" seals from Persepolis,[17] is fraught with significant consequences for our thoughts about the degree of co-operation, co-habitation, and the much advocated acculturation process between Elamites and Persians in the Anšan region.[18] Did the rising Persians and their king in the second half of the seventh century BCE want to distinguish themselves from the Elamites? Could they have afforded, at this early

14. The origin of Cyrus' tomb is still debated. Kleiss 1996, 135–140 favors the idea that the Sardis tomb was based on Persian models, that is, the tomb of Cyrus, and quite possibly for the burial of a Persian. This is followed by Boardman, although he also notes that Cyrus' tomb espoused western building designs (Boardman 2000, 54, 57–60), which allows him to conclude: "We seem then to have a royal Persian tomb invented in Lydia and adopted for one, perhaps two Persian kings, executed in techniques which are essentially not eastern, but Lydo-Iranian, and with features of Greek Ionic architecture" (Boardman 2000, 60). Compare Miller 2003, 304. See also Boucharlat in this volume.

15. For PFS 93*, see Garrison 2011, 375.

16. See Garrison 2011, 400–402.

17. For the seals PFS 93*, PFS 51, PFS 77* and PFS 1308*, see Garrison 2011, 381–390.

18. A point that has received less attention in the discussion of Cyrus' seal is the image itself, an armed horseman, two slain enemies on the ground and an additional wounded one fleeing away from him, not in regard to the artistic image, but to subject matter. The accompanying inscriptions mean that we ought to identify the rider as Cyrus I. He, then, wanted to be depicted as a leader and a warrior who destroys his enemies. Consequently, we may wonder whether early Persian habitation in Elamite territory may have been as peaceful as we have been led to assume.

stage of their development into a powerful polity, to do so? Whatever kudos Teispes, Cyrus I, and Cambyses I ought to receive for having laid the foundation of an emerging polity, they surely were still dependent on Elamites for at least military, if not also administrative, reasons, and on the Elamite elite, whose support they required. Compared to Darius' decisive push for a Persian identity, even the creation of a Persian "class," the Teispids' creation of a court style before a kingdom of some political significance and a seat of power are secured, seems perhaps premature, unless the Persian predecessors of Cyrus II were more powerful than our historical evidence allows us to recognize.

The inscription on the seal of Cyrus I, in combination with Cyrus II's genealogy provided in the text of the Cyrus Cylinder, at least allows us to secure Cyrus II's identity as king of Anšan. In the seventh and sixth centuries BCE, Anšan had been unoccupied, with only sparse evidence of settlement.[19] Notwithstanding its state of disrepair, Anšan as one of the former Elamite royal residences offered an immediate solution to a budding Persian/Teispid power in need of legitimizing itself by creating links to kingdoms that had ceased to exist in a more remote past, or in recent memory. The early Persian kings' claim on Anšan may be compared to Darius I laying claim to Susa shortly after his accession to the throne, in the latter's case manifested in the construction of a palace on the acropolis. One could not afford to leave a former royal capital "unattended," as some usurper, legitimate or not may have laid claim to it.

As for the Greek sources, we are aware of their preferred depiction of Cyrus' alleged humble upbringing. Herodotus and Xenophon preferred the variant in which he was presented as a cast aside offspring with links to a royal house, thus, as is implied, a legitimate heir to the throne of Media, but destined to spend his formative years growing up in humble surroundings. Nicolaus of Damascus and Justin make him the son of a brigand or of a herder, respectively, rising to the status of courtly servant and then to kingship.[20] According to Justin, Cyrus grew up with the herdsman of the king's cattle. Nicolaus of Damascus goes one step further (or lower on the social scale), claiming Cyrus to be a child of a certain Artadates, who was poor and lawless enough to earn his living as a brigand, while Cyrus' mother, called Argoste, was a goat herder. Nicolaus of Damascus also emphasizes Cyrus' nomadic descent from the Mardian tribe, in contrast to Herodotus' claim that Cyrus belonged to the most noble of the Persian tribes, the Pasargadae. Robert Drews has recognized the stories for what they are: literary motifs that ul-

---

19. Potts 2016, 310. Compare also Potts 2011, 35–43.
20. Nicolaus of Damascus *FGrH* 90 F66; Just. 1.4.7–10.

timately derive from the legendary story of Sargon I of Akkad, who had his own interest in having the story about his humble upbringing circulated – a matter of questionable legitimacy.[21] Drews thought that Nicolaus of Damascus took the story from Ctesias, who had heard it while at the Persian court, where he allegedly practiced as a physician. Yet, recently several scholars have placed considerable doubt on Ctesias ever having visited the Persian court.[22] If this were to be true, where would Ctesias, or any later writer of Persian histories, have heard it? In addition, while there is no doubt in Drews' mind that the story of Sargon I entered a "stream of tradition," which eventually brought it down to the Persian period,[23] this still constitutes a 1700-year span, and one which went beyond Mesopotamia to Persia. Alternatively, if we pursue the line of argument that Cyrus modeled his kingship on that of Assyrian kings, should we consider that he himself created yet another link to these rulers, by using a variant of Sargon's story? After all, he must have had access to knowledge about the kings of Assyria and their traditions following the conquest of Babylonia, most likely through Babylonian scholars he consulted. His reference to Aššurbanipal in the Cylinder alludes to the fact that he was aware, or rather, was made aware, of the Neo-Assyrian kings, and these will have included Sargon II (722–705 BCE), who bridged the widest chronological gap between him and his famous predecessor by choosing his name as his own throne name.

As for the story of Cyrus II's accession, it shares one element with that of the fictional hero Bourne. Both figures suffer mental manipulation at the hands of "higher" forces. Jason Bourne, outwardly an unassuming young man with a meek demeanor, has been brainwashed by a secret subdivision of the largest intelligence services, which has turned him into a ruthless assassin. Turning into an apparent rogue villain, he needs to be roped in by his "handlers." The Herodotean hero, too, seems to have been manipulated by a higher force, because Cyrus is being described as not actually fostering any idea of rebellion and conquest himself – the initiative came from the disenfranchised Median courtier, Harpagus, who was bent on exacting revenge for the murder of his son by Astyages.[24] Harpagus instilled in Cyrus the idea to lead the Persians in rebellion against the Medes, offering that he and his troops would desert Astyages' army, thus leading to the Median king's defeat. Cyrus clearly was manipulated and used by Harpagus. The lat-

21. Drews 1974, 387–393.
22. This doubt was expressed by several contributors to the conference volume. See Wiesehöfer, Rollinger, and Landfranchi 2011.
23. Drews 1974, 392.
24. Hdt. 1.123–124.

ter, however, may not have bargained on the fact that Cyrus, once he had rebelled, would keep on conquering the world. He became virtually unstoppable – a rogue hero of sorts.

But there is more: the figure of Jason Bourne possesses an exceptional physical and mental strength that in part stems from his ability to contain anger and channel the use of brutal force. He shares these traits with the historical Cyrus. In all appearance, a man of benign character, there is yet another side to Cyrus. Not only does the Nabonidus Chronicle record that he could occasionally act brutally, that is, destroy a city and its inhabitants if they failed to surrender in a timely fashion,[25] but Herodotus too tells us that Cyrus could be aggressive to the point of being volatile. In Babylonia, he "punished" the river Diyala when it did not do his bidding and he lost one of the sacred horses.[26] This comes very close to the actions of a mad king in Herodotean historiography, echoed in the numerous sacrilegious acts of Cyrus' son Cambyses II, and more markedly in the almost identical act of madness committed by Xerxes, whom we encounter whipping the Hellespont in anger after a storm destroyed part of the bridge that his troops en route to Hellas were supposed to cross.[27] As for Babylon itself, Herodotus' version stands strikingly in contrast to that of Near Eastern accounts. According to him, Babylon was not peacefully taken, but by cunning design (Cyrus ordered the flow of the waters of the Euphrates to be channeled off, and the city rendered accessible) and military force. Which source is closer to the historical truth? One should think our primary sources, the Nabonidus Chronicle and the Cyrus Cylinder, except for the fact that relevant events described in both were written post eventum, with Cyrus being the editor of the Cylinder text, and bearing in mind that this section of the Nabonidus Chronicle was written after Cyrus II had claimed the Babylonian throne. In contrast, Herodotus wrote some 120 years after the conquest of Babylon, yet he may have gathered his information on Babylonian affairs independently from Cyrus' propaganda.

If the last remarks emphasized the portrait of Cyrus as a harsh, brutal conqueror, we may counterbalance this image in pointing out his mental strength. The fact that it is Herodotus who alludes to these traits of character is perhaps unexpected, and we ought to wonder to what extent he was

25. The usually very supportive Nabonidus Chronicle still reports a massacre perpetrated by Cyrus' army against the Babylonian population at Opis: "In the month Tešrit, Cyrus having joined battle with the army of Akkad at Upû (Opis) on the bank of the Tigris, the people of Akkad fell back. He [Cyrus] pillaged and massacred the population. The fourteenth, Sippar was seized without struggle. Nabonidus fled" (Glassner 2004, no. 26, iii.12–15; 236–237).

26. Hdt. 1.189–190.1.

27. Hdt. 7.34–5.

conscious of Cyrus' "other" side.[28] He allows him to emerge in the *Histories* as the first conqueror who employs diplomatic skills in order to contain the extent of a military action. This is most poignantly expressed in the description of Cyrus' conquest of Lydia. Prior to the conquest, Cyrus sent messengers to the Ionians, offering them favorable conditions if they were to switch sides and surrender to him peacefully. They declined. Yet finding themselves on the wrong side, soon after Cyrus' victory over Croesus, the Ionians and Aeolians sent messengers (*angeloi*) to Sardis to ask that they be treated by the new sovereign on the same terms as those they had when they were under the overlordship of Croesus. Cyrus responded with an allegoric tale. There once was a flute player who saw some fish in the sea and played his flute to them in the hope that they would come ashore. When they refused to do so, he took a net, netted a large catch, and hauled them in. Seeing the fish jumping about he said to them: "You had best cease from your dancing now; you would not come out and dance then, when I played to you." The moral of the tale was to demonstrate to the Ionians and Aeolians that they were ready to obey him only after Cyrus' victory, but had refused to do so beforehand when Cyrus had asked them to revolt against Croesus. Thereupon, the Ionian cities began to prepare their defense against a Persian attack, except for Miletus, which had accepted the conqueror's terms in time.[29] Herodotus depicts a Persian king endowed with shrewd diplomatic skills: the catch is that this diplomacy worked as long as the other party acted according to the king's bidding. If they failed to comply with his demand, or, as in the case of the Ionians and Aeolians, came round to accepting it too late, military action replaced diplomatic negotiations.

We find Cyrus being similarly described conducting "peaceful negotiations" in his encounter with Croesus, in which Herodotus adds to the realistic atmosphere by referring to the interpreters who facilitated communication between the two kings.[30] The same Cyrus is also being described by Herodotus with the – altogether doubtable – ability to read and write.[31] These abilities add to Herodotus' intention to present Cyrus II as a well-educated political leader, not merely a conqueror. Overall, Herodotus must have been quite intrigued by the founder of the Persian empire, depicting him as an intellectual conqueror who favored peaceful means and mediating skills over violent ones.

28. The following remarks draw on a previous discussion on Persian diplomacy, for which see Brosius 2012, 150–164.

29. Hdt. 1.141. Brosius 2012. The story is a variant of Aesop's fable *The Fisherman with the Flute* (Fable 9).

30. Hdt. 1.86.

31. Hdt. 1.124–125.1.

Following his conquest of Media, Cyrus did what a (conquering) king in the ancient Near East considered good practice: marry the daughter of the (defeated) king, or at least keep the foreign princess at his court to avoid anybody else marrying her. Legitimate claim to the throne of Media still needed to be secured and ascertained. Accordingly, so Ctesias, he married Amytis, daughter of Astyages.[32] Of a Lydian princess, or indeed a Babylonian, sadly we know nothing. But Cyrus II is said to have married a Persian noble girl, Cassandane, daughter of Pharnaspes, himself a Persian, and an Achaemenid.[33] Cassandane was the mother of the heir to the throne, Cambyses II. Did Cyrus, at this point, have a sense of creating a dynasty, as Darius I will do so after him, and indeed did with the Achaemenids? Were "Persian" marriages favored over foreign ones, which may have been concluded merely maintain good diplomatic relations?

To return to Astyages and Cyrus II, and Herodotus' version of the familial link, the marriage between Mandane and the insignificant outsider Cambyses I:[34] by all accounts it is not very likely Astyages would marry his daughter Mandane to a socially and politically inferior Persian, Cambyses I. We know that in his time, and for centuries before him, political marriage alliances were standard practice among the royal houses of the eastern Mediterranean, Egypt, the Hittite empire, and the ancient Near East. The Lydian king Alyattes had married his daughter Aryenis to Astyages,[35] while previously a Median princess had been married to the Babylonian king Nebuchadnezzar.[36] These kings knew their self-worth and what they were worth to others. Marriage alliances were part of establishing and maintaining that status of the "brotherhood."[37] That meant to acknowledge each other as kings of equal standing. So, when we get to Cambyses I, he must have held a certain political status among these kings, in order for Astyages to give his daughter Mandane in marriage to him, in which case this event did not happen for the reasons Herodotus assumes. A small piece of supporting evidence that Cambyses' status may have been closer to that of Astyages may be gauged from the fact that the name Mandane re-appears among the names of royal princesses, as that of a daughter of Darius I.[38] If we accept this argument, then we ought to move the goalposts and conclude that Cyrus was able to build his

---

32. Ctesias *FGrH* 688 F9 (1) (= Lenfant 2004, F9 (1), 108–109). The name Amytis recurs as that of a daughter of Xerxes I in Ctesias *FGrH* 688 F13 (24) (= Lenfant 2004, F13 (24), 123.
33. Hdt. 3.2.2.
34. Hdt. 1.107.1; Xen. *Cyr.* 1.2.1.
35. Hdt. 1.74.4.
36. Jos. *Contra Appion* 1.19.141.
37. On this subject, see now Podany 2010.
38. Diod. Sic. 11.57.1; see also Schmitt 2011, no. 191, 234–235.

power on the foundation his father had already established, as he must have been politically strong enough to have attracted Astyages' attention, and be considered by him as a worthy partner in a political alliance. Going back to Mark Garrison's suggestion of a Teispid court, his idea of a strong Persian political power prior to the reign of Cyrus II gains further support.

Finally, both the historical and the fictional hero share the variant accounts of their respective deaths. Reports of Cyrus' death in the Greek sources range from a heroic death in battle to dying peacefully in bed surrounded by his family; whereas in Xenophon, Cyrus summons his sons to his bedside to divide his empire among them,[39] thus, presenting the happy end of a piece of historical fiction, Herodotus has him die in a battle against the Massagetae, his body being mutilated as an act of revenge by their queen Tomyris.[40]

What are we to conclude from this – rather broad – comparison between the historical and the fictional hero? On the one hand, it confirms that ancient historians, and especially historians of ancient Persia, have to make do with the scraps of information history has left them. Sometimes more "scraps" appear, and reveal fascinating new aspects, such as in the case of the copy, or possibly copies, of the Cyrus Cylinder,[41] which allow us to gain new and vital insights into certain historical facets. Specifically, in the case of the founder of the Persian empire we have to concede that information about the historical Cyrus is sparse, and much of it is borne out of the imaginative, creative, and literary-minded heads of ancient Greek authors. These were influenced at least in part by ancient Near Eastern literature, when we meet them in their early attempts at writing history, or shining as budding novelists or biographers, or impressing their views as philosophers and even as dramatists on their audiences. Yet, in their descriptions of the heroic, fictional figure of Cyrus they used techniques comparable to those still used today by creators of fictional modern heroes: a mysterious personal background, a nobility of character, a complex personality, an able fighter who, at the same time, exercises self-control and uses cunning and diplomacy to maximum effect. On the level of storytelling, the lasting appeal of the classics for a modern audience lies in their narrative technique. As to the historical figure of Cyrus we may conclude that it is our primary evidence, that is the Near Eastern sources, which provides us with a Persian king, who from the start of his conquering career displayed a considerable

39. Xen. *Cyr.* 8.7.

40. Hdt. 1.214.3–5. On Cyrus' death, see also Ctesias *FGrH* 688 F9 (= Lenfant 2004, F9 (7–8), 112–113).

41. Finkel 2013.

understanding of the power of manipulation and propaganda. Long before Darius I perfected that power of propaganda at Mount Bisotun, Cyrus II knew the importance of how to present himself as a peace-loving conqueror and to imbed his rule in the history of royal predecessors. He recognized the importance of his *Sitz im Leben*, his place in history as a ruler who – possibly – in the dissemination of his own childhood legend, in the use of his royal titulature, in the foundation of a new city, in the construction of his own royal palace and the architecture employed here, as well as in his account of the conquest of Babylon, complete with borrowings from Babylonian scholarship, even in the use of the cylindrical shape to document his Babylonian *res gestae*, wanted to be perceived as a king who continued the greatness of the kings of Assyria, as well as that of Lydia, and even Media and Elam.

Bibliography

Boardman, John. 2000. *Persia and the West*. London: Thames and Hudson.

Brosius, Maria. 2012. "Persian Diplomacy Between 'Pax Persica' and 'Zero-Tolerance.'" In *Maintaining Peace and Interstate Stability in Archaic and Classical Greece*, edited by J. Wilker, 150–164. Mainz: Verlag Antike.

Drews, Robert. 1974. "Sargon, Cyrus, and Mesopotamian Folk History." *Journal of Near Eastern Studies* 33:387–393.

Finkel, Irving. 2013. *The Cyrus Cylinder: The King of Persia's Proclamation from Ancient Babylon*. London: I. B. Tauris.

FGrH = Jacoby, Felix. 1954–1964. *Die Fragmente der griechischen Historiker*. 3 vols. Vol. III: *Geschichte von Städten und Völkern: Horographie und Ethnographie (A–C)*. Leiden: E. J. Brill.

Frye, Richard. 2010. "Cyrus the Mede and Darius the Achaemenid?" In *The World of Achaemenid Persia. History, Art and Society in Iran and the Ancient Near East*, edited by John Curtis and St. John Simpson, 17–19. London: I. B. Tauris.

Garrison, Mark B. 2011. "The Seal of "Kuraš the Anšanite, Son of Šešpeš" (Teispes), PFS 93*: Susa – Anšan – Persepolis." In *Elam and Persia*, edited by Javier Álvarez-Mon and Mark B. Garrison, 375–405. Winona Lake: Eisenbrauns.

Glassner, Jean-Jacques. 2004. *Mesopotamian Chronicles*. Edited by Benjamin R. Foster. Society of Biblical Literature Writings from the Ancient World, Number 19. Atlanta: Society of Biblical Literature.

Henkelman, Wouter F. M. 2011. "Cyrus the Persian and Darius the Elamite: A Case of Mistaken Identity." In *Herodot und das persische Reich / Herodotus and the Persian Empire: Akten des 3. Internationalen Kolloquiums zum Thema 'Vorderasien im Spannungsfeld klassischer und altorientalischer Über-*

lieferungen, Innsbruck 24.-28. November 2008, edited by Robert Rollinger, Brigitte Truschnegg, and Reinhold Bichler. Classica et Orientalia 3, ser. eds. Reinhold Bichler, Bruno Jacobs, Giovanni B. Lanfranchi, Robert Rollinger, et al., 577–634 Wiesbaden: Harrassowitz.

Jacobs, Bruno. 2011. "'Kyros, der grosse König, der Achämenide': Zum verwandtschaftlichen Verhältnis und zur politischen und kulturellen Kontinuität zwischen Kyros dem Grossen und Dareios I." In *Herodot und das persische Reich / Herodotus and the Persian Empire: Akten des 3. Internationalen Kolloquiums zum Thema 'Vorderasien im Spannungsfeld klassischer und altorientalischer Überlieferungen, Innsbruck 24.-28. November 2008*, edited by Robert Rollinger, Brigitte Truschnegg, and Reinhold Bichler. Classica et Orientalia 3, ser. eds. Reinhold Bichler, Bruno Jacobs, Giovanni B. Lanfranchi, Robert Rollinger, et al. , 635–664. Wiesbaden: Harrassowitz.

Kleiss, Wolfram. 1996. "Bemerkungen zum 'Pyramid Tomb' in Sardes." *Istanbuler Mitteilungen* 46:135–140.

Kuhrt, Amélie. 2010. *The Persian Empire. A Corpus of Sources from the Achaemenid Period*. New York: Routledge.

Lenfant, Dominique. 2004. *Ctésias de Cnide: La Perse, l'Inde, autres fragments*. Collection des Universités de France: Série grecque. Paris: Les Belles Lettres.

Miller, Margaret C. 2003 "Greece II: Greco-Persian Cultural Relations." *Encyclopædia Iranica* 11:304.

Podany, Amanda H. 2010. *The Brotherhood of Kings: How International Relations Shaped the Near East*. Oxford: OUP.

Potts, Daniel T. 2016. *The Archaeology of Elam: Formation and Transformation of an Ancient Iranian State*. Second edition. New York: Cambridge University Press.

———. 2011. "A Note on the Limits of Anšan." In *Elam and Persia*, edited by Javier Alvarez-Mon and Mark B. Garrison, 35–43. Winona Lake, Indiana: Eisenbrauns.

Schaudig, Hanspeter. 2001. *Die Inschriften Nabonids von Babylon und Kyros' des Grossen samt den in ihrem Umfeld entstandenen Tendenzschriften: Textausgabe und Grammatik*. Münster: Ugarit Verlag.

Schmitt, Rüdiger. 2011. *Iranische Personennamen in der griechischen Literatur vor Alexander d. Gr.* Vol. V: *Iranische Namen in der Nebenüberlieferungen indogermasnischer Sprachen*. Faszikel 5A. Edited by Rüdiger Schmitt, Heiner Eichner, Bert G. Fragner, and Velizar Sadovski. Iranisches Personennamenbuch – Iranische Onomastik 9. Wien: Verlag der Österreichischen Akademie der Wissenschaften.

Sekunda, Nicholas. 2010. "Changes in Achaemenid Royal Dress." In *The World of Achaemenid Persia. History, Art and Society in Iran and the Ancient Near East. Proceedings of a Conference at the British Museum 29th September - 1st October 2005*, edited by John Curtis and St John Simpson, 255–271. London: I. B. Tauris.

Stronach, David. 1978. *Pasargadae: A Report on the Excavations Conducted by the British Institute of Persian Studies from 1961 to 1963*. Oxford: Clarendon Press.

———. 1997. "Anshan and Parsa: Early Achaemenid History, Art, and Architecture on the Iranian Plateau." In *Mesopotamia and Iran in the Persian Period: Conquest and Imperialism, 539–331 BC: Proceedings of a Seminar in Memory of Vladimir G. Lukonin*, edited by John Curtis, 35–53. London: Trustees of the British Museum by British Museum Press.

———. 2001. "From Cyrus to Darius: Notes on Art and Architecture in Early Achaemenid Palaces." In *The Royal Palace Institution in the First Millennium BC*, edited by I. Nielsen. Monographs of the Danish Institute at Athens 4, 95–111. Aarhus: Aarhus University Press.

Stronach, David, and Hilary Gopnik. 2009. "Pasargadae." *Encyclopædia Iranica*, online edition, 2009, available at http://www.iranicaonline.org/articles/pasargadae (accessed on 30 April 2017).

Wiesehöfer, Josef; Robert Rollinger; and Giovanni B. Lanfranchi, eds. 2011. *Ktesias' Welt / Ctesias' World*. Classica et Orientalia 1. Wiesbaden: Otto Harrassowitz.

Cyrus the Great and Roman Views of Ancient Iran

Jason M. Schlude
College of Saint Benedict and Saint John's University

WHILE REFERENCES TO CYRUS THE GREAT are limited in Roman authors, they nevertheless provide us with an interesting and valuable line of research that stands to enrich our understanding of Roman views of ancient Iran. Most scholars today continue to emphasize that the Romans of the late Republic and early Empire cast the Parthians as an "other" people, against which they defined themselves. Often, such interpretations emphasize distance and hostility as a result of the opposition. A consideration of Cyrus in Roman thinking, however, may caution us from adopting this position in its entirety, leading us to see more complexity in Roman views. In short, the figure of Cyrus was important to these Romans, and they understood their Parthian neighbors (the new "Persians") as connected to it. Rather than totally rejecting the Parthians as an "other," the Romans also connected them to Cyrus the Great, a powerful individual whom they venerated. This process would have created and encouraged a level of familiarity with, and respect of, the Parthians – a conclusion in step with the trend of some more recent observations made on the basis of the material evidence. In the end, while Roman views of Cyrus the Great shed no new historical light on the career of this Persian king, they nevertheless demonstrate that in his afterlife Cyrus remained a meaningful and significant part of the ancient Mediterranean consciousness and imperial history.

I. Remembering Cyrus

The Roman world did not forget Cyrus the Great. Indeed, Cyrus surfaces in Latin writers of the Roman Republic and Empire. In the Augustan period, the poet Tibullus (or one in his circle) alludes to Cyrus' crossing of the Gyndes River.[1] In the reign of Tiberius, the historian Valerius Maximus recalled the famous dream of Cyrus' mother, which foretold his future power.[2] In the second century CE, the historian Tacitus notes a particular shrine in Hierocaesarea consecrated while Cyrus was king.[3] Possibly in the second

1. Tib. 3.7.141–142.
2. Val. Max. 1.7(ext.).5.
3. Tac. *Ann.* 3.62.

or third century CE, Justin, summarizing the Augustan historian Pompeius Trogus, compares the first Parthian king Arsaces with Alexander the Great, Romulus, and Cyrus.[4] In the fourth century CE, another historian, Ammianus Marcellinus, praises the intellectual power of the emperor Julian while comparing him to Cyrus.[5] And the philosopher Boethius, born in the fifth, and writing in the sixth, century CE, recalls Cyrus in the context of Croesus' unfortunate fate.[6] As these few nuggets suggest, Cyrus remained part of the Mediterranean consciousness.

A particularly entertaining entry point into the subject of Cyrus in the Roman world comes to us from Marcus Tullius Cicero. In late summer of 51 BCE, this Roman statesman and orator found himself in Asia Minor as governor of the Roman province Cilicia. It was a difficult time to be in the Roman east. In 54–53 BCE, Marcus Licinius Crassus, then the governor of Syria, carried out an ill-starred invasion of the Parthian empire. The Roman found himself outmatched by the Parthians, and his legions were slaughtered, standards captured, and his head lopped off, only to be carried to Armenia where it was used as a stage prop in a performance of Euripides' *Bacchae* for the kings of Armenia and Parthia.[7] Not long after in 52 BCE, the Parthians responded by engaging in a short-lived raid west of the Euphrates into Syria. But in August 51 BCE, it seems they were interested in slightly more substantial action, crossing again into Syria and briefly attacking Antioch.[8] Though Cicero and his troops saw no action against the Parthians, who remained near Antioch in Cyrrestice in winter 51–50 BCE before pulling back into the Parthian empire in the spring, the threat left a major impression on him and led him to write a flurry of letters to Roman colleagues making reference to Parthians in one way or another. Ultimately, fearful of the Parthians, Cicero launched an attack on a mountain people in the region of Amanus and then tried to secure a triumph back at Rome for it, claiming that his action had in fact scared the Parthians off. The senate was not persuaded. Even in a time of political gridlock and incompetence the prestigious body retained some good sense.[9]

4. Just. *Epit.* 41.5.5–6; cf. 38.7.1.
5. Amm. Marc. 16.5.8.
6. Boeth. *Consolatio Philosophiae* 2.P2.
7. The main ancient accounts are: Plut. *Crass.* 14–33; Dio Cass. 39.33.2, 40.12.1–28.2. For discussion, see Rawlinson 1872, 150–181; Debevoise 1938, 78–95; Tarn 1951, 604–612; Ziegler 1964, 32–33; Bivar 1983, 48–56; Sherwin-White 1984, 279–290; Sullivan 1990, 306–309; Wolski 1993, 128–133; Farrokh 2007, 135–140; Sampson 2008, especially 94–147; Sheldon 2010, 29–49; Traina 2011; Weggen 2011.
8. Dio Cass. 40.28.1–40.30.3. See also Schlude 2012, 16–19.
9. The relevant letters of Cicero include: *Fam.* 2.17, 3.3, 3.8, 8.5, 8.7, 8.10, 15.1–4; *Att.* 5.9, 5.11, 5.14, 5.16, 5.18, 5.20–21, 6.1–2, 6.4, 6.6, 6.8, 7.2, 7.26, 8.11. For a relatively recent discussion of Cicero in this context, see Engels 2008, 23–45.

For our purposes, these developments are significant, since they gave rise to an epistolary comment of Cicero referring to Cyrus the Great. In February 50 BCE, when Cicero still anticipated (incorrectly) a serious renewal of the Parthian invasion of 51 BCE, he wrote to his friend Papirius Paetus. The letter mainly deals with private affairs, but its opening refers to the Parthians and implies that Cicero had corresponded previously with Paetus on the issue:

> Your letter has made me a most excellent general. I was quite ignorant that you were so experienced in military affairs. I see that you often have read the books of Pyrrhus and Cineas. So I plan to obey your orders and, besides this, to have some little boat on the seacoast. They say that one cannot find any better defense against the Parthian cavalry. But why do we joke? You do not know with what general you are dealing! The Cyropaedia [Παιδείαν Κύρου], whose pages I had worn down in reading, I have fully exemplified in this command.[10]

In short, Cicero was saying that he was ready for the Parthians. The image conjured of Cicero trying to recall leadership lessons from Xenophon's treatise on Cyrus, perhaps even feverishly re-skimming parts of it to pick up pointers, while awaiting a Parthian attack, is amusing, ironic, and in the end quite telling.

This allusion to Cyrus in the Roman literary record is typical. It is rather off-hand, based on the Greek historiographic tradition, self-centered, and positive. The question is: what can we do with it – and other references in the same vein? Considering that Cyrus in the Roman world is a derivative of Greek accounts, it will shed little new light on the historical career of Cyrus. And as far as this holds, we face a quick dead end to one potential line of inquiry. With all this in mind, there may be little wonder that scholars have not worked heavily on the issue.[11] Yet the references that we have deserve more consideration. In this essay, I hope to begin the discussion on this issue and underscore one potential line of inquiry: how do we square Roman views of Cyrus, founder of the Persian empire, with Roman views of the Par-

---

10. Cic. *Fam.* 9.25.1: summum me ducem litterae tuae reddidere. plane nesciebam te tam peritum esse rei militaris. Pyrrhi te libros et Cineae video lectitasse. itaque obtemperare cogito praeceptis tuis; hoc amplius, navicularum habere aliquid in ora maritime; contra equitem Parthum negant ullam armaturam meliorem inveniri posse. sed quid ludimus? nescis, quo cum imperatore tibi negotium sit. Παιδείαν Κύρου, quam contriveram legendo, totam in hoc imperio explicavi. All translations are my own.

11. There remains little in the scholarship that focuses on the significance of Cyrus specifically in the Roman world. A possible exception to the rule is Rosivach 1984, 1–8, who discusses Roman views of Cyrus, but as part of an exploration of Roman views of Persians more generally and with an emphasis on the impact of the Greek literary tradition on Rome.

thians, inheritors of that empire? As the following will suggest, Cyrus may make our understanding of the latter subject more complex.

II. Previous Scholarship on Roman Views of Parthians

If there has been relatively little scholarship on the significance of Cyrus in the Roman world, there has been much discussion of Roman views of the Parthians. In general, the consensus is clear: the Romans viewed and constructed the Parthians as an enemy.[12] And most often as a result, scholars assume that Parthia served as a complete *other* for the Romans – a process that encouraged their opposition to, distance from, and hostility with, the Parthians. As part of this argument, scholars like Spawforth have noted how much the Romans placed the Parthians in the Persian mold, viewing themselves as the champions against the New Persians.[13] Merriam has written specifically that Latin poets cast the Parthians as Persians to heighten the conflict of the Romans and Parthians.[14] While others, such as Sonnabend and Shayegan, argue that Augustus aimed at coexistence with Parthia and, to support this policy, therefore portrayed the Parthians as the Persians of old and the Romans as the *defenders* against Persia (rather than *aggressors* – a fine, but important distinction that would not require proactive Roman military behavior), they still note that Romans generally viewed Parthians as an "imperial *other*," and their approach still emphasizes the Parthians as an alien *other*, to whom the Romans were opposed, and with whom they were in conflict.[15]

Finally, another prominent researcher's work on Roman sculpture, gems, cameos, and paintings would suggest that even the material record would support this picture.[16] Indeed on the one hand, Schneider learnedly and eloquently points out that Roman views of the "Orient" as represented in material depictions were not as one-sided and negative as many have assumed today, since many depictions consisted of stereotyped images (borrowed from the Greeks) of youthful, handsome Persians and Trojans, the latter being the ancestors of Rome. But on the other hand, he seems to mark out the Parthians as exceptional. While we have images of Parthians depicted in this positive Persian/Trojan tradition, sporting Phrygian caps,

12. Campbell 1993, 217, simply and directly summarizes the position: "the Parthians came to be seen as natural enemies of Rome, an idea which persisted through to the third century AD." See, more recently, Sheldon 2010, 194–196.
13. Spawforth 1994, 233–247.
14. Merriam 2004, 64–65.
15. Sonnabend 1986, 209–210; Shayegan 2011, xiii–xiv, 332–340, who uses the phrase "imperial *other*"; compare Lerouge 2007, 119–122.
16. See, for example, Schneider 2007, 50–86.

youthful clean-shaven faces, and double-belted tunics,[17] Schneider argues that Romans nevertheless saw their world as far distant from, and opposed to, Rome. For the tension, compare his final summary comments with his analysis elsewhere. In the conclusion of his 2007 article, he notes:

> ... the image of the handsome Oriental turned out to be a particularly successful icon as it became loaded with a set of different and inconsistent meanings. The image oscillated between Trojan friend, venerated Oriental deity and Parthian enemy, and embodied a strange conceptual overlap between the categories of friend and foe ... For Rome, the Oriental as friend and foe were not two opposing poles.[18]

Yet elsewhere he states:

> ... the Parthian was Rome's most distinctive cultural Other. The Roman idea of the Other world of the Parthians acquired its fixed form after the return of the standards in 20 BCE. It was a world at a vast distance from Rome, beyond the frontier of the Roman empire ... This *orbis alter* existed outside the *orbis Romanus* and did not impinge upon the Romans' view of their own supremacy. This Augustan concept of two opposing worlds reflects two apparently incongruent but interconnected issues of Roman imperial ideology, namely the asymmetry between Rome and the East, and Rome's interest in the (Parthian) Orient as her only true cultural counter-pole.[19]

The picture that emerges is one that seems to underscore an ambivalence in Roman views of various eastern figures, which included some very positive associations, but shows unwillingness to fully extend that favorable assessment to the Parthians. Despite being dressed in the same attractive garb as other easterners, the Parthians did not enjoy the same appreciation, according to Schneider. In this way, his general perspective aligns well with the other scholarship. The communis opinio is clear: the Parthians were a quintessential *other* for the Romans.

But another classical art historian takes a slightly different – and significant – stance.[20] In his extensive discussion of the image of Parthians in

17. Consider the glass gem in Berlin with Parthians offering up standards to Nike (Schneider 2007, 61, fig. 9) and the likely reconstructions of the standing Parthians in the Basilica Aemilia in Rome (Schneider 2007, 73, figs. 21–22). There were, of course, more historically accurate images of Parthians in the Roman world as well. The most famous example would be the Prima Porta Parthian with his beard and v-neck belted tunic (Schneider 2007, 55, figs. 2–3).
18. Schneider 2007, 79.
19. Schneider 2007, 60.
20. For what follows, see Rose 2005, 21–75.

Augustan Rome, in which he emphasizes Parthians as subordinate partners in peace with Rome, Rose also has noticed how Romans dressed Parthians in eastern/Trojan garb, which again had positive associations in Rome. And he is quick to point out how carefully Romans tried to distinguish Roman figures from Parthians on monuments as a result, the point being to highlight their essential difference. Yet, in contrast to Schneider, Rose concedes that the positive associations would have in fact rubbed off on the Parthians, about whose depiction, on the Parthian Arch of Augustus, he states: "The visual effect of the costume on the Augustan spectator would consequently have been much less pejorative than is usually assumed."[21] Rose's idea is simple, but persuasive: if it looks like a Persian/Trojan, it was probably viewed akin to a Persian/Trojan – in a more positive manner. Here then, the Parthians are not the quintessential Roman *other*. It is not as though they were not presented and viewed as hostile in many instances, as Rose would admit, but the picture was more complex. There was room perhaps for praise of Parthians.

With this in mind, we see two defined positions in modern scholarship. The first – and dominant one – is the Roman view of Parthians as *other*. The second – and perhaps emerging one – is the Roman view of Parthians as slightly more nuanced. I would like to suggest that this more nuanced view, which Rose illustrated on the strength of the material evidence, may find some corroborating support in the Latin literary tradition, and in particular in the way Cyrus the Great has been depicted therein for Romans.[22]

III. Roman Views of Parthians as Persians

First, however, we should point out how the Latin literary traditions, while underscoring the idea of a Roman and Parthian opposition, eventually presented the Parthians as neo-Persians who were threatening the Romans, with the consequence that the Romans must seek to harm or destroy them.

There is clear evidence from a range of sources that Romans identified the Parthians as Persians. Not only does Cicero at times make the connection,[23] as well as the historian Eutropius in the fourth century CE,[24] but also the Augustan poets equated the Parthians with the Persians. Before

21. Rose 2005, 34–35.

22. Along these lines, this paper is part of a scholarly trend aimed at problematizing the concept of the Other and appreciating all the complexity of identity construction and cultural borrowing. Good examples of this trend are Gruen 2005 and 2011.

23. E.g. Cic. *Dom.* 60.

24. Eutrop. *Brev.* 7.9 reviews the accomplishments of Augustus vis-à-vis Parthia, writing: Armeniam a Parthis recepit. obsides, quod nulli antea, Persae ei dederunt. reddiderunt etiam signa Romana, quae Crasso victo ademerant.

turning our attention to the poets Horace and Ovid, who make a number of such references, we shall first consider a public event in the same period that unequivocally confirms this association. In the year 2 BCE, there was a mock naval battle in Rome that reenacted the engagement of the Athenians and Persians at Salamis in 480 BCE.[25] Such a reenactment would seem peculiar perhaps except for the circumstances prompting and surrounding it.[26] In the same year, Augustus dedicated the temple of Mars the Avenger in his Forum in Rome, which henceforth would house the military standards lost to the Parthians by Crassus at Carrhae (as mentioned earlier). Augustus won them back through diplomacy in 20 BCE, relocated them from a monopteros of Mars on the Capitoline hill to this new temple for Mars the Avenger in 2 BCE, and had the battle of Salamis refought in Rome to celebrate the occasion. It was timed, no doubt deliberately, also to coincide with the departure of Augustus' grandson Gaius for a Parthian campaign (a campaign which ultimately did not take place). In short, the mock battle reflected and reinforced the fact that Romans viewed the Parthians as Persians – and themselves in the tradition of the Athenians.

And while one can already see in this equation the idea of the new Persians being aggressively malicious to Rome (as malicious as the Persians of old were against Hellas), with Roman bellicosity as the result, poets like Horace and Ovid indicate that this was not an uncommon Roman perspective. Two select examples suffice to make the point. To begin with Horace, in his first ode he praises Augustus as second only to Jupiter. He writes, "Whether he [Augustus] will drive in a just triumph the subdued Parthians who threaten Latium or the conquered Seres and Indians of the region of the East, second to you [Juppiter] he will rule fairly the happy world."[27] Here, Horace imagines Augustus riding in a future victory parade with the Parthians captive before him. Such an image necessarily implies that Augustus will have conducted a military campaign against the Parthians. And in case any Roman needs justification for the venture, he presents the Parthians as a threat to Rome. In fact, the two ideas are clearly linked. Parthian aggression (real or imagined) demanded Roman action.

The same motif of Romans conquering and triumphing over menacing Parthians surfaces in Ovid – although here the projected triumph is for Augustus' grandson Gaius to fulfill, the same who set out on the abortive

25. See Dio Cass. 55.10, specifically 55.10.7; *Mon. Anc.* 23; Ov. *Ars Am.* 1.171–172.
26. For some discussion of what follows, see Spawforth 1994, 238; Rose 2005, 45–50; Schlude *forthcoming*.
27. Hor. *Carm.* 1.12: ille seu Parthos Latio imminentis / egerit iusto domitos triumpho / sive subiectos Orientis orae / Seras et Indos, / te minor latum reget aequos orbem.

Parthian campaign of 2 BCE. In this case, the reference falls into Ovid's *Ars Amatoria* (*The Art of Love*), in which the author is giving Roman men advice on how to win over Roman women. In his introduction to the part of the poem addressing the art of seduction at a triumph, Ovid writes:

> Look! Caesar prepares to add to the conquered world that which was missing. Now Far East, you will be ours! Parthian, you will pay the penalty! You Crassi who lied buried, rejoice! And also the standards that harshly have suffered barbarian hands! An avenger is on hand and, though in his early years, announces himself the general, and wars that should not be waged by a boy, a boy carries out.[28]

Next, while discussing how Gaius' youth shall not be a liability, Ovid describes in more detail the Parthian enemy, adept at casting arrows from horseback, and forecasts victory and triumph:

> Therefore that will be the day, on which you, most beautiful of all, will go forth golden with four snow-white horses. Before you will go commanders, burdened with chains upon the neck in order that they may not find safety in the flight previously used.[29]

Finally, he concludes by imagining the Roman men pretending to know, and informing their love interests of, the identities of all the captives and symbols of the defeated, including among them "Persia" and "a city in Achaemenid valleys."[30]

In short, Ovid writes of the Parthians as Persians, emphasizes their hostility, which resulted in the defeat of Crassus and capture of Roman standards, and assures his audience that young Gaius will give them their just deserts. The image is clearly one of violent opposition.

Many other references could be mustered to make the same general point,[31] but one final reference aptly shows how deep the opposition ran. To return to Horace, in *Odes* 3.5, he encourages Augustus once again to conquer the Parthians, to right the wrongs committed when they defeated Crassus –

28. Ov. *Ars Am.* 1.177–182: ecce, parat Caesar domito quod defuit orbi / addere: nunc, oriens ultime, noster eris. / Parthe, dabis poenas: Crassi gaudete sepulti, / signaque barbaricas non bene passa manus. / ultor adest, primisque ducem profitetur in annis, / bellaque non puero tractat agenda puer.

29. Ov. *Ars Am.* 1.213–216: ergo erit illa dies, qua tu, pulcherrime rerum, / quattuor in niveis aureus ibis equis. / ibunt ante duces onerati colla catenis, / ne possint tuti, qua prius, esse fuga.

30. Ov. *Ars Am.* 1.225–226: hos facito Armenios; haec est Danaëia Persis: / urbs in Achaemeniis vallibus ista fuit.

31. E.g. Hor. *Carm.* 3.6.9–12, 4.14.41–52; *Epod.* 7.9–10; cf. Verg. *Aen.* 12.843–860, where one of the Furies, sent down by Zeus as an omen of defeat for Turnus and the Rutulians, is likened to a dangerous Parthian arrow.

a theme with which we are all too familiar. But here, Horace focuses on the Roman captives that the Parthians took and settled within their empire:

> Have the soldiers of Crassus lived as husbands shamefully joined to barbarian wives and (o corrupt senate and customs!) grown old in service of enemies turned fathers-in-law under a Median king, the Marsian and Apulian forgetful of the holy shields and name and toga and eternal Vesta, even while the temple of Jupiter and the city of Rome remain unharmed?[32]

Indeed, using the Romans now living in the Parthian empire, Horace betrays how in the thinking of some Romans Parthia was wholly an *other*. To be a Parthian, one must forget all that Rome holds dear: its history, citizenship, and gods. In short, a review of the Latin literary traditions finds much to support the scholarly consensus on Roman views of Parthia as marked by hostility and distance.

IV. The Significance of Cyrus

Yet, to return to Cyrus, consideration of that particular Persian in Roman thinking may suggest that the picture drawn above is perhaps too dire, too wrought with rejection, hostility, denigration, and distance that all necessarily ensued from the proposition that Parthians were the Roman *other*.

The references to Cyrus mentioned at the outset may have been offhand, but they are not without significance. Even if Romans only mentioned Cyrus sporadically, that small quantity of references cannot be used to suggest that Cyrus was rejected or unimportant to them. On the contrary, the Romans (especially in the late Republic and early Empire) thought about Cyrus frequently. To be sure, it was no coincidence that Cicero was paging through the *Cyropaedia* (or at least pretending to) when expecting another Parthian attack in the Roman east in 50 BCE. Other writings of Cicero – as well as other sources – suggest he and other Romans frequently thought about the life and career of Cyrus. Elsewhere, reflecting on effective oratory and the advantages of fluency, charm, and passion in pleading a case, Cicero contrasts the simplicity of some Roman authors "whom no one reads" with "that famous *Cyropaedia*" which they do read.[33] And certainly one of those who also read this work was Julius Caesar, as Suetonius tells us:

---

32. Hor. *Carm.* 3.5.5–12: milesne Crassi coniuge barbara / turpis maritus vixit et hostium, / pro curia inversique mores! / consenuit socerorum in armis / sub rege Medo Marsus et Apulus, / anciliorum et nominis et togae / oblitus aeternaeque Vestae, / incolumi Iove et urbe Roma?

33. Cic. *Brut.* 29.112: at Cyri vitam et disciplinam legunt, praeclaram illam quidem. See also Cic. *QFr.* 1.2.7.

Clearly almost everyone knew that a death befell [Caesar] of just
the sort that he had preferred. For at one time, when he had read in
Xenophon that Cyrus in his final illness had issued certain orders for
his funeral, [Caesar] despised so slow a form of death and wished for
himself a sudden and swift one.[34]

All such references indicate that the *Cyropaedia* was central to the aristo-
cratic Roman reading list.

With this in mind, it is interesting to consider what connection, if any,
the Romans made between Cyrus and the Parthians. As we have seen, they
saw the Parthians as the new Persians. And if Cyrus was the most famous
Persian known to them, then many Romans must have linked the two, their
view of the Parthians being informed to some degree by Cyrus – especially
Xenophon's Cyrus.

Fortunately, we can go beyond mere speculation in this matter. We have
references where the Romans explicitly connected Cyrus and the Parthians.
For example, in *Odes* 2.2, Horace reflects on the qualities of generosity and
greed, looking at the Parthian king Phraates IV, who eliminated his brothers in his quest for the throne as an example of the latter. In this context,
he writes:

> When Phraates was restored to the throne of Cyrus, Virtue,
> disagreeing with the common folk, removed him from the number of
> the fortunate and taught the people to forget false words, inasmuch
> as it confers kingdom, a safe diadem, and lasting victory on the one
> who sees heaps of treasure, but without backward glance.[35]

Here we see Horace linking the Parthian king with the Persian throne, or
rooting the Arsacid house in the Achaemenid dynasty. The same conclusion
should be drawn from an oft-cited – and debated – passage from the later
Tacitus, who at one point discusses Parthian territorial ambitions in the
Near East in 35 CE:

34. Suet. *Iul.* 87: illud plane inter omnes fere constitit, talem ei mortem paene ex sententia
obtigisse. nam et quondam, cum apud Xenophontem legisset Cyrum ultima ualitudine man-
dasse quaedam de funere suo, aspernatus tam lentum mortis genus subitam sibi celeremque
optauerat. It is also noteworthy that if Caesar was reading *Cyropaedia* 8.7, which discusses the
end of Cyrus (one might compare Hdt. 1.201–214, where Cyrus the Great meets a rather different and more violent fate), he had read through nearly the whole work and made it to the
end!

35. Hor. *Carm.* 2.2.17–24: redditum Cyri solio Phraaten / dissidens plebi numero beatorum
/ eximit Virtus populumque falsis / dedocet uti / vocibus, regnum et diadema tutum / def-
erens uni propriamque laurum / quisquis ingenti oculo inretorto / spectat acervos. See also
Carm. 3.29.27.

Although he [Artabanus] out of fear of Germanicus was faithful to the Romans and just to his own subjects, soon he behaved with arrogance towards us and brutality against his people, since he was confident in his successful wars against his surrounding nations, despised the old age of Tiberius and his harmless nature, as he thought it, and was eager for Armenia. When the king [of Armenia] Artaxias had died, he imposed Arsaces, the oldest of his children, on it [Armenia], with insult added and envoys sent to demand back the treasure of Vonones that was left behind in Syria and Cilicia. And he threw about arrogant threats about the old boundaries of the Persians and Macedonians, (saying) that he would invade the possessions of Cyrus and then Alexander.[36]

This passage, which is frequently discussed in the context of the potential Achaemenid program of the Arsacids – an issue not necessarily of bearing on our present analysis[37] – makes it nonetheless clear that Romans in the first century CE perceived the Parthians as the inheritors of Cyrus' empire.

This is significant as it offers a new angle on Roman views of Parthians. Beyond being of great interest to Roman literati, Cyrus the Great also served as a model of political leadership to Roman elites. Of course this was not something new: as already mentioned, the Roman celebration of Cyrus was informed by the construction of Cyrus in the Greek literary tradition, specifically in the work of Xenophon, whose treatment of the monarch was exceedingly positive.[38] This notwithstanding, the Romans seem to have possessed a genuine respect and reverence for Cyrus, if Cicero's desire to emulate Cyrus' example (*totam in hoc imperio explicavi*) may serve as a gauge of Roman appreciation.

This is also reflected in other Latin writings, where Romans further complimented and looked to connect themselves to Cyrus. To continue further the discussion on Cicero, we might turn to his *Republic*, a famous dialogue on political institutions. While in it Cicero identified problems of monarchy, he still emphasized the excellence of Cyrus:

36. Tac. *Ann.* 6.31: is metu Germanici fidus Romanis, aequabilis in suos, mox superbiam in nos, saevitiam in popularis sumpsit, fretus bellis quae secunda adversum circumiectas nationes exercuerat, et senectutem Tiberii ut inermem despiciens avidusque Armeniae, cui defuncto rege Artaxia Arsacen liberorum suorum veterrimum imposuit, addita contumelia et missis qui gazam a Vonone relictam in Syria Ciliciaque reposcerent; simul veteres Persarum ac Macedonum terminos seque invasurum possessa Cyro et post Alexandro per vaniloquentiam ac minas iaciebat.

37. For discussion and bibliography, see Shayegan 2011, especially 39–41, 293–295.

38. See Gruen 2011, 53–65, which also reviews previous scholarship. In the *Cyropaedia*, Xenophon presents Cyrus as a most effective king.

Therefore, although the Persian Cyrus was a most just and wise king, yet this does not seem most desirable, since the property of the people (for that is the meaning of republic as I said before) is ruled by the nod and decision of one man.[39]

There may be little surprise then that the same author looked to establish cultural parallels between Roman practices and those of Cyrus. Hence, in a discussion of burial practices, Cicero notes the following.

> But indeed that form of burial seems to me very old, which Cyrus used, according to Xenophon. For his body was returned to the earth, and in this way having been placed and interred as if under the cover of his mother, he was buried. We learned that our King Numa was buried with the same ritual in that tomb which was not far distant from the Altar of the Fountain, and we know that the Cornelian family used this form of interment continuously up to our present time. The remains of Gaius Marius, which had been buried by the Anio River, Sulla in his victory ordered to be dispersed, driven on as he was by an excessively bitter hatred, to which he would not have yielded, if he had been as prudent as he was violent.

The fact that Cicero claimed Cyrus' preference for inhumation was echoed by Romans, including the impressive likes of King Numa Pompilius (founder of Rome's most important religious practices), the famed family of the Cornelii (the most successful Roman family of the Roman Republic), and the revered Gaius Marius (one of the most famous self-made Romans of the Republic) is telling.[40] Cicero associated Cyrus with effectiveness, justice, and brilliance, and he judged it as a mark of distinction when Romans exhibited cultural similarities.

Yet, not only Cicero made such connections. Consider also Livy. Reflecting on whether Alexander the Great would have been able to defeat Rome (clearly not, from the Roman perspective!), Livy first considers the fame of Alexander, saying that in large part it owed to his early death, while still vic-

---

39. Cic. *Rep.* 1.43: itaque si Cyrus ille Perses iustissimus fuit sapientissimusque rex, tamen mihi populi res (ea enim est, ut dixi antea, publica) non maxime expetenda fuisse illa videtur, cum regeretur unius nutu ac modo. See also 1.44.

40. Cic. *Leg.* 2.56: At mihi quidem antiquissimum sepulturae genus illud fuisse videtur, quo apud Xenophontem Cyrus utitur: redditur enim terrae corpus, et ita locatum ac situm quasi operimento matris obducitur. Eodemque ritu in eo sepulcro quod haud procul a Fontis ara est, regem nostrum Numam conditum accepimus, gentemque Corneliam usque ad memoriam nostram hac sepultura scimus esse usam. C. Marii sitas reliquias apud Anienem dissipari iussit Sulla victor acerbiore odio incitatus, quam si tam sapiens fuisset, quam fuit vehemens.

torious. To show what would have happened, had he lived longer, he notes that, "as for Cyrus, whom the Greeks celebrate with praise most of all, what else except a long life offered a changing fortune to him, just as recently Pompey the Great."[41] To be sure, Livy is interested in the fall of Cyrus in this passage, but we should not ignore the positive elements. Livy identified Cyrus as praiseworthy and comparable not only to Alexander, obviously, a sensational figure, but even to the Roman Pompey – one of the greatest Roman generals ever.

In the end, it is hard to view Cyrus as anything but positive among Roman intellectuals. And their interest (even if spotty in the literature) in connecting him to Roman customs and figures is notable. He may have been the founder of a foreign empire, but the Romans nevertheless celebrated him, established common ground with him, and looked to him as a model for themselves.

But we may even go farther than this. Since the Romans saw the Parthians as heirs to the Achaemenids and successors to Cyrus, we must concede that Roman views of the Parthians were not likely all characterized by distance, derision, and rejection. Yes, those elements were there, and there was opposition between Rome and Parthia, but placing the Parthians in the league of the Persians, and specifically Cyrus, would have lent them the familiarity, standing, and respect accorded to the Persians of old, and their archetypal king.

The use of foreign peoples in identity construction was a complex process that did not always produce forthright, linear projections. I would say that the tortuous Roman view of the Parthians is yet another example. That the Parthians, Rome's formidable enemies, were not reduced to the cliché of inferior foes in the Roman imaginary owes greatly to Cyrus' figure, which in his afterlife remained a meaningful and significant part of the ancient Mediterranean consciousness and imperial history.[42]

41. Livy 9.17.6: Cyrum, quem maxime Graeci laudibus celebrant, quid nisi longa vita, sicut Magnum modo Pompeium, vertenti praebuit fortunae. Here Livy is referring to the violent death of Cyrus in 530 BCE, while on campaign against the Massagetae in eastern Iran, as reported by Hdt. 1.204–214. Once again, this conflicts with the account of Xenophon's *Cyropaedia*, which speaks of Cyrus' peaceful death in old age; see n. 34.

42. I would like to thank Dr. Rahim Shayegan for the kind invitation to participate in the *Cyrus the Great: Life and Lore* international conference at UCLA. This paper comes of that participation. Dr. Shayegan's efforts to ensure that Cyrus the Great, as well as ancient Iran in general, be properly appreciated in our time have enriched the field. He is a consummate scholar, host, and friend. He has my gratitude.

Select Bibliography

Bivar, A. D. H. 1983. "The Political History of Iran under the Arsacids." In *The Cambridge History of Iran,* edited by E. Yarshater, 7 vols., 3.1:21–99. Cambridge.

Campbell, J. B. 1993. "War and Diplomacy: Rome and Parthia, 31 BC–AD 235." In *War and Society in the Roman World,* edited by J. W. Rich and G. Shipley, 213–240. New York.

Debevoise, N. C. 1938. *A Political History of Parthia.* Chicago.

Engels, D. 2008. "Cicéron comme proconsul en Cilicie et la guerre contre les Parthes." *Revue belge de philologie et d'histoire* 86:23–45.

Farrokh, K. 2007. *Shadows in the Desert: Ancient Persia at War.* Oxford.

Gruen, E. S., ed. 2005. *Cultural Borrowings and Ethnic Appropriations in Antiquity.* Stuttgart.

Gruen, E. S. 2011. *Rethinking the Other in Antiquity.* Princeton.

Lerouge, C. 2007. *L'image des Parthes dans le monde gréco-romain: Du début du Ier siècle av. J.-C. jusqu'à la fin du Haut-Empire romain.* Stuttgart.

Merriam, C. U. 2004. "'Either with Us or Against Us': The Parthians in Augustan Ideology." *Scholia: Studies in Classical Antiquity* 13:56–70.

Rawlinson, G. 1873. *The Sixth Great Oriental Monarchy: Geography, History, and Antiquities of Parthia.* London.

Rose, C. B. 2005. "The Parthians in Augustan Rome." *American Journal of Archaeology* 109: 21–75.

Rosivach, J. 1984. "The Romans' View of the Persians." *The Classical World* 78.1:1–8.

Sampson, G. C. 2008. *The Defeat of Rome: Crassus, Carrhae, and the Invasion of the East.* Barnsley.

Schlude, Jason M. 2012. "The Parthian Response to the Campaign of Crassus." *Latomus* 71:11–23.

Schneider, R. M. 2007. "Friend and Foe: The Orient in Rome." In *The Age of the Parthians,* edited by V. S. Curtis and S. Stewart, 50–86. London.

Shayegan, M. R. 2011. *Arsacids and Sasanians: Political Ideology in Post-Hellenistic and Late Antique Persia.* Cambridge.

Sheldon, R. M. 2010. *Rome's Wars in Parthia.* London.

Sherwin-White, A. N. 1984. *Roman Foreign Policy in the East, 168 B.C. to A.D. 1.* London.

Sonnabend, H. 1986. *Fremdenbild und Politik: Vorstellungen der Römer von Ägypten und dem Partherreich in der Späten Republik und Frühen Kaiserzeit.* Frankfurt.

Spawforth, A. 1994. "Symbol of Unity? The Persian-Wars Tradition in the Roman Empire" In *Greek Historiography*, edited by S. Hornblower, 233–247. Oxford.

Sullivan, R. D. 1990. *Near Eastern Royalty and Rome, 100–30 BC.* Toronto.

Tarn, W. W. 1951. "Parthia" In *The Cambridge Ancient History*, edited by S. A. Cook, F. E. Adcock, and M. P. Charlesworth, 12 vols., 9: 574–613. Cambridge.

Traina, G. 2011. *Carrhes, 9 juin 53 av. J.-C.: Anatomie d'une défaite.* Paris.

Weggen, K. 2011. *Der lange Schatten von Carrhae: Studien zu M. Licinius Crassus.* Hamburg.

Wolski, J. 1993. *L'empire des Arsacides.* Leuven.

Ziegler, K. H. 1964. *Die Beziehungen zwischen Rom und dem Partherreich: Ein Beitrag zur Geschichte des Völkerrechts.* Wiesbaden.

The Shaping of Political Memory:
Cyrus and the Achaemenids in the Royal Ideologies of the Seleucid and Parthian Periods[1]

Marek Jan Olbrycht
University of Rzeszów

Introduction

THIS STUDY FOCUSES ON THE ASSOCIATIONS of the Seleucids (312–64 BCE), Arsacids (248 BCE–224 CE), and minor post-Achaemenid dynasties with the figure of Cyrus the Great and the Achaemenids (550–330 BCE) after the demise of the dynasty. I consider Cyrus the Great as part of the Achaemenids, even though in the opinion of some scholars he represented another (Teispid) clan.[2] The development of royal ideology in Western Asia over several centuries is not an easy subject to present in a short paper. But I shall try to explain why rulers of the Seleucid and Parthian periods linked their dynasties with the Achaemenids, what the particular context of such associations were, and who their target audiences were. There have been many misunderstandings on all of these points, due to the scarcity of evidence, fallacious assumptions, and the misjudgments of historical facts.

The Achaemenids and Alexander of Macedonia

The Achaemenids established the world's first universal empire, spanning territories over three continents – Asia, Africa, and for some time Europe. Persian power was established by Cyrus the Great (559–530 BCE) – eulogized by the Iranians, Jews, Babylonian priests, Greeks, and others – who managed to make a not very numerous people inhabiting the lands along the Persian Gulf masters of an empire stretching from Afghanistan to the Aegean Sea, giving rise to the largest state of those times. The Achaemenid state grew at an astounding rate under Cyrus' successors, Cambyses and Darius I. In the course of about four decades from 550 to 510 BCE, it attained its maxi-

---

1. The present article was written thanks to funding from the Humboldt Foundation, the Gerda Henkel Stiftung (Germany), and the Institute for Advanced Study at Princeton (USA), that true paradise for scholars, which awarded me membership for 2017–2018.
2. See Waters 2014, 225; and Jacobs 2011.

mum extent, stretching from Egypt and Libya to the Indus Valley (Pakistan) and Syrdarya (Uzbekistan), from Macedonia and Thrace in Europe to the Persian Gulf. In many respects, the Achaemenids inherited the legacy of the Iranian Medes and other peoples of the Ancient East (Babylonia, Elam, Urartu, and Assyria). Their vast state, equipped with a good administrative structure, a developed economy, and magnificent royal residences at Pasargadae, Persepolis, Susa, and Babylon, provided a reference and model, on which subsequent Iranian empires, such as the Seleucids and Arsacids, drew. Achaemenid patterns were also imitated by minor rulers of Western Asia, including Media Atropatene, Armenia, Pontus, Cappadocia, and Commagene.

One of the contentious issues is the model of kingship and system of government that was replacing the Achaemenid empire in the period of the decline of the Achaemenids and the reign of Alexander in Iran. In the last phase of his reign, 330–323 BCE, Alexander pursued a pro-Iranian policy. He did not consider himself an Achaemenid, but he evidently assimilated the manners of an Iranian ruler, adopting the Iranian costume and regalia, and following Iranian practices in reforming his armed forces and building up the social elite of his empire. In fact, he was king over the Iranian world, and many of those in the upper social estates of the Iranian lands making up his empire supported him. His first and principal wife Roxana was Iranian, albeit not an Achaemenid, and Alexander IV, his son and heir, was half-Iranian.[3] So, for many Iranians Alexander was not just an invader and a representative of the Macedonian and Greek world, but regarded as one of their own, a monarch who cherished the cultural and religious traditions of Iran.

Alexander revered Cyrus II's memory and it is highly likely that his concept of equal rights for Iranians alongside Macedonians was modeled after the pro-Median policies of Cyrus II and his successors. In many specific actions, Alexander was in all probability inspired by the acts of Cyrus.[4]

The struggles following Alexander's death released powerful separatisms in Iranian satrapies. A process began in which Iranians from the Plateau and Central Asia became gradually independent from Macedonian domination, such as in Media Atropatene. A similar development took place in Cappadocia, Armenia, and Pontus, where Iranian dynasties were established that had significant impact on the situation in Iran proper.[5]

3. On Alexander's pro-Iranian policies, see Olbrycht 2010; 2013c. See also Briant 2010; Olbrycht 2008; Olbrycht 2010; and Olbrycht 2013a.

4. On Alexander as Cyrus' imitator, see Olbrycht 2013c, 52–54.

5. See Olbrycht 2013a, 159–182.

The Seleucids

Seleucus and his dynasty emerged out of the struggle over the succession to the legacy of Alexander. Political and military support from the Iranian elements within the empire was decisive both in elevating Seleucus I to power in Western and Central Asia, and shaping the Macedonian-Iranian empire of the early Seleucids. Seleucus I's Iranian wife Apame, daughter of the famous Spitamenes, and mother of Antiochus, heir to the throne, was Queen Consort for a quarter of a century (324–299 BCE). She was one of Seleucus' chief assets in the latter's political designs in Afghanistan and Transoxania, and certainly helped her husband develop good relations with the Bactrian and Sogdian aristocracy. However, Seleucus' skillful policy, so effective in Babylonia and western Iran, proved largely a failure in Bactria and Sogdiana.[6] The Bactrian Greeks and a part of the native Bactrians had been aiming at establishing an independent realm for some time. Within a single generation after the death of Antiochus I in 261 BCE, separatist movements in the Upper Satrapies, fueled by Iranian and Greek aspirations for independence, came into full force, and gave rise, among others, to the Graeco-Bactrian kingdom and the Parthian state in the mid-third century BCE. By 140 BCE, the Arsacid Parthians had subjugated countries from Bactria to Babylonia, putting the final seal on the revival of Iranian political and cultural traditions.

Seleucus associated himself with Iranian traditions, though not necessarily with the Achaemenids.[7] Seleucus may have claimed connections with the Achaemenids through his wife Apame,[8] although her genuine relation to the Persian dynasty remains unclear.

Seleucus, like later Diadochi, used a diadem which – as the symbol of royalty – clearly belonged to Achaemenid tradition. The diadem appears to have been an important component of Achaemenid regalia, usually worn in combination with tiaras.[9] Plutarch (*Dem.* 18.3) notes that Seleucus began to use the diadem also in his interviews with the Greeks but "with the Barbarians he had dealt as king before this." This shows that Seleucus changed his self-presentation for different audiences. Apparently, Seleucus used the diadem and – in all likelihood – the Iranian royal title vis-à-vis Iranians after the subjugation of western Iran ca. 310 BCE.

The first dynastic era in Western Asia, the "Seleucid era," was probably linked with the Zoroastrian system of religious eras. In Iran, the mission of

---

6. Olbrycht 2005, 231–235.
7. For possible Seleucid-Achaemenid associations, see Tuplin 2008, 109–136.
8. See Tarn 1929, 138–141.
9. See Olbrycht 2004, 282–293.

Zoroaster was envisaged as auguring a pivotal point in history, and the era of Zoroaster may well have been introduced in Zoroastrian circles already under the Achaemenids. But Seleucus may have decided to transform the era into a reference point for his ruling house.[10] If indeed the Seleucid era had an Iranian origin, we can understand why the Arsacids were ready to accept it. But the crucial factor must have been the practical aspect, since the established era was already in widespread use in the administrative system of Iran and Mesopotamia, there was no reason to abolish it.

Upon the consolidation of its authority, the Seleucid empire was perceived as the dominant power in Western Asia. The Seleucids, who assumed the imperial mantle after the glorious Achaemenids, were regarded as a point of reference by local dynasties; what is more, the figure of Alexander of Macedonia, who was associated with the Seleucids, served as another, genealogical, point of reference to the Seleucids.[11]

Patterns of Appropriation – Achaemenid and Seleucid Roots in Post-Achaemenid Kingdoms

In the third and second centuries BCE, in former Achaemenid lands, a restoration of local satrapal dynasties took place. This happened in Media Atropatene (Atropatids), Armenia (Orontids), Cappadocia (Ariarathids), and Pontus.[12] Initially these dynasts traced their roots back to the Achaemenid satraps exclusively, and the Seleucids were omitted in their genealogies.[13] For example, the Ariarathid kings of Cappadocia looked back to Pharnaces, who had married Atossa, sister of Cambyses II and daughter of Cyrus the Great (Diod. 31.19.1–2; Euseb. *Chron.* 1.251). However, later these rulers often stressed their ancestral connections both with the Achaemenids and the Seleucids.[14] Moreover, rulers of the post-Achaemenid (Hellenistic) period often used components of artificial genealogies.[15]

The Cappadocian king Archelaus I created a partly constructed lineage and stressed his links to the Achaemenid kings and Macedonian rulers as well

---

10. See Gershevitch 1995, 9; Henning 1951, 38–40.

11. The Seleucid era was usually ascribed to Alexander the Great in late antiquity and in the Middle Ages; see Bickerman 1983, 778–791.

12. See Schottky 1989; Michels 2008; Olbrycht 2013.

13. For a general view of the issue, see Panitschek 1987–1988; Michels 2008.

14. On the importance of blood-relationships in the dynastic ideologies of post-Achaemenid Western Asia, see Sullivan 1990, 321ff.

15. Thus, Jonathan, the rebel Maccabee high priest, claimed common descent for the Spartans and Jews from Abraham (I *Macc.* 12.21; ca. 144 BCE). A spectacular example is provided by an inscription of Ptolemy III (*OGIS* 54; Austin 2006, no. 268), where a double divine lineage of the king, beginning with Heracles and Dionysus as ancestors, is claimed.

as Heracles. His daughter Glaphyra boasted of her noble ancestry, descended on her mother's side from Darius and on her father's side from Temenus, the ancestor of the Macedonian royal house (Joseph. *BJ* 1.476). Her mother was a princess of Armenia (*Mon. Anc.* 27.2). Through this link, the royal house of Cappadocia under Archelaus was related to Pontus: Mithradates Eupator's daughter Cleopatra married Tigranes II, king of Armenia (Just. 38.3.2).

In the mid-third century BCE, kings from the Iranian dynasties of Anatolia (Pontus and Cappadocia) and Armenia began to contract dynastic marriages with the Seleucids, and thereby the ruling houses assumed a mixed character.[16] A case in point is Antiochus II Theos who gave his daughter Stratonice to Ariarathes III, king of Cappadocia, in marriage.[17]

The kings of Commagene harked back both to the Achaemenids *and* Alexander and the Seleucids. King Antiochus I of Commagene referred to the "two very fortunate roots" of his ancestry (*Nomos*, ll. 30–31) pointing to "Hellenes and Persians."[18] The terraces of Nemrud Dağı bristled with stelae bearing the names of Antiochus' forefathers. The sequence of his paternal ancestors begins with the Great King Darius I and goes up to Mithradates Callinicus; the group of his maternal ancestors embraces Alexander the Great, Seleucus I, and ends with his mother, Laodice Thea, who was the daughter of the Seleucid king Antiochus VIII Grypus.[19] Actually, the founder of the satrapal dynasty was Orontes I, the satrap of Armenia, who married a daughter of Artaxerxes II called Rhodogune.[20] It is noticeable that Rhodogune is identified as Ἀρταξέρξου τοῦ καὶ Ἀρσάκου θυγατέρα "the daughter of Artaxerxes, who is also Arsaces." By this, Antiochus I stressed his descendance from the Achaemenid Artaxerxes II, while alluding at the same time to his link to the alleged forefather of the Arsacids (see below).

Thus, we have two genealogical lines in Commagene called roots in the *Nomos* inscription, but ancestral connections did not determine evolving political concepts and were not identical with cultural and religious spheres. The Commagenian inscriptions are in a simplified, clipped Greek, with numerous dropped articles. It is not the cultural language of Commagene, but a foreign idiom. The deities invoked carry Greek and Iranian names, but the

16. On dynastic marriages between the Seleucids and the dynasts of Western Asia, see Panitschek 1987–1988, 88–89; Schottky 1989, 108–112.

17. Diod. 31.19.1–9. Euseb. *Chron.* I.251. On the origin of the dynasty of Cappadocia, see Panitschek 1987–1988, 80–82; Briant 2002, 132–135.

18. The full text of the *Nomos* is offered by Waldman 1973, 62–71.

19. On the ancestors of Antiochus I of Commagene, see Messerschmidt 2000; Facella 2006, 270–279, 291–294; and Facella 2009.

20. Xen. *An.* 2.4.8; Plut. *Artax.* 27; *OGIS* 392; see Schottky 1989, 80–81.

religion is Iranian with some local substratum. An enumeration (*Nomos* ll. 225–226) of gods from Persia, Macedonia, and Commagene demonstrates the religious and cultural background of the Commagenian kings.

The tradition about the genealogy of the Pontic royal house underwent substantial changes over time.[21] Initially, the rulers of Pontus traced back their ancestry to the satraps of Dascylion in Asia Minor, related to Achaemenids.[22] Sallust (*Hist.* fr. 2.73M) and Florus (*Ep.* 1.40.1) tell us that the Pontic rulers derived their origins from Artabazus, satrap of Dascylion appointed by Xerxes. He may have belonged to a clan participating in the conspiracy against Gaumāta. The Pontic prince Mithradates, called Ktistes, accompanied Eumenes and afterwards supported Antigonus Monophthalmus. This Mithradates I was the founder of what would later be the Pontic kingdom, and he was accompanied by six noblemen, a fact evoking the story of Darius I and the conspiracy of the "seven Persians" against Gaumāta.[23]

In terms of chronology, the very first version of Pontic genealogy comes from Polybius (5.43.2), and may mirror the claims of Pharnaces I, or his immediate successors. Polybius relates that the Pontic dynasty claimed its origin from one of the "seven Persians" and ruled over a dominion passed on to their ancestors by Darius the Great. Significantly, it is not until Sallust that the Pontic kings' lineage is traced back explicitly to Darius the Great. Sallust (*Hist.* fr. 2.73M) speaks of satrap Artabazus but also mentions Darius as ancestors of the Pontic kings: a Dario Artabazes originem ducit quem conditorem regni Mithridatis fuisse confirmat Sallustius Crispus ("Artabazes draws [his] origins from Darius, who was the founder of Mithridates' kingdom, as Sallust Crispus confirms").

Noticeable is a passage in Justin 38.7.1 that belongs to a speech of Mithradates Eupator in 89 BCE, and implies that Mithradates VI Eupator traced his lineage back to Darius and Cyrus in the paternal line, and to Alexander and Seleucus in the maternal line:

> Se autem seu nobilitate illis conparetur clariorem illa conluvie
> convenarum esse qui paternos maiores suos a Cyro Darioque
> conditoribus Persici regni maternos a magno Alexandro ac Nicatore
> Seleuco conditoribus imperii Macedonici referat.

21. The main sources are: Polyb. 5.43.2; Sall. *Hist.* fr. 2.73M; Tac. *Ann.* 12.18; App. *Mithr.* 112; Flor. *Ep.* 1.40.1; Iust. 38.7.1.

22. Ballesteros Pastor 2013, 275.

23. App. *Mith.* 9; 112; Diod. 19.40.2; 20.111.4; Plut. *Dem.* 4; *Mor.* 83a; Tert. *Anima* 46; Just. 1.10.11. On the so-called "dynasty of Kios" and the genealogy of the Pontic kings, see Panitschek 1987–88; and Ballesteros Pastor 2013, 272–280 (with further bibliography).

He [Mithradates Eupator] was superior to that motley rabble of refugees since he could trace his line back on his father's side to Cyrus and Darius, the founders of the Persian empire, and on his mother's to Alexander the Great and Seleucus Nicator, founders of the Macedonian empire.[24]

It is only Justin who mentions Cyrus as Eupator's ancestor. Eupator must have firmly aimed to include Cyrus and Darius into his partly fictitious genealogy, for two of his sons were called Cyrus and Darius. Moreover, Eupator is said to have inherited some items from Darius the Persian (App. _Mithr._ 112; 115–117). Mithradates VIII of the Bosporus, grandson of Eupator, proclaimed himself a descendant of the great Achaemenes (Tac. _Ann._ 12.18.2) in the mid-first century CE.

Apart from the Achaemenids, Eupator declared his genealogical links with Alexander and Seleucus. Both great Macedonians merged together into one ruling line in the political memory of Asian kings, a phenomenon resembling the connection between Cyrus the Great and Darius I. For Pontic kings, the Achaemenid genealogy was in terms of political claims more important than the Seleucid one.[25] Nevertheless, the Pontic kings paid heed to the importance of marital alliances with the Seleucids. Thus, Mithradates II married the sister of Seleucus Callinicus, and Pharnaces married Nisa, the daughter of Antiochus IV.[26]

Arsaces I and the Early Arsacids

More or less conscious Parthian references to Achaemenid traditions can be seen already under Arsaces I and II, such as in the use by Arsacid rulers of the diadem and the tiara (_kyrbasia_).[27] Another mark of continuity consisted in maintaining the Zoroastrian custom of lighting a coronation fire in Asaak, in clear reference to the Achaemenids (Isidorus of Charax, _Stathmoi_ 11).[28]

Apart from his name, Arsaces used on his coins the titles of _autokrator_ and _krny_ (*_kārana_-).[29] Arsaces' use of the title _autokrator_ ("self-appointed ruler") derived from the Greek and Macedonian traditions. With this title, Ar-

24. Translation by Yardley 1994. See also App. _Mithr._ 70, who gives a general statement about Eupator's ancestry.

25. See Ballesteros Pastor 2013, 278.

26. See Seibert 1967, 118–119.

27. According to Gaslain 2005b, the _kyrbasia_ of Arsaces I was no longer intended as the satrapal headdress but became a symbol of the new conquerors, "evocative of their nomadic origin."

28. On Iranian and specifically Achaemenid traditions in Arsacid ideology, see Wolski 1966, 63–89; Wolski 1976, 204–205; Olbrycht 1997, 42–44; Olbrycht 2013c; Wiesehöfer 1996, 55–66; Fowler 2005, 125–155; and Shayegan 2011, 41–331.

29. For a detailed scrutiny of these titles, see Olbrycht 2013c.

saces emphasized that he had gained power on the strengths of his own virtues and conquests, consciously setting an essential turning point in the history of Iran. The Iranian title *krny* (*kārana*-) definitely derives from the Achaemenid world.[30] Under the early Arsacids it must have evolved to mean an independent ruler not subject to any superior authority.

The ancient sources emphasize the significance of the very name of Arsaces (Just. 41.5.6; 41.5.8; Amm. Marc. 23.6.5). Ammianus (23.6.2-6) compares the Roman title of Augustus to the meaning of the name Arsaces. Justin (41.5.5-6) juxtaposes Arsaces with Cyrus, Alexander, and Romulus. With these testimonies in mind, one should conclude that Parthians did not intend merely to commemorate the name of the dynasty's founder Arsaces (Parthian *Aršak*), but to transform the name into a title binding on the successors of Arsaces I.[31]

Aršak was also a personal name used by some Achaemenids. Artaxerxes II (404-359 BCE) bore the name Aršak and it was probably he whom some Arsacids considered the forefather of the dynasty.[32] The name is transmitted in several variants as Arsikas/Ἀρσίκας (Plut. *Artax.* 1.4), Arsakas/Ἀρσάκας (Ktesias/Photius, *FGrH* 688 F15 [51] and Arsakes/ Ἀρσάκης (Ktesias/Photius, *FGrH* 688 F15 [55]. Dinon offers the form Oarses/Ὀάρσης (Plut. *Artax.* 1.4). Babylonian sources give the form *Aršu*, mirrored in Greek sources as Arses/Ἄρσης. It seems that the form Aršak is a hypocoristic from Old Persian *Ŗšā-.[33]

In Arrian's lost *Parthica*, fragments of which are captured by Photius,[34] the Parthians are called a "Scythian race," which had long been under the yoke of Macedonia, and revolted under the brothers Arsaces and Tiridates accompanied by five accomplices. Syncellus connects Arsaces and Tiridates with Persians, including Artaxerxes, "king of the Persians," and states that: "a certain Arsakes and Teridates [Tiridates], brothers tracing their lineage to Artaxerxes king of the Persians, were satraps of the Bactrians at the time of the Macedonian Agathocles, the eparch of Persis. According to Arrian, this Agathocles fell in love with Teridates, one of the brothers, and was eagerly laying a snare for the young man. But failing utterly, he was killed by him and his brother Arsaces. Arsaces then became king of the Persians, after whom the kings of the Persians were known as 'Arsacidai.'"[35]

30. Apart from Arsaces I the title of *krny* was used by the ruler of Persis Wahbarz/Oborzus; see Klose/Müseler 2008, 26-30.
31. More on this in Gaslain 2005a, 222; Olbrycht 2013c.
32. On the name Arsakes/Arses for Artaxerxes II, see Plut. *Artax.* 1-2. Compare also Schmitt 1982, 83-95, especially 92; Briant 2002, 589-590, 986; and Binder 2008, 96-98.
33. For details, see Schmitt 1982, 92; and Binder 2008, 97-98.
34. Arr. *Parthika* 1.2, ed. Roos 1912 = Photius, cod. 58, ed. Henry 1959.
35. *Ekloga*, ed. Dindorf 1829, 539-540 = ed. Mosshammer 1984, 343. Translation by Adler and Tuffin 2002, 412.

Syncellus' account is confused and contains legendary elements like a conspicuous love story. Moreover, there is no trace of the existence of an early Arsacid king named Tiridates in any classical source other than Arrian/Photius and Syncellus (and derivative accounts), nor does this name appear on known Parthian ostraca as a royal name.[36] Still it cannot be excluded that Syncellus' source, aware of a connection between the Arsacids and the Achaemenid king named Artaxerxes, may be reliable. Present in both traditions are legendary themes that clearly echo Herodotus. And so, the rebellion is sparked off by a tyrant's (satrap's) attempt on the life of an aristocrat, and the history is built in much the same way as that of the overthrow of the Peisistratides in Athens. The number of seven conspirators mirrors exactly the Persian plot against Gaumāta, who elevated Darius I to power (Hdt. 3.71).[37]

Ties between the Arsacids and the Achaemenids need not be fictitious. Crucial is the circumstance that the Arsacids did not perceive themselves as the continuators of a satrapal lineage from Achaemenid times, contrary to the (largely historical) common claims held by dynasties in Atropatene, Armenia, Pontus, Cappadocia, and Commagene. In Parthia, there are no traces of a direct dynastic continuity between Arsaces I and the Achaemenids or an Achaemenid satrap. A connection between the Arsacids and the Achaemenids may have resulted from a possible marital alliance between Artaxerxes II and a Dahaean ruler in the steppes. The founder of the Parthian empire, Arsaces I, was a "Scythian," or a nomad, a member of the Dahae, who were steppe-dwellers. This tribe had been within the sphere of Achaemenid power at least beginning with the fifth century BCE. In Alexander's time, the Dahae actively supported Darius III, and then the last Iranian ruler, Bessus (whose throne name was Artaxerxes) and Spitamenes, in opposing Alexander of Macedonia.[38] It is hence likely that Achaemenid princesses were at some time during this long relation married off to a Dahaean ruler, thus creating a blood relation between the Dahaean élite and the Achaemenids. We know that Artaxerxes II carried out an active marital policy. As a case in point, he married one of his daughters, Rhodogune, to Orontes, satrap of Armenia (see above). Such alliances probably also occurred among the Achaemenid house and steppe-rulers of Central Asia. Contacts between the Achaemenids and peoples of Central Asia were multi-faceted. This is visible in historical

36. Livshits 2010, 156.
37. Such themes are indicated by, among others, Wolski 1993, 56–57; 2003, 23. See also Shayegan 2016, 11.
38. Olbrycht 1996.

events,[39] and recent archaeological discoveries in western Kazakhstān and in southern Ural regions. Excavations at Filippovka point to the possibility of "diplomatic" marriages between nomadic rulers of the Southern Ural area and the Achaemenids.[40] The Dahae, wandering between the Syr Darya basin and the steppes of the southern Urals in Achaemenid times, must have played a significant role in the nomadic-Achaemenid relations.

It was no coincidence hence that the name of Artaxerxes was given to a royal vineyard mentioned in the Parthian documents of the first century BCE discovered at Nisa. The Nisan documents mention a series of vineyards: *Gōtarzakān* <gwtrzkn>, *Artabānukān* <ʾtbnwkn(y)>, *Miθrdātakān* <mtrdtkn(y)>, *Frahātakān* <prhtkn>, and *Friyapatikān* <pryptykn(y)>. These designations are derived from the names of the second- and first-century BCE kings of Parthia, starting with Friyapat. There is also a mention of a vineyard called *Artaxšahrakān* <rthšrkn>, most probably in honor of Artaxerxes II, an Achaemenid monarch regarded as an ancestor of the Arsacids. The names of the vineyards correspond to the names of the temples to which they purveyed their produce.[41] There are no records of a vineyard named after Arsaces/ Aršak, but this name occurs five times in the archive of Nisa, and three times in connection with a coronation.[42] Religious worship was certainly practiced at Nisa, since we know of the presence of magi and the cultic specialist called *ādūrbed* "the one in charge of the fire."[43]

Arsaces I's historical role was quickly appreciated not only in Iran, but also in the Greco-Roman world (Amm. Marc. 23.6.2–6; Suda s.v. *Arsakes*). Ammianus Marcellinus (23.6.7–8) names Cyrus and Darius as warlike kings of Persia, but they remain in the shadow of the great Arsaces, whose reign is shown as a major landmark in Iran's history. When Justin (41.5.5–6) compares Arsaces with Cyrus, Alexander, and Romulus, he is surely fascinated by the Iranian king. The choice of personages in Justin's comparison is no mere accident. Cyrus was the founder of the Achaemenid empire, a figure celebrated in Iran and beyond. But Arsaces' state lasted twice as long, and under less favorable political conditions (such as the confrontation with powerful Rome), than was true of Achaemenid Persia. Another figure in Justin's list, Alexander, was appreciated not only in Rome, but also among Iranians.

39. See Olbrycht 1996, 148–158.

40. Treister and Yablonsky 2013, 313–315. For new findings and conclusions regarding the contacts between Central Asian nomads and Achaemenid Iran, see also Stöllner and Samašev 2013, 715–731.

41. Schmitt 1998, 170.

42. Bader 1996, 255.

43. Bader 1996, 271.

While his conquests changed the face of the world, he was nevertheless unable to build a lasting state.

Arsaces' stature justified the high status of his descendants. The importance of Arsaces also acquired a religious dimension. According to Ammianus (23.6.4–6), Arsaces was included among the gods, hence the special respect in which the Arsacids were held in their country.[44] That worship had its social dimension: the king of Parthia and members of the royal Arsacid clan occupied the highest position in the structure of Parthian society and in the Parthian state. The Arsacids were treated as the only rightful kings of Iran for several centuries.[45]

The Parthian King of Kings

A hundred years after Arsaces' subjugation of Khorasan, Mithradates I's conquests turned the Arsacid state into an empire stretching from Bactria to Babylonia and Transcaucasia, defeating the Seleucids and local rulers.[46] The Parthians took a pragmatic attitude towards the Seleucids and contracted dynastic marriages with the now weakened rulers of Syria.[47] But in their genealogies, they never referred to blood relations with the Seleucids, which they treated more like a sophisticated diplomatic additive intended to embellish the dynasty and enhance the fold of peoples subject to the Imperium Parthicum.

A significant political reform occurred after Parthian victories in Central Asia and on Iran's eastern frontiers, when Mithradates II (123/122–87 BCE) adopted the old Achaemenid title of King of Kings. The title (written in Greek as ΒΑΣΙΛΕΩΣ ΒΑΣΙΛΕΩΝ) first appeared on Parthian coins of type S. 27, which includes silver drachms and bronze fractions (S. 27.1–13 and S. 27.28).[48]

The oldest undisputed evidence of the title of King of Kings is the Babylonian diary no. - 110 'rev.' i', dated to 111 BCE. (year 201 of the Seleucid Era), and the Goal Year text no. 93 flake 3', dated to the years 112–111 BCE

---

44. On the divinization of the Arsacids, see Invernizzi 2011; Olbrycht 2013c; Olbrycht 2016.

45. Strab. 16.1.28: Parthians as φιλαρσάκαι; Amm. Marc. 23.6.6: Quam ob rem numinis eum vice venerantur et colunt ea usque propagatis honoribus ut ad nostri memoriam non nisi Arsacides is sit, quisquam in suscipiendo regno cunctis anteponatur, et in qualibet civili concertatione, quae adsidue apud eos eveniunt, velut sacrilegium quisque caveat ne dextra sua Arsaciden arma gestantem feriat vel privatum.

46. See Olbrycht 2010a, 229–245.

47. Mithradates I gave his daughter to the Seleucid king Demetrius II in marriage (Iust. 38.9.3; App. *Syr.* 67). Phraates II married a daughter of Demetrius II (Just. 38.10.10).

48. S. = Sellwood 1980.

(year 200 of the Seleucid Era).[49] The title of King of Kings became ubiquitous throughout the Parthian empire. About a hundred years had passed since the death of Arsaces I, and in that time the Arsacid state had become not just the propagandistic pretender, but the real political and cultural heir to the Achaemenid legacy.[50]

The title King of Kings became an almost inseparable part of Arsacid titulature. Mithradates II greatly capitalized on his own political and military successes, but also built on his predecessors' strenuous efforts. In little more than 100 years, the Arsacids forged and stabilized a vast empire encompassing lands from Armenia to Bactria and Sogdiana and from the Syrian frontier (Dura Europus) to Arachosia. Parthian Iran became the greatest power in Western and Central Asia, while the Seleucids were reduced to the status of marginal, peripheral chieftains. The power of Rome was still not a concern for the Parthians, although Mithradates II keenly observed the situation in Syria and Anatolia. His interest in Anatolia is made evident in his alliance with king Mithradates VI Eupator of Pontus, concluded before 102/101 BCE.[51] In Transcaucasia, Armenia was a bastion of Parthian rule.

Media, the richest land on the Iranian Plateau, played a decisive role in Parthian policies since the rule of Mithradates I (165–133/132 BCE).[52] Even under the Achaemenids, the Medes held a status nearly equal to that of the Persians. That was not only because of the affinity between the two tribes but also because of Media's imperial traditions and its resources and riches, as many sources emphasize. Both linguistically and ethnically, the Medes and the Parthians had much in common; the nations were neighbors. Importantly, a note of Justin (41.1.1) states that the Parthian language was somewhere between "Scythian and Median." Owing to its strategic, political, and economic potential, Media was of key importance to the Parthians and was subjected to their direct rule. Ecbatana was one of the Parthian empire's capitals (Strab. 11.13.1). Under Mithradates I, this city became the residence of the king's brother Bacasis (*Bagayaša*), controlling the western provinces of the Arsacid kingdom.[53] Median mints (Ecbatana and Rhaga) struck an overwhelming majority of Parthian drachms and the country possessed rich silver deposits.[54] All this made Media a land of exceptional importance to the Parthians, a land, on whose culture – a repository of old Iranian (and

---

49. Sachs and Hunger 2006, no. 93 flake 3'. See Shayegan 2011, 43, n. 22.
50. See Wolski 1966, 74.
51. See Olbrycht 2009, 163–190.
52. On Media's wealth, see Strab. 11.13.7; and Amm. Marc. 23.3.5; 23.6.29; 23.6.31.
53. See Olbrycht 2010, 238–239.
54. See Nikitin 1983, 95–100.

Achaemenid) traditions – they amply drew. It seems that the Arsacids from Mithradates I onwards had recourse to Achaemenid traditions mainly through the agency of the Median heritage.

Once they had taken control of Media, the Arsacids were quick to integrate into the iconography of the mountain of Bisotun/Behistun. Several Parthian royal reliefs were engraved at Bisotun next to the inscription of Darius.[55]

Mithradates II had himself depicted on coins in a high tiara. They are effigies from S. 28 emissions encompassing drachms and bronze issues. The introduction of a new type of crown by the Arsacids could not have been merely incidental.[56] In its shape, perhaps slightly modified by a lengthening, the Parthian tiara was probably borrowed from the Median tradition. Tall, domed Median tiaras are known from many reliefs of Persepolis (a ribbon is often visible in the back of a tiara). In a side view, the Parthian tiara resembles the classic Achaemenid upright tiara. It is noticeable that other kings of the post-Achaemenid area, including the rulers of Armenia and Persis, used rather a cylindrical headgear with crenellations or spikes, unless some of them imitated Parthian type tiaras (as was the case in Persis). Achaemenid rulers used crowns of various types depending on the occasion. Thus, they wore a specific type of *kyrbasia* – the stiffed *tiara orthe*, and the cylindrical crown (crenelated on top), known from reliefs and coinage (probably identifiable as the *kidaris/kitaris*).[57]

Artabanus II, Cyrus and Alexander

Around 34 CE, the Parthian king Artabanus II (8/9–39 CE) returned to an active policy in Transcaucasia: upon the death of Artaxias III, king of Armenia, Artabanus set his son Arsaces on the Armenian throne (Tac. *Ann.* 6.31.1). The Romans were quick to respond, leading eventually to a drastic deterioration in relations between the two powers.[58]

Upon the conquest of Armenia, Artabanus sent an embassy to Rome to present Parthia's demands to the emperor Tiberius. The Parthians insisted on the return of Vonones' treasury, which was kept by the Romans in Syria and Cilicia. Artabanus' demands comprised also aggressive threats against Roman territories. The grounds for his claims went back to Alexander and the Achaemenids. Artabanus' strategic goal was offensive in character, since according to Dio (58.26.1), after invading Armenia, he intended to attack Roman Cap-

55. See Boyce and Grenet 1991, 91–94.

56. For details, see Olbrycht 1997, 40–44.

57. Olbrycht 2014, 75–85.

58. On the Arsacid policy in Armenia in the years 34–37 CE, see Chaumont 1976, 88–91; Chaumont 1987, 423; and Olbrycht 2012a.

padocia. There is nothing in Artabanus' embassy about Roman obligation to return specific territories. What Artabanus was threatening them with was an attack on lands controlled by Rome to the west of the Euphrates. Having a strong army at the time, Artabanus could expect to come out victorious from a confrontation with Rome. The reference to the borders in the age of Cyrus and Alexander was a propaganda ploy and it was obvious that their restoration was not intended or desired, but it rather served to underline that the Arsacids were more entitled than Rome to rule in Asia. Perhaps Tacitus' mention of Syria and Cilicia, and Dio's addition of Cappadocia, were done for a good reason. These regions had been within the Parthian sphere of interest and expansion ever since Mithradates II (123–87 BCE).[59] In the years 34–36, Artabanus' strategic aim was to take the borderlands along the Euphrates, pushing the Romans away from the river and therefore also out of Armenia and Mesopotamia, in order to secure a good bargaining position for subsequent negotiations. His main objective was control over Armenia, and his purpose was for Rome to recognize Parthian power in that country.

Most historians discussing Aratbanus' intervention in Armenia as reported by Tacitus (*Ann.* 6.31.1), concentrate on its reference to Achaemenid precedents. Indeed, Artabanus II, while sending an embassy to Rome, claimed a link to Cyrus the Great and Alexander as justification for his policies:

> Simul veteres Persarum ac Macedonum terminos seque invasurum possessa Cyro et post Alexandro per vaniloquentiam ac minas iaciebat.

> At the same time, he would boast about the ancient boundaries of Persia and Macedonia, and make blustering threats about invading the territories held first by Cyrus and later by Alexander.[60]

It should be observed that alongside the Persians, Tacitus also mentions Alexander and the Macedonians. Perhaps this double declaration may be attributed especially to the political tradition of Media Atropatene, which Artabanus had ruled before he won the throne of Parthia. He was a relative, or at least a kinsman, of the Atropatids, the reigning dynasty in Atropatene (for three centuries until the time of Phraates IV).[61] This house owed its origin to Atropates, a loyal satrap of Darius III (336–330 BCE), later Alexander's faithful governor and general. Atropates' daughter married Perdiccas, who became regent on Alexander's death.[62]

Thus, already Atropates, the founder of the dynasty, combined both the

59. Olbrycht 2009; 2011, 275–281.
60. Translation by Yardley 2008.
61. On Media Atropatene, see Schottky 1989.
62. Olbrycht 2013, 160–161,171.

Iranian and Macedonian political traditions. This episode shows that Alexander's image in Parthian Iran was not simply negative, but that there were also circles that saw him as one of the great rulers of Iran, who could be referred to in situations of conflict with Rome – a foreign power.[63]

Cyrus and Alexander were familiar figures in Rome, associated with the power and wealth of Asia. The image of Alexander served as a model for Roman leaders like Pompey and emperors like Caligula, Trajan, or Septimius Severus.[64] The connection to Alexander claimed by Artabanus II deprived Rome of the propagandistic bargaining card that appropriated the figure of Alexander and his heritage. The Arsacids must have been aware of the fact that Alexander the Great's memory was regularly used in Roman political propaganda alongside the Greco-Persian Wars of the fifth century BCE.

The Persian Wars constituted a point of reference for some Greek literary traditions of the Hellenistic and Roman worlds. In the Roman period, the Parthians became the reincarnation of "Achaemenid Persians" in some Roman political undertakings.[65] Thus, for example, Augustus and Nero staged sea-battles imitating the Athenian victory of Salamis. Such events receive much attention in scholarly studies but their impact on current politics should not be exaggerated.

A well-known phenomenon is that the Roman emperors or republican leaders sought to equate themselves with Alexander the Great, giving the contemporary Parthians the label of the (new) "Persians" (*Persae*) or "Medes" (*Medi*). Thus, Cicero refers to the Parthians as *Persae* (*De domo sua* 60). Likewise, Horace uses the terms *Persae*, *Medi*, and *Parthi* interchangeably (*Odes* 3.3.43–44; 3.5.2–3; 3.2.3). In some cases, the Achaemenid references are more elaborated. Horace describes the return of Phraates IV to the "throne of Cyrus" (*Carm.* 2.2.17–21). In his poem *Thebaid* (286–293), Statius makes an elaborate comparison of Theodamas' situation with the "Achaemenid boy" (*puer Achaemenius*). Statius uses the proper adjective *Achaemenius* and its derivative *Achaemeniae* (*Theb.* 1.718: *gentis Achaemeniae ritu*), as a reference to the Parthians, the contemporary lords of Iran, and not to the Achaemenids of the Battle of Salamis or Cunaxa. Sporadically, Statius uses the notion *Persae* and its variants (*Silvae* 3.62; 5.187). His terminology is archaic, but the reality referred to is Parthian.

At first glance, the references made by Artabanus II, Parthian King of Kings, to Cyrus and Alexander look extraordinary. But his overtures were addressed to the Romans, the enemies of Iran.

In his declaration, Artabanus appropriated two of the political traditions

63. Olbrycht 2010, 368.
64. On Alexander in Rome, see Panitschek 1990; Kühnen 2008; Shayegan 2011, 340–348.
65. Spawforth 1994, 237–243.

of Western Asia: Cyrus and the Achaemenids, and the tradition of Alexander. There are grounds to believe that in Parthian eyes these traditions intermingled. Alexander was perceived as part and parcel of the imperial tradition of Iran. But the figure of Cyrus, far more distant in time to Alexander, was also present in Artabanus' declaration.

The Arsacids and the Memory of the Past

What is the picture of the Arsacids against the backdrop of many sovereigns claiming descendance from the Achaemenids? Some historians have thought the Arsacid claims to the Achaemenid heritage to be rather vague, not as explicit as the monumental claims of other rulers in Western Asia. Indeed, the Arsacid appropriation of an Achaemenid and Seleucid past seems to be far less specific and conscious than the ostentatious references made by rulers such as Antiochus of Commagene. A local ruler, or petty king, like the king of Commagene, or later even the Seleucids, was bound to be more vociferous about his mighty family connections, precisely because he was a petty king. Many of these princelings appended the epithet *Nikephoros* "Victorious," *Theos* "God," or *Basileus Megas* "Great King" to their titles, even though they had scored no military victories. Great was the chasm between panegyrical pretence and reality;[66] but with the Arsacids that distance was not so great. The Arsacids were resolutely building up an empire and only occasionally needed to look back at ancient traditions in terms of genealogical constructs; for them political realities took precedence over ideology. Moreover, their main reference point remained Arsaces I.

Differences in ideology may be observed by juxtaposing the Arsacids with the mighty king of Pontus, Mithradates Eupator (120–63 BCE). With respect to the Arsacids, Eupator assumed the role of a humble petitioner. He highly respected Mithradates II of Parthia as his ally.[67] He never used the title of King of Kings in his self-presentation, as was the custom of his Arsacid contemporaries.[68] It was on the eve of a great war against Rome, with Parthian support, that Eupator included Darius and Cyrus (alongside Alexander and the Seleucids) in the circle of his ancestors, changing the tone of his propaganda. Eupator's claims to genealogical connections with Cyrus and Darius were to strengthen his new status as a reviver and defender of Asian might in the face of Roman expansionist activities.

The early Arsacids are said to have had connections with the Achaemenid Great King Artaxerxes II, not with Achaemenid satraps, as was the case

66. This pertains to the last Seleucids and minor kings of the first century BCE; see de Callatay and Lorber 2011, 424–426.
67. Olbrycht 2009, 163–190.
68. Olbrycht 2012b, 719.

with other princes in Anatolia and Armenia. Contrary to the claims of other post-Achaemenid dynasties, already by the early second century BCE, the Arsacids' main point of reference was Arsaces I, the founder of the Parthian dynasty, not the Achaemenids or Seleucids. Arsaces I was not a prince hemmed in by a narrow horizon, but the founder for a powerful state. Evidence for this is the establishment of the Arsacid era, and the adoption of the royal title. Arsaces was brilliant at blending the traditions of the steppes, whence he originated, with the political and cultural legacy of Iran.

This special status of Arsaces finds its place in the account of "Persia" by Ammianus Marcellinus. Cyrus and Darius appear in the narration; however, they remain mere figures of a remote past in contrast to Arsaces.

Cyrus was a figure celebrated in Iran and beyond. He was treated in antiquity as a great hero, and founder of one of the greatest empires (Justin 2.10.7: *non heredem, sed conditorem tanti regni*). In the *Epitome* of Justin, Cyrus appears alongside Alexander, Romulus and Arsaces among the founders of great empires (41.5.5). As they ruled in the stalwart and populous lands of Iran, the Arsacids were not forgetful of the Achaemenid legacy. Arsaces had acceded to the throne around three generations after the death of Darius III, when the memory of the Achaemenids and their grandeur must still have been vivid.

The Arsacids were able to develop a universal imperial ideology of their own. Their chief point of reference was Arsaces, not his links, real or fictive, with the Achaemenids. It is striking that the Arsacids harkened back to the Achaemenids in many respects, but their claim to Achaemenid descendance was sporadic, and their connection to Achaemenid satraps as forebears nonexistent. Indeed, we cannot find in Arsacid Parthia any trace of pretenses by great clans to have originated from Achaemenid satrapal families. The major Parthian clans, like the Sūrēn and Kārin, must actually have been newly established great families without particular links to the Achaemenid period magnates including the Hydarnids, Orontids, or Phrataphernes' line.

The Arsacids did not use Achaemenid dynastic names like Artaxerxes, Darius, and Cyrus.[69] Unlike the Arsacids, the post-Achaemenid dynasts ruling in Persis regularly used Achaemenid throne-names, including Artaxerxes and Darius.[70]

It is quite true that the Achaemenids and the Seleucids together with

69. One of the Arsacid princes was called Darius; he was the son of Artabanus II who represented an Arsacid royal branch closely connected to Media Atropatene. Among the rulers of Atropatene, there had been a Darius during the time of Pompey (first century BCE). For Darius, son of Artabanus II, see Karras-Klapproth 1988, 50–51; on Darius from Atropatene, consult Schottky 1989, 160, 188.

70. Wiesehöfer 2011, 107–122.

Alexander were key references and models of imperial powers, that many of the local princes of Western Asia followed. The "roots" mentioned in the inscriptions of the Commagene were complex and diffuse, as were the traditions linking post-Achaemenid rulers in Western Asia with the great kings of the past.

Bibliography

Adler, W., and P. Tuffin, eds. 2002. *The Chronography of George Synkellos: A Byzantine Chronicle of Universal History from the Creation.* New York/Oxford.

ANRW = Temporini, H., and W. Haase. 1976–. *Aufstieg und Niedergang der römischen Welt: Geschichte und Kultur Roms im Spiegel der Neueren Forschung.* Berlin/New York.

Austin, M. 2006. *The Hellenistic World from Alexander to the Roman Conquest: A Selection of Ancient Sources in Translation.* Cambridge.

Bader, Andrei. 1996. "Parthian Ostraca from Nisa: Some Historical Data." In *Convegno Internazionale sul Tema: La Persia e L'Asia Centrale da Alessandro al X Secolo (Roma, 9–12 novembre 1994).* Atti dei Convegni Lincei 127. Roma, 251–276.

Ballesteros Pastor, L. 2013. *Pompeyo Trogo, Justino y Mitrídates : Comentario al Epítome de las Historias Filípicas* (37,1,6–38,8,1). Hildesheim/Zürich/New York.

Bickerman, E. 1983. "Time-reckoning." In *Cambridge History of Iran,* edited by E. Yarshater. Vol. 3:2: *The Seleucid, Arsacid and Sasanid Periods,* 778–791. Cambridge.

Binder, C. 2008. *Plutarchs Vita des Artaxerxes: Ein historischer Kommentar.* Göttinger Forum für Altertumswissenschaft. Beihefte N.F. 1. Berlin/New York.

Boyce, M., and F. Grenet. 1991. *A History of Zoroastrianism.* Volume III: *Zoroastrianism under Macedonian and Roman Rule.* Leiden.

Briant, P. 2002. *From Cyrus to Alexander: A History of the Persian Empire.* Translated by P. T. Daniels. Winona Lake, Ind.

———. 2010. *Alexander the Great and His Empire: A Short Introduction.* Translated by Amélie Kuhrt. Princeton/Oxford.

de Callatay, F., and A. C. C. Lorber. 2011. "The Pattern of Royal Epithets on Hellenistic Coinages." In *More than Men, Less than Gods: Studies on Royal Cult and Imperial Worship: Proceedings of the International Colloquium Organized by the Belgian School at Athens (November 1–2, 2007),* edited by P. P. Iossif, A. S. Chankowski, and C. C. Lorber. Studia Hellenistica, 5 :417–455. Leuven.

Chaumont, M.-L. 1987. "Armenia and Iran II: The Pre-Islamic Period," *Encyclopaedia Iranica* 3:418–438.

———. 1976. "L'Arménie entre Rome et l'Iran : I. De l'avènement d'Auguste à l'avènement de Dioclétien." In *ANRW*. Vol. II: *Principat*, 9.1:71–194.

Dindorf, W., ed. 1829. *Georgius Syncellus et Nicephorus Cp.* 2 vols. Corpus Scriptorum Christianorum Historiae Byzantinae, vols. 30–31. Bonn.

Facella, M. 2006. *La dinastia degli Orontidi nella Commagene ellenistico-romana*, Pisa.

Facella, M. 2009. "Darius and the Achaemenids in Commagene " In *Organisation des pouvoirs et contacts culturels dans les pays de l'empire achéménide: Actes du colloque organisé au Collège de France par la 'Chaire d'histoire et civilisation du monde achéménide et de l'empire d'Alexandre' et le 'Réseau international d'études et de recherches achéménides' (GDR 2538 CNRS), 9-10 novembre 2007*, edited by P. Briant and M. Chauveau. Persika 14:379–414. Paris.

Fowler, Richard. 2005. "'Most Fortunate Roots': Tradition and Legitimacy in Parthian Royal Ideology." In *Imaginary Kings: Royal Images in the Ancient Near East, Greece and Rome*, edited by O. Hekster and R. Fowler. Oriens et Occidens: Studien zu antiken Kulturkontakten und ihrem Nachleben, Band 11, 125–218. Stuttgart.

Fraser, P. M. 1978. "The Kings of Commagene and the Greek World." In *Studien zur Religion und Kultur Kleinasiens: Festschrift für Friedrich Dörner zum 65. Geburtstag am 28. Februar 1976*, edited by S. Şahin, E. Schwertheim, and J. Wagner, 359–374. Leiden.

Gaslain, J. 2005a. "Arsaces I, the First Arsacid King? Some Remarks on the Nature of Early Parthian Power." In *Central Asia from the Achaemenids to the Timurids: Archaeology, History, Ethnology, Culture*, edited by V. P. Nikonorov, 221–224. St. Petersburg.

———. 2005b. "Le bachlik d'Arsace Ier ou la représentation du nomade-roi." *Bulletin of Parthian and Mixed Oriental Studies* 1:9–30.

Gershevitch, I. 1995. "Approaches to Zoroaster's Gathas." *Iran* 33:1–29.

Henning, W. B. 1951. *Zoroaster: Politician or Witch-Doctor.* London.

Henry, R. 1959. *Photius Bibliothèque.* Vol. I: *Codices 1-84.* Collection des Universités de France, Série Grecque – Collection Budé N° 137. Paris.

Invernizzi, A. 2011. "Royal Cult in Arsakid Parthia." In *More than Men, Less than Gods: Studies on Royal Cult and Imperial Worship: Proceedings of the International Colloquium Organized by the Belgian School at Athens (November 1-2, 2007)*, edited by P. P. Iossif, A. S. Chankowski, and C. C. Lorber. Studia Hellenistica 5, 649–690. Leuven.

Jacobs, B. 2011. "Kyros, der große König, der Achämenide: Zum verwandtschaftlichen Verhältnis und zur politischen und kulturellen

Kontinuität zwischen Kyros dem Großen und Dareios I." In *Herodot und das persische Reich / Herodotus and the Persian Empire: Akten des 3. Internationalen Kolloquiums zum Thema 'Vorderasien im Spannungsfeld klassischer und altorientalischer Überlieferungen,' Innsbruck 24.-28. November 2008*, edited by R. Rollinger, B. Truschnegg, and R. Bichler. Classica et Orientalia 3: 635–663. Wiesbaden.

Karras-Klapproth, M. 1988. *Prosopographische Studien zur Geschichte des Partherreiches auf der Grundlage antiker literarischer Überlieferung*. Bonn.

Klose, D. O. A., and W. Müseler. 2008. *Statthalter, Rebellen, Könige: Die Münzen aus Persepolis von Alexander dem Großen zu den Sasaniden*. Munich.

Kühnen, A. 2008. *Die imitatio Alexandri in der römischen Politik*. Münster.

Livshits, V. A. 2010. *Parfianskaīa onomastika*. Saint-Petersburg.

Messerschmidt, W. 2000. "Die Ahnengalerie des Antiochos I. von Kommagene: Ein Zeugnis für die Geschichte des östlichen Hellenismus." In *Gottkönige am Euphrat: Neue Ausgrabungen und Forschungen in Kommagene*, edited by J. Wagner, 37–43. Mainz am Rhein.

Michels, C. 2008. *Kulturtransfer und monarchischer "Philhellenismus": Bithynien, Pontos und Kappadokien in hellenistischer Zeit*. Göttingen.

Mosshammer, A. A., ed. 1984. *Georgius Syncellus: Ecloga chronographica*. Bibliotheca Scriptorum Graecorum et Romanorum Teubneriana. Leipzig.

Nikitin, A. B. 1983. "Monetnyĭ dvor goroda Ragi v pervye gody pravleniĭa Mitridata II," *Vestnik drevneĭ istorii* 1983, no. 2: 95–100.

OGIS = W. Dittenberger. 1903–05. *Orientis Graeci Inscriptiones Selectae: Supplementum Sylloges Inscriptionum Graecarum*. Leipzig.

Olbrycht, M. J. 1996. "Die Beziehungen der Steppennomaden Mittelasiens zu den hellenistischen Staaten (bis zum Ende des 3. Jahrhunderts vor Chr.)." In *Hellenismus: Beiträge zur Erforschung von Akkulturation und politischer Ordnung in den Staaten des hellenistischen Zeitalters*, edited by B. Funck, 147–169. Tübingen.

———. 1997. "Parthian King's Tiara – Numismatic Evidence and Some Aspects of Arsacid Political Ideology." *Notae Numismaticae* 2:27–65.

———. 2003. "Parthia and Nomads of Central Asia. Elements of Steppe Origin in the Social and Military Developments of Arsakid Iran." In *Mitteilungen des Sonderforschungsbereichs "Differenz und Integration" 5: Militär und Staatlichkeit*, edited by I. Schneider, 69–109. Halle/Saale.

———. 2004. *Alexander the Great and the Iranian world* [in Polish: *Aleksander Wielki i świat irański*]. Rzeszów.

———. 2005. "Creating an Empire: Iran and Middle Asia in the Policy of Seleucus I." In *Central Asia from the Achaemenids to the Timurids*, edited by V. P. Nikonorov, 231–235. Saint-Petersburg.

———. 2009. "Mithradates VI Eupator and Iran." In *Mithridates VI and the Pontic Kingdom*, edited by J. M. Hoejte, 163–190. Aarhus.

———. 2010. "Macedonia and Persia." In *Blackwell Companion to Ancient Macedonia*, edited by J. Roisman and I. Worthington, 342–369. Malden/Oxford.

———. 2010a. "Mithradates I of Parthia and His Conquests up to 141 B.C." In *Hortus Historiae: Studies in Honour of Professor Jozef Wolski on the 100th Anniversary of His Birthday*, edited by M. dzielska, et al., 229–245. Kraków.

———. 2011. "Subjects and Allies: The Black Sea Empire of Mithradates VI Eupator (120–63 BC) Reconsidered." In *Pontika 2008: Recent Research on the Northern and Eastern Black Sea in Ancient Times*, edited by E. Papuci-Wladyka, M. Vickers, J. Bodzek, and D. Braund. BAR IS 2240, 275–281. Oxford.

———. 2012a. "The Political-Military Strategy of Artabanos /Ardawān II in AD 34–37." *Anabasis: Studia Classica et Orientalia* 3:215–237.

———. 2012b. Review of R. Shayegan, *Arsacids and Sasanians*, Cambridge 2011. *Gnomon* 84:717–722.

———. 2013a. "Iranians in the Diadochi Period." In *After Alexander: The Time of the Diadochi (323281 BC)*, edited by V. A. Troncoso and E. M. Anson, 159–182. Oxford.

———. 2013b. *Imperium Parthicum: Kryzys i odbudowa państwa Arsakidów w pierwszej połowie I wieku po Chr.* [*Imperium Parthicum: Crisis and Revival of the Arsacid State in the First Half of the 1st Century AD*]. Kraków.

———. 2013c. "'An Admirer of Persian Ways': Alexander the Great's Reforms in Parthia-Hyrcania and the Iranian Heritage." In *Excavating an Empire: Achaemenid Persia in Longue Durée*, edited by T. Daryaee, A. Mousavi, and K. Rezakhani, 37–62. Costa Mesa.

———. 2014. "The Diadem in the Achaemenid and Hellenistic Periods." *Anabasis. Studia Classica et Orientalia* 5:75–85.

———. 2016. "The Sacral Kingship of the Early Arsacids: Fire Cult and Kingly Glory" *Anabasis: Studia Classica et Orientalia* 7:91–106.

Panitschek, P. 1987–1988. "Zu den genealogischen Konstruktionen der Dynastien von Pontos und Kappadokien." *Rivista di storia dell'antichità* 17–18:73–95.

———. 1990. "Zur Darstellung der Alexander- und Achaemenidennachfolge als politische Programme in kaiserzeitlichen Quellen." *Klio* 72:457–492.

RGDA = *Res Gestae Divi Augusti* = Scheid 2007.

S = Sellwood 1980.

Sachs, A. J., and H. Hunger. 2006. *Astronomical Diaries and Related Texts from Babylonia*. 6 vols. VI: *Goal Year Texts (2006)*. Österreichische Akademie der Wissenschaften, phil-hist. Klasse - Denkschriften, Band 346. Wien.

Scheid, J. 2007. *Res gestae diui Augusti : Hauts faits du divin Auguste*. Les Belles Lettres. Paris.

Schmitt, R. 1982. "Achaemenid Throne-Names," *Annali dell'Istituto Orientale di Napoli* 42:83–95.

———. 1998. "Parthische Sprach- und Namenüberlieferung aus arsakidischer Zeit." In *Das Partherreich und seine Zeugnisse: Beiträge des internationalen Colloquiums, Eutin (27. - 30. Juni 1996)*, edited by Josef Wiesehöfer. Historia Einzelschriften, Heft 122, 163–204. Stuttgart.

———. 2011. *Iranische Personennamen in der griechischen Literatur vor Alexander d. Gr.* Vol. V: *Iranische Namen in der Nebenüberlieferungen indogermanischer Sprachen*. Faszikel 5A. Iranisches Personennamenbuch – Iranische Onomastik 9. Wien.

Schottky, M. 1989. *Media Atropatene und Gross-Armenien in hellenistischer Zeit*. Bonn.

Seibert, J. 1967. *Historische Beiträge zu den dynastischen Verbindungen in hellenistischer Zeit*. Stuttgart.

Sellwood, D. 1980. *An Introduction to the Coinage of Parthia*. London.

Shayegan, M. R. 2011. *Arsacids and Sasanians. Political Ideology in Post-Hellenistic and Late Antique Persia*. Cambridge.

———. 2016. "The Arsacids and Commagene." In *The Parthian and Early Sasanian Empires: Adaptation and Expansion: Proceedings of a Conference Held in Vienna, 14-16 June*, edited by V. S. Curtis, E. J. Pendleton, M. Alram, and T. Daryaee. Archaeological Monographs Series, 8–22. Oxford/Philadelphia.

Spawforth, A. 1994. "*Symbol of Unity*? The Persian Wars Tradition in the Roman Empire." In *Greek historiography*, edited by S. Hornblower, 233–247. Oxford.

Stöllner, Th. and Z. Samašev, eds. 2013. *Unbekanntes Kasachstan - Archäologie im Herzen Asiens: Katalog zur Ausstellung des Deutschen Bergbau-Museums Bochum*. Bochum.

Sullivan, R. D. 1990. *Near Eastern Royalty and Rome 100-30 B.C.* Toronto.

Tarn, W. W. 1929. "Queen Ptolemais and Apama," *The Classical Quarterly* 23:138–141.

Treister, M., Yablonsky, L. 2013. *Einflüsse der achämenidischen Kultur im südlichen Uralvorland (5. - 3. Jh. v. Chr.)* Ancient Toreutics and Jewellery in Eastern Europe 5. Wien.

Tuplin, C. 2008. "The Seleucids and Their Achaemenid Predecessors: A Persian Inheritance?" In *Ancient Greece and Ancient Iran: Cross-Cultural Encounters: 1st International Conference (Athens, 11-13 November 2006)*, edited by S. M. Darbandi and A. Zournatzi, 109–136. Athens.

Wagner, Jörg. 1983. "Dynastie und Herrscherkult in Kommagene: For-schungsgeschichte und neuere Funde," *Istanbuler Mitteilungen* 33:177–224.

Waldmann, H. 1973. *Die kommagenischen Kultreformen unter König Mithradates I. Kallinikos und seinem Sohne Antiochos I.* Leiden.

Waters, M. 2014. *Ancient Persia.* Cambridge.

Wiesehöfer, Josef. 1994. "'King of Kings' and 'Phihellen': Kingship in Arsacid Iran." In *Aspects of Hellenistic Kingship*, edited by P. Bilde, T. Engberg-Pedersen, L. Hannestad, and J. Zahle. Studies in Hellenistic Civilization VII, 55–66. Aarhus.

Wiesehöfer, J. 2011. "Frataraka Rule in Seleucid Persis: A New Appraisal." In *Creating a Hellenistic World*, edited by A. Erskine and L. Llewellyn-Jones, 107–122. Swansea.

Wolski, J. 1966. "Les Achéménides et les Arsacides: Contribution à la forma-tion des traditions iraniennes," *Syria* 43:63–89.

Wolski, J. 1977. "L'idéologie monarchique chez les Parthes." In *Centro di ri-cerche e di documentazione sull'antichità classica. Atti VIII (1976–1977): Studi vari di storia greca, ellenistica e romana*, 223–235. Milano.

Wolski, Józef. 1993. *L'empire des Arsacides*. Acta Iranica 32 — Textes et Mé-moires XVIII. Leuven.

Wolski, J. 2003. *Seleucid and Arsacid Studies: A Progress Report on Developments in Source Research*. Kraków.

Yardley, J. C. 1994. *Justin: Epitome of the Philippic History of Pompeius Trogus.* Atlanta.

———. 2008. *Tacitus: The Annals.* Oxford.

On Forgetting Cyrus and Remembering the Achaemenids in Late Antique Iran

Touraj Daryaee
University of California, Irvine

A T THE APEX OF SASANIAN POWER in the sixth century CE, at the very time when Ērānšahr's national history, the *Xwadāy-nāmag*, or the "Book of Lords," was being composed, a Nestorian Christian ecclesiastical council had convened in Iran. In this council, which began its work with the mention of its political patron, Xusrōy Anōšag-ruwān, the Persian king of kings was hailed as the "New Cyrus."[1] Thus, Cyrus loomed large in the minds of the Christians of the Sasanian empire in the late antique world.

A century before, the great king of kings, Yazdgerd I, is reported to have entertained even closer relations with the realms' Christian and Jewish communities.[2] A token of Yazdgerd's affinity with the Babylonian Jewry was his apparent familiarity with the political leader of the Jewish community within the empire, the exilarch (*reš galūt*), Huna b. Nathan, who reportedly took liberties with Yazdgerd I, to the point of even advising him to adjust his undergarments![3] Arguably, this anecdote may be based in the belief that Huna b. Nathan was the king of king's brother-in-law, Yazdgerd I having married Nathan's sister.[4] This idea is certainly echoed in the Zoroastrian Middle Persian texts, such as the *Šahrestānīhā ī Ērānšahr* (ŠĒ 47), where it is stated:

> šahrestān ī šūs ud šūstar šīšīnduxt zan ī Yazdgerd ī šābuhrān kerd
> čiyōn duxt ī rēš-galūdag jahūdagān šāh mād-iz ī Wahrām ī gōr būd
>
> The city of Susa and šūštar were built by šīšīnduxt, the wife of Yazdgerd,
> the son of šābuhr, since she was the daughter of the *reš galūt*, the king of the Jews, and she also was the mother of Wahrām Gōr.[5]

Beyond the identity and family relations of Huna b. Nathan, the hailing of Yazdgerd I as the "new Cyrus" is of paramount importance, as it suggests

---

1. Chabot 1902, 69–70; Payne 2015, 99.
2. Widengren 1961,140–142; Neusner 1970, 8–13.
3. Neusner 1970, 253.
4. Neusner 1970, 253 opposed this notion.
5. Daryaee 2002, 20.

that the generally positive image of Cyrus the Great – as the liberator of the Babylonian Jewry – was projected onto Yadgerd I. The very fact of this favorable projection implies that cordial relations between the Jews and the Persian court existed under the rule of Yazdgerd I,[6] and furthermore that a possible path for transmitting ancient Iranian (Achaemenid) history to the Sasanian court could have been afforded by Jewish sages.

This, however, does not mean that the Sasanians did not encounter, or did not hear about, the Achaemenids from other and earlier accounts as well. The Talmud does provide points of contact from Šābuhr I's reign onwards, when intense discussions on law and traditions between rabbis and the king are reported.[7] Even on the margins of the Sasanian empire, at Dura Europos, we may find some intriguing evidence that pertains to the reign of Šābuhr I in 256 CE. Along the western walls of the city stood the Jewish synagogue that exhibits some twelve Middle Persian inscriptions on wall paintings, including a scene associated with the story of Purim. My reading of the Middle Persian inscription of the latter scene is as follows:

> māh mihr abar sāl 14 ud rōz frawardīn
> ka Ōhrmazd ī dibīr ud kardag ī zandak[8] ud dibīr ī dahm
> ud ēn zandak ī Jahūdān ō ēn payrāstag ī bay ī bayān ī
> Jahūdān āmad hēnd u-šān ēn nigār nīšīd
> u-šān nigīrēd ud *passandīd ... nigīrēd
> ... nigār ...

> In the month of Mihr, on the fourteenth year [of Šābuhr's reign], on the day Frawardīn,
> when Ōhrmazd the scribe, the Kardag (*chargé d'affaires*)[9] of the district, and the pious scribe

6. Widengren, 1961, 140–142; Neusner 1970, 8–13.

7. In terms of the discussion about law and tradition between the kings and the rabbis: Šābuhr discusses the messiah with Shmuel (b. Sanhedrin 98a). In b. Baba Metzia 119a, Šābuhr praises (using the Middle Persian *āfrīn*) a rabbi for ruling on an internal Jewish matter. In b. Avodah Zarah 76b, Šābuhr purifies a knife so he can serve pieces of a citron to a rabbi. Šābuhr II speaks with a Rav Hama, in b. Sanhedrin 46b, about the biblical prooftext for the requirement to bury the dead. In b. Zevahim 19a, Yazdgerd I fixes the belt of the rabbi Huna bar Nathan and quotes the verse "a kingdom of priests and a holy nation" (Exodus 19:6). There are also many of the stories about Šābuhr's mother "Ifra Hormiz," who asks the rabbis to inspect her menstrual blood (b. Niddah 20b), sends charity to rabbis to dispense to the poor (b. Baba Batra 8a-b and b. Baba Batra 10b-11a), and in one place encourages her son Šābuhr not to interfere with the Jews, because God protects them (b. Taanit 24b). I would like to thank S. Gross for his help in identifying these passages in the Talmud. See also Mokhtarian 2015, 79–80 and 83–84.

8. Grenet 1988, 151, reads <bndk> *bandag*.

9. The office of <krtk> *kardag* most likely pertained to the realm of the judiciary; see also Nyberg 1974, 113.

came to this district of the Jews, to this place of worship of the god of gods

of the Jews, they saw this painting, they observed and *liked? ... saw ... painting ...[10]

The Dura inscriptions and their choice of location points to the fact that the Sasanians may have had some knowledge of the Achaemenids in the late antique period. In a sense, one can see the Achaemenid ruler and personages on the wall painting sporting Arsacid garb. The visit to the Dura synagogue by the Sasanian officials should make us ponder the relations between the Jews and Sasanians and how biblical stories, specifically those related to the Achaemenids, may have been transmitted. No doubt, the local Jewish official would have informed the Sasanian officers of the Achaemenid tradition and their treatment of the Jewish population, as recorded in the Jewish tradition. The Sasanian encounter with Persians of old through Dura's synagogue paintings was only one of the possible avenues for the transmission of Achaemenid traditions.

We know the Sasanians made visits to Persepolis, and occasionally left inscriptions,[11] but what we see with the Middle Persian inscription at the Dura synagogue are Sasanian officials viewing the frescoes in the synagogue as if they were in a museum beholding objects that offered an insight into the distant past. Their guides were no doubt Jewish, providing them with the historical context of the Judeo-Persian (Achaemenid) past. The Purim panel would have been evidence of the close connection between the Jews and Persians at a critical moment in history, when the Sasanians had conquered Dura from their Roman adversaries. Since the treatment of the vanquished population depended on the goodwill of the Persian conquerors, every bit of context establishing Judeo-Iranian antecedents could have been advantageous to the community.

Aside from the Jewish community, the Armenians, who entertained close relations, and were involved in ways more than one, with the Sasanians, afforded ample space in their national history to Cyrus. The fifth-century Armenian logographer/historian Movses Khorenatsi provides some details on the episode of the Medes' overthrow by Cyrus, who, according to Khorenatsi, was aided in this by a certain mythical Tigran.[12] But how this information would have reached the Sasanian court and how the transfer of knowledge would have taken place in the fifth century is totally unclear. We are left in the dark as to the possible interest of the Sasanians in Achae-

10. For earlier studies, see Daryaee 2010, 32.
11. See Shayegan 2017, 437–438.
12. See Thompson 1978, 113.

menids. Among modern scholars, Arthur Christensen, whose historicizing tendencies are well known, believed the idea of Persians having continuously warred against Greece was perhaps the only enduring memory of the Achaemenid past in late antique Sasanian Persia.[13]

First, however, allow us briefly to review the evidence from the third century CE, when the Sasanian empire was established. Šābuhr I in his inscription on the Kaʿabe-ye Zardošt at Naqš-e Rostam mentions his ancestors – that is, MP. *ahēnag(ān)*/Pth. *hasēnag(ān)* – however, as shown by M. Rahim Shayegan, the king's lineage did not reach back beyond three generations, which, in the case of Šābuhr I, encompassed: his father Ardaxšīr, grandfather Pābag, and great grandfather (and eponymous founder of the dynasty) Sāsān.[14] So, Šābuhr's ancestors (*ahēnag*) beyond Sāsān may not be established. In contrast, the Middle Persian Zoroastrian texts, which pertain to the late Sasanian and the post-Sasanian period, chiefly among them the *Bundahišn*, as well as Persian historians writing (also) in Arabic, such as Ṭabarī, provided a more detailed genealogy of the Sasanian kings, which most likely had been constructed to give legitimacy to the dynasty.

Ardaxšīr ī Pābagān, the founder of the Sasanian dynasty in the late Sasanian and post-Sasanian period, was related to a Dārāy ī Dārāyān, which could have either been Darius III, or as P. Oktor Skjærvø has suggested a conflation of the memory of the last Achaemenid king – which is to be found in the Pahlavi texts – with that of the Persid petty king Dārāy, known from the coins of Persis.[15] Shayegan has put forth the idea that in fact after the collapse of the Achaemenid empire, and after the emergence within the Hellenistic and later Arsacid periods of the sub-dynastic rule of the *fratarakā* in Persis, there was yet another local Persid dynasty – that called itself *šāh* 'king' in contrast to the *fratarakā* – which ought to be called the Dārāyānīds on account of its dynastic name Dārāyān.[16] Hence, making the connection between the early Sasanians and the last of the Achaemenids, Darius III, is even more remote and farfetched.

This Sasanian connection with the Achaemenids, however, is well attested in the *Kārnāmag ī Ardaxšīr ī Pābagān* (the vita of Ardaxšīr, son of Pābag), a late Sasanian epic romance that exhibits few historiographical tendencies. It appears to have been a late sixth- or seventh-century redaction,[17] which, as Frantz Grenet has suggested, was read at the late Sasanian and Abbasid

13. Christensen 1932, 154.
14. Shayegan 2011, 2–3.
15. Skjærvø 1997, 102–103.
16. Shayegan 2005 [2009], 171; and Shayegan 2017, 415, 421–423.
17. This dating has been more recently questioned by Panaino 1994 [1996], 393.

courts.[18] Indeed, the *Kārnāmag ī Ardaxšīr ī Pābagān* presents Ardaxšīr as the *nāf ī Dārāy šāh* (the scion of king Dārāy), a connection between Dārāy (presumably the Achaemenid king Darius III) and the Sasanian sovereign Ardaxšīr I, which we also know from another reliable source, namely, the Greek Manichaean codex Heinrich and Koenen edited and published over four decades ago, and which attributed the intriguing name *Dārēw-Ardaxšīr to the founder of the Sasanian empire.[19] But even this document is dated to the fifth century CE,[20] and thus the question remains, what did the Sasanians know of the Achaemenids and Cyrus in late antiquity, and when precisely did this knowledge begin to form?

Sources inspired by the sixth-century CE *Xwadāy-nāmag*, be they Middle Persian writings, or be they accounts redacted by Persian converts to Islam, such as Ṭabarī and Balʿamī, offer a completely different worldview. From these Muslim writings Cyrus is wholly absent, but the presence of Dārā (Darius) and Dārāy ī Dārāyān (Darius son of Darius), respectively representing Darius I and Darius III, suggest a partial knowledge of the Achaemenids, although we do not know when and how it emerged. Was it through the *fratarakā*, who ruled in the province of Persis during the Seleucid and Arsacid periods that Darius I and Darius III were remembered, or was it through the agency of Zoroastrian magi who remembered the coming of Alexander and the death of Darius III and the dispersion of the sacred traditions, as well as the destruction of the fire-temples? This is a difficult question to answer, but our medieval Persian sources provide some interesting information on the Achaemenids, which suggests a historiographical path to the remote past. Where it not for the polymath Abu Reyhan Bīrunī's account of Achaemenid genealogy,[21] or other sources, such as Ibn Balkhī's *Fārsnāme*, from the homeland of the Achaemenids, mentioning Darius and his building of roads and the postal system,[22] we would have to conclude the Sasanians had long forgotten the Achaemenids and no memory of them remained in late antique Iran. But late antique historians possessed this knowledge and carried it on well into medieval times, on the eastern and western frontiers of the Iranian world. So how could the Sasanians not know or remember them? If the Jewish, Armenian, and Christian communities remembered them, how is it possible the Persians themselves did not?

The key, I believe, is to understand the nature of historiography in the

---

18. Grenet 2003, 29.
19. Henrichs and Koenen 1970, 121; also cited in Dodgeon and Lieu 1991, 354.
20. Sunderman 1986, 290–291.
21. Yarshater 1976, 49–65.
22. Le Strange and Reynold 1921, 55.

late antique world. In this period, history unfolded according to a sacred, religious narrative. Armenian and Byzantine historiography followed the Christian worldview, while in Iran, Zoroastrianism provided the intellectual foundation for the sacred historiographical narrative. As Armenia's ancient history received a "Christian orientation," and later as Islamic history received a "Quranic orientation," one can argue that Iranian history took on a "Zoroastrian/Avestan worldview." Jean Kellens has reminded us that if the *Avesta* is the main corpus of Zoroastrian religious hymns and rituals, the term itself (*abēstag*) and its being put into writing as a *text* is a late antique phenomenon, from the late Sasanian period.[23] But if we also take into account the further possibility that the Avestan alphabet was likely invented under the reign of Šābuhr II,[24] then the fourth century represents a fortuitous moment for the Avesta to have emerged as a late antique textual body.

By the sixth century, when the *Xwadāy-nāmag* (Book of Lords/Kings) was redacted, variegated (epic) traditions were captured that served as a historical framework for the Iranian people. According to Kellens, the Avesta provided the mythical history of the Aryā, or the Iranians.[25] If one views the *Avesta* with a historical eye, one can deduce that the *Yašts*,[26] among others *Yašt* 5 (*Ābān Yašt*), *Yašt* 10 (*Mihr Yašt*), and *Yašt* 19 (*Zamyād Yašt*), provide glimpses of a narrative, which the Sasanians considered to be their ancient history. It is significant that the *Avesta* took its final form during the Sasanian period, synchronous with the "national history of the Iranians," the *Xwadāy-nāmag*, being put into writing.[27] Thus, it is not surprising that the *Xwadāy-nāmag* was heavily influenced by the Avestan lore. It is important to note that both its geographical horizon and the register of past kings and heroes began to be increasingly associated with the Iranian plateau in its late antique garb. One can go even further and state that many of the Sasanian kings acted and conducted themselves according to the customs of the ancient kings and potentates of the Avestan *Yašts*. In a way the Sasanians

23. Kellens 2012, 551.

24. Hoffmann 1987; and more recently Cantera 2004, 135–162.

25. Kellens 2005, 240: "L'adjectif *airiia-*, par lequel les chantres avestiques désignent l'éthnie à laquelle ils appartiennent, est indubitablement hérité puisqu'il correspond, et à mon avis exactement, à scr. *árya-*. Mais il est probable que tout sentiment de son sens étymologique était perdu et il apparaît que le mot est intégré avec précision dans l'histoire mythique des origines iraniennes. *Airiia-* a donc été réinterprété dans le cadre spécifique de la culture iranienne et ne prend de sens que dans la mesure où il est évocateur d'une série d'événements qui fondent l'identité du peuple à qui il sert de nom."

26. For the *Yašts*, see Skjærvø 1994, 217–220.

27. For the study of Iran's national history, see still Nöldeke 1896–1904; Yarshater 1983, 359–480; and Shahbazi 1990, 208–229.

were taking part in the epic history that was taking place, while the Achaemenids were absent.

From the fifth century CE on, Sasanian kings and princes began adopting Avestan names and titles, such as: Kawād, Kāwūs, Husraw (Xosrōy), Rāmšahr, and Kay that were all connected with the new historiographic traditions. The inclusion of the word *xwarrah* 'glory' or 'fortune' is a further indication of the Sasanian preoccupation with their mythical past. Indeed, something had changed in the ideological orientation of the Sasanians because of events in the fifth CE. This "ancestral" past was connected with the tragic murder of Dārā/Darius (III), and the destruction of the *Avesta* by Alexander of Macedon.[28] Whatever the origin of this memory – it could well be a genuine priestly tradition – it not only preserved the figure of Dārā, but also the coming of Alexander as an important caesura in history. From then onward Alexander became Dārā's half-brother, hence his legitimate successor within the Iranian national epic traditions, and Cyrus was nowhere to be remembered. Then, the Arsacids made a brief appearance: the late Sasanian compilation *Dēnkard* reports the Arsacid king Walāxš, who is credited with collecting the sacred scriptures, and a short list of Arsacid names. How the memory of the Arsacids had almost entirely elapsed by the time of the *Šāhnāme* is best captured in the following famous passage (*Šāhnāme* 6:82–83)[29]:

چو کوتاه بد شاخ و هم بیخ شان

نگوید جهاندیده تارخ شان

ازیرا جز از نام نشنیده ام

نه در نامه خسروان دیده ام

Since their genealogy and lineage was short
No worldly person can retell their history

From them I have heard nothing but their name,
Nor have I seen anything in the Book of the Kings.

What is interesting in Arsacid imperial ideology is the shift away from a philhellenic perspective towards Iranian traditions, specifically those associated with the Achaemenids.[30] But this connection, assuming it was known

28. For the intricate development of Darius III's image and memory in the Irano-Islamic traditions, see Briant 2003, 443–486.

29. Cited after Khaleghi-Motlagh 2005, 139.

30. Neusner 1963, 56; for the connections with Cyrus the Great, see Wolski 1988, 160; for Cyrus and Arsacid connections, Wiesehöfer 1996, 59. For "Achaemenid reminiscences" under the Arsacids, see Shayegan 2011, and more recently, Shayegan 2017, 424–426 and 433–436.

to the Sasanians, would have generated little interest in them preserving it. In Zoroastrian memory, the Arsacids were never rehabilitated. In a unique and interesting late Middle Persian text (manuscript MU29), the memory of the Arsacids makes an appearance:

> ud seyom tāg brinǰēn ka dīdē kē pādixšāyīh ī *aškānīyān ast kē abar *rāh ud *ristag [ī] druwand padīd dārēnd ud abar askandar ī xēšmtohm andar ērānšahr pādixšāyīh kunēnd ud dēn ī weh rāy tawāh kunēnd ud az pas xwad andar dušox az gēhān nigūn ōftēd.

> And the third, the brazen branch, which you (o Zoroaster) saw, is the rulership of the Arsacids (*aškyānīyān), who conducted (themselves) in an evil way and manner, and who ruled in Ērānšahr (such as) Alexander, whose seed is from wrath, and who destroyed the good religion, and then fell back into hell from the material world.[31]

This clear indictment of the Arsacids, however, in a late Pahlavi text, certainly expresses a great disdain for this dynasty that ruled over most of the Iranian world for close to five centuries. By the late Sasanian period, the sacred history was refashioned, by coupling the topography and monuments of western Iran with *Avesta*-inspired traditions stemming from eastern Iran, shifting the *lieux de mémoire* pertaining to locations in the Iranian east and central Asia to new loci on the Iranian Plateau. In this way, Zoroastrianism and Zoroastrians refashioned Iran's textual and topographical history, from what the Judeo-Christian and Greco-Roman knew of the past.[32]

In the eastern tradition, the *Avesta*-inspired narrative had certainly impacted the history and worldview of the Sasanians. The emphasis was on the antiquity of this history, but in fact, much of it was new, and refashioned the Zoroastrian tradition to justify Sasanian rule in the late antique world. In this new scheme of historiography, not only the Achaemenids were forgotten, but also the founder of the first Persian empire, Cyrus the Great. A Dārā(y) ī Dārāyān was the only remembrance of the Achaemenid past, and their monuments were associated with Kayanid and mythical heroes and rulers of the past, or the paladins of the Iranian epic. Cyrus the Great was remembered by the Jews and Christians, but the empire chose to forget him and replace the remote past with another one.

31. See Daryaee 2016, 9.
32. Canepa 2013, 319–372.

Bibliography

Briant, Pierre. 2003. *Darius dans l'ombre d'Alexandre*. Paris: Fayard.

Canepa, Matthew. 2013. "The Transformation of Sacred Space, Topography, and Royal Ritual in Persia and the Ancient Iranian World." In *Heaven on Earth: Temples, Ritual, and Cosmic Symbolism in the Ancient World*, edited by Deena Ravagan, 319372. Chicago.

Cantera, Alberto. 2004. *Studien zur Pahlavi-Übersetzung des Avesta*. Edited by Maria Macuch. Iranica, Band 7. Wiesbaden.

Chabot, Jean-Baptiste. 1902. *Synodicon orientale ou recueil de synodes nestoriens: d'après le MS syriaque 332 de la Bibliothèque Nationale et le MS K. VI, 4 du musée Borgia, à Rome*. Notices et Extraits des Manuscrits de la Bibliothèque Nationale et autres Bibliothèques, vol. 37. Paris.

Christensen, Arthur. 1932. *Les Kayanides*. Det Kgl. Danske Videnskabernes Selskab, Historisk-filologiske Meddelelser, XIX, 2. København: Andr. Fred Høst and Søn.

Daryaee, Touraj. 2016. "Alexander and the Arsacids in the Manuscript MU29." *DABIR* 1:8–10.

———. 2010. "To Learn and to Remember from Others: Persians Visiting the Dura-Europos Synagogue." *Scripta Judaica Cracoviensia* 8:29–30.

———. 2002. *Šahrestānīhā ī Ērānšahr. A Middle Persian Text on Late Antique Geography, Epic and History*. Costa Mesa, CA.

Dodgeon, Michael H., and Samuel N. C. Lieu. 1991. *The Roman Eastern Frontier and the Persian Wars (AD 226–363): A Documentary History*. London/New York.

Grenet, Frantz. 2003. *La Geste d'Ardashir fils de Pâbag: Kārnāmag ī Ardaxšēr ī Pābagān*. Die.

———. 1988. "Les Sassanides à Doura-Europos (253 ap. J.-C.): Réexamination du matériel épigraphique iranien du site." In *Géographie historique au Proche-Orient*, edited by Pierre-Louis Gatier, Bruno Helly, and Jean-Paul Rey-Coquais. Notes et Monographies Techniques 23:133–158. Paris: Éditions du C.N.R.S..

Henrichs, L., and L. Koenen. 1970. "Ein griechischer Mani-Codex." *Zeitschrift für Papyrologie und Epigraphik* 5:97–216.

Hoffmann, Karl. 1987. "i. The Avestan Script," online edition, 1987, available at http://www.iranicaonline.org/articles/avestan-language (accessed on 11 October 2017).

Kellens, Jean. 2012. "Les Achéménides et l'Avesta." In *Séptimo centenario de los estudios orientales en Salamanca*, edited by A. Agud, et al. Estudios Filológicos 337: Ediciones Universidad de Salamanca, 551–558.

———. 2005. "Les *Airiia-* ne sont plus des *Āryas* : Ce sont déjà des Iraniens." In *Āryas, Aryens et Iraniens en Asie Centrale*, edited by G. Fussman, J. Kellens, H.-P. Francfort, and X. Tremblay, 233–252. Paris.

Khaleghi-Motlagh, Djalal, ed. 2005. *Abuʾl Qasem Ferdowsi: The Shahnameh (The Book of Kings)*. 8 vols. Vol. 6. Persian Text Series, n.s. 1–8, ser. ed. Ehsan Yarshater. New York.

Mokhtarian, Jason Sion. 2015. *Rabbis, Sorcerers, Kings, and Priests: The Culture of the Talmud in Ancient Iran*. S. Mark Taper Foundation Imprint in Jewish Studies. Oakland, California.

Neusner, J. 1970. *A History of Jews in Babylonia*. Vol. V: *Later Sasanian Times*. Leiden.

———. 1963. "Parthian Political Ideology," *Iranica Antiqua* 3:40–59.

Nöldeke, Theodor. 1896–1904. "Das iranische Nationalepos." In *Grundriß der Iranischen Philologie*. 2 vols. Vol. II, edited by Wilhelm Geiger and Ernst Kuhn, 130–211. Strassburg: Karl J. Trübner.

Nyberg, H. S. 1970. *A Manual of Pahlavi*. Vol. II. Wiesbaden.

Panaino, Antonio. 1994 [1996]. "Two Astrological Reports of the *Kārnāmag ī Ardašīr ī Pābagān* (III, 4–7; IV, 6–7)," *Die Sprache* 36, no. 2:181–98.

Payne, Richard E. 2015. *A State of Mixture: Christians, Zoroastrians, and Iranian Political Culture in Late Antiquity*. Edited by Peter Brown. Transformation of the classical heritage LVI. Oakland, California: University of California Press.

Shahbazi, A. Shapur. 1990. "On the Xwaday-namag." In *Iranica Varia: Papers in Honor of Professor Ehsan Yarshater*, edited by D. Amin, M. Kasheff, and A. Sh. Shahbazi. Acta Iranica 30. Troisième Série, vol. XVI : Textes et Mémoires, 208–229. Leiden.

Shayegan, M. Rahim. 2017. "Persianism: Or Achaemenid Reminiscences in the Iranian and Iranicate World(s) of Antiquity." In *Persianism in Antiquity*, edited by Rolf Strootman and Miguel John Versluys, 401–557. Stuttgart: Franz Steiner Verlag.

———. 2011. *Arsacids and Sasanians: Political Ideology in Post-Hellenistic and Late Antique Persian*. Cambridge.

———. 2005 [2009]. "Nugae epigraphicae." In *Iranian and Zoroastrian Studies in Honor of Prods Oktor Skjærvø*, edited by Carol Altman Bromberg, Nicholas Sims-Williams, and Ursula Sims-Williams. Bulletin of the Asia Institute 19, 169–179. Bloomfield Hills, MI: Bulletin of the Asia Institute.

Skjærvø, Prods Oktor. 1997 [2000]. "The Joy of the Cup: A pre-Sasasnian Middle Persian Inscription on a Silver Bowl." *Bulletin of the Asia Institute* 11:93–104.

——. 1994. "Hymnic Composition in the Avesta" *Die Sprache* 36, no. 2:199–243.

Le Strange, Guy, and Reynold Alleyne Nicholson, eds. 1921. *The Fársnáma of Ibnu 'l-Balkhí*. E. J. W. Gibb Memorial Series – New Series 1. London: Cambridge University Press/Luzac.

Sundermann, Werner. 1986. "Kirchengeschichtliche Literatur der Manichäer II," *Alt-Orientalische Forschungen* 13, no. 2:239–317.

Thomson, Robert W., ed. 1978. *Moses Khorenatsʻi: History of the Armenians.* Harvard Armenian Texts and Studies, 4. Cambridge, MA/London: Harvard University Press.

Widengren, Geo. 1961. "The Status of the Jews in the Sassanian Empire," *Iranica Antiqua* 1:129–131.

Wiesehöfer, Josef. 1994. "'King of Kings' and 'Phihellen': Kingship in Arsacid Iran." In *Aspects of Hellenistic Kingship,* edited by Per Bilde, Troels Engberg-Pedersen, Lise Hannestad, and Jan Zahle. Studies in Hellenistic Civilization VII, 55–66. Aarhus: Aarhus University Press.

Wolski, Józef. 1988. "Le titre de "Roi des Rois" dans l'idéologie monarchique des Arsacides." *Acta Antiqua Academiae Scientiarum Hungaricae* 1–4 :159–166.

Yarshater, Ehsan. 1983. "Iranian National History." In *The Cambridge History of Iran*. VII vols. Vol. III, 1. Edited by Ehsan Yarshater. Cambridge: Cambridge University Press, 359–477.

——. 1976. "The List of Achaemenid Kings in al-Biruni and Bar Hebraeus." In *Biruni Symposium*, edited by E. Yarshater and D. Bishop, 49–65. New York.

Traces of Poetic Traditions about Cyrus the Great and his Dynasty in the *Šāhnāme* of Ferdowsi and the Cyrus Cylinder

Olga M. Davidson
Boston University

THE *ŠĀHNĀME* OF FERDOWSI, a monumental poem composed near the beginning of the eleventh century CE, features an episode that tells how the would-be king Key Khosrow destroyed a fortress occupied by demons, and established there a flourishing new city that centered on a magnificent fire temple he built and then tended for a whole year. The narrative of this episode contains details that may derive from old Iranian literary traditions that may have also informed some Achaemenid inscriptions, and I argue that there are corresponding details to be found in the text of the Cyrus Cylinder as well.

Let me begin by quoting my own translation of the relevant episode about Key Khosrow in the *Šāhnāme* of Ferdowsi:[1]

> When he was near the fortress he mounted up,
> put on his chainmail and belted it.
>
> From on high, he called for a scribe
> and ordered him to write a letter upon Chinese paper (*qartās-e čīn*)
>
> with ambergris, and in Pahlavi,
> as befitting a royal proclamation:
>
> "This letter comes from the Almighty's slave –
> From noble Key Khosrow, the world-seeker,
>
> who, escaped from evil Āharman's (Ahreman's) bondage,
> and who, with the help of God, has washed his hands from all evil.
>
> God, who is eternally the Lord, most high,
> holder of the world, giver of all things good, our guide,

---

1. Based on the Persian text of Khaleghi-Motlagh 1990, 464–467 (vv. 619–663).

the Lord of Mars, of Saturn, and the Sun,
the Lord of Grace (*farr*), the Lord of Strength,

who gave the throne and Grace (*farr*) of kings to me,
and fierce lions' claws and an elephantine body (*tan-e pīl*).

The whole world is my kingdom, all is mine,
from Pisces downward to the Bull's head.

If this fortress (*dez*) be in the province of Āharman,
Who is the enemy of the World-Creator,

(then,) by the Grace (*farr*) of holy God, and by his command,
I will smash it all into the dust with my mace.

And if the magicians are the cause of this machination
I shall not need an army to defeat their sorcery

For when I throw my leather lasso
I will capture the heads of magicians in my noose.

And if the blessed Sorūš himself is here
The army will be united as one under the command of God.

I am indeed not of the seed of Āharman;
For my soul has Grace (*farr*), my body has stature and elegance.

By God's command you shall reduce this (fortress) to nothing,
Such is the message of the 'king of kings.'"

Khosrow then seized a long spear with his hand
And bound the letter to the tip of that spear;

He raised the spear straight up like a banner.
He asked for nothing on earth save the Grace of God

and ordered Gīv to hasten with the spear
and stride up to the lofty walls.

He said to him: "Take this letter of admonition,
And bring it to the wall of the lofty fortress.

Plant there the spear, call on the name of God,
then quickly turn around and hurry back."

That worshipper of God, that glorious chief, Gīv, took the spear
in hand and went his way,
Filled with blessings from the best of souls, the worshipper of
God,

When he set the letter by the wall of the fortress (*dez*)
and delivered the message of Khosrow,

He uttered the name of God, the beneficent,
And fled on a fast horse like the wind.

That noble letter vanished.
There was big tremor, the ground of the fortress erupted (*bar
    damīd*).

At the same time by command of Holy God
the walls of the fortress cracked apart.

You would say: "It was a thunderstorm in spring."
A clamor rose up from the plain to the mountaintop.

The earth became black as a black man's face.
What of the walls of the city, what of the army?

You would say "A dark cloud has come,
The surrounding air is like a mighty lion's maw."

Then Key Khosrow urged on his black horse,
And shouted to the captains of the army:

"Make arrows rain in showers upon the fortress,
make the air be like a cloud in spring."

Immediately a fog rose laden with hail,
A cloud that brings on a hail of death.

Many demons (*dīvs*) met their death by these arrows
And many fell to earth, their courage shattered.

After a while, a brilliant light began to shine,
And all the heavy darkness vanished completely.

The world became like the shining moon,
by the name of God, and by the glory of the *šāh*.

A wonderful breeze sprang up;
the heavens above and all the face of earth began to smile.

The demons (*dīvs*) left at the command of the *šāh*.
The entry to the fortress appeared in the center.

The *šāh* of the Free entered from there
with old Gōdarz, the offspring of Kašwād.

He saw a city inside that large fortress,
full of gardens, plazas, halls, and palaces.

On that spot where that brilliant light had first shone,
where there was no longer any trace of the fortress,

Khosrow decreed that in that very place,
there be a dome, reaching up to the dark clouds.

It was ten lassoes long and wide,
Encircled by high vaulted chambers.

Its periphery was to be half a rapid Arab steed's course.
He brought and placed there (the fire of) Āzargašasp,

And round it sat the *mōbad*s.
Astrologers, and the men of wisdom.

He stayed in that city for as much time it took
for that Fire-temple (*ātaš-kade*) to attain to good reputation
    (good aroma and color).

When a year had passed, he prepared his army for departure,
Having packed up all his goods, and getting all to mount up.

In presenting my findings about this episode from the *Šāhnāme*, I build on
the earlier findings of Parivash Jamzadeh[2] in a study comparing this same
text with the texts of two Achaemenid inscriptions glorifying the Persian
king Xerxes, who was son of Darius the Great and who ruled the Achaemenid
Empire from 486 to 465 BCE.

The themes and possibly the language of these two inscriptions (XPf
and XPh) might have been shaped by a poetic tradition that has also survived into the era of New Persian epic poetry as represented by the *Šāhnāme*
of Ferdowsi. Indeed, in one of the inscriptions (XPf), where Xerxes provides
his genealogy, he also alludes to his being chosen as crown prince and heir
over other potential contenders, that is, other sons of Darius and potential
rivals, but it was Ahuramazdā's explicit wish (*A^huramazdām avaθā kāma āha*
"Ahuramazdā thus wished it") that Xerxes become king:

King Darius had other sons as well (*Dārayavahauš puçā aniyaiciy āhatā*).
Ahuramazdā thus wished it (*A^huramazdām avaθā kāma āha*). Darius,
my father, made me greatest after himself (*Dārayava^huš haya manā pitā
pasā tanūm mām maθištam akunauš*). When my father Darius went to his
abode (heaven), (then) by the greatness of Ahuramazdā I became king,
seated on my father's throne.

XPf §4: B–K[3]

2. Jamzadeh 2004.
3. Old Persian text follows the most recent editio minor by Schmitt 2009; translation by
Shayegan.

Similarly, as we may see from the text of the *Šāhnāme* episode I have translated, Key Khosrow is competing for the status of crown prince (Khaleghi-Motlagh 1990, 460, vv. 557–565), and the testing ground for him and his competitor, a prince named Farīborz, is the fortress inhabited by demons (Khaleghi-Motlagh 1990, 461, vv. 576–582). Intriguingly, the key to Key Khosrow's success is his *farr* – "the throne and Grace (*farr*) of kings" – bestowed upon him by God – "God, who is eternally the Lord, most high | holder of the world, giver of all things good, our guide || the Lord of Mars, of Saturn, and the Sun | the Lord of Grace (*farr*), the Lord of Strength||". As we can see, the *farr* is given to Key Khosrow by God, who is in this context defined by such epithets as the "Lord of Grace (*farr*)." In other words, Key Khosrow is able to overcome his rivals, as Xerxes overcame his brothers, because it was God's (Ahuramazdā's) express wish. Key Khosrow's rival, Farīborz, does not have the *farr*, and that is why he fails when the first attempt is made to capture the fortress of demons.

Another similarity between Key Khosrow's deeds in the *Šāhnāme* and Xerxes' actions relates to their opposing evil. In another inscription of Xerxes (XPh), the famous *Daiva*-Inscription, the king is quoted as saying, and I quote again:

> And among these lands there was a place where previously the
> demons (*daivas*) were worshipped. Afterwards, by the greatness
> of Ahuramazdā, I destroyed that den of the demons (*daivas*), and I
> proclaimed: "the demons (*daivas*) shall not be worshipped." Where
> previously the demons (*daivas*) had been worshipped, there I
> worshiped Ahuramazdā according to the order in the heights / at the
> right time and with the proper ritual (*artācā brazmaniy(a)*).

> XPh §5: A–I

Just as Xerxes converts a "den of demons (*daivas*)" (*daivādāna-*) into an abode where Ahuramazdā would be worshiped "according to the order in the heights," or at the right time and with the proper ritual – depending on how one interprets the sequence *artācā brazmaniy(a)*[4] – so also does Key Khosrow convert the fortress of demons [*dīvs*] into a holy city that is centered on the Fire of Gošnasp, known as *Ādur Gušnasp* in Middle Persian. Here I cite again the relevant lines of the *Šāhnāme*:

> On that spot where that brilliant light had first shone,
> where there was no longer any trace of the fortress,

---

4. See discussion in Schmitt 2014, 241–242.

> Khosrow decreed that in that very place,
> there be a dome, reaching up to the dark clouds.
>
> It was ten lassoes long and wide,
> Encircled by high vaulted chambers.
>
> Its periphery was to be half a rapid Arab steed's course.
> He brought and placed there (the fire of) Āzargašasp,
>
> And round it sat the *mōbad*s.
> Astrologers, and the men of wisdom.
>
> He stayed in that city for as much time it took
> for that Fire-temple (*ātaš-kade*) to attain to good reputation
>   (good aroma and color).

I should emphasize that the wording of the *Šāhnāme* indicates that this aetiological narrative about the institution of the Fire of Gošnasp stems from a West Iranian tradition, centered in Persis (modern day Fārs), just as the narratives of the comparable Achaemenid inscriptions are of course West Iranian by origin, centered in Fārs. As Jamzadeh emphasizes, the point of departure for the action of the episode about the conquest of the fortress of demons by Key Khosrow is ostentatiously specified as a place named Stakhr, which is in Fārs (Khaleghi-Motlagh 1990, 456, v. 505), and, just as ostentatiously, the narrative specifies that Key Khosrow returned there after having spent a year performing the sacred task of building and maintaining the new city that centers on the Fire of Gošnasp (Khaleghi-Motlagh 1990, 468, v. 675). So, the spatial frame for the entire narrative is Western Iran.

Moving beyond the two Achaemenid inscriptions we have considered, I propose to adduce further comparative evidence from a third Achaemenid inscription. Of course, I am speaking here of the text of the Cyrus Cylinder, which is written in the Neo-Babylonian language, by Babylonian scribes, for a Babylonian audience, at the behest of Cyrus the Great, but which may *also* reflect Achaemenid ideological tenets.[5]

I start my argumentation by highlighting a detail that we can see in the episode I cited from the *Šāhnāme* of Ferdowsi. I argue that the "letter" of Key Khosrow, as reportedly dictated by the prince to a scribe, is a text that mirrors oral traditions that may have been embedded in the texts of Achaemenid inscriptions.[6] I highlight the fact that the letter is not addressed to

5. On the Babylonian *Vorlagen* of the Cyrus Cylinder, see the contribution of Schaudig in this volume.

6. On the interactions of Iranian oral traditions and Achaemenid inscriptions, see Shayegan 2012.

anyone in particular. Rather, it is a general declaration – we may think of it as a declaration addressed to the world. And, in the context of this universalizing declaration, the crown prince quotes himself as an exponent of his own sovereignty as the destined ruler of the Iranian Empire. Further, as I will now argue, the wording of this universal declaration echoes elements of Cyrus' foundational inscription, which, as shown in detail by Schaudig in this volume, was strongly influenced by the Babylonian literary traditions in both structure and formulation. Such an influence, I propose, affected the Iranian oral traditions, and from there the Achaemenid inscriptions, and, eventually the *Šāhnāme* itself.

The facts of archaeology tell us that the Cyrus Cylinder had been placed as a foundation deposit.[7] And this particular building inscription was laid down inside the sacred wall of Babylon, the Imgur-Enlil, as we read in the inscription written on the cylinder.[8] The text of the Cyrus Cylinder also indicates that Cyrus, as the Persian king who overthrew the last king of Babylon, Nabonidus, instituted a restoration of the correct worship of Marduk at the god's temple – a correctness that the narrative pointedly contrasts with the abuses allegedly committed by his predecessor Nabonidus, last king of Babylon, who had supposedly neglected and corrupted the rituals of worshiping this all-important god of Babylon:

(5)   He (Nabonidus) ma[de] a counterfeit of (Marduk's temple) Esaĝil [. . . .
.....] . . . for (the city of) Ur and the rest of the sacred cities,

(6)   rites, which were inappropriate to them (i.e. the sacred cities and the gods), [improper] sac[rifices . . .]. He spoke [*insolence*] every day and was not afraid (of Marduk's wrath). As an insult,

(7)   (Nabonidus) brought the daily offerings to a halt and inter[fered with the rites. He s]et up [. . .] in the midst of the sacred cities. In his heart he br[oug]ht to an end the worship of Marduk, king of the gods.[9]

And:

(25)   For Babylon and all its sacred places I (Cyrus) took care in peace and sincerity. The people of Babylon [. . .], onto whom (Nabonidus) had imposed an inappropriate yoke against the wil[l of the g]ods,

(26)   I brought relief to their exhaustion and did away with their toil.

7. On the discovery of the Cyrus Cylinder, and its placement, see Talylor 2013, especially 59; and Schaudig in this volume. For the particular passage mentioning the Imgur-Enlil, see Schaudig, again in this volume, lines 38b–44.

8. For the text of the Cyrus Cylinder, see the edition and translation by Finkel 2013; and more recently, Schaudig in this volume.

9. Translation follows Schaudig in this volume.

(27–28a) Marduk, the great lord, rejoiced at [my good] deeds, and sent friendly blessings to me, Cyrus, the king who reveres him, to Cambyses, my son, the fruit of [my] loins, as well as to all my troops, and so we w[alked] in peace and happiness before him.[10]

Similarly in the narrative of the *Šāhnāme*, the "dictated" text of Key Khosrow that is deposited at the base of the walls of the fortress of demons proclaims that this king will institute the correct worship of God. With a thunderous blast, as we read in the vivid wording of Ferdowsi, the text that is deposited at the base of the walls of the fortress of demons now literally explodes these walls, thus setting the groundwork for the institution of the correct worship of God, centering on the Fire of Gošnasp, which then becomes the center-point of a flourishing city.

Just as the text of the Cyrus Cylinder shows a political opposition expressed in terms of *restoring* as opposed to *abusing* the rituals of worshiping the god Marduk, even though both sides of the opposition are in essence adherents of the same god (still, Nabonidus is accused of neglect), so also the text of the episode in the *Šāhnāme* concerning the quest of Key Khosrow shows traces of a political opposition between rival adherents of Zoroastrianism.

As Parivash Jamzadeh has noticed in her study of the episode about this quest of Key Khosrow, the name of the fortress of demons reveals an adherence to perfectly correct Zoroastrian ideology – but this ideology has been demonized in the narrative – demonized as a foil for rival adherents of Zoroastrianism who have singled out Key Khosrow as their heroic representative. In the narrative of the *Šāhnāme*, the name of the fortress of demons is *dež-e Bahman*. And the Zoroastrian pedigree of this place-name, which is *Wahman diz* or "fortress of Wahman" in Middle Persian, is clear: the divine name that is embedded in this place-name is Bahman in Persian and Wahman in Middle Persian, and both of these forms derive from Avestan *vohu- manah-*, meaning "Good Thought," which is the name for a divine abstraction that is second only to the supreme god Ahura Mazdā in the Zoroastrian constellation.

Conversely, the credentials of Key Khosrow in this episode of the *Šāhnāme* where he demolishes the fortress of demons at *dež-e Bahman* is likewise perfectly Zoroastrian. The fire temple that this king establishes after he demolishes the walls of the fort is viewed retrospectively as a landmark of Zoroastrian worship. In the Pahlavi *Vispred*, which features a Zoroastrian "litany to fire" (*Ātaš ī Bahrām niyāyišn*), it is said that Ādur Gušasp, "whose

10. Translation follows Schaudig in this volume.

function pertains to the class of warriors" (*u-š kār ī Arteštārīh*), assisted Kay Husrōy in securing victory at a place named *Wahman diz* (which is the *dež-e Bahman* in Persian): *ud šāh ī Kay Husrōy abar wahman diz pērōzgarīh ayāft pad hayārīh ī ēn ātaxš ud pad pēš Ohrmazd nālīd ud frayād kerd ōy ēn ādur Gušasp būd*, "and king Kay Khosrow obtained victory over the Fortress of Wahman with the help of this fire (and it was this very fire Gušasp that in the presence of Ōhrmazd groaned and called for assistance)" (Taraf 1981, 5.5.16–17).

In a number of Pahlavi texts, including the *Bundahišn*, *Mēnōg ī xrad*, the *Dēnkerd*, and the *Pahlavi Rivayat*, it is reported that Kay Husrōy abolished an "idol-temple" at Lake *Čēčast* – *Kay-Husrōy uzdēs-zār ī war Čēčast hamē kand* "Kay Khosrow destroyed the temple of idols of the Čēčast Lake" – which the narrative situates in Western Iran – and it is also reported that he established at that site "the fire of Gušasp" after he abolished the "idol-temple" – *Ādūr Gušasp bē ō dādgāh nišāst* "he established the Fire Gušasp in the proper place/fire temple" (Bd. 18.8). [11]

In the corresponding episode as narrated in the *Šāhnāme*, it is clear that Key Khosrow is acting as a representative of Zoroastrian orthodoxy when he demolishes the city walls of the fortress of demons and establishes "the fire of Gošnasp" in the city. Furthermore, Key Khosrow is described in this context as an exponent of Soruš, who is figured as a messenger of religious rectitude. The name Soruš is of course overtly Zoroastrian, derived from the Avestan form Sraoša, meaning "(correct) religious observance" and conceived as a Zoroastrian divinity.

So, like Cyrus in the text of the Cylinder, Key Khosrow in the text of the *Šāhnāme* is a representative of the correct way to worship a divinity, as opposed to a supposedly incorrect way of worship that a victor attributes to a demonized enemy he has just defeated.

Finally, just as the Cyrus Cylinder functions as a sacralized foundation deposit for the re-established temple of Marduk – and I have in mind here not only the cylinder itself as a sacred object but also the sacralized wording that is written on the cylinder in order to indicate the re-establishment – so also the letter that is supposedly dictated by Key Khosrow and is notionally quoted by the poet of the *Šāhnāme* has a comparable function. Not only the letter as an object but also the wording that is written in the letter functions as a sacralized foundation deposit: it is destined to establish "the fire of Gošnasp" while at the same time exploding the fortress of demons that had previously occluded the sacred fire and the city that can from now on sustain it forever.

11. For the text of the *Bundahišn*, see Pakzad 2005, 231–232, and 232, n. 90.

Bibliography

Finkel, Irving, ed. 2013. *The Cyrus Cylinder: The King of Persia's Proclamation from Ancient Babylon.* London: I. B. Tauris.

Jamzadeh, P. 2004. "A Šāhnāme Passage in an Achaemenid Context." *Iranica Antiqua* 39:383–388.

Khaleghi-Motlagh, Djalal, ed. 1990. *Abu'l Qasem Ferdowsi: The Shahnameh* (The Book of Kings). 8 vols. Vol. II. Persian Text Series, n.s. 1-8, ser. ed. Ehsan Yarshater. New York: Bibliotheca Persica.

Pakzad, Fazlollah. 2005. *Bundahišn: Zoroastrische Kosmogonie und Kosmologie.* Vol. I: Kritische Edition. Edited by Hassan Rezai Baghbidi. Ancient Iranian Studies Series 2. Tehran: Centre for the Great Islamic Encyclopaedia.

Schmitt, Rüdiger. 2009. *Die altpersischen Inschriften der Achaimeniden: Editio minor mit deutscher Übersetzung.* Wiesbaden: Reichert Verlag.

———. 2014. *Wörterbuch der altpersischen Königsinschriften.* Wiesbaden: Reichert Verlag.

Shayegan, M. Rahim. 2012. *Aspects of History and Epic in Ancient Iran: From Gaumāta to Wahnām.* Edited by Gregory Nagy. Hellenic Studies Series 52. Washington, D.C./Cambridge, Mass.: Center for Hellenic Studies – Harvard University Press.

Taraf, Zahra. 1981. *Der Awesta-Text Niyāyiš mit Pahlavi- und Sanskritübersetzung.* Vol. Beiheft 10. Edited by Bernhard Forssman, Karl Hoffman, and Johanna Narten. Münchener Studien zur Sprachwissenschaft. München: Kitzinger.

Taylor, Jonathan. 2013. "The Cyrus Cylinder: Discovery." In *The Cyrus Cylinder: The King of Persia's Proclamation from Ancient Babylon,* edited by Irving Finkel, 35–68. London: I. B. Tauris.

Index

Abu Reyhan Bīrunī, 225
Achaemenid(s):
  administration, 26, 108, 111,
    132–133;
  connection with nomadic rulers
    of the Southern Urals, 207;
  connections with the Seleucids,
    12, 198–204;
  demise of, 12, 198–199;
  descendance, 12, 202, 213–214;
  dynastic names, 214, 224;
  dynasty/house/monarchy, 3,
    9–10, 12–13, 117–118, 123–
    129, 160, 163, 178, 192, 198,
    206–207, 223;
  ethno-class, 13, 159;
  garden(s), 2, 6, 138–142, 234;
  genealogy, 1, 4, 12, 31n18, 50n12,
    84n36, 98, 174, 201–204, 208,
    213, 224–225, 227, 235;
  graves of elites, 77, 132, 137;
  Great Kings, 13, 30, 47, 72, 154,
    202, 213, 215;
  heirs to Ancient Near Eastern and
    Median polities, 2, 5, 11, 34–37,
    46–63, 72, 93, 99, 102–103, 132,
    157, 160, 171–172, 175, 178,
    180;
  hydraulic installation (in
    Pasargadae), 2, 7, 134, 137,
    142–146;
  imitated by minor rulers of
    Western Asia, 198–215;
  in Arsacid (Parthian) ideology, 12,
    204–215;
  in Commagenian genealogical

constructs, 12, 199, 202–203,
  206, 213, 215;
in early new Persian literary
  traditions, 4, 235;
in Jewish traditions, 9–11, 13, 94,
  106–129, 221–228;
in Pontic genealogical constructs,
  12, 199–204, 206, 209, 213;
in Sasanian traditions, 1, 4, 13,
  153n15, 221–228;
inscriptions, 5, 13–14, 26n2, 27,
  30–31, 34–39, 49–50, 50n12, 53,
  69–70, 86, 93, 102, 147, 152n9,
  156, 159, 172, 174, 210, 232,
  235–240;
kidaris/kitaris (headdress), 210;
kyrbasia (headdress), 204, 210;
masonry, 132, 137, 143–144;
princess(es), 178, 206;
relation with the Teispid line,
  1–6, 11–12, 27, 30–31, 49–50,
  163, 171, 173–174, 179, 198;
Roman views of, 3–4, 12–13,
  183–195, 207, 212;
rule in Egypt, 50, 52n21, 58, 63,
  126–128, 162, 164, 199;
satraps, 12, 199–206, 211, 213–
  214;
titles in Babylonia, *see* Assyrian
  and Babylonian titles
Achilles, 170
Aeolians, 177
Afghanistan, 198
Agathocles (Seleucid governor), 205
ahēnag (Middle Persian)/*hasēnag*
  (Parthian), 224. *See also* Šābuhr I

243